BITTER VICTORY

Wesley (Wes) Olson was born in 1960 in Perth, where he still lives with his wife, Dale, and their children, James, Caitlin and Claire. He joined the Western Australian Government Railways in 1977 and completed training to become a locomotive driver in 1983. He left Westrail in 1995 to join the National Rail Corporation.

In 1992, fascinated by the public interest in HMAS *Sydney*, he began studying naval history. The following year he embarked on research into the loss of the Australian cruiser, leading to the publication of two reports by the Western Australian Maritime Museum (1995 and 1996) and *Bitter Victory* in 2000.

BITTER VICTORY

THE DEATH OF
HMAS SYDNEY

WESLEY OLSON

NAVAL INSTITUTE PRESS
ANNAPOLIS, MARYLAND

First published in 2000 by
University of Western Australia Press
Nedlands, Western Australia 6907
www.uwapress.uwa.edu.au
This edition reprinted with amendments and additions 2002

Published and distributed in the United States of America
and Canada by Naval Institute Press, 291 Wood Road,
Annapolis, Maryland 21402-5034

Library of Congress Catalog No. 2002115448

ISBN 1 59114 066 8

Cover: *First Salvo* watercolour painting by Ross Shardlow

Produced by Benchmark Publications, Melbourne
Consultant editor: Jane Arms, Melbourne
Designed by Robyn Mundy Design, Perth
Typeset in 10.5 point Schneidler Light by Lasertype, Perth
Printed by Daniels Printing Craftsmen, Perth

CONTENTS

ACKNOWLEDGEMENTS

This book would not have been completed without the advice and help of a great number of people. The project as a whole, however, would not have even started were it not for two people, Dr Mike McCarthy and the late Mr W.H. (John) Ross.

Mike has been both friend and mentor. Despite his busy life, he always found time to give me encouragement and advice, give praise when I was producing good work, and to admonish me when I was not. Mike has been instrumental in transforming a train driver into an historian, and *Bitter Victory* could not have been written without him.

If Mike was my 'physical' teacher, Mr Ross was my 'spiritual' teacher. Having served in HMAS *Sydney* for over six years, Mr Ross lost many friends and colleagues when his former ship was sunk, and through our 'chats' I discovered something of his inner strength and character. Although perhaps entitled to be bitter about the circumstances of *Sydney*'s loss, he harboured no hatred for his former enemy. Consequently, he was able to keep an open mind and offer constructive advice whenever I sought his counsel. I endeavoured to apply Mr Ross's philosophy to my research and writing and sincerely hope that he would have approved of the end result.

Very special thanks to the following former *Sydney* crew members for their invaluable assistance: Bill Bain (RAAF); Tom Fisher; Vic Gibson; the late Jack Heazlewood; John Mahney; Ean McDonald; George Ramsay; Ernie Ryding; Alaistair Templeton, and Gordon White, MID.

I must also give thanks to the following people and organizations for helping make my research easier and more pleasurable: Barbara Poniewierski; the staff at the ACT, NSW, Victorian and WA offices of the National Archives of Australia, in particular, Mark Brennan, Esther Carey and Richard Summerrell; Sue Cox (Western Australian Maritime Museum); the office of the Honourable Kim Beazley, MP; and the staff at the Australian War Memorial Research Centre.

I was given further invaluable help from Commander Geoff Vickridge, RANR and the WA Chapter of the Naval Historical Society of Australia. The 'navalizing' of a pongo must have been quite tedious.

There are many other people too numerous to name who gave me help, but I feel the following are deserving of a mention in despatches: Martin Brice, Vic Jeffery; David Kennedy; Karl King; Dr Karin Margolius; Lieutenant Commander David Plummer, RAN; Ross Shardlow for his wonderful artwork; Ted Fletcher, Rex Turner and Geoff Williams for reminding me that failure is not an option.

My heartfelt thanks go to University of Western Australia Press for ensuring that failure did not become an option.

Despite the large number of 'advisors' who have helped shape this book, the views expressed, and the interpretations of evidence given, are mine, and I alone bear responsibility for any errors in fact or judgement.

Last, but by no means least, I would like to thank my wife Dale and children James, Caitlin and Claire for their patience and understanding.

Wesley Olson

AA	anti-aircraft
ACH	Area Combined Headquarters
ACNB	Australian Commonwealth Naval Board
AFO	Admiralty Fleet Order
AMC	Armed Merchant Cruiser
AOC	Air Officer Commanding
ASIS	Australia Station Intelligence Service/Summary
AWL	Average Water Line
AWM	Australian War Memorial
CAFO	**Confidential Admiralty Fleet Order**
C-IN-C	Commander-in-Chief
CNS	Chief of Naval Staff
COIC	Combined Operational Intelligence Centre
CPBC	Common Pointed Ballistic Capped
CWR	Central War Room
CZM	Commander-in-Chief Netherlands East Indies Naval Forces
DCNS	Deputy Chief of Naval Staff
DCT	Director Control Tower
DF	Direction Finding
DNI	Director of Naval Intelligence
DNO	Director of Naval Ordnance
DNOWA	District Naval Officer Western Australia
FOCAS	Flag Officer Commanding the Australian Squadron
FRUMEL	Fleet Radio Unit Melbourne
G	'Golf' time—GMT plus seven hours
GC&CS	Government Code and Cypher School
GMT	Greenwich Mean Time
H	'Hotel' time—GMT plus eight hours
HACP	High Angle Calculating Position
HACS	High Angle Control Station
HE	High Explosive
HK	*Hilfskreuzer* (auxiliary cruiser)
HMAS	His Majesty's Australian Ship
HMCS	His Majesty's Canadian Ship
HMNZS	His Majesty's New Zealand Ship
HMS	His Majesty's Ship
HSK	*Handelsschutzkreuzer* (trade protection cruiser), or *Handelsstorkreuzer* (cruiser for harassing merchant ships)
HT	Hired Transport
K	'Kilo' time—GMT plus ten hours
Kriegsmarine	German Navy
KTB	*Kriegstagebuch* (War Diary)

Luftwaffe	German Air Force
NID	Naval Intelligence Division
RAAF	Royal Australian Air Force
RACAS	Rear Admiral Commanding the Australian Squadron
RAN	Royal Australian Navy
RANR	Royal Australian Navy Reserve
RANVR	Royal Australian Navy Volunteer Reserve
RN	Royal Navy
OIC	Operational Intelligence Centre
PWSS	Port War Signal Station
SAP	Semi Armour Piercing
SFTS	Service Flying Training School
SWACH	South West Area Combined Headquarters
TBS	Talk Between Ships
TS	Transmitting Station
USS	United States Ship
VAI	Vessels in Area Indicated (shipping plot)
WAMM	Western Australian Maritime Museum
Wehrmacht	German Army
WIR	Weekly Intelligence Report
WRANS	Women's Royal Australian Naval Service
WS	Weekly Summary
W/T	Wireless Telegraphy
Z	Zulu (Greenwich Mean Time)

BRITISH AND GERMAN RANK EQUIVALENTS

ROYAL NAVY	KRIEGSMARINE
Admiral	Admiral
Vice-Admiral	Vizeadmiral
Rear-Admiral	Konteradmiral
Commodore	Kommodore
Captain	Kapitän zur See
(No equivalent)	Fregattenkapitän
Commander	Korvettenkapitän
Lieutenant-Commander	Kapitänleutnant
Lieutenant	Oberleutnant zur See
Sub-Lieutenant	Leutnant zur See

INTRODUCTION

IN the relatively brief history of the Royal Australian Navy two cruisers have borne the title His Majesty's Australian Ship *Sydney*, and in peace and war both ships carried the name with distinction and honour.

The first *Sydney*, a Chatham (Town) class light cruiser, gained fame early when, on 9 November 1914, it intercepted and destroyed the German light cruiser *Emden* off the Cocos-Keeling Islands. In doing so, it became the first RAN ship to engage an enemy warship.

The second *Sydney*, a light cruiser of the Modified Leander (Perth) class, upheld the tradition in the Second World War. On 19 July 1940, in what was to become known as the Cape Spada action, *Sydney II* destroyed an Italian light cruiser, the *Bartolomeo Colleoni*, and damaged another, the *Giovanni Delle Bande Nere*. It was the first cruiser duel of the war and won Captain J.A. Collins, RAN, and his crew national acclaim. When *Sydney* returned home in February 1941, captain and crew received a hero's welcome.

After a short refit the ship took up quieter duties on the Australia Station. Based at Fremantle, Western Australia, *Sydney* was given the unglamorous but

no less important task of training new personnel, patrolling the shipping lanes and providing escort for merchant ships.

It was while engaged in the latter work that another battle honour was won.

At 1340 on 11 November 1941 *Sydney*, under the command of Captain Joseph Burnett, RAN, sailed from Fremantle on a routine escort mission. Burnett was given the task of escorting the troopship *Zealandia* to the Sunda Strait, where he was to hand over the escort to the British cruiser HMS *Durban*. *Sydney* was to return independently to Fremantle.

Zealandia, carrying troops of the 8th Australian Division, should have sailed on 10 November, but crew troubles delayed departure.

Sydney and *Durban* rendezvoused at midday on 17 November in position 7° 56' South 104° 40' East. After handing over the escort, Burnett turned his ship about and set course for Fremantle.

Sydney should have returned to port on the afternoon of 20 November, but the Australian cruiser failed to arrive.

On the evening of Sunday 23 November, *Sydney* was instructed to break W/T silence and report its estimated time of arrival.

Nothing was received.

Search aircraft were despatched from RAAF Pearce the following day with orders to locate *Sydney*. When they failed to find any trace of the ship, it was decided to escalate the search.

The first, albeit indirect, news of *Sydney* was received that Monday afternoon. The Navy Office in Melbourne learned that German Naval personnel had been recovered from a raft that had been found in the Sunda Strait–Fremantle shipping lane. The survivors claimed their ship had been sunk by a cruiser.

In the days that followed, as the search spread northwards, more German survivors were found. All told the same story. They had been involved in an action with a Perth class cruiser on the afternoon of 19 November. Their ship, the auxiliary cruiser *Kormoran*, was set on fire and had to be abandoned. The cruiser, badly damaged by shellfire and torpedo, was also set on fire, and was last seen as a glow on the horizon.

It was later established that the cruiser was *Sydney*. Although over three hundred Germans survived the sinking of the *Kormoran*, *Sydney* and its entire complement of 645 officers and men were never seen again.

— 1 —

HMAS SYDNEY

H IS MAJESTY'S AUSTRALIAN SHIP *Sydney* (II), was one of three light cruisers of the British Modified Leander (Perth) class.[1] Laid down at the works of Swan Hunter & Wigham Richardson Ltd, Wallsend on Tyne, on 8 July 1933 as HMS *Phaeton*, the ship was bought by the Commonwealth government while it was still under construction. *Phaeton* was transferred to the Royal Australian Navy and renamed *Sydney*.

Launched on 22 September 1934, *Sydney* had an overall length of 555 feet and a beam of 56 feet 8 inches. *Sydney* had a light displacement of 6,701 tons, a deep displacement of 8,940 tons, and a standard displacement of 7,250 tons.[2]

MAIN ARMAMENT AND FIRE CONTROL

Sydney's main armament consisted of eight 6-inch Breech Loading Mark XXIII guns mounted in four twin turrets. Two turrets, designated 'A' and

HMAS *Sydney*, approaching Circular
Quay, Sydney, on 10 February 1941.
G. Vickridge

'B', were mounted forward, and the remaining two turrets, designated 'X'
and 'Y', were mounted aft. The Mark XXIII gun, mounted in the Mark XXI
twin turret, had a maximum range of 24,800 yards at a maximum
elevation of 60°.[3]

Each turret had its own shell room, and each pair of turrets shared a
common magazine. The shell rooms, as their name implies, were used
only for the storage of 6-inch shells. The cordite charges, used for firing
the shells from the guns, were stored in the 6-inch magazines. For safety,
the shell rooms and magazines were located below the waterline.

During the Second World War, the Royal Navy used turret-mounted
guns of various calibres, up to 16-inch, and these large guns, down to the
8-inch guns of the heavy cruisers, were operated and loaded by
hydraulics. Battleships and heavy cruisers were provided with a hydraulic
system for these purposes, but the 6-inch cruisers, owing to space and
weight limitations, used individual turret pumps. The electrically driven
hydraulic pumps were located in the pump space below each gunhouse

and provided the power to train the turret and to elevate and depress the guns. Although hydraulic and electrically driven shell and cordite hoists were provided, the 6-inch shell, weighing 112 pounds, was deemed light enough for hand loading. A well-trained gun crew was expected to be capable of achieving a rate of fire of eight rounds per minute.

The larger gunned warships, because of their slower loading, normally fired salvoes consisting of half the available guns. *Sydney*, like other 6-inch cruisers, normally fired full gun salvoes. In other words, if four turrets could bear on the target, a salvo would consist of eight guns.[4]

Two methods could be used to fire the guns. If fired from the director control tower (DCT), an electric current supplied by the low-power system would fire the guns via electric firing tubes. If fired in local control (each turret operating and firing as an individual unit), the turret batteries would supply the necessary current to fire the guns, again via electric firing tubes. In the event of a complete loss of power, these batteries provided sufficient power for the emergency lighting and the firing of the guns. The guns themselves would be elevated or depressed, and the turret trained, by hand-operated gearing. Similarly, the shell and cordite hoists could also be operated by hand.

Each turret was equipped with a local sight and had the ability to operate as an individual unit in local control under the direction of the turret officer. Normally, however, the turrets were operated under director control.

Director control was basically a centralized fire-control system. The DCT was the 'eye' of the gunnery system and was placed as high as possible on the ship's superstructure so as to be above smoke and spray and in a position where it had an all-round view.

The personnel manning the DCT were accommodated in three compartments. The front compartment housed the director layer (who could fire the guns via an electric firing pistol), the director trainer, the range to elevation unit operator and the cross-level operator. The second compartment, known as the gunnery control compartment, was located above and abaft the front compartment. It was occupied by the control officer (the gunnery officer), the rate officer, the spotting officer, a telephone number, and if required, a wireless telegraphist. Below the gunnery control compartment was the rangefinder compartment, which

housed the main 15-foot rangefinder. Two men, the rangetaker and the rangefinder operator, were accommodated in this compartment. Protection for these key personnel consisted only of bullet-proof plating with a maximum thickness of half an inch.

From the DCT, the target's speed, bearing, and range was passed electrically to the 6-inch transmitting station (TS) where additional information such as wind speed and air temperature was added as well as the difference of angle of each individual turret in the space of the ship's length. The TS, located below the waterline immediately forward of the No.1 low-power room, was the nerve centre of the gunnery system. It contained the Admiralty Fire Control Table Mark V, the fire control telephone exchange and a W/T table with remote control keys for the Type 45 W/T set in the auxiliary W/T office and the Type 49 W/T set in the second W/T office.

The fire control table was essentially a calculating machine that converted all available information into a target range and bearing. It also provided a plot on moving paper, which gave the TS officer a visual representation of the battle, what every spotter could see and what each rangefinder was recording. From the TS, the relevant range and bearing data were passed electrically to each gun turret.

When director firing was used, the guns were fired by the director layer by means of a firing pistol. The director layer's sight could be gyro stabilized to compensate for the pitch and roll of the ship. If gyro firing was employed, linking the firing circuits to a gyroscope, the director layer had to ensure that he kept the firing pistol pressed until the gyro system closed the firing circuits. This ensured that the guns would only fire when the ship reached a certain point in its motion, thereby providing more consistent and accurate shooting.

It was originally proposed that the Leander and Modified Leander class carry two DCTs, one above and to the rear of the bridge and the other on the after superstructure. This proposal would have provided director control when firing on after as well as forward bearings and would also have permitted divided control so that two targets could be engaged simultaneously. Budget restrictions, however, forced the abandonment of the second DCT and, despite the objections of the Director of Naval Ordnance (DNO), only the single forward DCT was

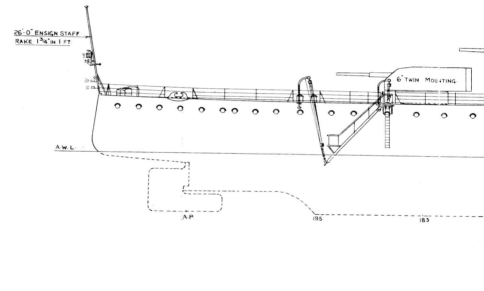

26'-0" ENSIGN STAFF
RAKE 1³⁄₄" IN 1 FT.

6" TWIN MOUNTING.

A.W.L.

A.P.

195

183

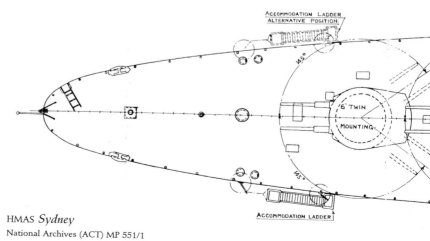

ACCOMMODATION LADDER
ALTERNATIVE POSITION.

145°

6" TWIN
MOUNTING.

145°

ACCOMMODATION LADDER.

HMAS *Sydney*
National Archives (ACT) MP 551/1

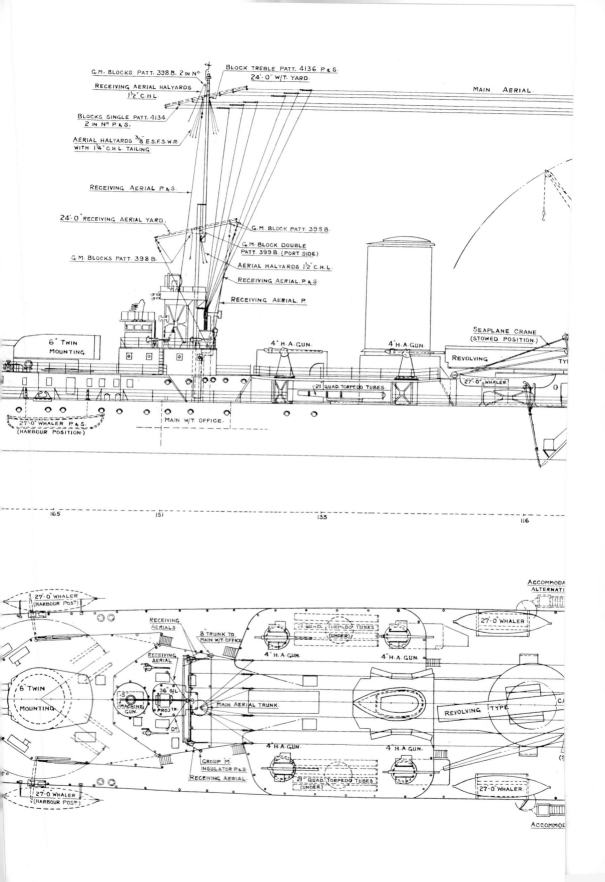

G.M. BLOCKS PATT. 398 B. 2 IN Nº

RECEIVING AERIAL HALYARDS
½" C.H.L.

BLOCK TREBLE PATT. 4136 P&S.
24'-0" W/T. YARD.

MAIN AERIAL.

BLOCKS SINGLE PATT. 4134
2 IN Nº P & S.

AERIAL HALYARDS ⅜" E.S.F.S.W.R.
WITH ¼" C.H.L. TAILING.

RECEIVING AERIAL P&S.

24'-0" RECEIVING AERIAL YARD.

G.M. BLOCK PATT. 398 B.

G.M. BLOCK DOUBLE
PATT. 399 B. (PORT SIDE)

G.M. BLOCKS PATT. 398 B.

AERIAL HALYARDS ½" C.H.L.

RECEIVING AERIAL. P & S.

RECEIVING AERIAL. P.

6" TWIN
MOUNTING

4" H.A. GUN.

4" H.A. GUN.

SEAPLANE CRANE
(STOWED POSITION.)

REVOLVING

TY

27'-0" WHALER.

O

21 QUAD. TORPEDO TUBES.

27'-0" WHALER P & S.
(HARBOUR POSITION.)

MAIN W/T. OFFICE.

165   151   135   116

27'-0" WHALER
(HARBOUR POSⁿ)

RECEIVING
AERIALS

8" TRUNK TO
MAIN W/T. OFFICE

21 QUAD. TORPEDO TUBES
(UNDER)

ACCOMMODA
ALTERNATI

27'-0" WHALER

RECEIVING
AERIAL

4" H.A. GUN.

4" H.A. GUN.

6" TWIN

MOUNTING

5"
MACHINE
GUN.

36" S/L.

PROJ TR.

Dº

MAIN AERIAL TRUNK.

REVOLVING TYPE

CA

GROUP M.
INSULATOR P&S.
RECEIVING AERIAL.

4" H.A. GUN.

4" H.A. GUN.

21 QUAD. TORPEDO TUBES
(UNDER)

27'-0" WHALER.

27'-0" WHALER
(HARBOUR POSⁿ)

ACCOMMOD

fitted. The DNO had objected on the grounds that if the single DCT were damaged, control of the guns would pass to the turret officers. Consequently, there would be a loss of central control and the efficiency of the main armament would be measurably lower.[5]

As a compromise, instead of a second DCT, it was proposed to fit a small non-revolving control position on the aft superstructure. This position, designated the after control position, was equipped with a Mark II training sight. The position was also provided with a gun range receiver, a gun deflection receiver and an Evershed target-bearing indicator and gong, as well as telephonic communication with the TS, DCT and the bridge. Although a cease-fire bell was also provided, there was no provision for centralized firing.

The other drawback of not having a second DCT was the loss of a rangefinder on the aft superstructure. The Leander and Modified Leander class carried the main 15-foot rangefinder in the DCT plus two 12-foot type UK 1 rangefinders on either side of the upper bridge, where a single hit could conceivably knock out all three rangefinders.

ANTI-AIRCRAFT, SALUTING AND SUB-CALIBRE ARMAMENT

Sydney's long range anti-aircraft weapons consisted of four 4-inch Quick Firing Mark V guns mounted on four high angle Mark IV mountings. They were mounted on the 4-inch gun deck immediately forward of the aft superstructure. Two guns were mounted on the port side (P-1 and P-2) and two on the starboard side (S-1 and S-2).

Although designed for high-angle firing, the Mark IV mounting was fitted with platforms for low-angle loading, allowing the guns to be used against low-flying aircraft and surface targets. In the high-angle role, the gun could fire a 31-lb high explosive shell to a maximum height of 28,750 feet. The maximum range for engaging surface targets was 16,300 yards.

Ammunition supply arrangements consisted of twelve ready-use lockers, each containing twenty rounds, mounted around the 4-inch gun deck. Approximately 800 rounds of 4-inch shell were carried, most being stored in the 4-inch magazine, which was situated abaft 'B' shell room.

For fire-control purposes, the Mark IV mounting was fitted with elevation and training receivers, which received height/range and bearing data from the high-angle control station (HACS) via the high-angle calculating position (HACP). This was basically a smaller version of the 6-inch fire-control system. The HACS was mounted on a tower above and abaft the DCT and housed a 15-foot type UD4 heightfinder. The HACS, operated by a five-man team, provided height and bearing data to the HACP, which was located in the hold immediately forward of the 6-inch TS.

The close-range anti-aircraft weapons comprised twelve 0.5-inch Vickers machine guns mounted on three Mark II quadruple mountings. One mounting was fitted on top of the after control position and the remaining two were mounted on platforms either side of the flag deck.

Augmenting the 0.5-inch machine guns were nine 0.303-inch Lewis machine guns, which could be mounted on pedestals on the aft 36-inch searchlight platform, the midships 36-inch searchlight platforms and the lower bridge.

Sydney was also equipped with four Quick-Firing 3-pounder Hotchkiss guns for saluting purposes, although it appears that these were removed in July or August 1940. *Sydney* also carried four 3-pounder sub-calibre practice guns, which fitted inside the firing chambers of the 6-inch guns, one gun being stowed in each 6-inch gunhouse.

TORPEDOES AND SEARCHLIGHTS

Sydney's torpedo armament consisted of eight 21-inch QR Mark VII above-water torpedo tubes mounted in quadruple sets. Housed in the tubes were eight 21-inch Mark IX torpedoes, each carrying a 750-lb warhead. No reloads were carried. The tubes were mounted on the upper deck, port and starboard, immediately below the 4-inch gundeck and could be fired locally or remotely from the bridge.

For illumination purposes, three 36-inch diameter Mark V searchlights were provided. One was mounted on a platform above the aft super-structure, the other two were mounted on platforms positioned on the port and starboard sides of the forward funnel.

ANTI-SUBMARINE EQUIPMENT

As completed, *Sydney* was equipped with Type 125 Asdic housed in a pattern 3069 dome, which could be retracted, or housed, when the Asdic was not in use.

For offensive action, *Sydney* carried five Mark VII depth charges on a rail at the stern. Each depth charge contained a 300-lb explosive charge of TNT or Amatol. The charge could be detonated at 50, 100, 150, 250, 350 or 500 feet by means of a depth-setting key. When the depth charges were not required for immediate use, the depth-setting keys were set to the 'safe' position. When at sea, the depth charges were primed for use but disarmed by means of the depth-setting key. The primers would be removed before entering harbour.[6]

BOILERS AND MACHINERY

For steam production and propulsion, *Sydney* was equipped with four Admiralty-type Yarrow three-drum boilers. The boilers supplied super-heated steam at a maximum pressure of 300 pounds per square inch to four Parsons geared turbine sets. At full power, these turbine sets, coupled through gear cases to the four propeller shafts, were capable of producing 72,000 shaft horse power. During power and fuel consumption trials in October 1938, the following speeds were calculated:

FULL SPEED	31.5 KNOTS
WITH ALL DESPATCH	30.4 KNOTS
WITH DESPATCH	28.2 KNOTS
WITH ALL CONVENIENT DESPATCH	25.9 KNOTS
WITH MODERATE DESPATCH	21.1 KNOTS
AT MOST ECONOMICAL SPEED	12.0 KNOTS

The forward boiler room housed 'A1' and 'A2' boilers as well as a small auxiliary boiler, which produced steam and hot water for the ship's galley and other domestic purposes. 'A1' and 'A2' boilers were mounted side by side, and the auxiliary boiler was mounted forward of these on the

centreline of the ship. 'A1' and 'A2' boilers supplied steam to the forward engine room. The forward engine room supplied power to the two outer (forward) propeller shafts.

The aft boiler room housed 'B1' and 'B2' boilers, these boilers being mounted in line on the centreline of the ship. 'B1' and 'B2' boilers supplied steam to the aft engine room, which supplied power to the two inner (aft) propeller shafts.

Boilers and turbine sets were cross-connected, enabling any boiler to supply steam to any turbine set, although when at sea each boiler room normally only supplied steam to its corresponding engine room.

Each boiler room was equipped with four steam-driven (turbo) forced-draught fans, which supplied the necessary draught for the boilers. This supply of air effectively pressurized the boiler room. Access to the stokehold was via an airlock, two of which were fitted in each boiler room. These airlocks allowed men to enter or leave the boiler room without creating a sudden drop in air pressure.

The forced-draught air was circulated through air preheaters mounted on the outside of each boiler before entering the boiler furnace. The draught would then force the exhaust gases produced by the combustion process up through the funnel uptakes. When more steam was required for an increase in the ship's speed, the speed of the turbo fans would also be increased to keep up with the boilers' demand for air.

The boilers were oil-fired and of the water tube type. Basically, distilled feed water was circulated through water tubes inside the boiler. The hot gases created in the furnace boiled the water in these tubes to create saturated steam, which was then piped through the furnace again to remove excess moisture. The steam thus produced had a temperature in the order of 600° Fahrenheit and was called 'superheated' steam.

Feed water for the boilers was also preheated and was delivered to the regulators by turbo-driven main feed pumps, two being fitted in each engine room. A single electrically driven auxiliary feed pump was also fitted in each boiler room.

Oil was supplied to the boilers by electrically driven pumps, two being fitted in each engine room. Like the air and the feed water, the oil was also preheated before delivery to the registers on the front of the boilers. The registers, mounted in rows, contained the oil sprayer, which

permitted the fuel-oil to be atomized and sprayed under pressure into the combustion chamber or furnace.

In normal operation, the oil-air mixture would be regulated so that little or no smoke was created and emitted from the funnel(s). There were occasions, however, when heavy smoke development was required, such as when laying a smoke screen. For this purpose a separate burner, which delivered a jet of unatomized oil into the furnace, was used. The flame from the normal sprayers would ignite this jet but, owing to incomplete combustion of the excess oil, heavy black smoke would be produced. Where possible, boilers would be alternated when making smoke because the prolonged use of a single boiler could lead to a buildup of unburned oil on the furnace floor or in the bilges if there were any defects in the boiler brickwork or casing. Such a buildup of oil constituted a serious fire hazard and was to be avoided.

Another potential hazard was a sudden loss of air pressure in the stokehold. This could cause the flame in the boilers to flash back, with potentially fatal results for the boiler-room men. Flashbacks, however, were relatively rare. The sudden loss of draught required to produce such a phenomenon would, in most cases, have been caused by a far more serious event, such as a breach of the surrounding hull plating or deck, or the simultaneous stopping of all fans because of shellfire, torpedo or bomb damage.[7]

Similar forced-draught fans were fitted to the engine rooms. These were known as supply and exhaust fans and were for the purpose of ventilating the engine room and reducing the engine-room temperature to an acceptable level. Two electrically driven 30-inch supply fans and two electrically driven 35-inch exhaust fans were provided in each engine room.

The superheated steam produced by the boilers was fed to the turbine sets through manoeuvring valves and a system of steam pipes or leads. This system of pipes and leads was designated the 'main steam system'. The system also supplied steam to the turbo generators, or dynamos, and certain auxiliaries, such as pumps, ejectors, fire extinguishers and the turbo fans. Exhaust steam from these auxiliaries was then used to heat the feed water for the boilers, the condensed steam being returned to the feed water system or tanks. The steam supplied to the turbines was exhausted

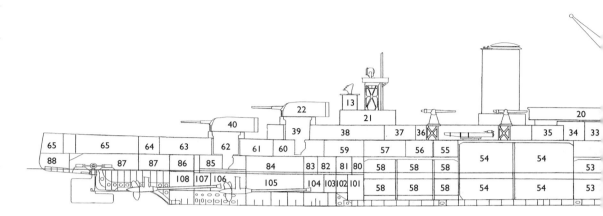

HMAS *Sydney*. Internal profile.

National archives

1	High-angle control station	30	Sickbay
2	Director control tower	31	Ship's galley
3	Compass platform	32	Bakery
4	Wheelhouse	33	Mail office (S)
5	Plotting office		Aircraft store (P)
6	Remote-control office	34	Shipwrights' workshop
7	Chart house	35	Vegetable store
8	Silent compartment	36	Torpedo parting shop
9	'B' turret	37	Officers' WCs
10	Captain's sea cabin (S)	38	Captain's cabin (S)
	Navigating Officer's cabin (P)		Senior officers' cabins (P)
11	Armament office (S)	39	'X' turret pump room/lobby
	Dental surgery (P)	40	'Y' turret
12	Signal distribution office	41	Paint store
13	After control position	42	Shipwrights' store
14	'A' turret	43	Cable locker flat
15	'B' turret pump room/lobby	44	No.1 lower mess
16	Seamen's heads	45	Ammunition lobby
17	Recreation space	46	No.2 lower mess
18	Blacksmith's shop	47	No.3 lower mess
19	Seaplane crane	48	No.4 lower mess
20	Catapult	49	Stokers' mess
21	Officers' galleys	50	Forward ('A') boiler room
22	'X' turret	51	Fan chamber
23	Paint room	52	Engineer's workshop
24	Capstan engine flat and prison (S)	53	Forward ('A') engine room
25	Messdeck (Stoker PO, PO &	54	Aft ('B') boiler room
	Canteen staff)	55	Fan chamber
26	'A' turret pump room/lobby	56	Cabins
27	CPO, ERA messdeck	57	Main W/T office (centre)
28	Ammunition lobby	58	Aft ('B') engine room
29	Upper mess	59	Cabins

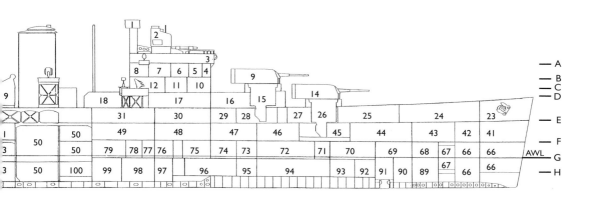

HMAS SYDNEY

60	Ammunition lobby	
61	Cabins (S)	
	Wardroom (P)	
62	'Y' turret pump room/lobby	
63	Cabins	
64	Capstan engine compartment	
65	WOs' cabins	
66	Water-tight compartments	
67	Cable locker	
68	Canvas room and petrol control compartment	
69	No.1 store	
70	Compressor room	
71	Band instrument room	
72	Pump lobby	
73	Chart and chronometer room	
74	Lobby	
75	Lower steering position	
76	Auxiliary W/T office	
77	Lobby	
78	Telephone exchange	
79	2nd W/T office (centre)	
	No.2 low power room (S)	
	Switchboard room (P)	
80	Storeroom	
81	Artisans' chest flat	
82	WO's store	
83	Gyro compass room	
84	After compressor room and pump lobby	
85	Ammunition lobby	
86	Fresh water tanks	
87	Steering gear compartment	
88	Officers' baggage room	
89	Aviation spirit room	
90	Fresh water tanks	
91	Asdic compartment	
92	Small arms magazine	
93	'A' shell room	
94	6-inch magazine	
95	'B' shell room	
96	4-inch magazine	
97	High-angle calculating position	
98	6-inch transmitting station	
99	No.1 low-power room	
100	Auxiliary boiler	
101	Gland compartment	
102	Warhead room	
103	Bomb room	
104	'X' shell room	
105	6-inch magazine	
106	'Y' shell room	
107	Gunners' store	
108	Spirit room and inflammable store	
A	Upper bridge	
B	Lower bridge	
C	Superstructure deck	
D	Forecastle deck	
E	Upper deck	
F	Lower deck	
G	Platform deck	
H	Hold	
AWL	Average water line	

into condensers bolted to the undersides of the low-pressure and astern turbines. Again, the water produced was returned to the feed water system or tanks. The primary source of feed water on *Sydney* were the evaporators in the aft engine room. They used exhaust steam to boil sea water to produce distilled water.

Protecting these vital components was a 3-inch layer of armour plate, known as an armour belt, which was attached to the 1-inch hull plates surrounding the boiler and engine rooms. Hull plates fore and aft of the armour belt were ⅞-inch thick.

PUMPING, FLOODING AND DRAINING

Just as there was a system for producing steam, there was also one for pumping, flooding and draining compartments. The functions required of this system were to clear the ship of drainage and bilgewater; provide sea water, under pressure, for fire-fighting purposes, the sanitary service, for cooling purposes and for washing decks and cables; permit deliberate flooding of certain compartments below the waterline to correct heel or trim arising from damage or to prevent fire or explosion; and pump out large quantities of water entering the hull through damage.[8]

For pumping out compartments, a 5-inch diameter pipe, designated the 'main suction', was fitted inside the ship on the port side about 4 feet above the average water line (AWL). A series of branch pipes and hoses provided access to all principal compartments on the platform deck. Valves were fitted to the main suction where main transverse bulkheads were pierced in order to preserve watertight subdivision.

Pumping was performed by various types of pump and ejector. In *Sydney*, each boiler and engine room was equipped with an electrically driven fire and bilge pump mounted on the port side and connected to the main suction by a 4-inch pipe. These pumps had a capacity of between 50 and 75 tons of water an hour. Each engine room was also fitted with an electrically driven oil-fuel transfer pump, which could also be employed as a fire and bilge pump. Supplementing these pumps were six steam bilge ejectors, each capable of discharging 200 to 300 tons of water an hour. Two were fitted in each boiler room and one in each engine room.

Outside the machinery spaces, *Sydney* had two 50 ton per hour electrically driven centrifugal pumps. One was mounted forward on the platform deck directly below 'B' turret; the other was mounted aft on the platform deck, approximately below 'Y' turret.

The water dealt with by the main suction could be discharged overboard, transferred to other parts of the ship for correction of trim or heel, or fed into the main service pipe by the use of cross connections. Portable electrically driven submersible pumps, which could be used in areas where the main suction was damaged or had failed, supported the main suction system. It is understood that *Sydney* carried two of these pumps, each with a capacity of 50 tons of water an hour.

To deal with fire and to provide salt water to various installations around the ship, there was a similar 5-inch diameter pipe, designated the 'main service'. This pipe ran fore and aft under the upper deck on the starboard side except in the machinery spaces, where it crossed over to the port side to connect with the fire and bilge pumps via 4-inch pipes. In normal circumstances, pressure in the main service was maintained by one of the fire and bilge pumps located in the machinery spaces.

Valves and hose fittings at the main transverse bulkheads enabled watertight integrity to be maintained and permitted damaged sections of the main service to be isolated or by-passed with canvas fire hoses. Cross connections between the main suction and the main service allowed each system or parts of each system to alternate. In this way, both systems could be used for extracting or supplying seawater, both systems sharing the common fire and bilge pumps.

The main service supplied water for fire fighting and was sometimes referred to as the fire main, but it also provided salt water for other shipboard purposes. They included servicing urinals, flushing soil pipes, filling practice torpedo heads, supplying the deck wash service and providing cooling water for various pieces of machinery, such as the air compressing plant, the steering gear, capstan bearings and the refrigerating plants.

In its fire-fighting role, the main service supplied salt water to numerous hose connections throughout the ship, each connection having a fire hose and nozzle stowed adjacent to it. The main service also provided salt water for the overhead spraying arrangements in the magazines and ammunition lobbies.

Flooding also played a key role in the system, either for the fighting of fire or for the correcting of heel or trim. All *Sydney*'s magazines and shell rooms, the bomb room, the spirit rooms, and the inflammable store were fitted with flooding arrangements, which allowed these rooms and magazines to be flooded from two positions. Geared rods connected to the seacocks and valves allowed flooding to be accomplished from the deck immediately above the relevant room or magazine, or from flooding cabinets on the weather decks. The bottom compartments in the machinery spaces and the oil-fuel tanks outside the machinery spaces could also be flooded in the event of an emergency.

THE ELECTRICAL SYSTEM

Sydney's electrical system consisted primarily of a ring main circuit, feeder cables to supply electricity beyond the ring main, four dynamos to generate the electricity and a single switchboard for the control and distribution of the electricity. This system was known as the 'main supply system'.

The 220-volt ring main consisted of two single conductors, which ran around the midship section to embrace the four dynamos. These conductors, one positive, the other negative, were paper-insulated, lead-sheathed and armour-encased stranded copper cables. To protect this vital component, the ring main and all of its switches were made watertight and were run within the ship's armour belt.

The two turbo-driven dynamos, one in each engine room, were connected to the athwartship sections of the ring main, and two diesel-driven dynamos, which were located in rooms abreast the aft boiler room, were connected to the port and starboard sections of the ring main. The ring main could thus be divided into four sections, any of which could be isolated from the system in the event of damage.[9]

Under normal circumstances, only the turbo generators were placed on line. When *Sydney* went to action stations, the two diesel generators were started and brought on line. The ring main was then split, with each section and its generator supplying a quarter of the ship and one of the turrets, thus minimizing the effects of battle damage. Outside the ring

main, feeder cables were used to supply power to the various motors, pumps and electrically operated components of the ship.

The main switchboard allowed the whole supply and distribution of lighting and power for the ship to be controlled from one central position. This switchboard was divided into two distinct parts, the dynamo supply panel and the distribution panel. Strangely, this vital component was housed in a compartment with little protection, the switchboard room being located on the port side of the platform deck immediately forward of the forward boiler room. In this position, the room was above the waterline and forward of the armour belt, and protected only by the ⁷⁄₈-inch hull plating.

The main supply system also supplied power to the 14 kW motor generators, which provided power for the low-power supply system. There were three motor generators, situated in the No.1 low-power room. Two obtained their 220-volt supply from the turbo dynamos via the main supply switchgear, and the third obtained its 220-volt supply from the diesel dynamos, also via the main supply switchgear. The low-power supply system was of critical importance because it supplied the power for the armament control and firing systems, the torpedo and searchlight controls, the gyro compass and the internal communications system.

Two low-power rooms were provided. The more important No.1 room, which contained the main armament firing generator, the gun elevation transmitter motor, the gyro-firing alternator and the master gyro compass (in an adjoining compartment), was located below the waterline immediately forward of the forward boiler room. The No.2 room, which contained the torpedo controls, the searchlight controls and the internal communications system controls, was situated on the starboard side of the platform deck immediately forward of the forward boiler room. This room also housed a motor generator for battery charging. Like the switchboard room, the No.2 low-power room was protected only by the ⁷⁄₈-inch hull plating. The two low-power rooms and the switchboard room thus formed an inverted triangle of electrical compartments immediately forward of the ring main.

WIRELESS TELEGRAPHY AND VISUAL SIGNALLING

As completed, *Sydney* was fitted with the following wireless telegraphy (W/T) transmitting sets:

MAIN W/T OFFICE	TYPE 48 SET
SECOND W/T OFFICE	TYPE 49 SET
AUXILIARY W/T OFFICE	TYPE 43 AND TYPE 45 SETS

Despite wartime proposals to upgrade some of these sets, it is believed that no alterations were effected before the ship's loss.

The main W/T office, which could receive and transmit messages, was located on the centreline of the ship on the lower deck immediately below the mainmast. This office, which incorporated the coding office, was fitted with a Type 48 transmitter set. An adjoining annexe on the port side housed the central receiving room, which contained the battery-powered W/T receiver sets. The aerials were trunked to the top of the after superstructure. Six insulated main transmitting aerials were strung between 24-foot wide W/T yards on the main and fore masts. Five insulated receiving aerials were suspended from the mainmast. Located in the flat immediately forward of the main office were the warning telephone (Wa/T) panels.[10]

The second W/T office was located on the platform deck directly above the No.1 low-power room and almost immediately below the foremast, which supported its aerials. This office, which could also receive and transmit messages, was fitted with a Type 49 transmitter set and battery-powered receivers.

The auxiliary W/T office was also located on the platform deck. It was fitted with receivers and Type 43 and 45 transmitter sets, the latter being used primarily for gunnery control purposes.

A Type 512 internal buzzer system was provided for communication between the W/T offices. It is understood that all W/T offices received their electrical power from the 220-volt system via feeder cables, this supply being converted locally.

In addition to the W/T offices, a remote-control office, located in a compartment on the lower bridge, was provided for the remote

controlling of the various W/T installations. For this purpose it was fitted with a Type 532 remote-control outfit.

Sydney's construction plans indicate that the auxiliary office was to house an emergency W/T transmitter and receiver set, although there is some doubt if a set was actually installed in this compartment.[11] Related documents show that the emergency set was Type 6E, although there is evidence to suggest that this may have been replaced in 1941 with a Type 60E emergency set.

In January 1938, an Admiralty order (CAFO) highlighted the need for an emergency low-power all-wave transmitter and receiver, driven by batteries, to be installed in a position near the commanding officer. For cruisers and above, this set was to be a semi-portable Type 60E, which was to be known as the 'standard emergency W/T equipment'. In addition, for protracted emergencies it was recommended that a transportable Type 52T set be fitted, which would serve as an 'after action' set as well as a transportable set. These requirements were reiterated in CAFO 1612 in 1940 and then brought to notice again in CAFO 2045 of 14 November 1940. This latter CAFO provides a rare insight into the realities of W/T communications in the early war years and is reproduced in part.

1. Several cases have occurred in which no W/T Enemy Report or distress message was received by other ships or shore authorities from HM Ships which have been lost in enemy action.

2. In the case of the loss of HM Ships GLORIOUS, ACASTA and ARDENT only one transmission was received from HMS GLORIOUS but nothing was heard from the other two ships. Nothing was heard from HM Ships EXMOUTH and DARING.

3. The transmission from HMS GLORIOUS was heard by one ship only but was so weak and corrupt that it was not recognised as an 'Enemy Report'.

4. It is considered probable that the main and second W/T transmitters in HMS GLORIOUS were destroyed in the early stages of the action and that an attempt was made to transmit a report on a portable W/T set.

5. The most probable causes of W/T failures in action were:
    (a) Failure of electric power.
    (b) Serious damage to main W/T equipment.
    (c) Destruction of aerial system.

6. All HM Ships, other than auxiliary vessels are equipped with some form of emergency W/T equipment working off batteries.

10. If a portable set is carried on board it is to be stowed away from the main W/T office. The portable set is to have tuning adjustment for all ship-to-shore frequencies covered by its wave frequency range.[12]

An alteration and addition list for *Sydney* dated 31 January 1941 indicates that Type 60E standard emergency W/T equipment was requested for installation in the ship's remote-control office to satisfy subparagraph 10 of CAFO 2045.[13] As this request was approved, it is assumed that the specified equipment was provided and installed before November 1941.

When at sea *Sydney*, like all other warships, maintained wireless silence, the primary task of the W/T organization being that of listening. When there was a requirement to break W/T silence, messages were transmitted in encoded Morse, there being no means by which to send voice messages.

Supplementary to this listening task was direction finding (D/F). The equipment, which enabled bearings to be taken on intercepted W/T transmissions, was installed in a compartment to the rear of the lower bridge.[14]

The W/T system catered for both ship-to-shore and ship-to-ship communications, but visual signalling (V/S) was normally used for short to medium range ship-to-ship signals traffic. For these purposes, signal flags or pennants could be displayed on the signal halyards, or signal projectors could be used to transmit Morse light signals. For light signalling, *Sydney* was equipped with four 10-inch and four 18-inch diameter signal projectors. One 10-inch and one 18-inch projector were mounted on each of the port and starboard signal projector platforms to the rear of the upper bridge, and one 10-inch and one 18-inch projector were mounted on each of the port and starboard extensions of the flag deck.

These projectors, sometimes known as daylight lamps, were used for both day and night signalling. The 10-inch projector was the more commonly used, though for close-range signalling at night a hand-held Aldis lamp was usually employed.

NAVIGATION AND STEERING

Sydney's navigation equipment consisted of two Sperry electro-mechanical gyro compasses. Although very accurate, the gyro compasses were totally reliant on the ship's electrical system. One compass was located forward in the No.1 low-power room, and the other was located aft in the after gyro compass room.

The bearing provided by the gyro compass was relayed electrically to auxiliary compasses called 'gyro-repeaters'. These were provided on the aft searchlight platform, in the lower steering position, in the wheelhouse on the lower bridge and on the compass platform on the upper bridge. The gyro signal was also fed to the navigation compass, known as the 'Pelorus'. For gunnery control purposes, a gyro compass receiver and a compass-bearing receiver were installed in the TS. Four azimuth repeaters were also provided, two being located to the rear of the upper bridge and two being provided on the lower bridge.

A magnetic compass was provided as a backup to the gyro compasses. This was the standard compass and was housed in the wooden binnacle and mounted on a wooden platform to the front of the upper bridge. Small portable magnetic compasses were also carried for use in the ship's boats.

On *Sydney*, conning was performed from the semi-enclosed compass platform to the front of the upper bridge via voicepipe and telephone to the wheelhouse and the lower steering position. Steering was normally performed from the wheelhouse, but when at action stations the helm was transferred to the lower steering position, this being located on the platform deck immediately below the bridge. An aft steering position and emergency hand-steering gear was provided in the steering-gear compartment at the stern. The emergency conning position appears to have been the aft 36-inch searchlight platform.

The compass platform, as its name indicates, housed the Pelorus and the binnacle. It also housed an array of instruments and switches, including engine room order repeat receivers from the lower steering position. A network of voice pipes linked the compass platform with all major compartments and positions in the fore part of the ship, telephones being provided for communication with the more remote parts. In contrast to many other British warships, *Sydney*'s compass platform was semienclosed with a 'roof' of bulletproof plating.

Conning was performed by the captain or the officer of the watch. Helm orders were normally passed via voicepipe to the quartermaster, or helmsman, stationed at the steering pedestal (wheel) in the wheelhouse.

The lower steering position, which was essentially a duplication of the compass platform and wheelhouse, was provided for the purpose of controlling the ship should the compass platform or wheelhouse or both be put out of action. To this end, the action station of the second in command (executive officer) was the lower steering position. In the event of the bridge being destroyed, the executive officer would make his way aft to the emergency conning position and command the ship from there.

The steering pedestals in the wheelhouse and lower steering position were connected hydraulically to electro-hydraulic steering gear located immediately above the rudder head on the platform deck. This gear was located in the steering gear compartment, or tiller flat, which also contained the telemotor control equipment and the electrically driven variable delivery pumps. Located in a compartment within the steering gear compartment was a third steering pedestal and telephone, which formed the emergency steering position.

AIRCRAFT AND CATAPULT ARRANGEMENTS

For gunnery spotting, anti-submarine patrols, and general reconnaissance *Sydney* was provided with an amphibious aircraft. Before July 1940 the ship carried a Supermarine Seagull V. At the time of its loss, *Sydney* was carrying a Walrus aircraft, serial No. L-2177. The Walrus was essentially a British version of the Seagull V.

The aircraft was normally launched from a 53-foot revolving catapult mounted amidships between the funnels, although it could also be lowered over the side for water takeoffs. A 6–7 ton electric seaplane crane, mounted on the centreline abaft the forward funnel, was provided for this purpose. The crane was also used for lowering and recovering the ship's boats.

Petrol for the aircraft was stored in the aviation spirit room, which was located in the bows. From here it was piped as required to the upper deck in the vicinity of the catapult support. Compressed air from the general air system was used to transfer the fuel.

Seagull A2-18 being hoisted
aboard *Sydney* at Fremantle.
WAMM

BOATS AND LIFESAVING EQUIPMENT

As completed, *Sydney* was equipped with the following boats and Carley floats:

BOATS

NUMBER	TYPE	LIFESAVING CAPACITY
I	36-FOOT MOTOR AND PULLING PINNACE	76
2	35-FOOT MOTOR BOAT	2 X 46
2	32-FOOT CUTTER	2 X 59
I	30-FOOT GIG	26
2	27-FOOT WHALER	2 X 27
I	16-FOOT SKIFF DINGHY	14

CARLEY FLOATS

NUMBER	TYPE	LIFESAVING CAPACITY
2	PATTERN NO. 17	2 X 45
2	PATTERN NO. 18	2 X 67
2	PATTERN NO. 20	2 X 20
TOTAL LIFESAVING CAPACITY		644*

* Documents dating from 1938 indicate that the 16-foot Skiff was replaced with a 16-foot Vosper motor boat (Jolly boat). The relevant Admiralty seamanship manuals indicate that the 16-foot motor boat could only accommodate seven people, thus reducing the total lifesaving capacity to 637.

As can be seen, there was ample lifesaving capacity for *Sydney*'s peacetime complement of approximately 505 officers and men, and almost sufficient to accommodate its enlarged wartime complement.

The lifesaving capacity of the Carley float, essentially a large oval-shaped life preserver, however, is somewhat misleading. The small Pattern No. 20 float, for example, was designed to provide life support for twenty men, although only twelve men could be accommodated inside the float. The remaining eight were expected to hang onto the rope lifeline secured to the outside of the float.

All of *Sydney*'s boats, with the exception of the two cutters and the two whalers, were stowed amidships abreast the forward funnel. These boats, and the two whalers, were hoisted in and out of the water by the ship's crane. The two cutters, however, were stowed on the forecastle deck abreast the foremast and could be lowered and recovered by davit. These cutters were *Sydney*'s sea boats, and were swung out on the davits, ready for instant use when at sea. All boats were of timber construction.

The Carley floats, despite the size and weight of the larger patterns, were placed in positions where they could be manhandled over the side. The two Pattern No.17 floats were originally stowed horizontally on the 4-inch gundeck between the guns and outboard of the ready-use ammunition lockers. The two larger Pattern No.18 floats were stowed vertically on the centreline of the 4-inch gundeck and secured to the timber stowage rack to form a rudimentary blast screen. The two Pattern No.20 floats were originally stowed horizontally (stacked) on the boiler room vent forward of the forward funnel.

The number and type of Carley float allotted to *Sydney* after the outbreak of war is difficult to determine. Although additional men were assigned to *Sydney* in September 1939 to increase the size of the crew for war service, it is understood that the ship did not receive any additional Carley floats. There is also little to suggest that *Sydney* received an increased allocation of Carley floats when it began operating in the hostile Mediterranean theatre, although photographs taken in mid to late 1940 reveal that the floats that were carried were repositioned.

Of interest was the repositioning of the two Pattern No.20 floats. These were relocated to the port side of the forecastle deck abreast the forward funnel and outboard of the 36-foot pinnace, in the place normally occupied by the 30-foot gig. The 30-foot gig appears to have been removed from the ship entirely, although when, and for what purpose, is unknown.

In addition to the Carley floats, circular type lifebuoys were carried. Photographs show that two lifebuoys were carried abaft the torpedo space, with another two stowed on the forward superstructure. It is possible that more were carried elsewhere on the ship.

Sydney's P-1 4-inch gun crew conducting a
practice shoot. Note the two Pattern No.20
Carley floats outboard of the 36-foot
pinnace.
WAMM

MISCELLANEOUS

One of the more distinctive features of the ship was its tall pole masts. *Sydney*, like other British cruisers, was designed for scouting and trade-protection duties. As these tasks could entail operating alone and far from home, a reliable W/T transmission range was needed. This meant that either the W/T sets carried should be more powerful than those carried by vessels designed for operations in home waters or the W/T aerials should be raised as high as possible. As the increased size of more powerful W/T sets was difficult to accommodate in the already cramped conditions aboard British cruisers, the easy option was to increase the height of the masts.

Mention must also be made of the deck coverings. All weather decks were covered with 7-inch wide planks of Borneo whitewood, partly for appearance, but primarily for the purpose of reducing the temperature in the living spaces below. The decks in the living areas were covered with linoleum, or corticene, which was a mixture of powdered cork and linseed oil. A similar material called korkoid was used in the officers' quarters and in certain compartments such as the sick bay. Cork was also applied to some overhead fittings and deckheads to reduce 'sweating'.

Leaded paint was applied to all metal fittings, bulkheads and plates to reduce the deterioration of the structure by rust. According to former *Sydney* crew members, on the outbreak of war, the pre-war enamelled paintwork was simply painted over with standard naval grey. Successive coats, including the two camouflage schemes, were also painted on over the existing paintwork.

At the time, it was not fully understood that the deck coverings and the layers of paint constituted a serious fire hazard. Most of the furniture, which was made of timber, also constituted a fire hazard. In 1943, when HMNZS *Leander* was undergoing repair at the US Navy base at Pearl Harbor, a firefighting committee inspected the ship and recommended that all its timber furniture be removed and replaced with steel office furniture.[15]

PROPOSED ALTERATIONS AND WARTIME MODIFICATIONS

In the early 1930s, a twin 4-inch gun mounting was designed and developed for the anti-aircraft role. The result was the Mark XIX high-angle/low-angle twin mounting, which entered service with the Royal Navy in 1936.

The question of rearming *Sydney* with these mountings was given consideration in 1938. In a confidential memo to the Australian Commonwealth Naval Board (ACNB), the Captain Superintendent HMA Naval Establishments Sydney (Captain G.R. Deverell, RN) considered that this rearmament could be conducted in the ship's refit period between December 1939 and January 1940.

The principal alterations to be carried out in connection with the rearmament were the fitting of twin 4-inch guns in lieu of single 4-inch guns and the fitting of blast screens between the 4-inch mountings. To accommodate the larger ammunition allowance, stowage in the 4-inch magazine was to be increased and a second shell hoist fitted. These alterations were to be carried out on the same lines as the alterations made to HMAS *Hobart* in 1938.

In October 1938, while the question of rearmament was still pending, *Sydney*'s Commanding Officer, Captain J.W.A. Waller, RN, prepared a report on the ship's fighting efficiency. In a letter to the Rear Admiral Commanding the Australian Squadron (RACAS), Waller echoed the DNO's views that a single 6-inch DCT was unsatisfactory and that, if possible, a second DCT be provided. The report noted that the principal components of the centralized fire-control system were poorly protected and located in such a manner that a single hit could put the whole system out of action. He explained that, if the DCT were knocked out, control of the guns would pass to the aft control. As this position was not equipped for centralized fire control, the fighting efficiency of the ship would be seriously impaired. Waller also pointed out that it was not only the single DCT, which was an 'Achilles heel', but also the wiring that ran from the DCT to the TS. Although this wiring ran down the centreline of the ship, it was insufficiently protected and could be severed by a single hit, blast or splinter damage.[16]

Waller was also concerned about the protection arrangements for the TS, HACP and the attendant low-power rooms. Although placed below the waterline, the TS, HACP and the No.1 low-power room were only about 12 inches below the AWL. They were also located forward of the armour belt, which meant that they were protected only by the hull plates and the oil-fuel tanks. If the hull plates and fuel-tank bulkheads were ruptured the TS, HACP and the No.1 low-power room could become flooded with salt water or oil-fuel or both.

The equally vital main switchboard room and the No.2 low-power room received even less protection. These rooms were located above the waterline and forward of the armour belt, being protected only by ⅞-inch plating. Waller, however, acknowledged that these shortcomings could not be rectified. All warships of the time embodied design compromises and *Sydney* was neither a singular victim nor an exception. The only practicable modification that was possible was increased protection for the wiring that linked the DCT and the HACS with their respective trans-mitting and calculating positions. Waller therefore proposed that these control cables be encased inside 40-lb (1-inch) high-tensile steel plate for 'protection against all but major fragments of shell or bombs, or direct hit'. With *Sydney* due for a refit late in 1939, Waller perhaps raised the issue with a view to having his recommendations implemented during the ship's refit period.

Waller's report prompted RACAS to recommend that added protection and an after DCT be provided. The matter went to the ACNB and from there to the Admiralty, although it is not known what their final recom-mendation was. As a second DCT is not mentioned in the rearmament proposals or the subsequent alteration and addition lists, it is probable that the matter was deferred indefinitely. Although the protection for the electrical cabling would have been a simple remedy and could have been completed during a refit, it is unclear if Waller's proposal was ever carried out.

Unfortunately, because of the outbreak of war on 3 September 1939, *Sydney*'s proposed rearmament was deferred, archive documents indicat-ing that it was still pending in September 1940.

Throughout 1940, the general shortage of cruisers, and *Sydney*'s good fortune in not sustaining any serious damage, effectively prevented the

ship's withdrawal from service for a major refit. The ship entered dock at Alexandria on 20 July for limited repairs to the minor damage resulting from the Cape Spada action in July 1940. This involved patching a shell hole in the forward funnel and numerous small splinter holes in the superstructure and upper deck. Three of the ship's boats were also damaged by splinters and required attention.

During July and August 1940, 20-lb (½-inch) plating was bolted to the guard-rail stanchions surrounding the 4-inch gundeck. This 3-foot high plating was added to provide the gun crews with some measure of protection against splinters and shrapnel. Photographs from this period reveal that for added protection, splinter mats (similar in appearance to mattresses) were secured to the mounting rails of the 4-inch guns. These mats were also secured to the rails around the aft searchlight platform. It is understood that the four 3-pounder saluting guns were removed at this time, possibly to compensate for the added topweight of the 20-lb plating.

When this work was completed, the ship was painted in a camouflage scheme. This involved applying medium grey over the existing light grey in a disruptive pattern. *Sydney* was still carrying this scheme when it returned to Australia in February 1941 and retained it until September when a new disruptive pattern was applied.

On 24 December 1940 *Sydney* entered dry-dock in Malta. To enhance the ship's survivability, all the lower deck side scuttles, with the exception of one scuttle on each side of each mess deck and in each cabin flat, were plated over. The unplated scuttles were retained for escape purposes. This was an Admiralty recommendation, as war experience had shown that these scuttles could open under the stress from near misses and endanger the ship's watertight integrity. While in dry-dock, the fitting of degaussing (demagnetizing) equipment for protection against magnetic mines was completed, the work having been started in August.

If *Sydney* had received major damage while in the Mediterranean, the proposed rearmament would no doubt have been undertaken while the ship was being repaired. Then, with *Sydney*'s return to the Australia Station, where in 1941 the prospect of air attack was remote, the priority of rearmament was given to those vessels that were proceeding to, or were already in, a hostile war zone.

September 1941. *Sydney*, freshly painted
in its second disruptive pattern, departs
Princes Pier, Port Melbourne.
P. Jennings

The question of *Sydney*'s rearmament, however, was raised again in
June 1941. In a submission to RACAS, Captain J. Burnett, RAN, wrote that
the effectiveness of *Sydney*'s long-range fire against formations of aircraft
would be greatly improved by the rearming of the ship with twin 4-inch
mountings. The submission, however, indicates that Burnett was under
no illusions about the lack of priority for vessels on the Australia Station.
In the same paragraph he acknowledged that *Sydney*'s rearmament could
be deferred indefinitely on account of the time involved in fitting and the
fact that the ship was 'at long notice'.

As a means of enhancing *Sydney*'s short-range anti-aircraft capability,
Burnett proposed the fitting of additional Lewis and Vickers machine
guns. He also proposed that shields be fitted to the short-range weapons
(0.5-inch) and the 4-inch Mark V guns to provide some measure of
protection for the guns' crews from near misses and splinters. This was
thought to be a sensible proposal, and approval was given to fit shields

to the 0.5-inch mountings, the work being completed on 7 July 1941. Unfortunately, not even the Admiralty had considered the question of fitting shields to the Mark IV 4-inch mounting. As a result, there were no available patterns or plans for the manufacture of such shields. Incredibly, rather than designing and constructing the shields locally, the ACNB entered into correspondence with the Admiralty for the supply of design drawings.

Ironically, it was on 19 November 1941 that the Admiralty advised the ACNB that no drawings for a protective shield were available.[17]

—2—

THE SEARCH

HMAS *Sydney* sailed from the port of Fremantle at 1340 on 11 November 1941. The cruiser was given the task of escorting the Hired Transport *Zealandia* to the Sunda Strait where it was to hand over the merchant ship to the British cruiser HMS *Durban* for onwards passage to Singapore. Because of industrial trouble, *Zealandia*, carrying troops of the ill-fated 8th Australian Division, was thirteen days behind schedule.

At 1222, seventy-eight minutes before departure, Captain Burnett had sent a signal to the C-IN-C China Station (Singapore). This was to advise that, owing to delayed departure, the rendezvous in the Sunda Strait should be amended to 0001z on 17 November.[1] Four minutes later, Burnett sent another signal advising the ACNB, RACAS and the District Naval Officer Western Australia (DNOWA) that *Sydney*'s revised estimated time of arrival back in Fremantle would be PM Thursday 20 November.

Sydney rendezvoused with *Durban* on 17 November in position 7° 56' South 104° 40' East. Following the handover, *Sydney* turned away and set course for Fremantle.

SYDNEY FAILS TO ARRIVE

At 0940 on Friday 21 November, DNOWA, Captain C. Farquhar-Smith, RAN, sent the following signal to the ACNB in Melbourne:

HMAS SYDNEY 0426 II
HMAS SYDNEY HAS NOT YET ARRIVED.[2]

The signal was received by Lieutenant-Commander N.S. Pixley, RANR, who, after confirming the contents with Farquhar-Smith, took it to the Deputy Chief of Naval Staff, Captain F.E. Getting, RAN.[3]

Captain Getting was not unduly worried by the signal, however, as nothing had been heard from *Sydney* itself. The cruiser was expected to maintain W/T silence unless there was something vital to communicate, and its lack of a transmission and non-arrival were not a cause for concern. A late rendezvous with *Durban* or an unforeseen event on its return passage could have accounted for the delay.

On Friday evening, Navy Office learned that *Zealandia* had arrived in Singapore a day late. On receipt of this information, it was assumed that the rendezvous and handover were also a day late, thereby accounting for the delay in *Sydney*'s returning to Fremantle.

Saturday 22 November dawned and there was still no sign of *Sydney*. During the morning Farquhar-Smith contacted Navy Office and learned of *Zealandia*'s late arrival in Singapore. It appears that on the basis of this information no further action was taken.

DNOWA conferred with Navy Office again on Sunday morning, and it was decided to give *Sydney* another twelve hours before ordering the cruiser to break W/T silence. Farquhar-Smith assumed that '*Sydney* had had engine trouble and did not wish to break W/T silence'.[4] Navy Office considered that 'with a cruiser on the trade routes there are always possibilities of her being diverted to answer QQ messages'. There was also some doubt whether *Sydney* might have 'missed *Durban* at the rendezvous and gone on to Singapore'.[5]

At 1854 on Sunday evening, Navy Office ordered *Sydney* to report its ETA Fremantle.[6] On receiving the signal, *Sydney* should have responded. Its continued silence indicated that it had either not heard the signal,

could not reply, or for operational reasons did not wish to break W/T silence.

Sydney, however, was now seventy-two hours overdue. Navy Office decided to contact C-IN-C China to establish the time and place in which *Sydney* parted company with *Durban* and *Zealandia*. Farquhar-Smith made arrangements for an air search.[7]

MONDAY 24 NOVEMBER

At 0050 on Monday 24 November, the Air Officer Commanding Western Area, Air Commodore De La Rue, RAAF, ordered an air search for *Sydney* to start at 0801. Fifteen minutes later, South Western Area Combined Headquarters (SWACH)[8] contacted RAAF Base Pearce and ordered a fan-shaped search covering *Sydney*'s likely position as if it were still making for Fremantle. From a datum on Rottnest Island, six Hudson bombers from No.14 Squadron RAAF were to fly north on diverging courses for a distance of 300 miles. On completion, they were to land at Geraldton, about 270 miles north of Fremantle.[9]

At 0834, Navy Office, still waiting for a reply from C-IN-C China, instructed the naval W/T station at Darwin to continue to call *Sydney* at intervals. Seven minutes later, Navy Office sent a signal to Farquhar-Smith, instructing him that Perth Radio should also call the overdue ship.[10]

Clearly concerned now, and impatient for C-IN-C China's reply, Navy Office sent another signal at 1009 stating that *Sydney* was apparently thirty-six hours (*sic*) overdue at Fremantle and all attempts to contact the ship had failed. It also queried whether Singapore had any information.

With negative reports coming in from the Hudsons, a second search was authorized for 25 November. This operation was to start at 0801 and search further north.

At 1332, the Central War Room (CWR) in Melbourne was informed that Monday's air search had been concluded with no results. One vessel, the *Wanganella*, had been sighted by two of the Hudsons. The aircraft gave sighting positions of 31° 08' South 114° 08' East and 30° 43' South 113° 33' East only four minutes apart and prompted a query by the

A flight of four Hudson bombers from
No.14 Squadron RAAF circa 1940.
Aviation Heritage Museum of Western Australia

SWACH duty officer, as one, if not both, of the positions could not be
correct.

C-IN-C China's reply was received by Navy Office about the same
time. *Sydney* had handed over *Zealandia* on 17 November, four hours late
and 41 miles south of the agreed rendezvous position. Singapore had no
further information.

At 1417, Navy Office advised the Admiralty and the Dutch Naval
Commander, East Indies (CZM), Vice-Admiral Helfrich, that *Sydney* had
been due to return to Fremantle on 'Thursday 20th' but had 'not yet
arrived'. The signal added that the CZM had been asked to conduct an air
search of the area south of the Sunda Strait.

Shortly before 1600, SWACH received advice that the scheduled air
search for Tuesday had been cancelled and that the CWR would be
ordering a revised search operation later. No explanation was given for
the cancellation. Twenty minutes later, however, C-IN-C China sent a

'Most Immediate' signal to Navy Office, advising that the following signal had been received from the tanker *Trocas* at 1500:

> PICKED UP 25 GERMAN NAVAL MEN FLOATING
> RAFT REQUIRE GUARDS IMMEDIATELY.
> POSITION 024° 06' SOUTH 111° 40' EAST."

This was the first indication that *Sydney* may have been involved in an action, and Navy Office reacted by instructing all stations to stop calling the ship; *Sydney* was either incapable of replying or was still maintaining W/T silence for operational reasons.

At 1700, the CWR ordered the ACH Townsville to despatch two Catalina flying boats with well-trained crews from Port Moresby to Fremantle immediately to help in the search for *Sydney*. The aircraft, A24-11 from No.11 Squadron RAAF, and A24-14 from No.20 Squadron RAAF, were to be accompanied by two experienced United States Navy aircraft captains who were on exchange duty.[12]

Forty minutes later, the CWR sent a signal to SWACH officially cancelling Tuesday's scheduled search and ordering two parallel track searches of seven aircraft each. At 1852, a signal was sent to *Trocas*, asking it to report the details of the engagement and the name of the ship from which the survivors were rescued. Eight minutes later, Navy Office provided SWACH with the information received from *Trocas* earlier in the day.

At 1957, as a result of the report that Germans had been recovered off Shark Bay, the merchant vessels *Pan Europe, Saidja, Herstein, Sunetta* and *Centaur* were instructed to pass through *Trocas*'s reported position and keep a lookout for further survivors. Twenty minutes later, *Hermion* was instructed to proceed with all despatch to position 24° 06' South 111° 40' East to pick up survivors and to break W/T silence to report on the situation.

Navy Office then advised the CZM and C-IN-C China that *Trocas* had picked up twenty-five German naval men and that it was considered that *Sydney* was connected with the Germans. As a result, the CZM was asked to cancel the proposed air search from the Sunda Strait. Unfortunately, the signal was not received by the CZM, and the Dutch air search was not cancelled.

That *Sydney* was probably linked to the Germans recovered by *Trocas* was a view obviously shared by the CWR. At 2120, it sent a signal to SWACH saying that it considered that *Sydney* may have been involved in an action on 19 November in the approximate position of 25° South 110° 20' East. SWACH was also informed that *Hermion* had been ordered to close position 24° 06' South 111° 40' East with all despatch and was expected to reach this position by 0600 on 25 November. *Pan Europe, Saidja, Herstein, Sunetta* and *Centaur* had been ordered to pass through the position and keep a lookout for survivors.

The CWR also sent its orders for Tuesday morning's air search. The operation was to start at daylight and was to be a parallel-track search from datums 28° 50' South 114° 48' East and 29° 56' South 112° 30' East. The seven Hudsons allocated were to search to datums 24° 10' South 108° 53' East and 23° 00' South 111° 00' East then proceed to the coast and land at Carnarvon. The objective was to locate *Sydney* as well as the ships' boats.[13]

Meanwhile, all naval personnel in Perth were recalled and two naval auxiliaries were readied for sea. Three vessels actually sailed: HMA Ships *Yandra* and *Olive Cam* at midnight, and *Wyrallah* thirty minutes later. A fourth vessel, HMAS *Heros*, was expected to depart at 0700 on 25 November. *Yandra* and *Wyrallah*, each carrying an armed guard, were to sail along independent routes with orders to intercept the Shell tanker *Trocas*. *Olive Cam* and *Heros* were to proceed along the coast towards Geraldton from where they would receive further instructions by W/T.

TUESDAY 25 NOVEMBER

At 0100 on Tuesday 25 November, Navy Office received an answer to its signal to *Trocas*, via DNOWA. The twenty-five Germans had come from *Comoron* (sic) which had been sunk by a cruiser.

An hour later, the CZM advised Navy Office that the Dutch cruiser *Tromp* would be leaving Sunda Strait as early as possible and would search for *Sydney* along its probable route as far as Fremantle. Two Dutch Catalinas from Surabaya and one Dornier flying boat from Tanjong Priok would help. The air search would start at dawn, the Catalinas sweeping

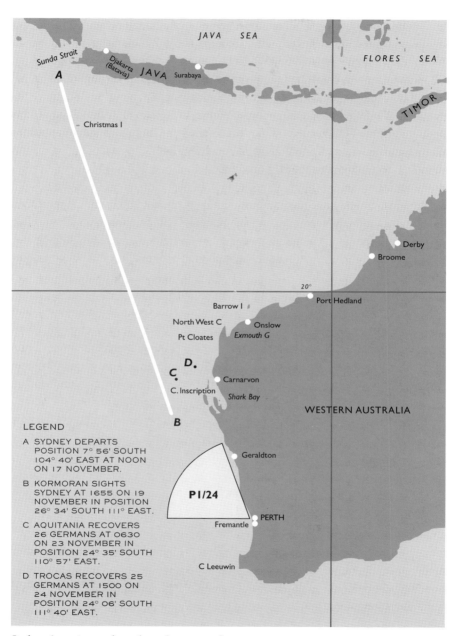

JAVA   SEA

FLORES   SEA

Sunda Strait
Djakarta
(Batavia)   JAVA   Surabaya
A

TIMOR

— Christmas I

Derby
Broome

20°   Port Hedland

Barrow I

North West C   Onslow
Pt Cloates   *Exmouth G*

D.
C.
C. Inscription   Carnarvon
Shark Bay

WESTERN AUSTRALIA

B

LEGEND

A SYDNEY DEPARTS
   POSITION 7° 56' SOUTH
   104° 40' EAST AT NOON
   ON 17 NOVEMBER.

B KORMORAN SIGHTS
   SYDNEY AT 1655 ON 19
   NOVEMBER IN POSITION
   26° 34' SOUTH 111° EAST.

C AQUITANIA RECOVERS
   26 GERMANS AT 0630
   ON 23 NOVEMBER IN
   POSITION 24° 35' SOUTH
   110° 57' EAST.

D TROCAS RECOVERS 25
   GERMANS AT 1500 ON
   24 NOVEMBER IN
   POSITION 24° 06' SOUTH
   111° 40' EAST.

Geraldton

P1/24

PERTH
Fremantle

C Leeuwin

Sydney's estimated track and extent of
air search conducted on 24 November.

either side of *Sydney*'s estimated line of advance of 160° before returning to Tjilatjap before nightfall. The Dornier would conduct a search from Tanjong Priok to Christmas Island. The aircraft failed to locate *Sydney*.

At 0531, RAAF Pearce relayed a departure signal for the first aircraft on Tuesday's search to SWACH. Although two aircraft were forced to withdraw from the operation because of engine trouble, the remaining aircraft met with some success. At 0724, SWACH received a report from Pearce that one aircraft had sighted a lifeboat in position 24° 52' South 111° 09' East. Another aircraft reported sighting *Herstein* about 70 miles north of this position.[14]

At 0815, Farquhar-Smith sent a signal to Navy Office advising that an aircraft had sighted a lifeboat in position 24° 52' South 111° 09' East. The same message was then broadcast to all British merchant ships in the vicinity. Forty-five minutes later, *Herstein* was ordered to close the position and locate the boat.

Just before this, Navy Office advised C-IN-C China and the CZM that *Trocas* had reported that the survivors were from *Comoron* (sic), which had been sunk by a cruiser. Navy Office added that there was no further news from *Sydney*. This signal created some confusion as neither C-IN-C China nor the CZM knew of any German ship with this name. Not having received Navy Office's signal transmitted at 2112 on 24 November, the CZM considered that the survivors picked up by *Trocas* were from the British armed merchant cruiser *Comorin*, even though this vessel had been lost in April. When the CZM realized that he had not received a copy of the earlier signal, he requested a repetition.[15]

At 0825 and 0837, SWACH received further reports from Pearce advising that the lifeboat sighted earlier was full, that the occupants were using white coats as a makeshift sail and that it was making about 3 knots on an easterly course. Less than an hour later, advice was received of the sighting of two more lifeboats. Flight Lieutenant Cook, flying one of the Hudsons, had radioed that he had sighted one boat off the coast 50 miles north of Carnarvon and another on the beach about 40 miles north of Carnarvon.

CONCERN FOR TROCAS

With the remaining aircraft returning negative results, SWACH appeared to be concerned by the fact that *Trocas* had not been sighted during the search. At 1000, Pearce was ordered to carry out another search as soon as possible for *Trocas*.

Amid growing concerns for the tanker, a signal was sent to Pearce. This was relayed to the Commanding Officer of No.14 Squadron, Wing Commander Lightfoot, now temporarily based at Carnarvon. Lightfoot was instructed to advise the local authorities that the occupants of the two lifeboats to the north of the town may be of enemy nationality.

At 1055, the CZM, still not aware that his air search had been cancelled, offered to extend his air reconnaissances to Western Australian harbours on Wednesday if required and if suitable flying boat facilities existed.

Meanwhile, Navy Office sent another signal to *Trocas* asking for the date, time and duration of the action and the condition of the cruiser after the action. Forty-five minutes later, the proposed search for *Trocas* was cancelled. No explanation was given, although it is clear from subsequent search objectives that its exact location was still the cause of some anxiety.

The concern for *Trocas* may have arisen because it had twenty-five German naval personnel on board who were probably capable of overpowering the tanker's crew and seizing the ship. The other possibility was that the ship might have fallen victim to an Axis submarine. On 21 November, the Admiralty transmitted a warning, saying that it was known that U-boats had been used as escorts for returning raiders, supply ships, and merchant vessels. The signal also included probable tactics and added that Vichy French submarines were probably being used as escorts for merchant ships. With *Sydney* and now *Trocas* missing, it might have been feared that both ships had become victims of a French submarine engaged in escorting *Comoron* (sic).[16]

On 24 November, the RACAS, Rear-Admiral J.G. Crace, RN, wrote in his private diary that the 'Naval Board are very worried about *Sydney* and think there is a possibility that a Vichy S/m [submarine] escorting a Vichy ship has torpedoed her'.[17]

The heavy cruiser HMAS *Canberra*, due to start a refit in Sydney, was ordered to remain ready to return to sea at four hours' notice. The cruiser

was also to make arrangements to fuel in this period in the event of an emergency.[18]

At 1145 on Tuesday, RAAF Pearce was given the revised details for the afternoon search, which were then relayed to Carnarvon. Six Hudsons were to conduct a parallel-track search from datums 24° 01' South 109° 08' East and 23° 00' South 111° 00' East to datums 29° 56' South 112° 30' East and 28° 50' South 114° 48' East. Although planned for six aircraft, only five were serviceable. A third operation, conducted by one Wirraway from No.25 Squadron RAAF, was to search the coastline from Shark Bay to the North West Cape. The aircraft were given the task of locating ships' boats or rafts. And one Hudson was asked to locate *Trocas*.

Shortly after 1400, SWACH received information from the CWR that *Tromp* was expected to leave Sunda Strait AM on 25 November for passage to Fremantle. The cruiser would be proceeding at 20 knots and would require fuel on arrival. Navy Office, however, changed this plan. At 1410, it formally acknowledged the CZM's earlier offer but recommended that he deploy his forces no further south than latitude 20°. The CZM was asked to cover the likely routes that *Sydney* may have taken if it were attempting to reach Singapore or Surabaya.

At 1533, SWACH received a departure report for the afternoon's search to seaward. Unfortunately, one aircraft had been unable to take part in the operation. Twenty minutes later, SWACH was informed that a second aircraft had been forced to shorten its patrol by 78 miles. Obviously concerned about the condition of the aircraft, Pearce was told to order all aircraft still engaged on the operation to return to Carnarvon after searching 170 miles from datum.

With the expected arrival of the two Catalinas early on Wednesday morning, the duty staff officer at Fremantle Artillery barracks was phoned and advised to warn the anti-aircraft defences. The aircraft, A24-14 and A24-11, reached Perth on the morning of 26 November and landed in Matilda Bay on the Swan River at 0745 and 0830 respectively.

On Tuesday evening SWACH informed the CWR that *Trocas* had reported in and had given its morning position, which was supported by D/F bearing. The CWR was also informed that *Wyrallah* would rendezvous with *Trocas* at approximately 0630 on 26 November to transfer the guard for the prisoners. *Trocas* would then sail to Fremantle, where it was

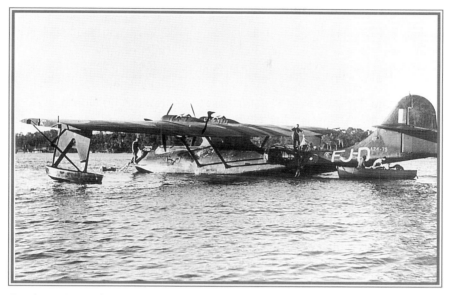

Catalina A24-75 from No.11 Squadron RAAF.
Aviation Heritage Museum of Western Australia

expected to arrive about noon on Thursday. *Wyrallah* was to continue northward to assist *Yandra, Olive Cam* and *Heros* in the search. With *Trocas* known to be safe, the focus of the search could return to *Sydney*.

At 1906, Pearce was ordered to mount a search of the coastline from North West Cape to Shark Bay starting at 0600 on Wednesday morning. Employing one Wirraway, the object was the location of ships' boats and rafts.

In a summary of the day's operations, the position of the morning's sighting of a lifeboat was amended to 24° 08' South 111° 09' East. This boat and the two ashore north of Carnarvon were described as brown in colour and clearly not from *Sydney*, its boats being painted naval grey. As only one of the vessels ordered to help in the search had been seen during the day's operations, arrangements were made to drop food and water to the lifeboat still at sea. It was also noted that a vehicle had been seen approaching the northernmost beached lifeboat, although it was not expected that any information would become available from these survivors until about 0400 on 26 November.

At about this time, the Naval Board received a sobering signal from the Admiralty. It considered that the only logical explanation for *Sydney*'s disappearance was that the cruiser had been torpedoed by the raider.

Shortly after 2005, the orders for a second search for Wednesday were issued. Conducted by four Hudsons, it was to be another parallel-track search of the area where the lifeboat had been sighted. The objective was to locate ships' boats or rafts.

At 2300, DNOWA telephoned Navy Office to advise that the following information had just been received from Carnarvon:

> Survivors number about 110. Mostly 70 miles north of Carnarvon. Germans are from a raider commenced an engagement with a British ship 'Perth' class which began 19th November 120 miles s-w of Fremantle. At midnight raider blew up. Germans rowed towards light of vessel which was in flames. Before they arrived British ship disappeared believed sunk. They turned and ran with the wind to land. Police are in charge of prisoners. One prisoner arriving midnight. Will report immediately. May they be transferred by vessel arriving Carnarvon 26th November.[19]

The timing of Farquhar-Smith's message was curious, because it predated an entry in the SWACH log by twenty-five minutes and the arrival of the first German in Carnarvon by nearly two hours.

It would appear that the originator of this important piece of information was a civilian, Mr Keith Baston, the manager of Quobba Station. After receiving Flight Lieutenant Cook's report, the RAAF (at Carnarvon) had apparently telephoned Baston and asked him to investigate the situation on the beach. He did this, and after talking to some of the English-speaking Germans, had driven back to Quobba and telephoned Carnarvon with the results.[20] This information was then sent by telephone to Farquhar-Smith, who immediately relayed it to Navy Office.

Such a sequence of events would appear to be supported by the text of the message. If the RAAF personnel at Carnarvon or Farquhar-Smith had studied the information more carefully, they would have realized that given the position of the lifeboats the action could not have occurred 120 miles south-west of Fremantle.

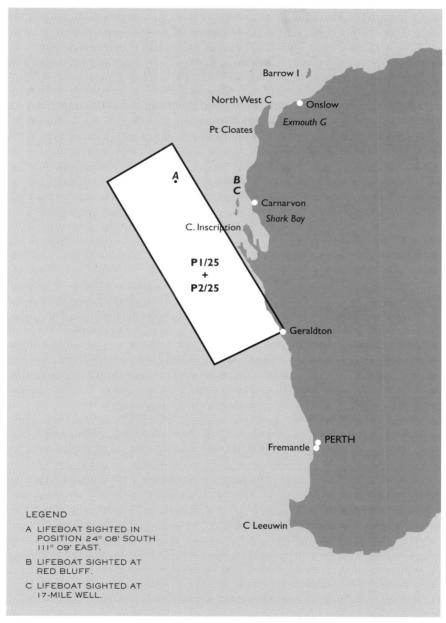

Barrow I

North West C

Onslow

Exmouth G

Pt Cloates

A

B
C

Carnarvon

Shark Bay

C. Inscription

**P1/25
+
P2/25**

Geraldton

PERTH

Fremantle

C Leeuwin

LEGEND

A LIFEBOAT SIGHTED IN
   POSITION 24° 08' SOUTH
   111° 09' EAST.

B LIFEBOAT SIGHTED AT
   RED BLUFF.

C LIFEBOAT SIGHTED AT
   17-MILE WELL.

Air operations conducted
on 25 November.

Twenty-five minutes later, SWACH received a relayed report from Carnarvon. Flight-Lieutenant Cook informed Pearce that:

> Survivors that were located not yet arrived in town number approximately 120 Germans. They state that an engagement between them, an armed raider, and a first class cruiser commenced Wednesday last at 1900H; their ship finally blowing up at midnight. Engagement took place approximately 120 miles S-W of Fremantle. They had three lifeboats and two rubber boats. When last seen the first class cruiser was on fire.[21]

Cook also reported that he had given instructions for an English-speaking survivor to be brought to town as soon as possible for questioning. This man was expected to arrive shortly after midnight, with the main body expected about five hours later. Cook added that he would call back at 0100 and suggested that the man selected be flown to Pearce for further questioning. This information was passed to the duty Staff Officer at DNOWA, Lieutenant-Commander J.L. Rycroft, RANVR, who in turn relayed the information to Navy Office.

If the German survivors north of Carnarvon were to be believed, *Sydney* sank on 19 November. The survivors, if there were any left, had been in the water for six days.

WEDNESDAY 26 NOVEMBER

During the night, Navy Office advised the CZM that his air search would no longer be required. *Tromp*, however, having departed Tanjong Priok at midday on 25 November, would continue with its search.

At 0030 on 26 November, SWACH informed Pearce that a naval intelligence officer and an interpreter were to be flown to Carnarvon, departing at 0500.

Shortly before 0300, SWACH received a signal from Pearce giving details of the information gleaned from Hans Linke, the English-speaking survivor who had been taken to Carnarvon ahead of the main party. Linke, a W/T operator, had volunteered the information that his ship was

the 6,000-ton *Komoran* (*sic*). His ship, an armed merchantman, had a crew of 'about 300' and was armed with '8-inch guns as well as AA guns'. The captain's name was Betlers (*sic*). They had been in the Indian Ocean about six months and their last victim had been the *Stomacos Embiricos* (*sic*), sunk about two months previously. At about 1730 on Wednesday 19 November, when in position 26° South 111° East, a cruiser escorting a convoy of five to seven ships was sighted. Linke was of the impression that the cruiser thought that his ship belonged to the convoy and approached to within half a mile. He said that the cruiser did not use its W/T but had signalled with flags. At 1740 *Komoran* (*sic*) opened fire; its first salvo silencing the cruiser's 8-inch (*sic*) guns. The gunfire continued until 1900. By this time his ship was burning fiercely amidships, and at midnight was blown up after the crew had escaped in boats. The cruiser vanished over the horizon burning amidships and astern and was believed to have sunk.

SWACH relayed the information to the CWR. Farquhar-Smith, however, received the information direct from Carnarvon at 0325, this later report recording the raider captain's name as Detmer.

At 0526, a Gannet aircraft, carrying Lieutenant-Commander Rycroft and an interpreter, Mr J. Lobstein, took off from Pearce. Two hours later, *Wyrallah* met and transferred the guard to *Trocas*. *Wyrallah*, *Yandra*, *Heros* (Group 53) and *Olive Cam* were then ordered to take up positions forty miles apart on the parallel of 26° 10' South and sweep northwards.

Less than eight hours after informing the CZM that his air search was no longer required, Navy Office changed its mind again. At 0816, it informed the CZM that *Sydney* had been in action with the German raider *Komoran* (*sic*) in position 26° South 111° East at 1730 on 19 November, the raider being sunk. Navy Office added that the German survivors had said that, when last seen, *Sydney* was burning amidships and aft. Navy Office went on to say that Australian aircraft and naval vessels would cover the area of the action but requested that the CZM reinstate the previously arranged air and sea search to cover the possibility of *Sydney* making for the naval dockyards at Surabaya or Singapore.

Meanwhile, the four Hudsons, which had started their search at 0600, had made several sightings. One lifeboat had been sighted in position 24° 39' South 112° 02' East at 0648, and a second boat at 0744 in position

24° 14' South 112° 24' East. At about the same time, another aircraft sighted a vessel with a grey superstructure, which identified itself with the code letters GMQP (*Centaur*). Then, at 1105, a report was received that the aircraft that had spotted the second lifeboat had sighted *Herstein* and *Pan Europe* in position 23° 31' South 111° 08' East.

As a result of the morning's discoveries, another search was ordered for the afternoon.

At 1125, the CZM advised Navy Office that in light of the changed requirements *Tromp* would sail no further south than latitude 20° South, this information being relayed to SWACH. Fifteen minutes later, Navy Office sent a signal to *Tromp* informing the cruiser of the situation.

Shortly after midday, Pearce received orders for the afternoon search. Seven Hudsons were to search to the south of the lifeboat positions. The object was to locate ships' boats or rafts. A fourth operation, to support the Hudsons, was to be a search of the coastline from Geraldton to North West Cape. It was to be conducted by Catalina A24-14, which was to return to Geraldton on completion, flying parallel to the coast but 50 miles to seaward.

Pearce then provided SWACH with an update on the lifeboat sightings. The first boat sighted was described as having a beam of about twenty-five feet (*sic*) and was carrying about fifty men. Initially reported as making for the coast on a course of 090°, it was now claimed to be on a course of 075°. The boat was described as being similar to the boats already ashore north of Carnarvon. The second boat was smaller, had a narrower beam and was carrying twenty to twenty-five men. SWACH instructed Pearce to arrange for the Gannet, now at Carnarvon, to drop water and supplies to the occupants of the two lifeboats.

Informed of the details of the lifeboats, and anxious to establish the identity of the survivors, the CWR then issued instructions that the aircraft taking part in the afternoon's search was to attempt to establish the identity and nationality of the men in the boats. This task was allotted to the Catalina. The aircrew, having been given the lifeboat positions, were instructed to make a water landing if possible and confirm the nationality of the boats' occupants.

At 1421, Pearce informed SWACH that the Wirraway search was complete but negative. This was followed by a completion report for the

morning's search to seaward. Underlining the urgent necessity of locating possible *Sydney* survivors was the following signal from SWACH:

ALL AIRCRAFT TO BE INFORMED SEARCH MUST
NOT REPEAT NOT BE REDUCED.[22]

Unfortunately this order could not be complied with, as a short time later SWACH was informed that the afternoon search would be reduced to four aircraft. Two Hudsons had become unserviceable, and a third was still being refuelled and would not be ready until 1600. As a result of the shortage of aircraft, No.4 Service Flying Training School at Geraldton was contacted and ordered to conduct a parallel-track search to seaward as soon as possible. Eight Anson training aircraft were to be employed, the object being to locate ships' boats or rafts. All tracks were to be flown on a bearing of 270° true for set distances, the maximum being 150 miles. The Ansons were then to return along these tracks and land at either Geraldton or Carnarvon. This search, which started at 1625 and finished at 2100, proved fruitless.

At 1547, Pearce received a signal from the Catalina. The signal, like an earlier one received at 1340, was indecipherable. Three minutes later one of the Hudsons reported its position. With uncertainty surrounding the contents of the Catalina's W/T transmissions, and possibly the ability of the aircraft to complete its mission, the Hudson was instructed to locate and identify the boats that had been sighted earlier in the day. Additionally, it was to locate and report the positions and actions of any search vessels encountered.

Just before 1800, SWACH was informed that the Gannet had returned to Carnarvon without having sighted the lifeboats. It had conducted a square search based on a visibility of 2 miles and had only sighted *Centaur*, reportedly heading towards Carnarvon.

At 1820, the situation with the Catalina became clearer. The aircraft had been unable to reach the datum position of the lifeboats before dusk.[23] Its search was completed at 1818, but the aircraft had found nothing. The second Catalina, A24-11, which had flown up from Perth during the afternoon, was ordered to go to Geraldton and refuel at the earliest opportunity.

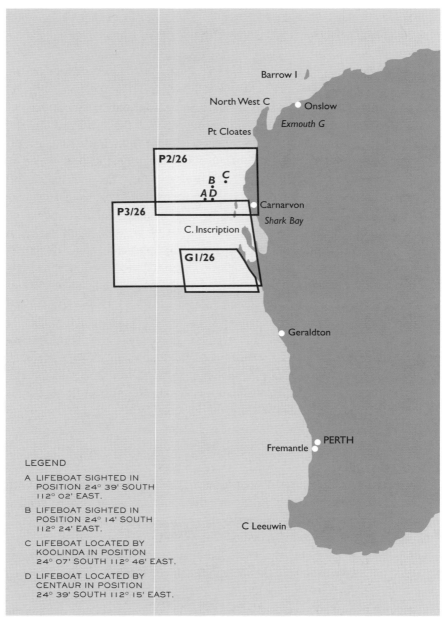

Barrow I

North West C

Onslow

Exmouth G

Pt Cloates

P2/26

C
B
A D

Carnarvon

P3/26

Shark Bay

C. Inscription

G1/26

Geraldton

PERTH

Fremantle

C Leeuwin

LEGEND

A LIFEBOAT SIGHTED IN
   POSITION 24° 39' SOUTH
   112° 02' EAST.

B LIFEBOAT SIGHTED IN
   POSITION 24° 14' SOUTH
   112° 24' EAST.

C LIFEBOAT LOCATED BY
   KOOLINDA IN POSITION
   24° 07' SOUTH 112° 46' EAST.

D LIFEBOAT LOCATED BY
   CENTAUR IN POSITION
   24° 39' SOUTH 112° 15' EAST.

Air operations conducted
to seaward on 26 November.

Earlier in the day, Rycroft had found and questioned *Kormoran's* Navigating Officer, Kapitänleutnant Henry Meyer, who confirmed the position of the action. At 1900, Rycroft advised SWACH that Meyer now gave the position of the action as 27° South 111° East.[24] Later in the evening, Farquhar-Smith passed this information to Navy Office with the comment that this position was thought to be approximately correct.

At 1924, the SWACH log recorded that one of the Hudsons on the afternoon search had sighted three vessels in the vicinity of position 25° 00' South 111° 15' East at 1852. SWACH then ordered the first search for the following day. Starting at 0730, the two Catalinas were to extend the search westwards to longitude 107° 40' East. They were to locate ships' boats or rafts. Orders for a second operation followed. This was to be a parallel-track search by five Hudsons. Starting at 0600, the Hudsons were to sweep due west from the coast between the datums 25° 43' South 112° 56' East and 26° 53' South 113° 32' East. After flying set distances to a maximum depth of 228 miles, the aircraft were to turn north, fly 84 miles, then return to the coast on parallel tracks. The aircraft were to locate ships' boats or rafts.

The orders for a third search were sent to No.4 SFTS at 1935. Starting at 0700, seven Ansons were required to conduct a parallel-track search from the coast between datums 24° 40' South 113° 15' East and 27° 00' South 113° 36' East. Like the Hudsons, the Ansons were to fly due west for '150 miles or as far as possible', then step aside 14 miles and return to the coast on a bearing of 090°. Again, the object was to locate ships' boats or rafts.

At 1938, Pearce received orders for a fourth search. Three Wirraways were to search the islands and coastline from Onslow to Geraldton with the object of locating ships' boats or rafts. The operation was to start at 0600. Orders for a fifth operation, employing one Anson from No.4 SFTS, followed. This aircraft was to take off at first light, locate the two lifeboats previously sighted in positions 24° 39' South 112° 02' East and 24° 14' South 112° 24' East, then guide search vessels to the boats. A relief aircraft was to be provided if necessary.

At 2020, SWACH recorded that an Anson had landed at Carnarvon after flying 85 miles on its leg of the afternoon search. The crew of this aircraft reported sighting oil on the surface of the water 18 miles from the coast.

No importance was attached to the report, however, as this was considered to be a common sight about the coast. Officially, the afternoon searches were completed with no sightings.

In a summary of the day's operations the CWR was advised that the lifeboats sighted earlier in the day had not been seen during the afternoon. The nationality of the occupants, therefore, was still unknown. Of the search vessels, only *Centaur*, *Herstein* and *Pan Europe* had been sighted. *Wyrallah*, however, had met *Trocas*, transferred the guard detachment, and was now proceeding northwards with *Heros* and *Olive Cam* in order to sweep the area off Carnarvon. The CWR was also advised that the prisoners from the beached lifeboats, and their guard, were to be taken from Carnarvon to Fremantle aboard *Centaur*.

At 2330, Farquhar-Smith sent a similar summary report to Navy Office. This was followed by a report that visitors to Dirk Hartog Island, who had returned to the mainland during the day, had seen a vessel on fire on 20 November. They reported that, at 1000 the previous Thursday, they had seen a destroyer 7 miles off steering south at high speed and throwing off a smokescreen. DNOWA added that the report was being investigated. It was subsequently ascertained that the sighting had been made on 19 November and that the tug *Uco* was probably the vessel in question.

As for the fate of *Sydney*, Farquhar-Smith had little further to add. All reports indicated that the boats thus far sighted, or accounted for, were from the raider. Regarding the raider, reports from Carnarvon indicated that *Sydney* had replied to the enemy fire with gunfire and torpedoes. The raider, named *Kormorant* (*sic*), was 'unreliably' said to have been armed with six 8-inch guns. It was further reported that the raider had carried an aircraft and had possibly been equipped with torpedoes, although two prisoners claimed that none had been fired. A follow-up report thirty minutes later indicated that *Sydney*'s torpedoes had missed the raider.

Thirty minutes earlier, *Centaur* had broken W/T silence to inform Navy Office that at 2220 it had discovered a lifeboat containing sixty-two German seamen. The boat had been located in position 24° 39' South 112° 15' East. Owing to the lack of armed guards, *Centaur* had taken the boat in tow and was heading for Carnarvon at 4 knots.

THURSDAY 27 NOVEMBER

At 0420 on 27 November, SWACH received a signal from the CWR informing them that three Netherlands East Indies Catalinas would be joining the search. These aircraft would cover the likely routes that *Sydney* would have taken if it were attempting to make Surabaya or Singapore.

Ninety minutes later SWACH advised No.4 SFTS that, as a result of the report that *Centaur* had taken lifeboats in tow, the dawn search by one aircraft was cancelled. It is not understood if *Centaur*'s signal had been misunderstood, or whether it had signalled again that it had two life-boats in tow. Either way, SWACH gained the impression that the two lifeboats sighted on Wednesday morning were now being towed by *Centaur*. In reality, only one of these boats had been located, and this had not been by design.[25]

The boat taken in tow by *Centaur* was commanded by *Kormoran*'s captain, Fregattenkapitän T.A. Detmers. Shortly after dawn, Detmers ordered the tow rope to be cut after the boat suddenly filled with water. Detmers later claimed that his boat had become swamped when *Centaur* increased speed and changed course.[26] Captain W.F. Dark, in command of *Centaur*, suspected, however, that the Germans had deliberately swamped their boat in an attempt to get aboard his ship. Not wishing to take on so many Germans without an adequate guard, Dark lowered two of his own lifeboats and had the survivors transferred into them. The swamped German boat, which had submerged but remained afloat because of its buoyancy tanks, was then hoisted aboard.

Thus, when search aircraft sighted *Centaur* at 0630, they observed that it was towing two lifeboats. When this was reported to SWACH, it was assumed that all four of the lifeboats sighted during the search operations were now accounted for. Two were beached north of Carnarvon, while the remaining two were assumed to be under tow by *Centaur*.

The State Shipping Service vessel *Koolinda*, however, had discovered a fifth lifeboat, on the evening of 26 November. At 0900 SWACH advised the CWR that *Koolinda* was travelling from Carnarvon to Fremantle with thirty (*sic*) prisoners on board.

It is not clear how SWACH obtained this information or exactly what knowledge it had of the prisoners, as there is no mention of *Koolinda* in

Shortly after dawn on 27 November.
German survivors transferring from their
swamped lifeboat to *Centaur*'s P-4 lifeboat.
Battye Library 5545B/4

the SWACH log. The only document that sheds any light is the master's report to DNOWA dated 29 November. Captain J.S. Airey reported that, on Wednesday 26 November, *Koolinda* received DNOWA's signal that two lifeboats were adrift off the coast. Speed was increased and at 1905 a boat was sighted in position 24° 07' South 112° 46' East. The boat and its thirty-one German occupants were recovered forty-five minutes later. *Koolinda* continued searching for the second boat, but at 2215 a vessel showing a single masthead light was sighted and challenged. Receiving no reply, Captain Airey turned away and set course for Carnarvon, arriving there at 0400 on Thursday morning.[27]

From this document it would appear that *Koolinda* maintained W/T silence and that SWACH only became aware of its discovery when it berthed at Carnarvon.

At 0823, SWACH received a signal from the CWR recommending that the search be moved north to latitude 20° South and extended to the maximum depth seaward. In the light of this recommendation and the numerous negative reports coming in, the AOC Western Area ordered that the area between 20° South and 24° South be searched during the afternoon. As a result, SWACH advised Pearce that once the Hudsons had completed their morning search all aircraft were to return to Carnarvon for refuelling and to be serviceable by 1300. At 1018, however, advice was received that one Hudson could not be made serviceable and might have to return to Pearce.

The morning search by the Hudsons produced only two sightings of *Herstein*. One aircraft reported the ship in position 24° 14' South 112° 12' East and making 10 knots on a course of 225°. The other aircraft reported *Herstein* less than an hour later in position 25° 09' South 112° 11' East and making 12 knots on a course of 180°. Clearly, navigational accuracy was a problem for the searching aircraft.

To plan the conduct of the afternoon search operations, the AOC signalled No.4 SFTS, requesting track charts of the areas searched by the Catalinas. This was followed by a call to RAAF headquarters asking for additional Hudsons from Darwin.

Meanwhile, HT *Aquitania*, which had steamed through the search area on 23 November, was negotiating Bass Strait en-route to Sydney. At 1320K the PWSS at Wilson's Promontory advised Navy Office that it had

received a signal from the troopship. Its master, Captain W. Gibbons, reported that at 0630 on 23 November he had rescued twenty-six Germans from a raft in position 24° 35' South 110° 57' East.

At 1134, news was received that an Anson had sighted a small boat containing about forty Germans in position 25° 04' South 112° 04' East. This was the missing boat that had been sighted on the morning of 25 November and which SWACH assumed had been taken in tow by *Centaur.*

The crowded boat had a white flag with the words 'No Water' in English and German painted in red on it. A small patrol vessel in the vicinity was contacted and led towards the boat, but the Anson could not remain on station to ensure contact was made owing to lack of fuel. A second patrol vessel steering an approximate course towards the boat was also sighted, and after checking that the position given for the boat was accurate, Flight Lieutenant Rooke departed for Carnarvon.

Another Anson sighted *Centaur* 15 to 20 miles from Carnarvon, as well as a tanker in position 24° 12' South 111° 38' East. The latter vessel, estimated at 6,000 tons and described as having a grey hull, grey superstructure, two masts and a single funnel aft, was later identified as *Sunetta.* A further sighting was made during the morning search, which was not recorded in the SWACH log or the ACH summary of the search operations.

At 1025, Flight Lieutenant Payne in Anson W-2124 landed at Geraldton and reported sighting oil stains between datum 27° 00' South 113° 32' East and the coast.[28]

At 1140, SWACH ordered that a third operation be mounted by No.4 SFTS starting at 1430. On a line from Cape Cuvier and extending approximately 85 miles to seaward, eight Ansons were to sweep north on parallel tracks on a course of 009° true for a distance of 250 miles before returning to Onslow. Supporting this operation, and fulfilling the CWR's desire to extend the search northwards, would be a fourth search. Starting at 1400, four Hudsons from Carnarvon were to conduct a step-aside parallel-track search of the area north of latitude 24° 14' South. Their objective was to locate ships' boats or rafts.

In addition, the AOC's request for extra aircraft had been acknowledged. At 1215, SWACH received word that three Hudsons were to be moved from Darwin to Port Hedland to help in the search. Ten minutes

later, Pearce warned the Catalinas that they could expect to encounter up to three Dutch Catalinas and the Dutch cruiser *Tromp* in their patrol area.

Carnarvon, concerned that there had been no report of the recovery of the lifeboat sighted by Flight Lieutenant Rooke, decided to contact SWACH. At 1226, SWACH was advised that although a search vessel had been seen heading straight for the boat, it was still some 15 miles distant when Rooke had been forced to depart. To ensure contact was made, SWACH ordered one Anson to be despatched from No.4 SFTS to position 25° 04' South 112° 04' East.

A short time later, another indecipherable signal was received from one of the Catalinas. Communication with the second Catalina, however, appears to have been satisfactory, as a position and negative sighting report was received from it at 1404.

At 1533, Pearce advised SWACH that the Gannet had returned from Onslow and reported sighting three pieces of white timber about 15 or 16 feet in length about 1 mile or so apart. This timber was about 20 miles due west from the coast in the approximate latitude of the southern end of Exmouth Gulf. The position was later logged as 22° 32' South 113° 18' East.

At about the same time, the Anson, tasked with ensuring the boat sighted by Rooke had been intercepted, was successfully completing its mission. *Yandra* was sighted in position 24° 54' South 112° 30' East towing the German boat. This information was passed to the CWR at 1558.

With the number of German survivors growing, the decision was made to send Commander E.F.V. Dechaineux, RAN, from the Directorate of Naval Intelligence to Fremantle to 'carry out special interrogation'. At 1436, Farquhar-Smith was advised that Dechaineux and an interpreter, Commander Salm of the Royal Dutch Navy, would be arriving by aircraft PM Friday 28 November.

At 1742, the CWR was advised that the Catalina search was complete but negative. A minute later, SWACH issued orders to No.4 SFTS for the mounting of the first search for Friday. From latitude 20° 08' South, five Ansons, now at Onslow, were to conduct a parallel-track search on a course of 189° true for a distance of 250 miles before returning to Carnarvon. Their objective was to locate ships' boats or rafts. This was immediately followed by orders for a second operation, another

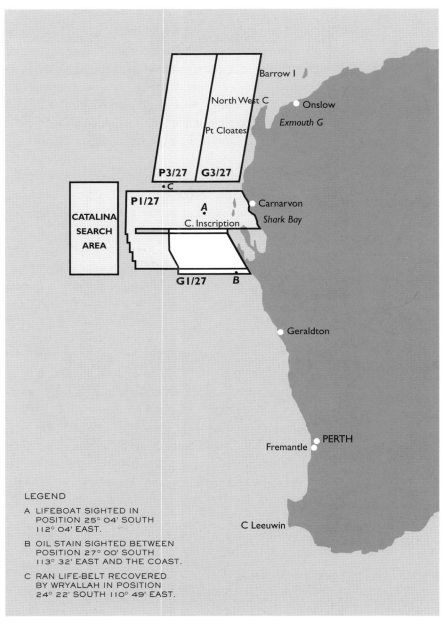

LEGEND

A LIFEBOAT SIGHTED IN
POSITION 25° 04' SOUTH
112° 04' EAST.

B OIL STAIN SIGHTED BETWEEN
POSITION 27° 00' SOUTH
113° 32' EAST AND THE COAST.

C RAN LIFE-BELT RECOVERED
BY WRYALLAH IN POSITION
24° 22' SOUTH 110° 49' EAST.

Air operations conducted
on 27 November.

parallel-track search using three Ansons from Carnarvon. They were to start their search from latitude 24° 14' South and fly on the reciprocal course of 009° true for a distance of 250 miles before landing at Onslow.

At 1813, Pearce was ordered to mount a search with the three Hudsons from Darwin that were now supposedly at Port Hedland. Starting at 0715, they were to conduct a second parallel-track search from latitude 20° 08' South then land at Carnarvon. Their objective was to locate ships' boats or rafts. Unfortunately, SWACH was unaware that the Hudsons had been unable to reach Port Hedland and had landed at Broome instead.

Fifteen minutes later, the orders for a fourth search, designated P2/28, were issued. Three Hudsons from Carnarvon, starting at 0715 and using a visibility distance of five miles, were to conduct a step-aside parallel-track search from latitude 24° 14' South to latitude 20° 08' South. This was followed by the orders for a fifth search, P3/28. The operation required two Hudsons from Carnarvon to conduct a step-aside parallel search to seaward.

At 1910, SWACH was advised that three Ansons had arrived at Onslow. Three minutes later, the orders for a sixth search, P4/28, were issued. This operation required the two Catalinas at Geraldton to search the area bounded by datums 24° 34' South 110° 00' East, 24° 34' South 113° 00' East, 28° 00' South 114° 00' East and 28° 00' South 110° 00' East. Starting at 0630 and using best visibility, the Catalinas were to search for ships' boats or rafts.

Shortly after 2000, SWACH received the first positive report about *Sydney*. A signal from one of the Hudsons on the afternoon search reported that a vessel had picked up an RAN life-belt in position 23° 06' South 110° 47' East. The report was immediately relayed to the CWR. The vessel in question was identified as the *Evagoras*. At 2055, the position for the life-belt was amended to 24° 06' South 110° 49' East.

Unfortunately, this first hint of success was overshadowed by the news that an Anson was two hours overdue at Onslow.

At 2115, DNOWA received a message from Carnarvon. Rycroft had located Detmers among the survivors brought in by *Centaur* and reported that:

Raider Captain can confirm previous report with addition action took place latitude 26° 32' longitude 111° HMAS SYDNEY two

Officers and men from Detmers's boat, now
accommodated in one of *Centaur*'s lifeboats,
prepare to be taken in tow. Their disgust at
being left in an open boat is obvious.
Battye Library 5545B/7

torpedoes missed. Raider torpedo hit forward and salvo amidships. HMAS SYDNEY badly on fire. Action began 19th at 1600 broke off 1830. Raider struck in engine room and on fire. HMAS SYDNEY last seen turning behind smoke screen bearing 153° 5 miles from raider and steering South 5 knots. Raider had 25 killed, remainder of 400 in boats and rafts experienced bad weather. Endeavouring obtain further information.[29]

Surprisingly, this important information, containing the action position, was not passed to SWACH until shortly before 0900 the following morning.

At 2153, Pearce was advised that a search for the missing Anson and its crew of two was to start at daylight. Three Wirraways were to be assigned to this operation and they were to conduct a coastal search up to 15 miles inland from Cape Cuvier to Robe River. If the Anson was not located, the Wirraways were to refuel at Onslow and search a further 15 miles inland.

Forty-five minutes later, Squadron Leader Cooper, the officer in charge of the Ansons at Onslow, advised Pearce that the missing Anson had been searching the area between Onslow and 20° 00' South 114° 50' East. He added that the other Ansons had experienced strong winds and ended up making a landfall in the vicinity of Barrow Island. A follow-up signal said that the Ansons were in need of maintenance and it was not considered desirable that they be sent on patrol over the sea. Cooper also asked that the datum for the search be moved further south, so that none of his aircraft would exceed four hours' flying time.

While SWACH had been arranging the search for the missing Anson, the CWR focused its attention on the life-belt discovery. At 2220, they advised SWACH that the Catalina search area was to be amended. The two Catalinas were now required to search the area bounded by datums 22° 00' South 109° 00' East, 22° 00' South 111° 00' East, 24° 00' South 111° 00' East and 24° 00' South 109° 00' East. Strangely, when previous search objectives were the location of boats or rafts, the Catalinas were asked to locate *Sydney* or ships' boats.

Trocas, meanwhile, had arrived at Fremantle. The Senior Naval Intelligence Officer at Fremantle, Commander V.A.T. Ramage, RAN, interviewed

Trocas's officers, interrogated a number of the prisoners, then prepared a summary of the information obtained. Ramage was able to provide Navy Office with a comprehensive report of the action, a description of the armament of the raider, and a brief history of the raider's activities and vessels sunk.

Of the action, he wrote:

> KORMORAN steering North, sighted on starboard bow ship steering South about 1600H/19th. Raider altered course to westward bringing cruiser on to starboard quarter. Cruiser altered course westward and closed rapidly challenging with daylight lamp. Raider made no reply but opened fire when cruiser was in comparatively short range. Estimated range varies from about one to five or six miles, one survivor stating he could see men on deck of cruiser. First shots from raider hit cruiser's bridge and started fire, cruiser altered course to port, survivors stating that it appeared she intended to ram, passed close round stern of raider and proceeded on parallel course gradually drawing ahead, on port side of raider. Cruiser was now heavily on fire in bridge and midship sections. Raider also badly damaged and on fire in engine room area. Hit in engine room put Diesel Electric Control out of action, rendering all electrical equipment, including fire-fighting, inoperative. Action commenced about 1730H, lasting about an hour. Raider abandoned ship about 1900H for reason that fire could not be put out and it was certain that fire would reach ammunition stowage. Survivors state that Captain and Officers were on board when they abandoned ship about 1900H. At this time cruiser was seen to be still heavily on fire, and shortly afterwards disappeared. No violent explosions on cruiser were seen or heard by raider. They believe three torpedoes were fired by raider, one of which is thought to have hit. Raider blew up about midnight.[30]

Ramage considered that, with few exceptions, the survivors had spoken the truth.

FRIDAY 28 NOVEMBER

At 0038 Pearce was provided with revised search parameters for the Hudsons at Carnarvon aimed at covering the area where the life-belt had been recovered. Five minutes later, a signal was sent to No.4 SFTS, authorizing Squadron Leader Cooper to direct the search for the missing Anson. In addition to the three Wirraways allocated, the Gannet would conduct a search of the coastline from Carnarvon to Onslow, this aircraft then being at Cooper's disposal.

In view of the state of the Ansons at Onslow, it was decided to withdraw them from the search to seaward. To compensate for the withdrawal of these aircraft, two of the Hudsons assigned to P2/28 were to be redirected into the Ansons' search area.

Two Ansons from Carnarvon were now required to conduct a parallel-track search from latitude 24° 14' South. Starting at 0630, they were to fly 250 miles on a course of 009° true then land at Onslow. Covering a strip of water approximately 60 miles to seaward, the Ansons were to locate ships' boats or rafts.

Another operation, P6/28, was to employ two Hudsons from Carnarvon. Starting at 0715, the aircraft were to search to the north-east of the Catalina search area. Their objective was to locate ships' boats or rafts. Due to an oversight, the Hudsons were not warned that *Tromp* could be encountered and one aircrew was very surprised when it found a foreign warship in its patrol area.[31]

At 0212, a general appreciation by Wing Commander McLean noted that due to the deterioration of both aircrew and control personnel at all headquarters and bases, it was becoming increasingly difficult to organize efficient operations. He considered that it would become necessary to stop operations for at least twenty-four hours before another twelve hours had elapsed to rest personnel and to enable aircraft maintenance to be carried out.

Later in the morning, news was received that the Onslow postmaster had reported that the missing Anson had been found by a Wirraway on a claypan on the southern edge of Exmouth Gulf. The Anson had been forced to land due to lack of fuel. With their mission completed, the three Wirraways returned to Carnarvon.

At 0855, SWACH received news of a signal from *Wyrallah*. It was the vessel that had recovered the life-belt the previous evening. *Wyrallah* reported that, at 1815 on 27 November, it picked up an inflated RAN-type life-belt in position 24° 22' South 110° 49' East. There was no name on the belt but 'OTRC 11/39' was found stencilled on the inflatable rubber tube. It was also noted that the securing tape was knotted as if the life-belt had been worn, but that the tape had been snapped.

Shortly after 1000, a report was received that reflected the problems that were arising in the field. Carnarvon had contacted Pearce to advise that, as soon as the missing Anson was recovered, all Ansons should be returned to Geraldton. It was considered that their condition and navigation equipment were inadequate for further work over water. A curt response, perhaps indicating the pressure under which the SWACH personnel were operating, was sent three minutes later:

ANSONS MUST NOT RETURN TO GERALDTON
WITHOUT ORDERS FROM THIS HEADQUARTERS.[32]

As if to compound the problems, the Gannet, which had flown out supplies of food and water to the stranded aircrew, landed on the claypan and became bogged.

While the exchange of signals had been occurring, SWACH received word that *Wyrallah* had made another discovery. At 0906, the vessel reported to DNOWA that it had picked up two Carley floats and one German body. The floats were small, made from steel, and obviously foreign, and the body was badly decomposed. After being stripped of all effects, the German was buried at sea. A further signal from *Wyrallah* reported that it had also picked up a foreign kapok life-belt in position 24° 10' South 110° 54' East. The belt was reported as being black, with indications that it had been on fire. It also had pieces of shrapnel embedded in it.

At 1040, Pearce was asked to signal all aircraft to report any sightings of patrol vessels. All pilots were to be questioned on completion of their flights and the reports forwarded to SWACH.

By midday, with only negative reports coming in, SWACH ordered another search. Employing six Hudsons, and using a visibility distance of

five miles, the aircraft were to search for boats and rafts between latitudes 24° South and 26° South. The operation, designated P7/28, was to start at 1315.

News was then received that a second Anson had landed on the clay-pan at Exmouth. It too was bogged. With three aircrews now stranded, it was decided to use a third Anson to drop food and water to the men.

A short time later, P6/28 was logged as complete. The only sighting was that of *Tromp* in position 20° 05' South 112° 42' East.

At 1417, SWACH received the requested reports of sightings of search vessels. The Hudson on P2/28 had sighted *Olive Cam*, *Heros* and *Sunetta*.

At 1550, SWACH was informed that the Anson search had been completed without result. Fifteen minutes later, another signal was received from Pearce reporting that an indecipherable message between the Catalinas had been intercepted at 1525. Forty minutes later, SWACH was informed that the signal between the Catalinas had been repeated. Although the whole message could not be deciphered, what could be heard concerned the investigation of smoke in an indistinguishable position.

Shortly after 1700, P3/28 was recorded as having been completed. Two vessels had been sighted during this operation: a trawler with no markings (*Wyrallah*) and a Dutch tanker exhibiting the letters PJER.[33]

With only negative reports coming in and hope of finding any more survivors fading, SWACH began issuing the orders for the following day's operations. At 1722, a signal was sent to the CWR and No.4 SFTS informing them that four Ansons would be needed for the first operation. The aircraft on G1/29 were to search between datums 22° 00' South 113° 35' East and 22° 00' South 112° 44' East. They were to fly on a course of 180° true for a distance of 120 miles then return to Carnarvon. No objective was recorded.

Shortly after this signal was sent, Carnarvon informed Pearce that heavy haze and heavy winds made it imperative that all aircraft should be on the ground before dark. In addition, fuel stocks were running low. It was estimated that only 2,000 gallons of petrol would be left by midnight.

At 1745, the CWR contacted SWACH and suggested the following areas be searched on 29 November:

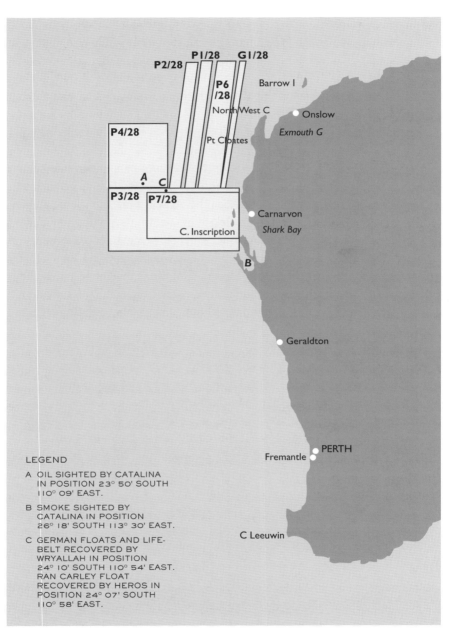

Air operations conducted
on 28 November.

Area 'A' – a 30-mile radius search from 24° 00' South 110° 54' East, with naval vessels supporting.

Area 'B' – a 60-mile radius search from 28° 00' South 110° 00' East. The object was to locate rafts or wreckage. It was suggested that if serviceability permitted, the Catalinas should conduct a square search.

Area 'C' – a low-altitude search of all beaches from Geraldton to Port Hedland, with the object of locating wreckage.

Search area 'A' would be covered by Catalina A24-11. Search area 'B' would be covered by Catalina A24-14. Both aircraft were tasked with locating rafts or wreckage.

Twenty minutes later, SWACH received a report from Pearce. A Catalina on P4/28 had reported sighting smoke but had sighted it too late to investigate.

At 1831, the orders for P2/29 and P3/29 were issued. P2/29 was to be a low-altitude search by one Wirraway of all beaches from Carnarvon to Port Hedland. P3/29 was to be a low-altitude search by one Wirraway of all beaches from Geraldton to Carnarvon. Both aircraft were to search for wreckage. These orders were followed by those for P1/29. Two Hudsons were to search for ships' boats or rafts between latitudes 22° South and 24° South. The orders for P4/29 were issued at 1859. Five Hudsons were to search between latitudes 24° South and 25° 43' South.

At 1910, the search by the three Darwin Hudsons was logged as having been completed with no sightings. Half an hour later, SWACH received two requests for information from the ACH in Darwin. He queried when the search involving his three aircraft would be completed and when he could expect them to be returned. The short and sharp reply was that they would be returned to Darwin when released from duty by Western Area.

At 2113, Pearce reported that operations P4/28 and P7/28 were complete. One Catalina had seen a 'patch of oil five miles south east of the position of reported action'. The other Catalina reported seeing a patch of oil outside its search area, a sighting report being passed by visual signal to two search vessels. In addition, the position of the smoke that had

been sighted earlier was given as approximately 26° 18' South 113° 30' East.

Although the SWACH and CWR logs did not record anything further on these oil sightings, the summary report submitted to Navy Office by Farquhar-Smith provided a latitude and longitude for the latter sighting, and the identity of the vessel which investigated the sighting.[34]

SATURDAY 29 NOVEMBER

By midnight Friday, it appeared that there was little more that could be done. The SWACH log reflected this state of affairs. Nothing was recorded from 2235 Friday evening until 0618 Saturday morning. At the latter time, the first of the departure reports was logged. These continued until 0750 when a signal was received from Pearce requesting that, if possible, the Catalinas be released on Sunday for rest and maintenance. This was followed by more departure reports and the first of the negative sighting reports for the day.

At 0856, however, a rather cryptic message was received from *Wyrallah* via Pearce, reporting 'one British and two German'. Fifteen minutes later, Pearce was ordered to mount a search from Carnarvon as soon as possible to locate *Wyrallah* and *Sunetta* if they were in the vicinity of Shark Bay. The aircraft was to obtain from *Wyrallah* the nationality of the Carley floats picked up on 28 November and to obtain from *Sunetta* a repetition of the message that it had made to a Wirraway the same day. The aircraft was also to instruct *Wyrallah* to pass on any information to *Sunetta*, and to instruct *Sunetta* to wireless any information received from *Wyrallah*. *Wyrallah* was considered to be within a 20-mile radius of 24° 05' South 110° 50' East.

Fifty minutes later, Pearce informed SWACH that the aircraft assigned to the above operation had become unserviceable and that another aircraft would not be available until 1200. At 1005, SWACH cancelled the proposed operation, the information required having been obtained.

At 1031, SWACH received a report from Geraldton that an Anson had sighted a 3,000 to 4,000 ton cargo vessel with passenger accommodation 10 miles from North West Cape on a course of 190°.

Half an hour later, another message was received from Pearce, which explained the earlier signal from *Wyrallah*. At 0725, a Hudson had reported sighting two patrol vessels in position 24° 00' South 110° 47' East. The pilot had then been ordered to intercept the vessels again to establish the nationality of the life floats recovered. The Hudson subsequently reported that the reply was 'one British, two German'.

A fourth vessel, identified as *Cape Otway*, was sighted by an Anson at 1030. Another sighting of a vessel of approximately 2,000 tons with no superstructure aft of the funnel, giving an island effect to the bridge, was also reported. The latter vessel identified itself as VJPK. This was *Cape Otway*. It was apparently sighted and reported by a second aircraft that did not realize that VJPK were the identification letters of the *Cape Otway*.

At 1112, SWACH authorized the release of the Catalinas on 30 November for rest and maintenance, subject to CWR approval. SWACH then provided the CWR with the latest available information. *Wyrallah* had reported that the Carley floats it recovered were obviously foreign. *Heros* had reported picking up one RAN-type Carley float at 1100 on 28 November in position 24° 07' South 110° 58' East. It was added that this float was badly damaged by gunfire. *Olive Cam* was returning to Geraldton and *Heros* would have to return after today due to shortage of fuel. *Wyrallah* would continue to search the area where it had recovered the life-belt and floats. HMAS *Gunbar* was being sent from Fremantle to assist.

While this information was being passed to the CWR, another sighting report was received. The Wirraway on P2/29 had reported sighting two vessels in the vicinity of North West Cape, as well as a plank, measuring approximately 1 foot by 3 feet, on the beach 1 mile east of Point Cloates.

At 1215, Pearce was ordered to mount another search. This was apparently prompted by a report from Carnarvon that six serviceable aircraft were available for operations. P7/29 was to comprise six Hudsons, which were to conduct a step-aside parallel-track search for boats or rafts between latitudes 26° South and 28° 24' South. On completion, the aircraft were to search Houtman Rocks then land at Geraldton.

Half an hour later, SWACH received a copy of a message sent to DNOWA by *Sunetta*. It had searched for two days without success and was now heading for its destination.

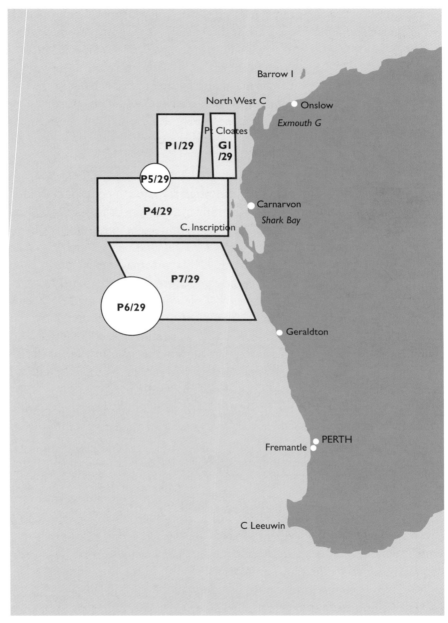

Air operations conducted
on 29 November.

By midday it was becoming clear that nothing more could be gained by continuing the search. At 1302, the following message from the CWR was logged:

> Search for SYDNEY to cease on conclusion operations 29th November unless sightings or new intelligence indicates necessity for further search. Aircraft from Darwin to return home station. Catalinas return home station Tuesday 2nd December. Advise Darwin & Townsville of ETD.[35]

In the following hour, completion reports for the morning's operations were logged. There were no new sightings. At 1455, Pearce advised that one of the aircraft assigned to P7/29 had become unserviceable and that only five aircraft could be deployed. Twenty minutes later, the AOC informed Pearce that the Darwin Hudsons were to be returned on 30 November if the search was to conclude on 29 November, and that the aircraft must be in readiness for this eventuality. Pearce was to advise Darwin of their expected departure time. And if the search was to conclude, all Pearce aircraft were to observe Sunday as a day of rest, although they must be prepared for a return to Pearce on 1 December.

At 1522, Geraldton was ordered to recall its Ansons. The search had been concluded.

While arrangements were being finalized for the return of the Catalinas and the Darwin Hudsons, the aircraft on the final search were reaching their patrol area. At 1620, one aircraft reported sighting *Sunetta*. A second vessel, identified as VQSC (*Evagoras*), was sighted ten minutes later. This was followed by the sighting of vessel PDJR at 1708 and *Havfru* at 1827.[36]

At 2145, SWACH received the completion signal for P7/29. Although several vessels had been sighted, the results of this, the final air search, were negative. On receipt of the completion report SWACH sent the following signal to the CWR and Pearce:

> P7/29 completed and negative 1300z/29. This completes air operations in connection SYDNEY. No further information of fresh sighting from naval or shore sources.[37]

Almost an hour earlier the ACNB had sent, apparently before learning of the final results of P7/29, the following message to the Admiralty:

> The NB regret that after intensive air and surface search of the area no evidence of HMAS SYDNEY has been sighted except two RAN life belts and one Carley float badly damaged by gunfire. It is concluded that SYDNEY sank after the action and further search has been abandoned.[38]

The final word on the search operations was sent to the CWR from SWACH on 4 December. Investigations had revealed that *Evagoras* had not picked up a life-belt. The search had only located two items from *Sydney*. One RAN-type life-belt recovered by *Wyrallah* and one RAN-type Carley float recovered by *Heros*.

—3—

AN OPEN WOUND

DESPITE the best efforts of the searchers, their support staff, and the various commands involved in the orchestration of the search, *Sydney* was not found. The pride of Australia's Navy was gone, and so too were 645 officers and men.

Taken in the context of the war, *Sydney* was a small loss; a relatively insignificant cruiser sunk in a remote part of the world by an unspectacular raider. In Britain, *Sydney*'s loss was overshadowed by the sinking of the aircraft carrier *Ark Royal* on 14 November and the battleship *Barham* on 25 November, the sinking of the latter vessel claiming the lives of 862 officers and men.

To the people of Australia, however, *Sydney*'s loss was a national disaster. The nation's most famous warship had been sunk with all hands. In terms of shock and damage to morale, the loss of *Sydney* was perhaps comparable only with the sinking of the battle cruiser *Hood* on 24 May 1941.

HMS *Hood*, for nearly two decades the largest warship in the world, had been the pride of the Royal Navy. *Hood*'s loss, in a matter of minutes, to

the German battleship *Bismarck* was a devastating blow to the British people, and one that fell harder when it was learned that only three men from the entire complement of 1,421 officers and men survived the sinking.

But the sinking of *Hood* was also different. *Hood*'s loss was announced by the Admiralty barely fifteen hours after the ship had been sunk. Rather than concealing the disaster, the British authorities used the battle cruiser's loss to harden the nation's resolve. Within three days, *Bismarck* was hunted down and destroyed. As far as the British public was concerned, *Hood* was avenged. As for the Royal Navy, two boards of inquiry were eventually conducted to ascertain the cause of *Hood*'s destruction and sinking.

In *Sydney*'s case, there was no immediate announcement and no board of inquiry. Although there were valid reasons for the former, the delayed announcement of *Sydney*'s loss permitted rumour and speculation to flourish, thus creating a great deal of uncertainty and anguish. By the time Prime Minister John Curtin announced the loss on 1 December, the damage was done.

Sydney's disappearance cut a deep wound in the nation's psyche. No one could comprehend how an armed merchantman could have defeated *Sydney* or why there were no survivors.

The Navy knew the how and why but was reluctant to explain the circumstances of *Sydney*'s loss to the Australian public. It was not until 1957, when George Hermon Gill's *Royal Australian Navy 1939–42* was released,[1] that the public received a full account of *Sydney*'s last action. Unfortunately, the questions had remained unanswered for too long, and many were not convinced that the true story had finally emerged.

Gill's work was followed in 1959 by an account of *Kormoran*'s exploits. Written by its captain, Theodor Detmers, *The Raider Kormoran* presented a basically similar account of the action but offered no explanation of why none of *Sydney*'s crew survived.

Perhaps, given time, the wound would have healed.

In 1981, however, the author Michael Montgomery released *Who Sank the Sydney?*[2] Montgomery challenged the accepted view of how *Sydney* was lost and proposed that a Japanese submarine had been involved and that there had been a conspiracy to conceal this alleged involvement.

Since 1981, the question of how *Sydney* was sunk has sparked debate, opened old and new wounds, and finally, in 1998, forced the Commonwealth government to conduct an inquiry into the circumstances surrounding the cruiser's loss.

Clearly, the Royal Australian Navy and the Curtin government sowed the seeds of public uncertainty and mistrust in late 1941. And just as clearly, if *Sydney*'s loss is ever to be fully understood, it is necessary to return to November 1941 to see how and why the situation developed.

THE SILENT SERVICE

Perhaps the single greatest contributing factor to *Sydney*'s loss with all hands was the wartime requirement for ships to maintain W/T silence. Despite claims to the contrary *Sydney*, quite correctly, maintained W/T silence after departure from Fremantle on 11 November. The last officially recognized signal, a response to a signal from FOCAS, was transmitted eight minutes before departure.

While on the Australia Station, *Sydney*'s whereabouts and daily movements, like other warships, were controlled and monitored by Navy Office in Melbourne. Once at sea, *Sydney* was expected to conform to pre-departure sailing instructions or intentions. If there were a requirement to cancel or alter these instructions after sailing, *Sydney* would be advised accordingly. Normally, this was done indirectly by the 'I' method. A signal intended for *Sydney* would be transmitted from one shore station to another. This signal would then be repeated to the originating station, thus providing *Sydney* with two opportunities to receive the signal. *Sydney*, of course, was not required to break W/T silence to acknowledge receipt. Despite the disadvantage of not being certain that the intended recipient had actually received the signal, the system generally worked well.

One serious flaw with the system, however, was that it engendered a belief that if nothing was heard from a ship it was not in trouble or behind schedule. In cases where a ship was delayed by weather, it merely resulted in an unheralded late arrival. But in cases where a ship was lost through enemy action and no enemy report or distress signal had been

transmitted, days or even weeks could pass before the authorities learned of the vessel's fate.

Although it was assumed that a ship in difficulties or under attack would be able to transmit a distress signal, the realities were often quite different, and there were a number of instances where merchant ships were sunk or captured without a warning or distress signal being transmitted. Similarly, there were cases where warships were damaged or sunk before they could report that they were under attack.

So, in the absence of signals from *Sydney*, it would have been assumed that all was well. Even when *Sydney* failed to arrive as scheduled, there would not have been any immediate cause for anxiety. Despite this, but perhaps because it was standard procedure, when *Sydney* had not arrived by the morning of 21 November, DNOWA advised Navy Office that the cruiser was overdue. Navy Office was not alarmed by *Sydney*'s non-arrival, however, and on learning that *Zealandia* had arrived in Singapore a day late decided to take no action.

The belief that *Sydney* was not in trouble because nothing had been received from the ship meant that another two and a half days passed before Navy Office decided to instruct the cruiser to report its ETA in Fremantle.

The first indication that *Sydney* may have been involved in an action came on the morning of Sunday 23 November. At 0630 *Aquitania* recovered twenty-six German naval men from two inflatable rubber rafts in position 24° 35' South 110° 57' East. But on ascertaining that the Germans were from a raider sunk by a cruiser, and fearing there may be another raider in the vicinity, Captain Gibbons decided to leave the area at once.[3]

Despite two of the Germans saying that the cruiser had been hit and was seen to be on fire, Gibbons subsequently claimed that it had not occurred to him that there was anything wrong with the cruiser. He also claimed that as *Aquitania* had not received any distress signals, any action signals, or anything else that could have been considered hostile, he decided not to break W/T silence to report his discovery. In other words, Gibbons also assumed that as the cruiser in question had not broken W/T silence it was not in trouble.

Captain Gibbons considered diverting to Fremantle to land the prisoners or closing with the Rottnest PWSS to make a visual report, but was

concerned that the raider may have mined the approaches. He therefore decided to maintain course and go straight to his destination of Sydney. As a result, Navy Office remained ignorant of the fact that *Sydney* had been in action.

Navy Office's first clue came late on the afternoon of 24 November, when it was learned that the tanker *Trocas* had recovered twenty-five German naval personnel from a raft in position 24° 06' South 111° 40' East. At 2052K, Navy Office asked *Trocas* to report the details of the engagement, obviously assuming the Germans' vessel had been sunk in an action.

It is not clear how or why Navy Office came to the conclusion that there had been an action, although the fact that the survivors were German naval men would have suggested they had come from a German naval vessel. Given that intelligence reports indicated that a German raider was thought to be operating in the Indian Ocean, it would have been logical to assume that the men had come from the raider or its supply ship. And given that these men had been recovered in the Sunda Strait–Fremantle shipping lane, which *Sydney* was expected to return along, it would also have been logical to assume that *Sydney* might have been responsible for the vessel's sinking.

That *Sydney* was considered to have been involved was indicated in a subsequent signal to the CZM, C-IN-C China, C-IN-C East Indies and RACAS. Transmitted at 2312K, the signal reported the details of *Trocas*'s discovery and added that it was considered *Sydney* was connected with the ship-wrecked Germans. Such a conclusion would explain why all W/T stations were instructed to stop calling *Sydney*. If *Sydney* were responsible, Burnett would have signalled Navy Office with the details if he wished. The fact that he had not perhaps indicated that he was conducting a search for other enemy vessels and did not wish to break W/T silence.

Significantly, in a 29 November report to the C-IN-C China, the British Naval Liaison Officer, Batavia, said that the CZM had come to the same conclusion regarding *Sydney*'s probable connection with the Germans. On receiving a copy of *Trocas*'s initial signal, the CZM considered that 'an action had occurred between *Sydney* and a German surface craft'. The CZM was of the opinion, however, 'that due to *Sydney*'s prolonged silence, she was either sunk or so badly damaged that she was unable to make use of any W/T.'[4]

A briefing note compiled by the Chief of Naval Staff, Vice-Admiral Sir Guy Royle, on 24 November, suggests that Navy Office was uncertain of *Sydney*'s fate. Addressed to the Minister for the Navy, Norman Makin, the note gave an overview of *Sydney*'s plight. Royle indicated that *Sydney* should have returned to Fremantle by the afternoon of 21 November at the latest, but no news had been received of the cruiser since the rendezvous on 17 November. He also informed Makin that 'it is unusual for a warship to break W/T silence except in an emergency', but added that 'every endeavour to contact *Sydney* by calling on W/T has been un-successful'. Royle's comment, 'It is most unlikely that she has received instructions from other Naval Authorities to proceed outside Australia Station', suggests that the Naval Board doubted that *Sydney* had been directed elsewhere by the Admiralty.[5]

On the morning of 25 November, a follow-up briefing note was prepared. Makin was informed of *Trocas*'s recovery of twenty-five German naval men from the vessel *Comoron* (sic), which had been sunk by a cruiser. A hand-written addendum provided the latest news that a search aircraft had sighted a lifeboat 40 miles south of the position where the raft had been found. The addendum advised that this information 'must be kept most secret as enemy are probably unaware of the situation'.

At 1810K Navy Office advised the CZM, C-IN-C China and C-IN-C East Indies of the latest developments and requested that they investigate the possibility of a severely damaged *Sydney* attempting to reach the docks at Singapore or Surabaya.

Clearly, *Sydney* was the cruiser that had sunk the *Comoron* (sic) and Royle, at least, was beginning to suspect that the cruiser might not have survived the encounter. A briefing minute from Frederick Shedden, Secre-tary of the Department of Defence Co-ordination, to the Prime Minister (dated 25 November) warned that Royle feared that *Sydney* had been sunk by the raider.

Royle had briefed Shedden via the 'secraphone' and added that he would be flying to Canberra on 26 November to discuss the matter. He also indicated that he wished to attend the War Cabinet meeting in the afternoon.

Royle's fears that *Sydney* had been lost probably stemmed from an Admiralty message received the same day. The Admiralty had signalled

that the only explanation they could think of for *Sydney*'s disappearance was that the raider might have torpedoed the cruiser. Shortly after 2130ᴋ on 25 November, Navy Office received a signal from C-IN-C China stating that he concurred with the Admiralty's explanation.

These fears appear to have been confirmed later that night by DNOWA. At 2300 (0100ᴋ), Farquhar-Smith advised Navy Office of the latest developments. Information received from Carnarvon indicated that the raider had been involved in an action with a Perth class cruiser on 19 November, 120 miles south-west (*sic*) of Fremantle. According to the German survivors' claims, the British ship was believed to have sunk.

In view of this news from the west, Navy Office was forced to agree with the Admiralty's appreciation. At 0234ᴋ on 26 November, it advised the Admiralty and C-IN-C China of this latest development, although, strangely, they were informed that the action was considered to have occurred in the forenoon of 21 November.[6]

There is nothing to indicate why Navy Office considered that the action had started on 21 November, although Farquhar-Smith's report that the action took place 120 miles 'south-west' of Fremantle may hold the key. If Navy Office had accepted this as the correct position of the action, then they may have considered that *Sydney* could not have reached the area until the forenoon of 21 November, given that the cruiser's ETA in Fremantle was 20 November.

While the Navy was trying to piece together what had happened, rumours of *Sydney*'s disappearance and possible loss were starting to spread.

It is now unclear when or where the first public rumours began, but 24 November was the probable starting day. With *Sydney* overdue and naval staff being urgently recalled to duty on the evening of 24 November, many would have speculated that the two events were related. While some recall they heard of *Sydney*'s disappearance earlier than 24 November, these claims have proven difficult to verify.

By the afternoon of 25 November, rumours that an Australian warship had been sunk began to circulate in Canberra. The Minister for Information, Senator Ashley, instructed the Chief Publicity Censor, Edmund Bonney, to prohibit publication or mention of HMAS *Sydney*. The censorship instruction was issued at 1430ᴋ. To ensure that nothing was

published in the afternoon papers, Bonney telephoned a number of the editors personally.

Earlier in the day the *Herald*'s Canberra representative had informed his Melbourne office of the rumour that an Australian warship had been sunk. When Bonney phoned to warn of the censorship instruction, the *Herald*'s editor put two and two together. *Sydney* had been sunk.

It was quickly realized that the reference to *Sydney* in the censorship instruction had been a mistake. In another ill-conceived attempt to keep the media silent, the Navy's Publicity Censorship Liaison Officer, Lieutenant-Commander G.H. Gill, RANVR, arranged for another censorship instruction to be issued. This said, 'No reference whatever press or radio to any statements or rumours regarding alleged naval activity in Australian waters'. The *Herald*'s editor now knew that *Sydney* had been sunk in Australian waters.

The War Cabinet met on 26 November, and Royle briefed the ministers about *Sydney*. From the available information (much of it based on the statements made by Linke), it appeared that *Sydney* had closed to within half a mile of a German raider named *Comoran* (*sic*). The raider had been sunk by gunfire on 19 November, but had managed to torpedo *Sydney*. When last seen, *Sydney* was on fire amidships and aft, but vanished so quickly that the cruiser was believed to have sunk. Information from Carnarvon indicated that *Sydney* had been escorting a convoy when first sighted by the Germans. They thought the cruiser had closed, thinking their ship was part of the convoy. Royle, however, said he thought it most unlikely that *Sydney* would have been escorting a convoy as it had no orders to do so. He also thought it 'most unlikely that an officer of Burnett's perspicacity would think that a ship would join up with his convoy in broad daylight'.[7]

The surviving background notes of the meeting suggest there was some incomprehension that *Sydney* could have been destroyed by a single raider. Royle apparently replied that although *Sydney* had 3-inch armour, at half a mile or even a mile it was no good against a raider armed with 6-inch guns. Despite this, there was speculation that a second raider was involved. It is not clear if these were the views of the ministers or Royle.

Curtin noted that much of what was being discussed was conjecture. But nothing would change the fact that *Sydney* was gone, and therefore

Cabinet needed to discuss the question of notifying the next of kin. This created a problem. It was thought that the enemy was probably unaware of the situation, and it was policy not to provide the enemy with any gratuitous information. Cabinet therefore decided that there would be no public statement about *Sydney*'s loss, but that the next of kin would be notified. The press was to be informed in confidence, but would be instructed 'not to publish'. It was also decided that when a public announcement was made, it should be in a form that did not convey any useful information to the enemy.

The meeting of the War Cabinet was followed by a meeting of the Advisory War Council, Royle again briefing those present. Once again it was decided to maintain the censorship and notify the next of kin. The former Minister for the Navy, W.M. (Billy) Hughes, however, dissented. He insisted that to tell the next of kin was to tell the world.

It would appear that the final decision to delay a public announcement was a ministerial one, as the Naval Board had already drafted a suggested statement for the Prime Minister should the government consider a release imperative. A copy of the statement had been sent to Royle from the Secretary of the Naval Board at 1242K on 26 November, presumably for presentation at the Advisory War Council meeting.

It is clear, however, that the Naval Board was also keen to delay a public announcement. The preamble to the statement said that the release, 'while undesirable at present, should, if contemplated, be subject to sufficient delay to permit informing next of kin and arranging simultaneous release by overseas authorities'.[8]

At 1428K, the Naval Board relayed the following message to all district naval officers, the naval officer in charge, Darwin, and RACAS:

It is desired to take press into confidence regarding HMAS SYDNEY. It is therefore requested that you will arrange for editors in your city to be secretly repetition secretly advised as follows. HMAS SYDNEY sank German raider late afternoon Wednesday 19th November five hundred miles north west Fremantle. Information received from German survivors picked up subsequent to action. Known SYDNEY damaged but extent unknown as no direct communication since received from her. All possible action being taken

to secure information. Meanwhile publicity most undesirable following reasons. (a) Fate of SYDNEY at present is [in] doubt. (b) Fate of enemy unknown to Germany and important to keep them in ignorance. (c) Undesirable advertise loss or damage to HMA Ship in view Pacific situation.

Press will be kept informed and cooperation requested needless to say. Next of kin will be advised immediately definite news received.

Late on the afternoon of 26 November, the next of kin were notified. The telegrams sent by the Naval Board said: 'With deep regret I have to inform you that your [relationship and name] is missing as a result of enemy action. Minister for Navy and Naval Board desire to express to you their sincere sympathy'. Similarly worded telegrams were sent by the Air Board to the next of kin of the RAAF personnel lost in *Sydney*.

PIECING THE STORY TOGETHER

Earlier in the day, Paymaster Lieutenant Baume, in charge of an armed guard of eleven men and one sick-berth attendant, boarded *Trocas* to take charge of the German survivors. While the SBA treated the numerous cases of sunburn, sores, swollen feet, conjunctivitis and constipation, Baume began questioning the prisoners. At 1335, he signalled the Naval Board that one prisoner had said that the cruiser had been struck by a torpedo, and when last seen was burning amidships.

In Carnarvon, Lieutenant-Commander Rycroft and Mr Lobstein had started the daunting task of interrogating the German prisoners. Their job was not easy. The two boatloads of survivors had been trucked into town in the early hours of the morning and secured in the town gaol's court-yard. Little effort had been made to search or segregate the officers and the ratings. As a result, by the time Rycroft and Lobstein reached them, Kapitänleutnant Herbert Bretschneider had gone through and ensured that anything of any military value had been destroyed. Worse, the two groups, which had left *Kormoran* at different times, had been allowed to mingle, thereby preventing Rycroft checking the statements of one group against the other.[9]

Meanwhile, *Centaur* was instructed to sail to Carnarvon to embark the prisoners for passage to Fremantle. At the same time, arrangements were being made to send an armed guard from Geraldton to Carnarvon. These troops, from the 11th Garrison Battalion, were to relieve the Volunteer Defence Corps guards at Carnarvon, then escort the prisoners to Fremantle.

At 2315, *Centaur* advised Navy Office that it had discovered a boat containing sixty-two German seamen and was proceeding to Carnarvon. Fifteen minutes later, Farquhar-Smith provided Navy Office with a summary of the days' developments, including the latest intelligence from Carnarvon. Rycroft had located *Kormoran*'s Navigating Officer (Meyer) who had given the position of the action as 27° South 111° East. It was also reported that the raider's captain was 'in one of two boats now approaching the coast'.[10] The source of this important piece of information is not clear, although it is possible that Meyer told Rycroft that Detmers's boat had left *Kormoran* shortly after his. Farquhar-Smith noted that this suggested that all boats sighted were from the raider.

At 0745 on Thursday, 27 November, Farquhar-Smith advised Navy Office that *Trocas* had arrived in Fremantle. From the surviving documents, it appears that Commander Ramage joined *Trocas* in Gage Roads, off Fremantle, to begin his interrogation of the prisoners. Baume, Captain Bryant, the ship's officers, and fourteen of the prisoners were questioned before *Trocas* berthed. On berthing, the prisoners were taken off and quartered in isolation in the Detention Barracks at Fremantle Gaol.

The interviews with *Trocas*'s officers revealed that the raider had left Germany in December 1940 and had operated in the Atlantic and Indian Oceans before being attacked by a cruiser on 19 November. The survivors said three torpedoes had been fired at the cruiser, one of which was seen to hit and explode. It was also reported that many of the survivors had come aboard carrying bottles of milk bearing Japanese markings.

Later in the day, Ramage telephoned Navy Office to make an initial verbal report of his findings. He then prepared and forwarded a comprehensive written report on the information obtained from the prisoners.[11]

Another summary report, of the information supplied by *Trocas*'s engineering officers, presumably compiled by Ramage, revealed more. Much of the information they supplied had come from Rudolph Lensch, one of the raider's engineers. He had been unconscious when picked up

and was questioned while in a semi-conscious state. Lensch said that at about 1630 on 19 November a cruiser had challenged his ship. They had replied to the cruiser's challenge but were then asked for the secret reply. He said that 'when they could not reply, they were ordered to stop'. Lensch also claimed that someone else in his boat had informed him that the cruiser had 'lowered a boat, presumably to investigate their ship'. The report noted that because Lensch was only semi-conscious when he provided this information he was possibly speaking the truth. When questioned again, however, Lensch claimed that he could not remember saying anything about a boat being lowered.

Regarding his ship, Lensch said it was formerly the Hamburg–Amerika Line *Steiermark*. On being taken over by the Navy, it was armed with six 5.9-inch guns and six torpedo tubes and renamed *Kormoran*. He also provided a great deal of information about *Kormoran*'s machinery, mechanical condition and damage received during the action. Lensch added that they had been bound for the Pacific, via the north of Australia.

Of the cruiser, he said that at approximately 2000 it appeared to be still moving slowly. About an hour later, the glow of its fires was replaced by what he described as a white flash, although he said he heard no sound of explosion.[12]

Shortly after 0900 on 27 November, Farquhar-Smith learned that *Koolinda* was sailing to Fremantle with thirty (*sic*) prisoners aboard. At 1155, HMAS *Yandra* recovered a further seventy-two survivors from a large lifeboat. After taking seventy Germans and two Chinese on board, *Yandra* set course for Carnarvon.

Centaur, towing survivors in two of its own boats, reached Carnarvon that afternoon. Captain Dark refused to allow the Germans to board his ship until an armed guard had been taken on board. Once that had been done, Detmers and his men were permitted to board *Centaur* and were put under guard in the forward hold.[13]

Rycroft boarded *Centaur* the same evening, found Detmers among the survivors, and began questioning him. At 2115, Rycroft signalled his findings to Farquhar-Smith. Detmers claimed that the cruiser had been torpedoed forward and struck amidships by salvoes. When last seen, it was badly on fire and steering south at 5 knots. From Rycroft, Detmers learned that HMAS *Sydney* had failed to return to port.[14]

Meanwhile, further information had been received at SWACH. It was now understood that at 1803 (1003Z) on 19 November the tug *Uco* had heard a faint Q signal. Two minutes later, its W/T operator heard 'QQQQ QQQQ' followed by an unintelligible group of figures badly made but possibly containing the figures 110. This was followed by '1000 GMT'. The operator estimated that the vessel sending the signal to be within a radius of 300 miles. *Uco*, at this time, was in position 26° 45' South 113° 20' East.

It was then discovered that Geraldton Radio had picked up a similar mutilated signal at the same time. At 1805 on 19 November, the operator heard a weak unintelligible message that ended with '7C 11115E 1000 GMT'. The operator waited two minutes, but there was no repetition. At 1815, Geraldton transmitted a message to all ships, asking if there was anything to report. No reply was received. A report of these signals was transmitted to the CWR at 1430 on 27 November.[15]

Although not realized at the time, the mutilated signal had originated from *Kormoran*. The raider had transmitted two Q signals shortly before the action.

While the search for possible survivors was continuing, the press was growing impatient. Now that the next of kin had been advised, members of the press were requesting permission to publish the names of *Sydney*'s crew. An urgent memo from the Secretary to the Naval Board to the Secretary to the Minister for the Navy requested that permission be denied. He considered it most undesirable at this juncture to inform the enemy of the loss of a large naval vessel. It would also give 'wing to present rumour within Australia'.

At 2105K, the Secretary to the Naval Board, Honorary Paymaster Commander G.L. Macandie, RAN, telexed a 'Most Secret' report to the Secretary to the Department of the Navy, for distribution to the Governor-General, the Prime Minister, the Minister for the Navy and Mr Shedden. The report was a summary of events since 11 November, incorporating the latest developments and intelligence.

On the interrogation of prisoners at Carnarvon, the report noted that 'such information as they have imparted is contradictory and some is certainly untrue' (referring to the information supplied by Linke), although it was hoped that the correct story would emerge after the *Trocas*

prisoners had been questioned. As for *Sydney*, it was noted that all of the prisoners seemed to agree that the cruiser was on fire when last seen. Among the latest developments was the news that *Aquitania* had passed Wilson's Promontory that afternoon and signalled the PWSS that it had twenty-six Germans on board.

Macandie's report claimed that *Sydney* had been due to return to Fremantle on 21 November, and that when it was learned that *Zealandia* had arrived in Singapore twenty-four hours late, it was assumed that *Sydney* would also be twenty-four hours late. In other words, Navy Office considered *Sydney* had not been due to arrive in Fremantle until the afternoon of 22 November.

It is difficult to comprehend how Navy Office could have reached such a conclusion. Before sailing, *Sydney* had advised Navy Office that its amended ETA would be PM on 20 November. Even if *Sydney* had been delayed twenty-four hours by *Zealandia*'s erratic speed, the cruiser should have reached Fremantle PM on 21 November at the latest. That this was understood was shown in Royle's memo to Makin on 24 November. Royle said that *Sydney* should have returned by the afternoon of 21 November at the latest.

The mix up in the date of *Sydney*'s return may have been a genuine error, but a later anticipated return date of 22 November would have conveniently explained Navy Office's lack of action over *Sydney*'s disappearance.

At 0510 on Friday 28 November, Rycroft advised Navy Office that there were now 163 prisoners at Carnarvon, with a further 72 expected from *Yandra*. And an inspection of *Centaur* revealed that it would be impossible to take on board and segregate each group of prisoners without leaving cargo behind. He requested permission to place all the ratings in No.2 lower hold and all the officers in No.3 between deck hold.

Prompted perhaps by the sheer number of prisoners now in custody, Royle ordered RACAS, Rear-Admiral J.G. Crace, RN, to go to Fremantle to conduct a complete investigation. To help co-ordinate the interrogations, the Director of Operations Division, Commander Dechaineux, and Commander Salm (interpreter) were also sent.

Later in the morning, Rycroft advised Farquhar-Smith of the arrival of *Yandra* in Carnarvon. He also reported that one of *Yandra*'s officer

prisoners was being kept isolated as he had 'told everything he knows of the ship and the action'. Rycroft added that *Centaur* would be sailing at noon but without the raider's captain and first officer. It had been considered too risky to leave these two men on the ship with the other prisoners. Detmers and Kapitänleutnant Kurt Foerster would travel the 560 miles to Perth by truck.

The officer prisoner mentioned in Rycroft's report was Leutnant Wilhelm Bunjes. He was described as being very unenthusiastic about the war and, unlike his companion, Oberleutnant Joachim von Gösseln, happily told all he knew of *Kormoran* and its activities. From Bunjes, Rycroft was able to compile the following narrative of the action.

Whilst in the approximate position 160 miles SW of NW Cape, steaming NNE, 14 knots, the masthead lookout sighted a ship on the starboard bow at 1600.

At first this was believed to be a sailing vessel afterwards confirmed as a 'grey cruiser'. It was believed in the raider that she had not been sighted by the cruiser and altered course to 240 and increased speed to 'full speed'. Raider 41 was then sighted by the cruiser who altered to the same course.

At 1740 the cruiser was abaft the starboard beam distance 1,200 metres (1,300 yds). Challenged by the cruiser she gave the false name STRAAT MALACCA Dutch nationality. After interchange and fumbling of signals to gain time, was given 'Proceed'. Then immediately was asked 'Hoist the Secret Signal'. This they were unable to do so the captain ordered 'Action'.

During this time the two ships were proceeding on parallel courses 1,200 metres apart and all the cruiser's guns and port torpedo tubes were trained on the raider.

At 'Action' the German flag was broken out and all the guns and tubes which would bear were trained and fired.

Apparently the raider fired first. Seconds later the cruiser fired but her first salvo missed over. Raider's first salvo struck about 'B' turret and bridge and 'Y' turret. This German officer stated that all salvoes appeared to hit and the cruiser took considerable time to find gun-hitting range.

Soon after engaging both ships altered to port, the raider about 30 the cruiser hard to port passing about 1,200 metres astern of raider. This manoeuvre appeared to be an attempt to ram the raider.

Action continued on opening course raider firing four gun salvoes which was seen to hit forward by a torpedo which caused a large fire and reduced speed considerably.

The raider was first hit in the engine room completely stopping the engines and causing an uncontrollable fire.[16]

Although clumsily worded, the account compared favourably with the one submitted by Ramage the previous day. It was now becoming clear *Sydney* had inadvertently closed with an enemy raider. Worse, it appeared that *Sydney* had been unprepared for the encounter and had paid dearly.

It was also on 28 November that the Advisory War Council met again. By this stage the press was desperate to publish news of *Sydney*'s disappearance and was urging an immediate release of information. Curtin, however, still mindful of the Navy's desire to delay any announcement, considered that no public statement should be made until the Navy considered it appropriate. While acknowledging the Navy's needs, however, Curtin also wished to keep the press on side. He asked the Navy to airmail to each state a complete casualty list for prompt release to the newspapers as soon as a public announcement was authorized.

Late on the evening of 28 November the Secretary to the Department of Navy, Alfred Nankervis, was informed that the search for survivors from *Sydney* had thus far proved unsuccessful.

Koolinda reached Fremantle shortly after 0800 on 29 November. Although a report indicated *Koolinda* had thirty prisoners aboard, the ship was actually carrying thirty-one. The prisoners, described as young and having no officer in charge, were disembarked and sent to the No.11 Internment Camp at Harvey, about 80 miles south of Fremantle. One prisoner, too ill to travel, was admitted to hospital.

Captain Airey subsequently submitted a report on the recovery of these survivors to Farquhar-Smith. Included in his report was a statement made by one of the survivors, who had told Airey that on 'Wednesday evening 19th November 1941 my ship Cormoran (*sic*) was challenged by a British cruiser. The cruiser opened fire first and we retaliated. After a

Kormoran survivors disembark from *Koolinda*.
Western Australia Maritime Museum

fight lasting about one and a half hours my ship caught fire. We took to the life boats at 7.20 PM approx; and both ships were then seen to be blazing. About midnight both ships sank. We looked around for survivors off both ships but none could be found'.

At 1030 on 29 November, Commanders Dechaineux and Salm, having arrived in Perth late the previous day, started their interrogation of the *Trocas* prisoners. Their opening questions were arranged in this way:

(a) Where were you when the action started?
(b) What time did you leave the ship?
(c) How did you get away?
(d) Did you see the British cruiser?

By midday, after having questioned only four prisoners, Dechaineux had given up. At 1430, after reconsidering their line of questioning,

Dechaineux and Salm proceeded to Harvey to begin questioning the *Koolinda* prisoners.

Later in the day, Dechaineux was advised (presumably by Farquhar-Smith) that if he wished to interrogate the *Centaur* party before they were sent to Harvey, he would need to do so on board the ship in Gage Roads. Dechaineux replied that he considered that the interrogation of the *Centaur* and *Yandra* parties should take place at Harvey. He added that he would be returning to Perth on Sunday in order to interrogate the raider's captain.

While Dechaineux had been trying to extract information from the *Trocas* prisoners in Fremantle, Captain H.B. Farncomb, RAN, Commanding Officer of HMAS *Canberra*, had been trying to do likewise with the *Aquitania* prisoners in Sydney.[17]

Farncomb questioned twenty of the twenty-six survivors recovered by *Aquitania* and did a remarkable job. In his report, he noted that several of the prisoners had been inclined to talk a lot about the action, but as most of these men had been serving between decks at the time, much of their information was hearsay. He added that their morale was good and all were 'confident that Germany would win the war within a year'. In reconstructing the action, Farncomb reported:

> The action with HMAS SYDNEY commenced about 1605H on 19th November. HMAS SYDNEY approached signalling with a daylight lamp and when the range had come down to about 3000 yards the raider opened fire. She appears to have hit SYDNEY near the bridge with the first salvo. One or two of the ratings even estimated the range, shortly after the action had started, at about 1500 yards. It was stated that the raider obtained at least one hit with a torpedo under SYDNEY's forecastle and after that she was firing at least three salvoes to SYDNEY's one. After about the raider's 15th salvo, SYDNEY ceased fire, but opened fire again shortly afterwards, apparently firing one or two salvoes. The action with SYDNEY lasted about one hour.
>
> When last seen SYDNEY was badly on fire amidships having sustained several hits. She appeared to be down by the bows and two of the survivors stated that they could see flames just abaft her funnels.

The raider was badly hit in the engine room and at about 1900H her magazines were flooded. The ship was scuttled and subsequently abandoned.

None of the prisoners knew what had happened to the SYDNEY. While they were in their boats, about 1930, they stated that they could still see SYDNEY burning some miles away, but owing to being in the boats they did not have a good view. One rating said that SYDNEY was last seen at 2100, but this information is open to doubt.

The following day (Sunday 30 November), Dechaineux submitted a report on the interrogations in the west. About the *Trocas* prisoners he claimed that 'this party is led by a truculent Gestapo agent and little more can be got from them'. From the five *Koolinda* prisoners, however, he was able to prepare a good account of *Kormoran*'s cruise and its supply ship arrangements. As for the action, Dechaineux reported:

The alarm was sounded in the KORMORAN at 1600/19. At that time SYDNEY appeared on the Northern horizon, distant about 15 miles. The KORMORAN then turned to the Westward, and increased to full speed. The SYDNEY gave chase, ordering the K to stop. The K on purpose made a great display of endeavouring to reply and also to comply with the instructions from the SYDNEY. It is reasonable to suppose that this apparent inefficiency in signalling by the K was a *ruse de guerre*, in the hope that the SYDNEY would close to investigate.

The SYDNEY came up on the starboard quarter of K to a distance of about 1500 metres when the K opened fire, the first salvo hitting the SYDNEY's bridge. K's second salvo hit the superstructure amidships and set the Cruiser on fire. Shortly after the first salvo K fired two torpedoes from her starboard tubes. It is believed one of these torpedoes hit.

SYDNEY's first salvo, fired after she was hit, missed the KORMORAN. The second salvo hit the KORMORAN's bridge. One subsequent salvo at least hit the K's engine room, setting a lubricating oil tank on fire and paralysing the fire fighting equipment.

The action was joined at about 1700 and lasted until 1750. The relative course of the SYDNEY took her from fine on the starboard

quarter, across K's stern and, on a parallel course up the K's port side. A third torpedo was fired when SYDNEY was on K's port beam. The trend of the action was to the westward. After action was broken off the SYDNEY turned away and steamed to the South East, heavily on fire. One gun aboard K fired 50 rounds.

Most evidence seems to show that the cruiser disappeared suddenly and most prisoners believe that she sank before midnight.

The first order to abandon ship in KORMORAN was given about 1810, when the engine room personnel got away. It appears that the personnel had ample time to equip the boats very thoroughly. The Captain and Officers did not leave the ship until much later. It is believed that K blew up at midnight.

The first hit on K destroyed the radio and no signal was sent to any German authority.[18]

Although Dechaineux admitted that this account incorporated evidence collected from various sources, it is extremely doubtful that he would have received a copy of Farncomb's report before he prepared his report. If this was so, Farncomb and Dechaineux independently produced two detailed accounts of the action from two widely separated groups of prisoners. Although differing in minor details, the two accounts were sufficiently alike to suggest that the information being supplied was genuine.

SUNDAY 30 NOVEMBER

By Sunday hopes of finding *Sydney* had faded. At 2254K on Saturday evening, the Naval Board had signalled the Admiralty that 'after intensive air and surface search of the area no evidence of HMAS SYDNEY has been sighted except two [sic] RAN life-belts and one Carley float badly damaged by gunfire'. The board concluded that *Sydney* had been sunk. The search was being abandoned.

Prime Minister Curtin was given the news on Sunday 30 November.

Although the search was over, there were still prisoners to be interrogated and a public announcement to be made. As for the prisoners, Navy Office ordered Detmers and Foerster to be separated, and not to be questioned before the arrival of Rear-Admiral Crace.

Centaur reached Fremantle on Sunday morning, and on arrival Rycroft submitted his report to Farquhar-Smith. Apart from producing formal versions of his previous reports on Linke, Meyer, and Detmers, Rycroft had little to add to what was now known. It was revealed, however, that twenty-five men had been killed in the action, and an undisclosed number had been lost when a 'raft had broken up and sunk'. Disturbingly, Rycroft considered that the prisoners had been 'instructed by their Officers to give incorrect answers to all questions regardless of their nature'.[19]

Yandra arrived in Fremantle on Sunday evening. Lieutenant J.A. Taplin, RANR, *Yandra*'s Commanding Officer, was able to provide the DNOWA with a very detailed five-page report on his ship's involvement in the search, the recovery of seventy-two survivors, and his interrogation of the prisoners. Taplin's account of the action was based primarily on the statements made by Bunjes. The report noted that one prisoner, Petty Officer Otto Jürgensen, 'gave very guarded information regarding the action'. Taplin considered that 'if he could be induced to talk he could be of inestimable value'.

A summary of the information supplied by Shu Ah Fah, one of the raider's four Chinese laundrymen, was also contained in Taplin's report to Farquhar-Smith. Surviving documents indicate that Shu Ah Fah was subsequently questioned by Ramage, who noted that his story of the action 'conforms in general to that told by SubLieut [*sic*] Bunjes from first sighting at 1600 to the time of opening fire, but differs considerably from that time onward'. A hand-written notation, possibly added by Dechaineux at a later date, indicates that Shu Ah Fah's claims of *Kormoran*'s minelaying activities and supply arrangements had been discredited.[20]

At 1959K, Farncomb advised the Naval Board that he had conducted further interrogations with the *Aquitania* prisoners. Farncomb reported that before the action *Sydney*'s catapult had been turned out and the aircraft's engine started. During the action, *Sydney* had its foremast shot

away and one of its boats destroyed. As for *Sydney*'s condition after the action, it was reported that the cruiser was burning fiercely, the screws were visible at times, and that the ship appeared to 'glow'. It was also ascertained that a rating from the propaganda service had captured the action on film, although there was no mention of what had happened to it.

Later Sunday evening, Royle received a personal message from the First Sea Lord, Admiral Sir Dudley Pound, who requested that when all the available information on the action had been gathered he would be grateful to 'know what happened so that we can deduce any lessons for the future'.

THE FIRST PUBLIC ANNOUNCEMENT

At 2100 on 30 November, Prime Minister Curtin gave the following brief statement to the Canberra press contingent:

> HMAS SYDNEY has been in action with a heavily armed enemy merchant raider, which she sank by gunfire. The information was received from survivors from the enemy vessel, who were picked up some time after the action. No subsequent communication has been received from HMAS SYDNEY, and the Government regrets to say that it must be presumed that she has been lost.

The statement was for publication only and was not to be broadcast by any Australian radio station for forty-eight hours. The ban was also to apply to overseas agencies. The statement and a casualty list were intended for Australian publication the following morning. What followed, could only be described as a public relations fiasco.

Some papers, unsure what they should or should not publish, simply published the Prime Minister's statement and the staggering 645-strong casualty list. Others published everything they knew, even managing to include stories from German prisoners. Three radio stations (2UW, 3KZ and 3AR) lifted the story from the papers and announced *Sydney*'s loss. As a result they were temporarily suspended from broadcasting.

While the nation read and heard the tragic news with stunned disbelief, the press began demanding further information from the Prime Minister. In turn, the Prime Minister's office asked the Navy what other information could be released. Besides asking if further stories from the German prisoners could be released, the question of *Sydney* survivors, possibly picked up by a second raider or supply ship, was raised. The press also wanted to know if the place and date of action could be revealed.

The question of further stories from German prisoners was quite embarrassing. None of the newspapers had been given permission to interview the prisoners, and it was thought that any statements made by them would be boastful and therefore most undesirable.

In response to the Prime Minister's question about a second raider, Macandie replied that the 'Naval Board have continuously had under review the possibility of two raiders, and this has been the principal reason for their desire to delay as long as possible the information that one raider has been sunk from reaching the enemy'. It was hoped that if a second raider or supply ship had been scheduled to rendezvous with *Kormoran*, and *Kormoran* failed to make that rendezvous, the other vessel would break w/t silence 'to inform somebody that she had not kept the rendezvous'. If this happened, the vessel would reveal its location through direction finding, thus permitting a second enemy vessel to be located and destroyed.

Macandie added that from the available information it appeared most unlikely that any of *Sydney*'s crew had been picked up by a second enemy vessel, but that there was a 'faint possibility that a ship passing through the area on 21–22 November may have a few survivors'. It was thought that if this was the case, however, such a vessel should have called at Fremantle or reported by w/t.

As for announcing the place and date of the action, it was considered undesirable to make this information public for security reasons.

Clearly, the Naval Board did not want any more information to be released. Unfortunately, this was not what the government wanted to hear. Although Curtin understood the Navy's reasoning, the press was still demanding more information for the afternoon papers.

At 1432k, the Minister for the Navy asked Macandie for the number of German survivors and asked whether this information could be made

available to the press. Makin was informed that there were 320 (*sic*) German survivors but, in view of the effect that this information would have on the next of kin, relatives and friends of *Sydney*'s crew, Macandie considered the number should not be published.

The question of a second raider was also raised during the afternoon War Cabinet meeting. Although there was no evidence of a second raider, the Navy had become confused by an Admiralty message referring to a raider named *Steiermark*. The initial reports from the German survivors indicated that they had come from a raider named *Cormoran* (*sic*). This created the belief that *Steiermark* and *Cormoran* (*sic*) were two different ships. When this was explained at the War Cabinet meeting, it led to speculation that *Sydney* survivors could be aboard the 'second' raider. Curtin asked Makin to clear up this matter.[21]

While the government and the Naval Board debated what information should be released, rumours and speculation continued to spread. One report mentioned that the wreck of the *Sydney* had been discovered on the Western Australian coast.

As for maintaining security, it was learned from the New Zealand Naval Board that Australian newspapers, containing news of *Sydney*'s loss, had arrived in New Zealand. As a result, the New Zealand press was now urgently requesting permission to publish the story. The request was denied.

Unknown to the Naval Board, their bid to maintain security was an exercise in futility. There was no second raider, and *Kormoran*'s supply ship (*Kulmerland*) was long gone.[22] Furthermore, German intelligence already knew that *Kormoran* was sunk and *Sydney* missing. Interception and decoding of the signal sent from Navy Office to *Trocas* (in Merchant Navy Code) on 24 November revealed there had been an engagement in Australian waters. Confirmation that *Kormoran* had been lost had come on 30 November when a deciphered Admiralty message of 26 November reported the sinking of a raider by the cruiser *Sydney*. As the only other raider at sea (*Atlantis*) had been sunk in the South Atlantic on 22 November, the raider sunk by *Sydney* could only be *Kormoran*.[23]

That news of *Sydney*'s loss had already leaked out was demonstrated on 28 November when it was learned that an American radio station had broadcast that *Sydney* had been lost in the Timor Sea off Broome, Western Australia.[24]

THE FORMAL INTERROGATIONS BEGIN

On 1 December, the formal interrogation of *Kormoran*'s officers began at Swanbourne Barracks, about five miles north of Fremantle. Detmers, Foerster, Bunjes, and von Gösseln were singled out for questioning on the first day; also selected were Leutnant Walter Hrich (cameraman), Oberleutnant Heinz Messerschmidt (mine officer and secretary to the captain) and Dr Hermann Wagner (meteorologist).

Detmers, presumably questioned by Crace, divulged that his ship had been disguised as the Dutch ship *Straat Malakka*. For the purpose of disguise, the hull and funnel had been painted black and the super-structure buff. At 1600 ship's time (1700H) on 19 November, a cruiser was sighted. They turned away, but the cruiser, subsequently identified as of the Perth class, gave chase. The cruiser allegedly signalled 'NNP', which Detmers claimed he did not understand. When he failed to reply, the cruiser ordered him to stop. The cruiser then signalled 'in plain language to give [the] secret call'. As he did not know the secret call he was left with no option but to fight.

At a range of 'somewhat more than a mile' the cruiser's first salvo went over, while *Kormoran*'s first salvo 'hit the conning tower [bridge] of the cruiser'. After some delay, they fired two torpedoes, 'one of which missed and one hit, about 20 metres from the bow. The fore turrets then stopped firing'. The cruiser's third turret then fired and hit them, damag-ing the fire-fighting apparatus and starting a fire. Detmers 'thought the cruiser was going to ram him, but it passed astern' and 'fired four tor-pedoes'. After firing torpedoes, the cruiser 'turned away behind a smoke screen—when seen later the second funnel was burning'.

He ordered the bulk of his crew away at approximately 2000, retaining about a hundred men. Owing to insufficient power they then spent three hours extracting the remaining boats from a hatch. At midnight he sank his ship.

As for who fired first, Detmers said that he thought that 'both ships opened fire at the same moment—perhaps [the] cruiser half a second earlier'. He added that the cruiser had approached with all guns and torpedo tubes trained on them. The aircraft, which had been warming up on the catapult, was hit as it was about to be launched.

When questioned about the Japanese milk found in the lifeboats, Detmers replied that they had received it from a 'German ship on its way from Japan to Germany'.

Crace learned little from Foerster. As the raider's second-in-command, he was below decks during the action and saw nothing. He did, however, express astonishment that the cruiser had come so near to his ship. The action, he said, lasted about twenty minutes, and that 'after the first salvo there was no fire-fighting equipment left in the raider'. He tried to rig up some emergency gear but after another hit in the engine room the raider stopped, then caught fire. He was then forced to flood the magazines.

The questioning of the other officers went from one extreme to the other. Bunjes was particularly helpful, as was Wagner. Messerschmidt and von Gösseln gave guarded information. Hrich refused to 'reveal anything to the enemy'.

Hrich's selection for interrogation on the first day would appear to be unusual, except that Farncomb had ascertained that the Germans had filmed the action.[25] It is not known if the interrogating officers had prior knowledge of Hrich's role aboard ship, but it would appear so. Hrich was the official cameraman who had been assigned to *Kormoran* by the German propaganda ministry for the purpose of producing a documentary film. His early selection for interrogation, therefore, may not have been coincidental. Clearly, Hrich would have been well placed to view the action, making him a particularly valuable witness. Unfortunately, he refused to talk about the ship or the action.

After a lengthy though somewhat unproductive day, Crace signalled his findings to the Naval Board. Both ships had opened fire almost simultaneously at a range of about a mile. While *Sydney*'s first salvo went over, the raider's first salvo hit. *Sydney* was then struck by a torpedo. Crace admitted that the raider's movements and organization of supply were not yet clear and considered that 'no further information will be gained by direct questions as officers will not talk and men know little of importance'. He decided to reorganize the interrogations. Two investigating teams of one officer and two interpreters would interrogate all the junior officers and the ratings. Crace also considered that the officer prisoners should be transferred to an eastern states POW camp in which decoy prisoners and listening devices had been installed. Crace added

Post-war photograph of Kapitän zur See
Theodor Anton Detmers. Awarded the Knight's
Cross of the Iron Cross for the action with
Sydney. Detmers was promoted in April 1943.
Bibliothek für Zeitgeschichte, Stuttgart

that Dechaineux would compile a report on the latter's return to Melbourne.

Crace questioned Detmers at length again on 2 December. The ship's doctor, Marinestabsarzt Friedrich Lienhoop, and *Kormoran*'s Torpedo Officer, Oberleutnant Joachim Greter were also questioned on this day. The rest of the ship's officers were transferred to Harvey and questioned by Ramage and Crace on 4 December. An exception was Leutnant Bruno Kube; he was interviewed in hospital on 9 December. In line with the policy of keeping groups and certain individuals segregated until they had been interrogated, some officers were quartered in isolation. Although questioned at Swanbourne Barracks, von Gösseln appears to have been quartered at the Fremantle Detention Barracks.

It is not clear why von Gösseln was isolated, although an earlier statement by Lensch may have had something to do with it. Lensch reported that von Gösseln and another officer, Oberleutnant Wilhelm Brinkman, had jumped overboard to save themselves while the other officers remained on board. It may have been considered that knowledge of this apparent act of cowardice could be used against von Gösseln.

Oberleutnant Heinfried Ahl also came in for special attention. He was initially questioned with the other officers at Harvey on 4 December. Athough it was known he was an aviation officer, Ahl refused to answer any questions about the raider's aircraft or its employment. The RAAF, however, was particularly keen to clear up reports of unidentified aircraft over Geraldton and over RAAF Pearce in early November. The RAAF requested the Navy to ask the prisoners 'whether supply ships carry aircraft' and if a supply ship had been responsible for the flights over Geraldton and Pearce.[26] Because he would not talk, Ahl was transferred to the Fremantle Detention Barracks and put in isolation. The tactic worked. When Ahl was interrogated again on 8 December, he was particularly helpful. Although it was not ascertained if supply ships carried aircraft, Ahl said that he had not flown over land while in the Indian Ocean and had not seen land from his aircraft. Clearly, *Kormoran* had not been responsible for the flights over Geraldton and Pearce.

After questioning the raider's senior officers, Crace issued his instructions for the interrogation of the ratings. The objective now was to obtain as much information as possible on the raider itself, other raiders, and

their supply-ship arrangements. These instructions, issued on 2 December, detailed the method of interrogation to be used and the specific information required. Crace acknowledged that it would be a 'dull laborious task', but stressed that it was 'most important to get all we can from the prisoners'. The information obtained may 'lead to the destruction of more than one enemy supply ship or raider'.

His work done, and his continued presence no longer necessary, Crace returned to Sydney, arriving there on 7 December. Dechaineux and Salm had already gone. They had left Perth on 3 December, Dechaineux returning to Melbourne to prepare his report for the Naval Board.

With the exception of thirteen prisoners who were in hospital and those ex-*Trocas*, all the prisoners from *Koolinda*, *Centaur* and *Yandra* were sent to Harvey. The questioning of these men was not completed until 9 December. The *Trocas* prisoners appear to have been interrogated at the Fremantle Detention Barracks before being sent to Harvey on 19 December.[27]

UNDER PRESSURE TO RELEASE MORE INFORMATION

Despite the Naval Board's desire to withhold further details of *Sydney*'s loss, events overseas were beginning to undermine its position.

On 1 December, the London *Daily Express* published an article by its naval correspondent, Bernard Hall. The article claimed that the Australian cruiser *Sydney* had been torpedoed while closing to rescue survivors from the raider *Steiermark*. Hall speculated that *Sydney* had 'shattered' the raider by gunfire then closed to pick up the survivors. This he claimed, was 'in the *Sydney* tradition', as it had 'withstood a terrific aerial bombardment' the year before while picking up survivors from the *Bartolomeo Colleoni*. Unfortunately, Hall used a considerable amount of journalistic licence to paint a misleading picture for his readers. *Sydney* had not picked up *Colleoni* survivors while under air attack, and there was no evidence to show that the cruiser was picking up *Steiermark* survivors when it was torpedoed. Similarly, his claim that the search for *Sydney* survivors, conducted 'all along the line between New Zealand and Malaya', was a little off track, to say the least. His detailed knowledge of the number of

men missing, the names of vessels sunk by the *Steiermark*, and its armament and complement, however, was uncannily accurate. Clearly, Hall,
who had served in the Royal Navy, had been provided with privileged
information from very reliable sources.

Hall's article was followed at 0700z on 2 December, when the Reuters
correspondent in Singapore broadcast the news that *Sydney* had been
sunk off Australia. Within hours, Germany was also announcing the
story. Then, since the Germans knew, the British authorities permitted the
BBC to include details of the action in a propaganda broadcast at 1300z.[28]
The broadcast named *Kormoran* and gave details of the raider's armament,
information that was still subject to censorship restrictions in Australia.

Although Hall's article attracted little attention, the Australian press
was understandably incensed when it learned that the BBC had broadcast
information that it was not permitted to publish. Naturally, the Prime
Minister's office bore the brunt of this indignation. Although the Commonwealth government subsequently cabled a strongly worded protest
to the Secretary of State for Dominion Affairs, the damage was done.

On 3 December, the Naval Board, apparently bowing to growing
public pressure, authorized the release of further information. Shortly
after midday, the following statement was sent to Canberra for broadcast
and release to the press. It was recommended that the Prime Minister
issue the statement in time for publication in the afternoon papers.

> The Prime Minister, (Mr Curtin) announced today that following
> the sifting and checking of evidence resulting from the interrog-
> ation of prisoners from the German raider KORMORAN, it was now
> possible to reconstruct, to an extent, the action between that ship
> and HMAS SYDNEY.
>
> In releasing the statement, Mr Curtin emphasized that in the
> absence of any information from HMAS SYDNEY one side of the
> picture only is given from direct evidence. Certain of the aspects on
> board HMAS SYDNEY must remain a matter of surmise as to details.
> The broad canvas can, however, be taken as giving an accurate
> picture.
>
> HMAS SYDNEY was on patrol duties some three hundred miles
> west of Carnarvon, Western Australia, when she encountered the

KORMORAN. The initial advantage lay with the German, since she was disguised as a merchant ship, and her identity had to be established before she could be attacked. The SYDNEY, on the other hand, was obviously a British cruiser and as such an undoubted enemy to the raider.

The encounter took place shortly before dusk. In the absence of direct evidence, it can only be assumed that some factor prevented the SYDNEY making use of her aircraft for reconnaissance from a distance. With dusk falling, she had to close the suspect to establish identity. She did this cleared for action, and in a state of readiness.

As soon as the raider was convinced that her identity would be known, she opened fire, simultaneously with the first salvo from HMAS SYDNEY. The raider's first salvo struck the SYDNEY full on the bridge, and put her at a temporary but vital disadvantage. In addition to doing grave damage to the central control, it started a fire which lasted throughout the action.

HMAS SYDNEY closed the range immediately, and fought fiercely, probably with independent firing. She was soon on fire amidships as the result of another salvo from the raider. She had, however, meanwhile crippled the enemy by a direct hit in the engine room, and set her heavily on fire also. By this time it was dark, and the enemy ceased fire and abandoned ship, which subsequently blew up.

From their boats, the Germans watched SYDNEY disappear over the horizon. She was then on fire amidships. That was the last seen of her.

Prisoners claim that a number of torpedoes were fired at the SYDNEY. It is not known if any struck. If they did so, they may have been the cause of the ship's eventual sinking.

It is possible that the fires on board the SYDNEY were the cause of no boats from her having been picked up. The fires were in the midship section, where boats and Carley floats were housed. It must be assumed that these were destroyed.

There is nothing in the evidence to point to the SYDNEY having blown up. The last evidence of her was her disappearance, still afloat, over the horizon.

The search for her, however, has been long and wide. It has produced nothing but two [sic] empty life-belts and one Carley float, badly damaged by gunfire. Her actual fate, in the absence of other evidence, must remain a mystery. All that we do know is that she fought gallantly, and successfully achieved her aim — the destruction of the enemy.

Despite the claim that the action took place 300 miles west of Carnarvon, the statement was a reasonably accurate, though guarded, summary of what was known. It is doubtful, however, that the press was satisfied with such a meagre offering.

The War Cabinet met again in Melbourne the following day. As Royle was en-route to Singapore, the Acting Chief of Naval Staff, Commodore J.W. Durnford, RN, represented the Navy. Durnford provided the ministers with a brief account of the action based on the information already collected. In the discussion that followed, Durnford said that although *Sydney*'s aircraft was reported as ready to fly off, it was not known whether Burnett had been suspicious, or had thought the ship genuine, although the preliminary naval intelligence view was that Burnett thought the supposed Dutch ship was genuine. Durnford added that the raider had fired fifteen salvoes into *Sydney* but that *Sydney* 'had got 12 hits' into the German. When last seen, *Sydney* was badly on fire, and it was assumed that the cruiser sank as a result of the punishment received.[29]

Curtin appears to have accepted Durnford's account of the action but asked if there was any explanation for the lack of survivors. It is not known if Durnford was able to reply to this question, although he did mention that the Navy no longer considered that a second ship was trailing *Kormoran*. This perhaps implied that there was little hope that *Sydney* survivors could have been picked up by a second raider or supply ship.

The Naval Board was certain that *Sydney* was gone, but others apparently still held out hope. At 2320 on 4 December, SWACH received a curious report from Geraldton. It was reported that a call, possibly from *Sydney*, had been received on the 24.5 metre wavelength, and Geraldton was requesting a D/F bearing from Darwin. Twenty minutes later, Squadron Leader Cooper (at Geraldton), reported that one of his wireless

operators had heard an R/T (radio telegraphy) message which he thought may be from HMAS *Sydney*. The message, however, appeared to be addressed to Darwin or a technical telegraph operator. Nevertheless, Darwin was immediately instructed to establish a watch on 24.5 metres.

At 2355, another report from Squadron Leader Cooper was logged. It now appeared that the message was emanating from Sydney Aeradio. Cooper reported that the following message had been heard at 1510z:

> Calling Darwin of Technical Telegraph Operator—Call from Sea Sydney calling send Carrier men on board—Calling Frazer D/F Darwin—Cannot detect you—Singapore call Darwin. This M S Sydney calling message received frequency satisfactory will put thru [*sic*] in morse.[30]

This message was also heard by several people on an ordinary shortwave receiver in Geraldton's Esplanade Hotel. Although it had been thought initially that the message was a distress call from HMAS *Sydney*, the text of the signal suggested otherwise. Additionally, the message heard had been a voice message. Although the Geraldton listeners appear not to have known, *Sydney*'s W/T sets used Morse and were incapable of transmitting voice messages.

The confusion and false hope was cleared up the following afternoon when it was ascertained that the message had originated from the Post Master General, Sydney, although not before the matter had been referred to the Combined Operational Intelligence Centre (COIC).

The Director of the COIC was Commander R.B.M. Long, RAN, who was also Director of Naval Intelligence. Long should have played a key role in the evaluation of the intelligence gathered from the *Kormoran* survivors, but circumstances prevented it. He had been in Singapore from 13 to 21 November, attending a conference of secret service staff members. Long returned to Australia on 27 November, but he does not appear to have taken an active part in the investigation into the loss of *Sydney* until early December. This is understandable. Long was heavily involved in preparing his intelligence network for the expected entry of Japan into the war.

On 5 December Long forwarded to Dechaineux and Getting, without comment, a report on the *Aquitania* prisoners. The report had been prepared and submitted by Staff Sergeant R. Alexander, who appears to have been the sergeant in charge of the prisoners after their recovery. It is clear from the report that Alexander had a difficult time trying to extract any worthwhile intelligence from the prisoners. He noted that they pretended not to understand English, although they clearly understood what was being said to them. He also noted that the prisoners 'appeared to have made up their story before being taken on board', and 'obviously had been warned not to tell anything'.

Yet Alexander was able report that one prisoner claimed that the raider had fired two torpedoes at 'a cruiser', one of which hit. The cruiser 'hit them by gunfire and they sank'. As for the fate of the cruiser, the prisoners claimed that it 'went away, blazing amidships and aft'. Alexander added that this story 'was adhered to by all prisoners excepting one who stated, and reiterated, that the cruiser turned turtle'.[31]

The prisoners made other claims: the action had taken place on Thursday (November 20), they had sighted the Australian coast four days before the action, the raider was laying mines, supplies had come from Hong Kong, and the previous name of their ship was *Stuttgart*.

Although these claims were obviously intended to mislead, the prisoners also divulged that their ship was armed with six 5.9-inch guns, two torpedo tubes, two aircraft, and was capable of making 18 knots.

Of interest was the report that the prisoners' rubber raft contained a 'portable wireless set', 'which was of the kind which is worn strapped to the back'. The wireless set was not recovered, and Alexander did not know if it could both transmit and receive.

On 6 December, Ramage prepared a brief summary of deductions of the interrogations already conducted. Although he reported that the previous general description of the action remained unaltered, Ramage was able to provide a clearer account of the sequence of events leading up to the action.

According to the statements made by Erich Ahlbach (Yeoman of Signals), *Sydney* had begun signalling by light 'Hoist your signal letters', from a distance of about 7 miles. *Kormoran* replied by hoisting the letters 'PKQI' (*Straat Malakka*) to the triatic stay between the foremast and the funnel. As the funnel prevented the signal pendants being seen clearly, *Sydney* made 'Hoist your signal letters clear'. *Kormoran* complied, but

when *Sydney* was approximately abeam, asked, 'Where bound?' Ahlbach said that the answer given was Batavia, and that this signal was sent by light. *Sydney* then apparently signalled the letters 'IK', which Ahlbach said they did not understand, as in International Code this meant, 'You should prepare for a cyclone, hurricane, or typhoon.'

Ramage noted that the secret call sign of *Straat Malakka* was 'IIKP', indicating that *Sydney* had sent the secret challenge. As Ahlbach did not know the correct response, he made no reply. *Sydney* then made the signal, 'Show your secret sign.' In response, the raider captain ordered, 'Drop screens' (*sic*) and opened fire.

Ramage also reported that some time before the action started, the raider had broadcast 'QQQQ 26 S. 111 E. STRAAT MALAKKA' and repeated it once.

Ramage thought fit to add that according to 'Lieutenant Skerries' (*sic*), the raider's anti-aircraft guns and smaller armament were concentrated on

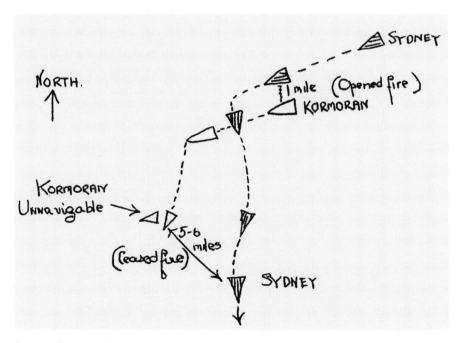

Ramage's track diagram.
National Archives (VIC.) MP 1049/5, 2026/19/6

Sydney's torpedo tubes and '1-inch' gun positions. This claim, he noted, was supported by the condition of the Carley float recovered by HMAS *Heros*. The float had a number of holes in it which appeared to have been 'caused by shells of small calibre (3.7cms and under)'. Ramage said that by the end of the action *Kormoran* was 'unnavigable' and that the last shots were fired with *Sydney* on a relative bearing of 225°.

Ramage's report, which included a track diagram of the action, was forwarded to the Naval Board by Farquhar-Smith on 12 December.[32]

Although the interrogations were still underway, and Dechaineux's report had not yet been received, the Naval Board chose the afternoon of Sunday 7 December to send an interim report of the interrogations to the Admiralty. The following account of the approach and the action was included in the signal.

> First sighting range 15 miles. Raider, speed 15 knots, altered course from 000° to 250°. SYDNEY bore north from No.41. SYDNEY chased and apparently made no other signal than NNJ repeat NNJ Raider did not reply or hoist signal letters. No stop signal was received by enemy. When SYDNEY was at close range raider made Straad Malakka [*sic*] by light, which ship she was impersonating. Dutch flag flown.
>
> At 1650H/19 SYDNEY was just abaft No.41 beam, distant 1.25 miles, both ships 15 knots, course 250°. Cruiser now made 'Make your secret letters' in plain language.
>
> Raider immediately dropped concealing gun ports and opened gun and torpedo fire. SYDNEY was at Action Stations and armament trained. She opened fire simultaneously. 'Steirmark's' [*sic*] first salvo hit cruiser's bridge. SYDNEY's first salvo over. Very early in action torpedo hit cruiser under 'A' turret, jamming 'A' and 'B' turrets. Action lasted 25 minutes and was broken off at range of 4 miles. No.41 stopped. SYDNEY proceeding at 5 knots. Believed SYDNEY sank, due shell and torpedo fire damage, at 2300H/19. Raider scuttled at 2359 H/19. Position of action 25° South 111° East.
>
> Identity confirmed No.41 'Steirmark' [*sic*] alias 'Kormorant' [*sic*]. Speed 18 knots. Six 15-centimetre guns. Two 2-centimetre A A guns. Two above water and one submerged tube each side. About 250 Type Y mines of which a large number still on board when

scuttled. 1 Arado seaplane with bombs. Air propelled torpedoes [with] contact pistols. Believed no repeat no [torpedo] direction system. Reputed to carry fast motor boat capable of laying 3 mines.

This report, which also included details of *Kormoran*'s cruise, was, in essence, the same as that presented by Durnford to the War Cabinet on 4 December.

JAPAN ENTERS THE WAR

On 8 December, the tragedy of *Sydney*'s loss was overtaken by far greater events. On this day the nation learned that the United States Pacific Fleet had been crippled at Pearl Harbor in a surprise attack by the Japanese.[33] Within hours the British colony of Hong Kong was under attack, and Malaya and Thailand were being invaded. Suddenly, there was a lot more to worry about than the loss of a single warship.

Two days later, the world was stunned by the news that the British battleship *Prince of Wales* and the battle cruiser *Repulse* had been sunk off the coast of Malaya by Japanese aircraft. While the news shocked Britain, Australia had to come to terms with the alarming fact that there were now no Allied capital ships left standing between it and the extremely powerful Japanese Navy.

The already thinly spread and sparsely resourced Royal Australian Navy now had to make hurried preparations for the defence of Australia. Although the investigation into *Sydney*'s loss continued, it became less of a priority.

The interrogations in Western Australia were concluded on 10 December. On 11 December, Ramage wrote the following personal letter to Crace:

Dear Admiral Crace

I enclose a brief summary of deductions from interrogations which were concluded yesterday. Copies have been forwarded to Naval Board, to whom complete statements of all POWs are being

forwarded. Unfortunately no light has been thrown on what the final fate of SYDNEY was. My own view is that she sank in flames about 2300H, or earlier, and that such of her gallant crew who were alive at this time were swallowed up by the sea. The action ended in daylight. If there was any attempt by SYDNEY to abandon ship before dark, and if they had any boats in which to do this, I can only assume that the ruthless Hun shot them up. The remark in REIZER's diary that 'we should remember the words of the Captain, "For every German we shall kill a thousand Englishmen"' indicates that they would not be beyond such brutality.

The lesson for all to learn is that even when the odds are against him the Hun knows the value of bluff and surprise. His sending out the QQ- undoubtedly allayed B's suspicions.

In general the crew were a mixed crowd. A few arrogant ones were easily tamed by a night in cells without food or bedding, and the old Diggers revelled in firing a few shots near the cells at dusk or dawn. Some of the older men were quite willing to talk of past activities, and outline particulars of their ship. To obtain a clear picture of the whole action was impracticable, mainly, I think, because they were surprised by their own comparatively good fortune.

If you would care for a complete copy of all interrogation please ask Ridley to write me for it. Have had a spare copy made. Am writing to you personally as I think it desirable that though most NO's [Naval Officers] probably realise that SYDNEY was taken by surprise, the details should be confined to as few as possible.

Segregation of batches of prisoners has proved most valuable. Any new point, e.g. last supply ship being KULMERLAND disguised as American LUCHENBACH [sic] with American colours painted on side, could be ascertained by re-interrogating a suitable man from a batch who could have had no contact with informer since abandoning ship.

Have just heard with joy that [Admiral] Tennant is among 2,000 survivors from REPULSE and P. of W.[34]

A candid letter from a Commander to an Admiral is rare, but the fact that this letter contained the personal views of one of the interrogating

officers makes it remarkable. That such a letter has survived makes it even more so.

Clearly, Ramage had no love for the Germans. He also appears to have been professionally embarrassed by the manner of *Sydney*'s loss. Furthermore, Ramage's remarks that '*Sydney* was taken by surprise' and 'the details should be confined to as few as possible' give a clear indication of the direction in which he thought the investigation should go.

On 13 December, *Kormoran*'s officers were embarked in the *Duntroon* for passage to Melbourne, arriving there on 20 December. The ratings were also transferred, but these men, sent in two batches, travelled by train. The first group left Harvey on 27 December, and the second group left in early January. It is not clear why the prisoners were transferred out of Western Australia, although the fear of Japanese invasion is a likely factor.

All the prisoners were initially quartered at the No.13 Prisoner of War (POW) camp at Murchison in northern Victoria, where the *Aquitania* prisoners were already interned. At Murchison, *Kormoran*'s officers were temporarily housed in quarters that had been suitably 'bugged' with hidden microphones. When it was realized that little real information was being obtained the officers were moved to Dhurringile, about 10 miles away.

On 21 December Dechaineux submitted his report on the loss of *Sydney* to Royle, Getting, and Long. Contained in it were:

(A) Interim Report of investigation in the loss of HMAS *Sydney* by Commander Dechaineux.

(B) Summary of interrogation of prisoners from Raider No.41, carried out subsequent to that of Commander Dechaineux. [Ramage's report of 6 December]

(C) Complete notes of interrogation of prisoners carried out under the direction of RACAS, and the supervision of District Naval Officer, Western Australia. [These had been submitted to the Naval Board by Farquhar-Smith on 16 December]

(D) Track Chart of action compiled from narratives; and sketch of raider.

(E) Track Chart of movements compiled from Admiralty sources and interrogation.

(F) The file containing information already passed to Admiralty.

The interim report was a five-page document containing a table of events before the instigation of the search for *Sydney*, a description of the action, and a very detailed study of Raider No.41. Although Dechaineux had access to a great deal of new information, his description of the action was essentially only a rehash of what was already known. Although Ramage had reported on 6 December that *Kormoran* carried two guns of 3.7-centimetre calibre, Dechaineux failed to include this information in his description of the raider's armament. Yet Dechaineux did report that '... Dettmers [*sic*] and other prisoners have frankly told the story of the action, and there is every reason to believe the authenticity of their story'.

Dechaineux proposed that the first action should be to complete the story for the Admiralty. His second proposal was that the DNI should 'sift and prepare the final report'. Thirdly, he recommended that on compilation of the final report, 'the final study should be made to extract all benefits and further lessons learnt'.

Dechaineux reported that the 'Captain of SYDNEY was deceived and placed himself in [a] tactically unsound position'. Dechaineux considered that the 'contributory cause of this is the admitted inefficiency of Merchant Ships in challenge and reply procedure'. For unknown reasons, this point was deleted in the final draft of his report.

It would appear that Dechaineux's report and recommendations were accepted, because two days later the Naval Board signalled this information to the Admiralty:

1. Captain of SYDNEY was deceived and placed himself in tactically unsound position.

2. The fundamental importance of good challenge and reply procedure by merchant ships. Desirable to make it compulsory for independently routed merchant ships to carry daylight lamp range 10 miles. Some merchant ships of Allied nations do not

carry secret call signs. All ships trading in Allied interests should possess these. Admiralty 1223/20 refers.

3. The necessity for being ready to open fire at a moment's notice when approaching a merchant vessel and for keeping a close watch for the dropping of screens or other devices for concealing guns.

There will usually be a delay of 20 to 25 seconds whilst the guns of the M.V. are being trained on to the correct object.

4. Apparently the fires could not be fought due probably to fire amidships. Consider the wide separation of fire pumps desirable.[35]

This signal, transmitted at 1030z, also included amendments to the previous signals sent to the Admiralty. Eleven minutes later the Admiralty was advised that, with reference to their signal of 1115A/30 November (the signal from Pound to Royle), 'All material information obtained has now been communicated to Admiralty in ACNB messages 1700z/27 November, 0222z/28 November, 0604z/28 November, 0700z/7 December and 1030z/23 December.'

It is not clear why Dechaineux failed to include the latest intelligence in his interim report, although it is possible that he was under pressure to close the investigation as soon as possible. It is also conceivable that other tasks were demanding his attentions and reducing the amount of time he could allocate to the *Sydney*.[36]

Long also appears to have had more pressing matters to deal with. Although Dechaineux had recommended that the DNI should prepare the final report on the loss of *Sydney*, there is no evidence to show that this occurred. Instead, Mr F.B. Eldridge, a senior master at the Royal Australian Naval College, was asked to compile the report. Eldridge took on the mammoth task of sifting through the mass of material collected and presented his findings to Long on 28 January 1942. Long examined Eldridge's work and informed Royle that, 'The report has been checked through. There appears to be no errors.'[37]

Eldridge's report was, and still is, a remarkable document. Indeed, Macandie, on behalf of the Naval Board, wrote: 'The compilation of this

Report entailed a detailed survey of a mass of material containing the results of interrogation of Prisoners of War ex-KORMORAN; and the Naval Board consider that the work performed by Mr Eldridge in preparing the Report is deserving of commendation.'

The report included a detailed analysis of *Kormoran* and its equipment, previous movements, co-operation with other raiders and supply ships, use of neutral ports, and the treatment of prisoners. Of the action, Eldridge reported:

> The story of the action between the SYDNEY and the raider was frankly told by the Captain, Fregatten Kapitan Dettmers [*sic*] and other prisoners, and the story as told seems to ring true, though there is no explanation on the surface as to why SYDNEY came so close, or why she came so close before attempting to launch her aircraft.
>
> At about 1600G/19 the raider in position approximately 26° S. 111° E. was proceeding northward at a speed of about ten knots (14 knots according to Sub-Lieutenant Bunjes) when what at first appeared to be a sail was sighted by the lookout to the north on the starboard bow. (About NNE according to Sub-Lieutenant Bunjes). The stranger was soon identified as a cruiser and Commander Detmers immediately turned away into the sun (250°) and increased to full speed which was estimated at 15 knots. The cruiser had obviously sighted them for she too turned and came up on the starboard quarter at high speed, repeatedly making the signal by daylight lamp NNJ, for about half an hour, no reply being made by the KORMORAN as the Commander was of the opinion that the use of a powerful signalling lamp would have betrayed his identity as he was at the time posing as the Dutch ship STRAAT MALAKKA, and merchant ships did not carry such lamps. In addition, he said, he did not understand what the signal NNJ meant.
>
> Some time before the action was joined, KORMORAN broadcast QQQQ 26 S 111 E, STRAAT MALAKKA and repeated it once. Pachmann, an operator, stated that this message was given twice, about ten minutes before the action began. It is worthy of note that a QQ message was picked up by Tug UCO, at about 1000 GMT on

19 November, but the position and ship's name could not be read by the PO Telegraphist in UCO. Geraldton also read a mutilated time and position message at 1005z/19. No Q's were distinguished and when after ten minutes there was no repetition, a message was sent out to ships asking if there was anything to report, but no reply was received.

At a distance of about 7 miles SYDNEY made the signal by flashing 'Hoist your signal letters'. In reply KORMORAN hoisted PKQI (STRAAT MALAKKA) on the triatic stay between the foremast and the funnel, but the funnel prevented the message being clearly seen aboard the SYDNEY. When SYDNEY made the signal 'Hoist your signal letters clear', Ahlbach the Yeoman of Signals stated that he lengthened the halyard and drew it towards the starboard side. It is reasonable to assume that this apparent inefficiency in signalling by the KORMORAN was a 'ruse de guerre', in the hope that SYDNEY would close to investigate, for SYDNEY's signal had to be repeated continuously before it was complied with.

SYDNEY came up with the KORMORAN with all guns and torpedo tubes bearing and when she was approximately abeam of the Raider she asked by flags and flashing 'Where bound?' According to Ahlbach this was spelt in English by flashing. KORMORAN answered BATAVIA, and SYDNEY apparently made 'IK' which KORMORAN could not understand as in the International Code this means 'You should prepare for a cyclone, hurricane or typhoon', but which was in fact the two interior letters of the secret call sign [of] STRAAT MALAKKA (IIKP). To this KORMORAN made no reply.

SYDNEY then made by flashing 'Show your secret sign'. Having no reply to this the raider Captain decided to fight, which up to this time he had tried to avoid doing. According to Ahlbach SYDNEY did not order the raider to stop, and this statement is made by other prisoners, but Captain Detmers mentions an order to stop immediately before the signal by searchlight in plain language to give the secret call.

At about 1700G/19 when the two ships were proceeding on parallel courses in a westerly direction at approximately 15 knots, the SYDNEY being on the KORMORAN's starboard beam at a distance

of 'somewhat more than a mile' (Commander Detmers) (or at a distance of 1200 or 1500 metres according to other prisoners-of-war), KORMORAN dropped her gun-concealing plates and hoisting the German flag, opened fire with four of her six fifteen centimetre guns. (The particulars obtained by the Military authorities upon further inquiry would reduce the range still further to about 1100 metres.) The first salvo hit the SYDNEY's bridge. Almost simultaneously, but probably just afterwards, SYDNEY's first salvo hit the raider amidships. Her second salvo found the raider's engine-room and fuel tanks and caused a fire. In the meantime the raider had fired two torpedoes, one of which struck the SYDNEY forward (about 20 metres from the bow according to Commander Detmers), at the same time that a salvo struck her amidships.

The SYDNEY's forward turrets were apparently put out of action by the explosion caused by the torpedo, and SYDNEY's aircraft, which is reported to have been warming up at the time that the engagement began, was shot to pieces. The range was so close that prisoners stated that they could see men about the plane, and an anti-aircraft gunner stated that the A.A guns were used against the cruiser so that her A.A. guns and torpedoes might not be used.

SYDNEY now altered course to port across the stern of the raider and continued on a slightly diverging course from the raider. She must have been very close as some of the raider's crew thought that she was going to ram. According to Ahlbach (Yeoman of Signals) who was on the bridge of the KORMORAN, SYDNEY turned about 90° to port, passed close under the stern of the KORMORAN and maintained her course in a southerly direction. At this stage apparently, though a fire was raging and could not be put out because all fire-fighting appliances had been destroyed, KORMORAN's guns were all in action and one of her guns is stated to have fired fifty rounds while all guns fired a total of about 450 rounds.

SYDNEY's X and Y turrets were still in action. SYDNEY now fired four torpedoes which KORMORAN turned to meet, and three passed ahead and one astern. A torpedo fired by the raider about the same time also missed its mark. Both ships were now on fire, SYDNEY being heavily afire amidships and on the bridge, and down by the

bows about six feet. The raider's bridge had been hit but not put out of action. SYDNEY's first hit had destroyed the radio and a large fire was burning in the engine room. Approximately half an hour after fire opened the action was over, KORMORAN was stopped, SYDNEY proceeding in a south easterly direction at a speed of about five knots, and throwing out a dense cloud of smoke which some of the prisoners interrogated thought was a smoke screen, but which was probably simply result of fire. At about 1900 the Captain of the raider ordered his engine-room personnel and those of the ship's company who were not required, to abandon ship, retaining aboard about 100 men and all his officers. At about 2300/19 Captain Detmers decided to abandon his ship which was blown up about midnight. The cruiser was still in sight distant about 10 km. when the first boats left the KORMORAN, and for some time the glow of the fire could be seen. Before midnight it had disappeared. No explosion was heard. According to Bohm (one of the survivors picked up by TROCAS) three wooden lifeboats and three rubber rafts were launched first, leaving one boat for those still on board. Commander Detmers mentioned that it took three hours to get lifeboats out of a hatch because of the lack of power. The motor-boats had been destroyed and even if the big boat which it carried had not been destroyed, there was no power available to move it. One of the floats collapsed; men jumped overboard and though a number of these men were picked up by the life-boats that had been launched it would appear that about eighty were lost.

Commander Detmers expressed the opinion that the SYDNEY sank as the result of the punishment she had received, and that there could be no survivors as the whole of the superstructure had been so smashed, boats on deck must have been destroyed, while any boats stowed below must have been burned by the fires which were raging. At the time that Commander Detmers was preparing to abandon ship the blaze from SYDNEY was still to be seen, but when he looked around before leaving the ship it had disappeared. This evidence is supported by other statements which go to show that SYDNEY disappeared somewhat before midnight, and that

KORMORAN's sinking was hastened by an explosion after midnight. The weather at the time was rough, as it had been for two or three days before the encounter.

The first definite information to the outside world was received at 0816Z/24 when the Tanker TROCAS reported by W/T that twenty-five German Naval men on a floating raft had been picked up in position 26° 06' S. 111° 40' E [*sic*].

As Macandie's letter of commendation also carried Long's signature, it would appear that Eldridge's report, and in particular his account of the action, was accepted by the Naval Board and Long as a true and accurate report on the loss of the *Sydney*. Although it is yet to be determined, it would also appear that the Eldridge report became the official final report on the loss of the *Sydney*. This hypothesis is based on the fact that an Admiralty account of *Sydney*'s loss (contained in Battle Summary No.13 of 1942[38]) was quite clearly prepared from information contained in Eldridge's report.

On 18 March 1942, the Advisory War Council discussed *Sydney* for the last time. The Prime Minister asked a question about a 'Court of Inquiry' into *Sydney*'s loss, and Royle responded by outlining the findings of a 'full inquiry'. The resulting minute from the meeting noted that:

> The SYDNEY had worked into a position approximately 1500 yards from the raider. The raider opened fire and launched two torpedoes, one of which hit SYDNEY. The raider had given a wrong name and was not on the daily list. The Captain of the SYDNEY was 24 hours late in arriving at his rendezvous and had taken a risk in getting so close to the raider. In doing so he had not followed his orders. Further, the Gunnery Officer of the SYDNEY was not ready. He should have been able to fire first and get in two salvoes before the raider attacked.[39]

Although the claim that *Sydney* was twenty-four hours late arriving at its rendezvous with *Durban* was incorrect, few could have argued with the remaining statements and conclusions. Clearly, in the Navy's view, Burnett had made a gross error in judgement in closing with a vessel that

was not on the list of vessels expected (VAI). It appeared that this error was compounded by *Sydney*'s gunnery officer, who was apparently not ready to open fire as soon as the raider began to unmask its guns.

Curiously, no one seems to have asked what might have prompted Burnett to close. If he had been deceived into thinking that the *Straat Malakka* was genuine, there should have been no reason to close. Conversely, if he were suspicious he should have kept his distance.

JAPANESE INVOLVEMENT?

The other issue that should have been addressed at this time was the question of possible Japanese involvement. Although there was no direct evidence of Japanese involvement in the sinking of the *Sydney*, the discovery of Japanese milk bottles in the German lifeboats led many to believe that the German survivors had had contact with a Japanese vessel. While the interrogations revealed that the *Kormoran* had been resupplied in October by *Kulmerland*, which was carrying provisions obtained in Japan, some remained unconvinced. Although this *was* the explanation for the Japanese milk, the fact that some of the bottles recovered contained milk that was still drinkable after such a long period of time led to the belief that the milk had been obtained more recently. In fact, an annotation on the bottom of an attachment to a report on the milk queried the possibility of *Kormoran* having been resupplied by a Japanese submarine.[40]

It also appears that consideration was given to the possibility that the lifeboats had been supplied by a passing Japanese ship. This led to speculation that such a vessel might have picked up *Sydney* survivors. When questioned on this point on 7 January 1942 Detmers replied, 'I do not think so at all. I do not think there was a Japanese ship within six days sail of where the action took place.'[41]

Such speculation was, however, unfounded. The milk was months old, but had been specially processed in a manner which baffled the dairy bacteriologist at the Department of Agriculture.

Unfortunately, the public was not informed that *Kormoran* had been resupplied by a German supply ship carrying Japanese provisions. Many

saw (and souvenired)[42] the Japanese milk bottles and, in the absence of any official explanation, became convinced that the Japanese had a hand in the sinking of *Sydney*. An inaccurate newspaper report, claiming that the German raider responsible for the sinking of *Sydney* had been fitted out in Japan, would have done little to dispel this conviction.[43]

Further encouragement came from the Japanese themselves. For reasons still unknown, in late 1941 or early 1942 the Japanese broadcast the claim that *Sydney* had been captured and towed to Japan. Then on 17 February 1942 a Chinese radio station, possibly repeating an earlier Japanese announcement, broadcast the claim that *Sydney*'s officers were interned in Tokyo.[44]

Amid the rumours and claims of possible Japanese involvement, Military Intelligence attempted to make sense of some strange symbols contained in sketches drawn by one of the prisoners. Dr Fritz List, a war correspondent assigned to *Kormoran*, had made several sketches of key events on pieces of toilet paper. These included a vessel on fire, a lifeboat under sail, a lifeboat approaching the coast and a cave with two entrances. Although there was nothing of obvious significance depicted in the drawings, it was thought that some of the unusual symbols could contain shorthand messages. Captain J. Hehir enlisted the help of a German shorthand expert, Mrs H. Kevin. She found what appeared to be German shorthand characters in six of the sketches and, with the assistance of Sergeant E. Caminer, attempted to produce an interpretation of her findings. While some of the sketches were thought to contain references to the action and the aftermath, the cave sketch allegedly contained this hidden message:

SHORT HONOUR CONFERRED ON KORMORAN FOR WORKING ACCORDING TO IDEALS OF UNITY OF THE GERMAN PEOPLE. (UNTIL) REINFORCEMENTS ARRIVED (D)

IF (WHEN) (UNTIL). . . IN THE EVENING CONQUER (S) (ED) THE VICTIM.

A JAPANESE GUNFIRE ATTACK (OR)

A JAPANESE TRANSPORT... GUNFIRE ATTACK)
FROM (or VIA) JAPAN ITSELF.

TWO AIRCRAFT CARRIERS ... GERMAN/TRANSPORT
UNSELFISHNESS IS EVERYTHING.[45]

When questioned on the subject, List claimed that his drawings were simple sketches, and that the alleged shorthand symbols 'depict rocks surrounding the caves'. Subsequent post-war examinations of the sketches have failed to identify the shorthand characters supposedly found by Kevin and Caminer.[46]

Although there was never any real evidence of direct Japanese involvement, it is understandable that many grieving families would have wanted to believe the rumours and the propaganda. According to the Australian authorities, there were no *Sydney* survivors, but according to the Japanese claims, there were.

Such hopes, that survivors from *Sydney* were prisoners of the Japanese, would have been raised later in 1942 when it was learned that survivors from HMAS *Perth* were in Japanese POW camps.

Perth, like *Sydney*, had seemingly vanished without trace in March 1942. Nothing had been heard from *Perth* after the night of 28 February when the cruiser reported that it was engaging enemy forces in the Sunda Strait. When *Perth* failed to make an Allied port, it was posted as overdue. Later it was presumed that the cruiser had been lost. The ship's entire complement of 682 officers and men were posted as missing. The nation, still trying to come to terms with the loss of *Sydney*, was forced to accept the possibility that *Perth* had also been lost with all hands.

About six months after *Perth*'s sinking, however, Japanese propaganda broadcasters began announcing the names of *Perth* survivors. That these reports were factual was confirmed in September 1944 when four *Perth* men were found among the survivors of the torpedoed Japanese transport *Rakuyo Maru*.

Understandably, the release of thousands of Allied POWs at the end of the Pacific war again raised expectations that *Sydney* survivors would be found. As a result, Commodore J.A. Collins, RAN (former captain of *Sydney*), who had gone to Japan as Commander of the Australian Squadron and had

stayed on to arrange entry for the British Commonwealth Occupation Force, was sent the following signal:

> Personal for Commodore Collins from First Naval Member. The rumour that crew of HMAS SYDNEY may have fallen into the hands of the Japanese has been revived here.
>
> The Minister desires that you should make such inquiries as you are able to ascertain whether Japanese can give any lead as to the fate of HMAS SYDNEY and her crew.
>
> Request you will report result by signal.

Raising hopes even further, and perhaps giving unjustified credibility to the rumours, was the decision to inform the media of Collins's instructions. On the night of 13–14 September 1945, the Australian Broadcasting Commission announced that Commodore Collins was making inquiries in Tokyo about the fate of HMAS *Sydney*.

On 1 October, as a result of these inquiries, the First Naval Member, Admiral L.K.H. Hamilton, RN, presented this to Makin:

> German Naval attaché at Tokyo knows only that HMAS SYDNEY was sunk some hundreds of miles off Perth. He does not know whether ship was torpedoed but stated that subsequent Japanese broadcast that she was towed to Japan was definitely incorrect.
>
> Further, no survivors were picked up by any Axis vessel and none were brought to Japan.
>
> The Japanese Navy Ministry have stated that nothing is known there but enquiries on our part are continuing.
>
> Commodore Collins feels, however, that no information is known anywhere in Japan which could support hopes that any personnel of HMAS SYDNEY are alive.

On 19 October, Makin was informed that Collins had reported that 'All possible contacts and enquiries in Japan have been made and Japanese naval records have been inspected. Results are negative in every case'.[47]

A week earlier, Lieutenant-Commander Rycroft, still serving as the Staff Officer, Intelligence, Fremantle, had sent a letter to Long. Rycroft

wrote that the 'recurrent publicity can only cause distress to those who normally would have allowed the lapse of time to heal their sorrow'. He proposed that a detailed account of the action and the wide-ranging search for possible survivors which followed be published. This he considered 'should result in completely setting at rest any rumours or speculation concerning possible survivors from the *Sydney*'. Perhaps anticipating a favourable response, Rycoft included a suitable account prepared by Third Officer Westhoven, WRANS.

Unfortunately, the Deputy Director of Naval Intelligence, Lieutenant-Commander A.G. Monteith, RANR, did not agree. In a handwritten memo to Long, Monteith wrote:

> I cannot agree with S.O.(I)'s contention that to officially release this story would set the matter at rest because:
>
> (a) the papers would not publish the whole.
>
> (b) the account is by no means conclusive.
>
> (c) it would tend to arouse further speculation and criticism.
>
> (d) it would be derogatory to the service in that it infers that the SYDNEY was far from being alert.
>
> (e) the best course of action to put the matter at rest is to take no action. To publish would only resurrect the whole matter to no good purpose.

Lieutenant-Commander Gill concurred, and advised Long that 'we should write nothing unless and until pressure is brought by the press for a Ministerial Statement'. As a result, on 23 October 1945, Long wrote to Rycoft to inform him that his proposal had been rejected. Long said:

> Continous investigation has been carried out into the facts relating to the action between HMAS SYDNEY and the German Raider KORMORAN There has now been accumulated a mass of confirmatory information which leaves no doubt that there are no survivors from HMAS SYDNEY. There are a number of reasons, however, why the full analysis should not be published, the principal that such an

analysis would still not be accepted by some people as being absolute confirmation of the loss of all the SYDNEY's complement. It is intended not to publish anything further concerning this action, and its results, unless the Board is forced by Ministerial pressure to write a Ministerial Statement.[48]

The recurrent publicity to which Rycroft referred was not limited to Japanese claims. On 24 September 1945, the *Argus* in Melbourne published a story of a German account of the action. *Kormoran*'s second doctor and surgeon, Dr Siebelt Habben, had returned to Germany in 1943 as a result of a POW exchange. On reaching Germany, he provided the German authorities with reports on *Kormoran*'s final battle and of life in an Australian POW camp. Although the authorities considered that the latter report was not suitable for general publication, on 13 August 1944 the German newspaper *Volkischer Beobachter* published the story of how *Kormoran* sank *Sydney*. The *Argus* wrote that the German account threw new light on the disappearance of HMAS *Sydney*, then provided a condensed version of the German account of the action. The story, according to the *Argus*, confirmed 'that told [to] the Commonwealth authorities by other survivors of *Cormoran* [*sic*]'.

Three days after the *Argus* story was published, the Perth newspaper, *The Daily News*, published a letter submitted by Mr H. Clarke, who was commenting on a statement made by Makin on 18 September. Clarke wrote:

> Mr Makin says he has given instructions for the Germans survivors of the ship sunk by the *Sydney* to be questioned again. I suggest that the German survivors be handed over to the relatives of the men on the *Sydney* and will guarantee to get results. All islands within a 1000 miles or more of where the *Sydney* was last seen should be visited. Not only men of the *Sydney* may be found but also other missing men.

Because the press never learned of Long's decision, a ministerial statement was not forthcoming. As a result, the Australian public had to wait another twelve years before a full account of *Sydney*'s loss was published.

With hindsight, it is clear that the Naval Intelligence Division's decision to 'say nothing' was wrong. Although the Navy's motives for withholding the details of *Sydney*'s loss in the weeks following the action were understandable, the Naval Intelligence Division's motives for withholding the story after war are not.

Lieutenant-Commander Monteith's views, which were supported by Gill and Long, perhaps provide an insight into why there was opposition to the release of the full story. Monteith wrote that to officially release the story would arouse further speculation and criticism. He also considered that such an account would be 'derogatory to the service in that it infers that the *Sydney* was far from being alert'. From these comments, it is clear that there was a question of professional pride. Burnett was seen to have blundered. He had not only lost his life and his command, but he had blemished the Royal Australian Navy's otherwise proud war record.

If this was what Monteith, Gill and Long truly believed, it perhaps explains why they did not want to see the story revived. Yet it is also conceivable that these men did not wish to see a fellow officer's reputation further tarnished by a public disclosure of how *Sydney* was lost. Either way, they denied the Australian public the truth.

The sixteen years that passed between *Sydney*'s loss and the release of Gill's account of the action allowed half-truths and speculation to harden into conviction. Many people would not have been convinced by Gill's account. Many more would not have bothered to read it.

The wound had been left open for too long.

—4—

THE TONNAGE WAR

THE Royal Australian Navy, which held Captain Joseph Burnett in high regard, was clearly perplexed by his handling of HMAS *Sydney* on 19 November 1941.[1] Neither Navy Office, Naval Intelligence, nor brother officers appear to have been able to offer a logical explanation for Burnett's having closed with a suspicious vessel.

When viewed as an isolated incident, it is difficult to comprehend Burnett's actions. His decision to close would appear out of character for a man who was described as thorough, cautious and prudent. Perhaps the key to understanding Burnett's actions is not to treat *Sydney*'s loss as an isolated incident, but to study it in the context of the war at sea.

THE 'TONNAGE WAR'

When Great Britain declared war on Germany on 3 September 1939, the Royal Navy found itself in less than ideal circumstances. Britain, by virtue

of its geology and geography, was heavily dependent on imports of raw materials to maintain its industries and foodstuffs to feed its population. The nation's survival was dependent upon the Royal Navy's ability to keep the trade routes open and the merchant fleet safe from attack. Germany, albeit to a lesser extent, was also reliant on imports, and as part of Britain's war strategy the Royal Navy was given the added burden of imposing a blockade on enemy shipping.

Cruisers played a key role in defending the trade routes and enforcing the blockade, and as a measure of the strain under which the Royal Navy found itself one need only look at its cruiser strength at the outbreak of war.

At the end of the First World War, it was estimated that the minimum number of cruisers required for trade protection alone was seventy. In September 1939 the navy had only sixty-four, of which twenty-seven were First World War vintage and of limited endurance. Six vessels that had been converted into anti-aircraft cruisers for employment with the fleet reduced the number to fifty-eight.[2]

To help alleviate the shortage, a number of passenger vessels were armed with obsolete guns and commissioned as armed merchant cruisers (AMCs). On 23 August 1939 the Admiralty obtained permission to requisition twenty-five such vessels.[3] By February 1940, the demand was so great that forty-six AMCs had been pressed into service.[4]

The German Navy (*Kriegsmarine*), however, had not been rebuilt with the intention of challenging the Royal Navy for command of the seas. Pre-war construction had concentrated on warships suited for war with continental neighbours and commerce raiding, and Germany's wartime programme of U-boat construction was simply an extension of this strategy. Thus, from the start of the war, indeed from the first day, the *Kriegsmarine* began a campaign against the British and Allied merchant fleets.

Before the war, the British merchant fleet totalled nearly 21,000,000 tons. By 8 April 1940, the Germans had sunk 668,521 tons of British shipping from a combined Allied total of 1,251,168 tons.[5] Despite the start of an emergency shipbuilding programme, it soon became obvious that new construction would not be able to keep pace with losses.

The large numbers of foreign ships that joined the Allied cause when their countries were over-run by the Germans temporarily alleviated the crisis. There were also some small gains as a result of the blockade. The masters of German ships attempting to run the blockade were instructed to scuttle their ships if intercepted by the Royal Navy, but some captains, believing that the war would be short and Germany victorious, were reluctant to do so. Others, inexperienced in these matters, failed to complete the job before anti-scuttling parties came on board to halt the process and seize the ship.

Essentially, the scuttling process involved the use of water and fire. Holds and engine rooms were flooded by opening sea cocks and water inlet valves or by fracturing water inlet pipes. Explosive charges could also be used to speed up proceedings, and flammable cargoes and wooden fittings were set on fire to complete the destruction.

It was soon learned, however, that if an anti-scuttling party could get aboard quickly enough it was sometimes possible to stem the flooding and to control or extinguish the fires. Besides plaudits for a successful capture, there was the added incentive of prize money. By the end of 1939, fifteen German ships totalling 75,000 tons had been captured and pressed into British service.[6]

Despite these small gains the future for Britain looked bleak. By 1 September 1940, 749 ships totalling 2,795,995 tons had been sunk. Of this total Britain lost 1,561,193 tons. During the same period, fifty-eight German ships totalling 259,167 tons were captured.[7] The Germans were clearly winning the battle for the Atlantic.

In a letter to US President F. D. Roosevelt dated 8 December 1940, the British Prime Minister, Winston Churchill, summed up the situation:

> The danger of Great Britain being destroyed by a swift, over-whelming blow has for the time being very greatly receded. In its place there is a long gradually maturing danger, less sudden and less spectacular, but equally deadly. This mortal danger is the steady and increasing diminution of sea tonnage.[8]

In the same letter Churchill stated that at best, Britain's shipyards could produce 1,250,000 tons a year. This potential total appeared to offset the losses, but between 1 September and 1 December 1940 Britain lost another 867,229 tons of shipping of a total of 1,132,006 tons sunk through enemy action.[9]

Compounding the problem was Britain's need to import the raw materials to build ships. It was estimated that the annual tonnage of imports required to maintain the war effort at full strength was 43,000,000. The rate entering Britain in September 1940 would provide only 37,000,000 tons. Clearly, it was to be a war of attrition.

The Germans, however, were also having problems. As of September 1939, the *Kriegsmarine* had 56 U-boats in commission, of which twelve were required for training purposes. By the end of 1940, the total had fallen to 46. Fourteen new boats had been constructed, but 24 had been lost.[10]

From the beginning of 1941 through to the middle of 1943, however, new construction exceeded the loss rate, allowing Konteradmiral Dönitz, head of the U-boat arm, to have more and more boats on patrol each month. Between January and April 1941, 30 new U-boats were commissioned. By January 1942, the number of operational U-boats rose to 91. Twelve months later 212 boats were available. By April 1943 no less than 240 U-boats were in commission.

To counter this formidable force, the Allies built large numbers of anti-submarine vessels. During 1942, the point was reached where convoys could be provided with escorts for their entire journey. More importantly, a surplus of escort craft permitted support groups to be formed, the first of these being formed in September 1942. A support group was, in effect, a hunter-killer group whose task, once a U-boat had been detected, was to hunt it down and destroy it while the convoy sailed on under the protection of its assigned escort.

With the new anti-submarine frigates came escort carriers which would provide vital air cover in the mid Atlantic. Unfortunately, owing to logistical problems, the newly acquired support groups and escort carriers had to be transferred to other theatres. It was not until the end of March 1943 that the support groups and escort carriers could be returned. Their impact was enormous. In April 1943, 15 U-boats were destroyed. The following month 41 were destroyed. In June the figure dropped to 17, but in July it rose again to 37 U-boats destroyed. From mid 1943, the balance swung in favour of the Allies, allowing the convoys to take to Britain sufficient men and material to permit the build up for the invasion of Europe.

By the end of 1943, the crisis had eased. The size of the Allied merchant fleet, predominantly because of the industrial might of the United States, was steadily increasing while the number of operational U-boats was steadily decreasing. It had, however, been a closely run race. If the *Kriegsmarine* had succeeded in reducing the size of the British and Allied merchant fleet to the point where the reduced imports could not maintain Britain's war effort or sustain the population, Britain would have been forced to capitulate.

Admiral Max Horton, Flag Officer Submarines from January 1940 to November 1942, had a clear understanding of the situation. In a letter to the Admiralty, dated 26 February 1942, Horton wrote succinctly: 'Control of the sea is vital to the British Empire. If we lose it, we lose the war.'[11]

This 'control of the sea' involved having an accurate knowledge of the shipping that plied the world's waterways. To help the Royal Navy with its daunting task of protecting the merchant fleet and enforcing the blockade, a world-wide system was established whereby every convoy and every independently routed Allied or neutral vessel was reported and recorded on a shipping plot. Warships, before going to sea, could be advised which vessels they could expect to encounter in their operational area. This information was recorded on a plot (VAI) and once the warship was at sea would be regularly updated by W/T. Occasionally, vessels were encountered which, for various reasons, were not on the VAI. In such instances, these vessels were to be treated as suspicious until they had been positively identified. The Admiralty had great faith in the system and expected captains to trust the information supplied and to be extremely cautious of vessels not on the plot.

Once a warship sighted another vessel at sea, procedure demanded that the vessel be requested to identify itself. In the early war years, this was usually accomplished by making the signal 'SC' or 'VH'. The former was the two-letter code group for 'What is the name of your vessel', and the latter was the two-letter code group for 'You should hoist your signal letters'. These signals could be sent by signal lamp, flag hoist, or both. The three-letter code group signal 'NNJ', which meant 'You should make your signal letters', was also used, but less frequently.[12]

Vessels normally identified themselves with a code group of four letters. If the name given was on the VAI, and the vessel appeared genuine,

there was often no need for further questioning and the vessel could be permitted to proceed. If the vessel was not on the VAI, or acted suspiciously, further questioning could be conducted. This was normally in the nature of 'Where are you bound', 'Where are you from', or 'What is your cargo?' The procedure was simple enough when dealing with ships whose captain and crew were conversant with the codes, but many of the vessels encountered were crewed by foreigners who only had a basic grasp of the International Code of Signals and the Royal Navy's challenge procedures.

If a vessel failed to respond to a challenge, or acted suspiciously, it would be ordered to stop. If the vessel still failed to respond, a warning shot would be fired. Once the vessel was stopped, a close examination might prove sufficient to confirm its identity. If not, boarding would be necessary.

There were, however, risks attached to stopping and boarding suspicious vessels. To lower and recover a boat with a boarding party, the warship had to slow down or stop, thus providing an ideal target for any U-boat that happened to be in the vicinity. Much less likely, but a factor that had to be considered, was the possibility that the intercepted vessel was a disguised merchant raider covertly armed with guns and torpedoes.

If a vessel failed to respond to signals, or failed to stop after warning shots had been fired, the warship would be left with no option but to open direct fire. Misunderstandings in the challenge procedure, however, were relatively common, and no warship captain wanted to fire on a vessel that could subsequently prove to be Allied or neutral. Significantly, when confronted with suspicious vessels which proved to be enemy raiders, the captains of HMS *Cornwall* and HMS *Devonshire* displayed a reluctance to open direct fire.

More often than not, the captain of a genuine blockade runner or supply ship would scuttle and abandon his vessel when intercepted. If this occurred, and conditions were favourable, the warship was expected to close to despatch an anti-scuttling party. But there was still the danger that the warship could be closing with a disguised merchant raider pretending to abandon ship.

This act of pretending to abandon ship had been a favourite British ploy in the First World War. Decoy ships, or Q-ships as they were later

called, would allow themselves to be shelled, or even torpedoed, by an attacking U-boat. A 'panic party' would then abandon ship in the hope that the U-boat would surface, if it had not already done so, and close with its victim. Once the U-boat was within range, the decoy ship would unmask its guns and open rapid fire in the hope of destroying the U-boat before it could dive to safety. The ruse proved so effective that eleven U-boats were destroyed in this manner.[13]

Q-ships were again employed by the Royal Navy in the Second World War, but for various reasons met with little success. On 25 January 1940, however, one Q-ship had been presented with a very tempting target. Unfortunately, the potential victim was the British cruiser HMS *Neptune*.

HMS *Botlea*, in the guise of the Royal Fleet Auxiliary *Lambridge*, had been sighted by *Neptune* while on patrol off Sierra Leone. *Neptune*, not satisfied by the initial exchange of signals, closed to investigate. The supposed *Lambridge* was ordered to stop so that a boarding party could be sent aboard to examine the ship's papers. The boarding party, satisfied that all was in order, then returned to *Neptune*, which was lying stopped several hundred yards off the supposed merchantman's beam.[14] *Botlea*, its concealed weapons undetected by the boarding party, was permitted to proceed. *Botlea*'s captain, in his subsequent report to the Admiralty, claimed that if *Neptune* had been German he could have 'disabled her with two torpedoes and swept her upper deck'. Because of the secrecy surrounding the work of the Q-ships, the report was never circulated.[15]

Despite the risks, the need to make up for lost merchant ship tonnage was crucial, and commanding officers were actively encouraged to capture blockade runners and enemy supply ships. Even before the end of 1939, the Admiralty was instructing its commanding officers on the procedures to be adopted in order to prevent the Germans scuttling their vessels.

On intercepting known enemy ships, the masters were to be ordered to stop and cast loose their lifeboats. They would then be informed that, if they attempted to scuttle, they would have their lifeboats destroyed, and the crew left aboard to burn or drown if they abandoned ship. If the Germans were preparing to, or had already abandoned ship, machine-gun fire was to be directed close to the lifeboats in an attempt to drive the Germans back on board. Another method involved directing fire at

the enemy's bridge. This could be in the form of a frightening near miss to discourage scuttling, or the complete destruction to prevent the order to scuttle being issued.[16]

These instructions ran counter to the widely accepted rule of the sea that every effort should be made to assist those in distress, and it is doubtful that they were followed with much enthusiasm or fervour. But they were followed.

On the morning of 12 February 1940, the destroyer HMS *Hasty* intercepted a merchantman 500 miles off the coast of Spain. When challenged, the vessel claimed to be Danish. The vessel was in fact the German *Morea*, which had sailed from the Spanish port of Vigo on the night of 10–11 February and was attempting to run the blockade. *Hasty* made a wide Asdic sweep to ensure there were no U-boats present, then closed and lowered a whaler with an anti-scuttling party. *Morea*'s captain, realizing that his ship was going to be boarded, ordered his crew to scuttle and abandon ship.

Seeing his quarry being abandoned, and in accordance with Admiralty instructions, Lieutenant-Commander L.R.K. Tyrwhitt, RN, ordered his 0.5-inch machine guns to be fired across the bows of the merchant ship and then into its bridge. Lewis gun fire was then directed close to the lifeboats already launched in an attempt to drive the Germans back to their ship. A short time later, *Hasty*'s anti-scuttling party clambered aboard. Despite the efforts of the Germans, prompt action by the anti-scuttling party in checking the scuttling process meant that *Morea* was saved.[17]

Less than a month later, on the afternoon of 6 March, in response to a W/T report the previous day, the heavy cruiser HMS *Berwick* found and intercepted a suspected blockade runner in the guise of the American registered *Argosy*. On closing, the *Argosy* transmitted an SOS in the name of the Hamburg-Südamerika Line *Uruguay*. Whether this was done to divert the cruiser's attention elsewhere is not clear, but it did increase suspicion. *Berwick* closed, and the Germans, realizing that they were going to be boarded, scuttled and abandoned their ship. The anti-scuttling party eventually got aboard, but the German ship was beyond salvage.

Clearly, speed was essential if a scuttled vessel was to be saved.

On the night of 7–8 March 1940, the light cruiser HMS *Dunedin*, acting on intelligence reports, intercepted the German cargo liner *Hannover*.

Dunedin, under the command of Captain C.E. Lambe, RN, was patrolling the Mona Passage to the east of the Dominican Republic. At 0220, the yet to be identified *Hannover* was sighted. On closing the range, the vessel was seen to be on fire and being abandoned.

Three days previously, *Dunedin* had attempted to capture the German freighter *Heidelberg*, which had also scuttled on being approached. Unfortunately, the anti-scuttling party could not get across quickly enough and *Heidelberg* was lost. Given a second opportunity to seize a German blockade runner, Lambe was determined to make a successful capture. Knowing that he had to act quickly, Lambe took *Dunedin* alongside the burning merchantman so that the anti-scuttling party could scramble across. While an armed party headed for the bridge, telegraphists raced to the W/T office to seize the vessel's books, documents and codes before they could be destroyed. Meanwhile, other specialists made their way to the engine room to try to check the flooding.

As the anti-scuttling party were racing to their designated points, fire parties aboard *Dunedin* played their hoses into the liner's hatchways in an attempt to quell the fires. At about 0430, the Canadian destroyer *Assiniboine* came to *Dunedin*'s assistance. For the next five days, the two warships and their desperate crews struggled to keep *Hannover* afloat. The fires were gradually brought under control, but the flooding, compounded by the water from the fire hoses, reached a critical level. Portable pumps were manhandled across and rigged. Once the pumps were in operation, the flooding was checked and reduced. On 13 March, after a 700 mile ordeal, *Dunedin* and *Assiniboine* nursed *Hannover* into Kingston, Jamaica.[18]

The Australia Station was not without incident either. When Italy entered the war on 10 June 1940, there were two Italian vessels, *Romolo* and *Remo*, in Australasian waters. *Remo* was berthed in Fremantle and was seized without incident. *Romolo*, however, was at sea, having departed from Brisbane on 5 June.

With the expectation that Italy would enter the war, the AMC HMS *Manoora* was ordered to shadow *Romolo*. Contact was lost on the evening of 6 June but re-established the following morning. Close contact was then maintained to prevent *Romolo* slipping away again. Unfortunately, on 9 June, *Manoora*'s captain, Commander S.H.K. Spurgeon, RAN, received

instructions to stop shadowing and to head for Singapore. These orders were cancelled the following day when Spurgeon was instructed to resume shadowing *Romolo*.

It was not until 12 June that *Manoora* sighted *Romolo* again. With Italy and Britain now formally at war, *Manoora* closed to intercept. Spurgeon signalled by lamp and W/T to 'Stop instantly or I will fire. Do not attempt to sink ship. Do not abandon ship because I will not pick you up'. In response, Captain Gavino stopped his engines, hoisted the Italian flag, and began transmitting an SOS. He then gave orders to abandon ship.

As the Italian vessel was well beyond *Manoora*'s gun range, there was little that Spurgeon could do to prevent the Italians abandoning ship. Then a rainsquall hid *Romolo* from view. When Spurgeon sighted his quarry again fifteen minutes later, *Romolo* was seen to be stopped, on fire, listing to port and being abandoned. By the time *Manoora* reached the scene, *Romolo* was deemed to be beyond salvage. After picking up the passengers and crew, Spurgeon fired seven 6-inch shells into the burning hulk then stood by until it sank.[19]

THE ARRIVAL OF THE RAIDERS

On 21 March 1940, the Admiralty issued Confidential Admiralty Fleet Order (CAFO) 422. Entitled German Surface Vessels, CAFO 422 provided a list of almost 700 German merchant vessels and categorized them to show their potential war value. From this categorization it was considered possible, 'given the age, speed and size of a ship whose "dangerousness" is not specifically mentioned, to form an opinion as to her capabilities'.[20] It was also stated that *'It must not be assumed that the ships mentioned are armed. Definite information as to the arming of a ship will be passed to all concerned as soon as it is received and will be included in any amending CAFO'* (author's emphasis).

The threat of the Germans arming certain merchant ships and operating them as auxiliary cruisers became a reality when the first confirmed report of their active employment reached the Admiralty in July 1940.

The first of these disguised merchant raiders, *Schiff 16* (*Atlantis*), had sailed on 11 March 1940. *Atlantis* was formerly the 7,862 ton, 17-knot,

Goldenfels, which had been built in 1937 for the Bremen Hansa Line. Within three months, *Atlantis* was followed by five others:

> *Schiff 36 (Orion)* sailed on 6 April 1940. Formerly the 7,021 ton, 13-knot *Kurmark*, which had been built in 1930 for the Hamburg-Amerika Line;

> *Schiff 21 (Widder)* sailed on 6 May 1940. Formerly the 7,851 ton, 14-knot, *Neumark*, which had been built in 1929 for the Hamburg-Amerika Line;

> *Schiff 10 (Thor)* sailed on 6 June 1940. Formerly the 3,862 ton, 17-knot, *Santa Cruz*, which had been built for the Oldenburg-Portuguesische Line in 1938;

> *Schiff 33 (Pinguin)* sailed on 15 June 1940. Formerly the 7,766 ton Hansa Line ship *Kandelfels* (sister ship to *Goldenfels*). Built in 1936, *Pinguin* was also capable of 17 knots; and

> *Schiff 45 (Komet)*, the last raider of the first wave, sailed on 3 July. *Komet* was formerly the 3,287 ton Norddeutscher Lloyd ship *Ems*. Although built in 1937 *Komet* was capable of only 14 knots.[21]

All of these raiders were armed with six 15-centimetre (5.9-inch) guns and all were fitted with torpedo tubes. For firing warning shots they were also equipped with either a 7.5-centimetre or 6-centimetre gun. For defence against aircraft they carried varying arrangements of 3.7-centimetre and 2-centimetre guns. In this regard they were better armed than most Royal Navy warships.

The task of the raiders was to destroy or capture enemy merchant ships, to force the Allies to use safer but longer shipping routes, and to make the already hardpressed Admiralty redeploy its forces to counter the threat. Their tactics of using disguise to launch surprise attacks on unwary merchantmen, which sometimes could not transmit warning signals in time, often left the Admiralty unaware of their exact location. That overdue ships could not automatically be attributed to raider activity further hindered the Admiralty's attempts to locate these raiders. In addition to the normal U-boat menace, the shortage of merchant ships led

to many older vessels of doubtful seaworthiness being pressed into service. The disappearance of such vessels therefore left the Admiralty pondering whether a raider or U-boat was responsible or whether the vessel's loss could be attributed to the normal hazards of the sea.[22]

The threat of raiders also brought a new problem. At the start of the war, merchant ships, if attacked by an enemy warship, were to signal by W/T the three-letter code group 'RRR' followed by their signal letters and position. If attacked by a U-boat the three-letter code group 'SSS' was to be transmitted, while 'QQQ' was to be transmitted if a suspicious ship approached. With the appearance of the raiders, there was now a need to differentiate between an attack by a regular warship such as a pocket battleship and an attack by a disguised merchant raider. The three-letter code group was therefore changed to a four-letter code group. 'RRRR' was to be transmitted if attacked by regular or conventional warship, while 'QQQQ' was to be transmitted if attacked by a disguised merchant raider. 'SSSS' was to be transmitted if attacked by U-boat or submarine.[23]

Naturally, the Germans did their utmost to prevent these signals, which betrayed their whereabouts, being transmitted or received. Victims would be ordered not to use their W/T. Those that refused to obey were fired upon. If the merchantman continued to transmit, the German W/T operators would attempt to jam or drown out the signal by transmitting on the same frequency.

By the end of 1940, the six German raiders had sunk or captured fifty-four merchant ships totalling 366,644 tons. In the same period, the Royal Navy had managed to intercept the raiders only twice, and on both occasions came off second best.

On 28 July 1940, the AMC HMS *Alcantara* was on patrol south-west of Trinidade Island in the South Atlantic, searching for a raider which was feared to be heading south to prey on shipping in the Rio de la Plata area. The day was fine and clear and at 1000 masts were sighted fine on the starboard bow. Captain J.G.P. Ingham, RN, ordered course to be altered to intercept the unidentified vessel which appeared to be steering NNW.

The stranger was the raider *Thor*, commanded by Fregattenkapitän Otto Kähler. *Thor's* lookouts had sighted *Alcantara* an hour earlier but, fearing that the other vessel could be a British auxiliary cruiser, Kähler kept his distance and maintained a diverging course. Kähler's fears were

realized when the other ship turned and began pursuing him. His instructions, like those of the other raider captains, were to avoid British warships. At about 1300, *Thor*'s W/T operators intercepted and jammed a coded signal being sent by *Alcantara*, which was steadily gaining. By 1400, it was evident to Kähler that he could not outrun his pursuer and that he would have to fight.

When the range reduced to 17,000 yards, *Alcantara* signalled by lamp 'What ship?' In reply, *Thor* altered course to starboard, decamouflaged, hoisted the German flag, then opened fire with a two-gun salvo. This was quickly followed by a full, four-gun salvo. *Alcantara* immediately followed suit with two salvoes that fell short.

Thor's salvoes, however, were on target, one shell bursting over *Alcantara*'s quarterdeck. Splinters from this shell killed the trainer of the P-4 6-inch gun, severed the range, deflection, fire and cease-fire leads at the gun (short-circuiting the entire system to all guns), and brought down the W/T aerials. Another air-burst damaged the boat hoists, fans and ventilators, and cut the searchlight cables.

Thor's third salvo also hit. One shell struck the hull to starboard, ripping a 4-foot hole in the plating, and sending splinters tearing through the ship. A short time later another shell struck *Alcantara* on the starboard side on the waterline abreast the engine room. Water poured in and short-circuited three of the four condenser extractor pumps. Within thirty minutes, speed had to be reduced from 20 to 10 knots. Not long after, speed had to be reduced again until *Alcantara* was almost dead in the water.

All the time *Thor* kept up a rapid and accurate fire, scoring another three hits. One of these shells struck the bridge and knocked out the already damaged fire-control system. Local control was then ordered while the gunnery officer tried to re-establish centralized control.

The battle, however, was not altogether one-sided. *Thor* was struck twice. One shell, which failed to detonate, tore through the ship, damaging electrical cables, pipes, and the forward ammunition hoist. The second exploded on the starboard motor boat, sending splinters through the torpedo flat below. Three men were killed and four wounded.

Thirty minutes after fire had been opened, *Thor* had hammered *Alcantara* almost to a standstill. Kähler deemed the time right to make his

escape. He turned and withdrew under cover of smoke. Kähler had been tempted to close and destroy the AMC, but the chance of further damage to his ship outweighed any advantage that could be gained by the destruction of the British vessel.

Kähler had gained the upper hand almost from the start of the action, managing to upset *Alcantara*'s fire-control arrangements with his second salvo. While *Alcantara* had struggled to maintain co-ordinated and controlled fire, *Thor*'s gunnery system remained unaffected, except for mechanical defects with the guns when they became overheated. As a result, Kähler had a decisive advantage and was able to dictate the course of the battle.[24]

On 5 December 1940, the Royal Navy had its second clash with a raider, under almost identical circumstances. It was *Thor* again, and once more Kähler's lookouts made the first sighting. The vessel was the AMC *Carnarvon Castle* and Kähler, identifying the ship correctly, turned away to port.

HMS *Carnarvon Castle*, under the command of Captain H.N.M. Hardy, RN, was on patrol 700 miles north-east of Montevideo. When an unknown vessel was sighted at a range of about 19,000 yards, Hardy turned to intercept. While speed was being increased the signal 'What ship?' was made. There was no reply, so Hardy instructed his signalman to order the stranger to 'Stop instantly'. When there was still no reply and no slackening of speed, Hardy ordered a warning shot to be fired. The shell, however, fell well short. In response, Kähler raised his war flag, dropped his disguise, and opened fire with a two-gun salvo at a range of over 16,000 yards. *Thor* was then turned to starboard to bring its four-gun starboard battery to bear. The raider was on target with the fourth salvo.

As with *Alcantara*, *Carnarvon Castle*'s fire-control system was damaged early in the engagement and its shooting throughout the action accordingly poor. Kähler was again in control of the action and turned alternately port then starboard under cover of smoke. The turns permitted Kähler to use both batteries and to allow the guns on the lee side to be cooled. The old 15-centimetre guns were not up to rapid firing and as they overheated the recoil systems began to fail. This prevented the

barrels returning to their normal position after firing, which meant that the hot barrels had to be pushed into position before they could be fired again. Kähler also managed to fire two torpedoes, but Hardy avoided these by turning towards the threat.

As *Carnarvon Castle* was being struck repeatedly, Hardy decided to retire under cover of smoke and maintain contact out of range of the German guns. Kähler, however, turned under cover of smoke and steamed off at full speed.

In a battle that lasted just over an hour, Kähler's gunners fired 593 rounds of 15-centimetre shell and scored 23 hits. *Thor* escaped without damage.

THE RAIDERS REACH AUSTRALIAN WATERS

By December 1940, three of the German raiders had reached the Australia Station.

On 7 October *Pinguin*, working the Sunda Strait–Cape Leeuwin shipping lane, came across the Norwegian *Storstad*, and captured the tanker without firing a shot. *Storstad* was then taken to the north-west of North West Cape and converted into an auxiliary minelayer. The two vessels then sailed south into the Great Australian Bight. In late October and early November, the two ships mined Bass Strait and the approaches to Sydney, Melbourne, Hobart and Adelaide. Once the mining mission was completed, *Pinguin* and *Storstad*, renamed *Passat* by the Germans, returned to the Indian Ocean.[25]

In the Pacific, *Komet* (disguised as the Japanese *Maebasi Maru*) and *Orion* (disguised as *Manyo Maru*) joined company. On 25 November, the two raiders, supported by the supply ship *Kulmerland* (disguised as *Tokyo Maru*), captured then sank the small freighter *Holmwood*. Two days later, they sank the liner *Rangitane* to the east of New Zealand. The trio then sailed north to prey on the phosphate shipping around the island of Nauru. On 6 December, the phosphate carrier *Triona* was intercepted between the Solomon Islands and Nauru and sunk. The following day the Norwegian *Vinni* was sunk off Nauru. Then, on 8 December, *Triadic*, *Triaster* and *Komata* were sunk. The w/t operator on Nauru alerted the

Australian authorities, but with no warships in the area there was little Navy Office could do.

As a result of *Komet*'s and *Orion*'s successes, the Germans had captured 675 prisoners. Because of the difficulty of feeding and caring for such a large number of people, it was decided to land most of them on Emirau Island before the three German ships went their separate ways. On 1 January, the released prisoners reached Townsville aboard the Australian steamship *Nellore*. Interviewed by the naval authorities, they said that the raiders had been disguised as Japanese ships. Only *Kulmerland* was positively identified, the Weekly Intelligence Report for 30 May 1941 naming it as the Pacific raiders' supply ship.[26]

The seventh raider, *Schiff 41* (*Kormoran*), sailed from Gotenhafen (Gdynia) on 3 December 1940 under the command of Korvettenkapitän Theodor Anton Detmers.[27] Formerly the Hamburg–Amerika Line ship *Steiermark*, *Kormoran* was the first of the second wave of raiders. Displacing 8,736 tons, and 515 feet in length, *Kormoran* was also the largest.

Like the previous raiders, *Kormoran* had as its main armament, six 15-centimetre guns. These guns, Model C/13s of First World War vintage, had a maximum range of 18,100 yards. Two were mounted beneath the forecastle and were concealed behind hinged, counterweighted steel plates that opened upwards, the starboard gun being designated No.1 gun and the port gun No.2 gun. Another two guns were similarly mounted at the stern beneath the poop deck. The No.5 gun was to starboard and the No.6 gun was to port. The other two guns, Nos 3 and 4, were mounted on the centreline of the ship in Nos 2 and 4 cargoholds, and were concealed behind collapsible hatch walls. This arrangement gave the vessel a very clean profile, but it also had a disadvantage. Due to the wide beam of the ship (66 feet) and their low mountings, guns 3 and 4 could not be depressed sufficiently to engage targets at close range. At maximum depression, the wide deck screened the target and rendered the gunsights useless.[28]

It was planned that *Kormoran* would also carry a single 7.5-centimetre gun for firing warning shots, but this weapon was removed before sailing.

Owing to a shortage of 3.7-centimetre anti-aircraft guns, the raider's air defence and secondary armament were to have only consisted of five 2-centimetre C/30 automatic cannon. The 2-centimetre guns, two forward,

two amidships and one aft, were mounted on hydraulic platforms that were raised into position as required. Detmers, however, wanted a secondary weapon with greater range and penetration for use against surface targets. He sought and successfully obtained two 3.7-centimetre anti-tank guns from the army. These weapons were mounted on either side of the bridge and concealed behind light steel plates. In addition to these weapons, a number of 7.92-millimetre MG-34 machine guns were carried.

Kormoran was also equipped with six torpedo tubes. Like the 15-centimetre guns, these were of First World War vintage. Two sets of twin tubes were mounted port and starboard above the waterline and forward of the bridge structure. The tubes were concealed behind steel plates and had to be pushed into the firing position after the covering plates had been raised. The other two torpedo tubes were mounted below the waterline in the No.3 hold immediately forward of the bridge. These two tubes, one to port and one to starboard, were mounted at an angle of 35° abaft the beam.[29]

The underwater tubes were not fitted with extension sleeves for firing while the ship was underway, and it appears that the angled mounting was introduced to overcome this deficiency. The arrangement, however, proved unsatisfactory. Trials revealed that 3 knots was the maximum speed at which the ship could travel when firing the underwater tubes. It is believed that *Kormoran*'s torpedo tubes fired 50-centimetre (19.9-inch) diameter torpedoes.[30]

For mining operations *Kormoran* is believed to have carried 360 (EMC) moored type contact mines and 30 (TMB) magnetic ground mines. The former could be deployed in coastal waters up to the 200 fathom line, but the latter, which rested on the seabed, could only be laid in water with a maximum depth of 10 fathoms. The mines were stowed on the mine deck, which ran aft from No.4 hold. The mine deck, situated one deck below the upper deck, ran for almost a third of the ship's length.

To enable the magnetic mines to be safely deployed, a light speedboat was carried and stowed in No.6 hold. The *Leichtes-Schnellboot* (LS) series boats were originally designed as small torpedo boats, but technical problems with the 45-centimetre torpedoes they were to carry meant that the first two boats, LS2 and LS3, were completed as minelayers. *Kormoran* received LS3, which was capable of carrying four magnetic mines.

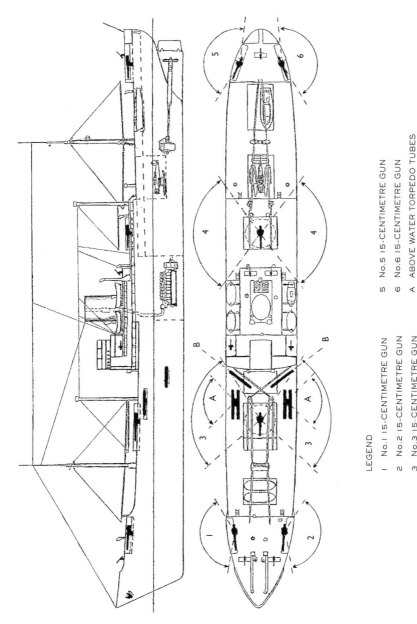

LEGEND

1 No.1 15-CENTIMETRE GUN
2 No.2 15-CENTIMETRE GUN
3 No.3 15-CENTIMETRE GUN
4 No.4 15-CENTIMETRE GUN

5 No.5 15-CENTIMETRE GUN
6 No.6 15-CENTIMETRE GUN
A ABOVE WATER TORPEDO TUBES
B BELOW WATER TORPEDO TUBES

HSK *Kormoran*. Arrangement of armament and arcs of fire.

Kormoran's diesel-electric propulsion system consisted of four Krupp 9-cylinder four stroke diesel engines, each of 3,600-bhp, coupled to four 2,600-kva, 3,800-volt alternators. These supplied current, via a central distribution point, to electric motors on the two propeller shafts. The alternators also supplied electricity for auxiliary machinery via two 500-kva transformers. To provide supplementary power for the auxiliaries, two small diesel generators were installed in the No.3 hold. Although capable of making 18 knots, a 10-knot cruising speed, coupled with a capacity to carry 5,200 tons of fuel-oil, gave *Kormoran* a potential radius of action of 70,000 miles.[31]

For reconnaissance purposes, two Arado 196 floatplanes were stowed in No.5 hold. In addition to the four ship's boats, which were carried on the bridge superstructure, two large steel lifeboats were stowed in No.1 hold. The extra boats were carried to help accommodate the raider's 400 crew. These lifeboats were supplemented by a boat taken from one of *Kormoran*'s victims plus a boat from the supply ship *Kulmerland*. For transferring supplies and torpedoes to U-boats a number of large inflatable rubber dinghies were carried.

A SECRET CALL SIGN IS INTRODUCED

In December 1940, the Admiralty amended the shipping identification procedure to include a secret call sign. As before, the merchant ship would be asked to make its signal letters, but with the new procedure the letters would then be converted, using a code book, into a secret call sign of four letters. The warship would then signal the two inner letters of the secret call sign. The merchant ship was expected to reply with the two outer letters. Failure of the merchant ship to reply, or reply correctly, would produce the demand to stop. Twelve months later, the secret call sign was still not fully implemented and was applicable only to British and some Dutch vessels. It has been estimated that only about half of the British ships challenged during this period managed to reply correctly.[32]

On 23 January 1941, the Admiralty issued CAFO 143, which was an update to CAFO 422. Entitled 'Raider Identification', CAFO 143 provided further information on the identification of disguised German raiders.

CAFO 143 noted that at the outbreak of war Germany had 890 motor-ships but, of these, only about 35 per cent would be useful for raiding purposes. Because of the large number of more recently built ships, it was considered that any vessel over fifteen years of age would not be used. It was thought that smaller ships of about 5,000 tons, in particular fruit ships, might receive preference for use as raiders. This was because they were fast (17 knots) and because their between decks (3 forward and 2 aft) were useful for carrying stores, ammunition and prisoners.

In addition to a table of vessel types likely to be used as raiders, CAFO 143 included notes on the methods of disguise, and general observations on raiders.

Under general observations, it was noted that, because of a greater endurance, the type of ship likely to be employed as a raider would be diesel driven, although geared turbine, water tube boiler, oil burners were not to be overlooked.

CAFO 143 indicated that raiders would be difficult to identify from a distance and that in most cases boarding would be necessary to confirm suspicions. The boarding parties were advised to examine the auxiliary equipment on the bridge, the refrigeration plant (if equipped) in the engine room, notices and builders plates, signs of recent removal of dummy funnels and evidence of false superstructure.[33]

CAFO 143, therefore, was a recipe for a disaster. The Admiralty had not been able to provide definite information on which German merchant ships were armed and was now recommending that commanding officers board suspect vessels to confirm their suspicions.

Fortunately, the two recent encounters with a raider had revealed no reluctance on the part of the Germans to open fire at extreme range. It was only a matter of time, however, before hesitation on the part of the enemy would induce a British warship to close in order to confirm suspicions. If a close-range action ensued, any advantages in speed, armour and superior armament that the British ship might posses would be lost.

COURTING DISASTER

At 1037 on 27 February 1941, the light cruiser HMS *Leander*, patrolling to the east of Mogadishu, sighted a merchant ship directly ahead. Captain R.H. Bevan, RN, ordered speed to be increased from 20 to 23 knots to close the vessel. As the range decreased, it could be seen that the vessel, which resembled an Italian 'RAMB' class freighter, had a gun mounted on the forecastle. Intelligence reports revealed that the Italians had armed these banana freighters with 4.7-inch guns.

International law provided for merchant ships to be armed, for self-defence, with a gun mounted on the stern. A gun mounted on the forecastle was deemed to be for offensive purposes. A vessel equipped in this way lost its civil status and became, for all intents and purposes, a warship.[34] It must have been obvious to Bevan, therefore, that he was dealing with a belligerent.

Leander went to action stations, although its 6-inch turrets were left trained in the fore and aft position. By 1115, the range had reduced to 11,000 yards. Ten minutes later, the range was 10,000 yards. Bevan ordered the vessel to identify itself. Four minutes later, the vessel hoisted the Red Ensign. The vessel was ordered to hoist its signal letters. After a delay of about five minutes, the vessel hoisted the letters 'GJYD'. After searching through the relevant shipping recognition books, it was found that these letters represented the British ship *Grosmont Castle*. No details of this vessel could be found.

At 1141, the secret challenge was made. When no reply was received, the vessel was ordered to stop instantly. This signal was also ignored.

While the exchange of signals was taking place, an armed boarding party was assembled. Then at 1150, just as Bevan was preparing to fire a warning shot, the vessel hoisted either the Italian mercantile or naval ensign and began training its guns on *Leander*.

Bevan was now in an extremely awkward position. He had intended to take station on the vessel's bow, in preparation for boarding, but was now slightly before the Italian's beam, at a range of about 3,000 yards. The main armament, which was still in the fore and aft position, was quickly ordered to train onto the target. At 1153, the enemy vessel opened fire. *Leander* responded thirty seconds later.[35]

The Italians managed to fire about six rounds from their 4.7-inch guns before five rapid salvoes from *Leander* discouraged them from continuing. Although the Italian fire was described as erratic and short, one shell struck *Leander* on the funnel and blew a 12-inch diameter hole in the casing.

Leander's aim was better. Several hits were scored on *Ramb I*, all before the bridge. Bevan checked fire and signalled the Italian to surrender. No reply was received, but the Italians struck their colours and the crew began abandoning ship.

With *Ramb I* stopped and being abandoned, Bevan hove to on the starboard quarter and despatched a boarding party to seize the ship. Before the cutter reached the vessel, an Italian officer warned the party that his ship was on fire and was laden with ammunition. The boarding party, quite reasonably, lay off the Italian vessel to reassess the situation.

A fire in the fore of the ship could be seen to be spreading aft. Any thought of trying to fight the fire was quickly dispelled when a heavy explosion shattered the fore part of the ship. As *Ramb I* began to settle by the bows, there was another heavy explosion aft and the raider quickly sank.

Despite closing with what was clearly an offensively armed enemy vessel, Bevan received praise from the Commander-in-Chief, East Indies, Vice-Admiral R. Leatham, RN, for 'ridding the seas of a potential raider'.[36] But the action could easily have gone the other way. A few well-directed shells and *Leander* could have sustained heavy casualties and been badly damaged.

On 2 March, *Leander* joined HMAS *Canberra*, having received orders to search the Saya de Mahla Bank for enemy shipping. When Bevan met Captain Farncomb, the action with *Ramb I* was no doubt discussed. How much, if at all, this influenced Farncomb's handling of *Canberra* two days later is open to conjecture.

Leatham considered that the Saya de Mahla Bank was an ideal place for a raider to refuel, and D/F bearings on W/T transmissions indicated that enemy vessels were in the area. His reasoning and decision to send *Canberra* and *Leander* there were sound, as there was an enemy tanker to the north of the bank. This was *Ketty Brövig*, a Norwegian tanker captured by *Atlantis* a month earlier and now in the charge of a prize crew.

On 4 March, *Canberra*'s Seagull reconnaissance aircraft sighted the tanker with a merchantman in company. The merchantman was the German blockade runner *Coburg*, refuelling after having broken out of the port of Massawa on 22 February. On sighting *Canberra*'s aircraft, the two ships quickly parted. *Ketty Brövig* headed south, and *Coburg* headed north. As *Canberra* pursued the latter ship, Farncomb ordered Bevan to close and intercept the tanker, which was being harassed and bombed by the Seagull.

Farncomb believed he was chasing a German raider, which was known to be operating in the area, so when the freighter refused to stop, he opened fire at a range of 21,100 yards. Probably mindful of the Royal Navy's two previous encounters with German raiders and Bevan's clash with an Italian raider, Farncomb continued to fire at extreme range until the vessel was well ablaze and being abandoned.[37]

With the supposed raider done for, Farncomb turned his attentions to the tanker. *Leander*, still closing the position, was ordered to pick up *Coburg*'s survivors.

Ketty Brövig's prize captain could see that escape was impossible, and to prevent the ship's recapture, promptly scuttled it. *Canberra* closed and despatched an anti-scuttling party, but the tanker was deemed to be beyond salvage.

Canberra had effectively destroyed two enemy ships, but through several minor errors in gunnery drill, expended 215 rounds of 8-inch shell. Leatham, in his report of the action, commented that Farncomb had been overcautious in his action with *Coburg* and that if he had closed to a more effective range the 'enemy might have been identified sooner and much ammunition saved'.[38]

Navy Office in Melbourne agreed with Leatham's comments, but it was easy to be wise after the event. Although *Coburg* was unarmed, the freighter was listed as an express cargo ship of 17 knots, and could conceivably have been selected for conversion to a raider. Therefore, Farncomb was justified in believing he had cornered a raider. Considering that in the Royal Navy's two previous encounters with a German raider, the raider had opened fire at extreme range, Farncomb was also justified in keeping his distance.

THE CONTINUING NEED TO MAKE UP FOR LOST TONNAGE

In the three months to 1 March 1941, Allied merchant shipping losses totalled 1,079,130 tons. On 6 March, the Admiralty reiterated its views on the capture of enemy merchant ships. CAFO 480 ('Enemy Merchant Ships, Capture Of—Procedure') stated:

> *No enemy merchant ship captured should be sunk unless the strongest military reason exists.* Every ship may be of the greatest value as the war progresses. If a prize crew cannot be spared at the moment, one possibility is to leave the ship stopped with caretakers on board (author's emphasis).[39]

Less than a month later, the Royal Navy was involved in its third clash with a German raider. On 4 April 1941, HMS *Voltaire* was about 900 miles west of the Cape Verde Islands, on passage from Trinidad to Freetown. Just after sunrise, *Voltaire* was spotted by *Thor*, which failed to identify the ship as an AMC. *Voltaire* also made a sighting. Both vessels turned toward each other, challenged, then fired warning shots. Kähler immediately realized that he had turned towards an enemy auxiliary cruiser. With escape impossible, he knew he would have to fight.

Kähler took full advantage of his longer ranged guns and fired his first salvo at 0649, immediately scoring hits on *Voltaire*'s W/T office and generator room. The latter hit cut the power to the fire-control system, forcing Captain J.A.P. Blackburn, RN, to order his 6-inch guns to go into local control. With *Voltaire*'s gunnery critically impaired, *Thor*'s fast and accurate salvo firing quickly dominated the duel. By the time the range had reduced to 7,000 yards, *Voltaire* was a blazing wreck.

Fortunately for *Voltaire*, the raider's guns overheated again, forcing Kähler to cease fire. In order to finish the AMC, Kähler closed to within 2,000 yards and began manoeuvring for a torpedo attack. It proved unnecessary. *Voltaire*'s remaining guns were now silent, white flags could be seen, and the crew was abandoning ship. Kähler stood off cautiously while his boats went in to pick up survivors, the crews armed with rifles and machine guns to keep the sharks away. When *Voltaire* sank, Kähler

moved in and spent five hours picking up survivors, secure in the knowledge that no signal had been sent by the AMC's W/T operators.

In the eighty-minute action *Thor* expended 724 rounds of 15-centimetre shell. The raider suffered only superficial damage and there were no casualties. *Voltaire* sank with the loss of seventy-two officers and men.

Because *Voltaire* had not been able to transmit an action report, the Admiralty remained unaware of the AMC's fate until the next day when the German propaganda ministry boasted that one of their raiders had sunk the British AMC *Voltaire*. On the strength of this report, HMCS *Prince David* was ordered to search along *Voltaire*'s track. On 7 April the Canadian AMC sighted wreckage and a patch of fuel-oil covering an area of 3 square miles. There were no survivors in the water and the Admiralty had to fear the worst.[40]

In the three encounters with German raiders, the Royal Navy had two of its AMCs badly damaged, a third sunk, and had little to show in return. The fourth encounter in May 1941 was almost another disaster.

On 7 May, *British Emperor* was attacked by *Pinguin*, although the merchantman managed to transmit a fairly comprehensive raider report before the W/T operator was silenced. The 'Q' signal was received by the heavy cruiser HMS *Cornwall* approximately 500 miles to the south. Captain P.C.W. Manwaring, RN, immediately altered course to intercept.

At about 0200 on 8 May, *Pinguin*'s lookouts sighted an unidentified object to port. Fearing that it was a warship, Kapitän zur See Felix Krüder decided to turn away. The object was indeed a warship. It was *Cornwall*, but Manwaring's lookouts had failed to see the darkened raider.

At dawn, *Cornwall*'s two Walrus aircraft were launched to conduct a search. Just after 0700, one of the aircraft was spotted by *Pinguin*. The aircrew, having sighted *Pinguin*, and under orders to maintain W/T silence, returned to *Cornwall* to make their report. Manwaring increased speed and altered course to intercept.

The Walrus was relaunched later in the morning, the aircrew under instructions to establish the identity of the vessel. Shortly after midday, the Walrus returned to report that the vessel had reluctantly identified itself as the Norwegian *Tamerlane*. Photographs taken during the flight revealed a ship with a strong resemblance to *Tamerlane*, though this vessel

was not listed on the VAI. The aircrew also reported an unusual absence of normally curious crewmen on deck when they flew over.

Manwaring was not convinced of the merchantman's *bona fides* and increased speed again to ensure a visual sighting before nightfall. Although there was nothing to suggest that this was the raider responsible for the attack on *British Emperor*, he also thought the lack of crew odd. The Walrus was launched again at 1345 with orders to regain contact with the vessel and report its movements.

Just after 1600, Manwaring sighted his quarry hull down at 30,000 yards. Closing rapidly, he ordered the vessel to heave to, reinforcing the order with two warning shots.

Krüder could easily identify the warship by its three prominent funnels, a British heavy cruiser, armed with 8-inch guns. Escape was impossible as the cruiser was superior in speed and armament. The only option was bluff. Krüder therefore ordered a raider report to be transmitted on the captured British W/T set, which *Pinguin* carried. An experienced W/T operator could distinguish a British set from a German one, and it was hoped that the use of a British set would allay the warship's suspicions. The ruse appeared to work as Manwaring later admitted that he had been forced to consider the possibility that the vessel was the Norwegian *Tamerlane*.

The possibility that *Tamerlane* was genuine created a dilemma. The only way that Manwaring could establish whether this was the *Tamerlane*, apart from boarding the merchantman, was to break W/T silence and consult the C-IN-C East Indies. The trouble was that if *Tamerlane* were genuine, breaking W/T silence would disclose his presence to the real raider and perhaps allow it to escape.

Cornwall was low on fuel, darkness was only hours away, and Manwaring was the man on the spot. He still had a Walrus aloft, but the aircraft was of limited value and he had to take action himself.

According to the German account of the action, *Cornwall* signalled repeatedly 'Heave to and await boarding party', although Manwaring's action report indicated that the signal was 'Heave to or I fire'. As there are some serious inconsistencies between Manwaring's action report and *Cornwall*'s log, there is an element of uncertainty about Manwaring's intentions and the actual signal sent.[41]

By 1710, *Cornwall* was well inside the known gun range of the German raiders (18,000 yards) and closing rapidly. At 1713, Manwaring ordered an alteration of course. From being almost bows-on during the approach, *Cornwall* was swung to port to open A-arcs, to allow the after turrets to bear on the target. Krüder saw the cruiser alter course and apparently believed it was manoeuvring to fire a broadside. He therefore swung *Pinguin* to port, unmasked his guns, hoisted the German flag, and opened fire at a range of 10,500 yards.

On *Cornwall*, Manwaring was caught off guard. Possibly due to the manoeuvring of both ships, *Cornwall*'s guns were not bearing on the target when the order to open fire was given. With 'x' and 'y' turrets not yet able to bear, 'a' and 'b' turrets were ordered to follow director. Unfortunately, before *Cornwall* could fire its first salvo, *Pinguin* managed to fire two. Although the first salvo fell short, the second was on target. One shell struck *Cornwall* on the waterline forward and exploded between the marines' messdeck and the flour store. Although this hit caused only superficial damage, splinters penetrated into the lower steering position, wounding the chief quartermaster and one other rating, as well as temporarily disabling the steering.

Cornwall's first salvo, under director control, was then fired. To Manwaring's consternation, the shells fell 50° off bearing. 'a' and 'b' turrets were immediately ordered to continue in local control while the fault in the fire control system was investigated.

For a short time *Cornwall* was out of control and incapable of bringing effective fire to bear. Helm orders were quickly passed to the after steering position and a few minutes later the cruiser was swinging away to port again and opening the range. As soon as 'x' and 'y' turrets could bear they began firing in group control.

Meanwhile, Krüder had ordered two torpedoes to be fired. Fortunately for Manwaring they missed, *Cornwall* being warned of their approach by the Walrus. *Cornwall*'s alteration in course also served to upset the Germans' aim, as *Pinguin*'s shells began to fall short.

The fault in *Cornwall*'s fire-control system was traced to a training circuit fuse in the transmitting station, the fuse apparently having been knocked out by the shock of the 15-centimetre shell striking forward. Once rectified, director firing was resumed. *Cornwall* then began

delivering effective fire from a range of about 14,000 yards and increasing.[42]

Krüder realized that *Pinguin* would soon be out-ranged. With little hope of inflicting any more damage on his adversary, he issued his scuttling orders. Moments later *Pinguin* was shattered by a tremendous explosion that sent flame, smoke and debris thousands of feet into the air.

Cornwall's eighth salvo had been responsible. Of the four shells fired, one hit forward, another destroyed the meteorological office under the bridge, and a third burst in the engine room. The fourth shell exploded in No.5 hold, detonating the raider's mines. *Pinguin* sank in seconds.

Cornwall, however, was also in difficulties. Water entering through the shell hole on the waterline had shorted the electrical system, causing a loss of power throughout the ship. When power was eventually restored, *Cornwall* closed and rescued *Pinguin's* survivors.

Sixty Germans from a complement of 401 survived the sinking. Among the Germans, pools of oil and floating debris, British and Indian seamen were also found. It was sobering to discover that in destroying the raider, *Cornwall* had also killed 213 captured Allied seamen.

The Admiralty was critical of Manwaring's handling of the situation. It considered that despite the fact that *Cornwall* was engaged in a raider hunt, Manwaring had placed too much emphasis on maintaining W/T silence. Valuable time had been wasted in getting the reconnaissance aircraft to return to the ship to make sighting reports, and that once the vessel had given its signal letters these should have been passed on to the C-IN-C for confirmation. It was also considered that Manwaring had made a serious error in judgement in closing a suspicious vessel, the error compounded by the inability to open fire immediately the vessel declared its true identity.

With hindsight, these criticisms would appear to be valid. They failed, however, to take into account Manwaring's concern that the *Tamerlane* was genuine. The concern was undoubtedly heightened by the vessel's transmission of a raider report on a British W/T set. Given Manwaring's predicament, it would have been unwise to break W/T silence to confirm the vessel's identity, as this would have betrayed *Cornwall's* presence to the raider if *Tamerlane* was genuine.

If Manwaring had doubts about *Tamerlane's bona fides*, and did not wish to break W/T silence, his only other means of identifying the vessel was by

visual inspection or boarding. That the former was Manwaring's intention is supported by his orders for the vessel to heave to and his manoeuvring of *Cornwall*. At 1714, *Cornwall* was approximately 10,500 yards off the suspect vessel's port quarter. Manwaring then altered course to port, presumably in order to position *Cornwall* off the merchantman's port beam.

Such a position, 10,500 yards off the beam, would have provided Manwaring with a perfect silhouette of the supposed *Tamerlane*. At 10,500 yards all of the merchantman's identifying features would have been visible. These, checked against the details and silhouette of *Tamerlane*, provided in the relevant shipping recognition books, would have enabled Manwaring to make a positive identification from a relatively safe distance.

Unfortunately, before Manwaring could complete the manoeuvre, Krüder decamouflaged and opened fire. Given that Admiralty instructions (CAFO 143) indicated that boarding was considered necessary if a vessel could not be identified, it is tempting to speculate what would have happened had Krüder not disclosed his ship's identity.

THE INTELLIGENCE WAR

On the same day that *British Emperor* was sunk by *Pinguin*, the Royal Navy, in an operation planned to provide information and material for the Operational Intelligence Centre (OIC) of the Admiralty, captured the German weather ship *München*.

From the start of the war, the OIC and the Government Code and Cypher School (GC&CS) at Bletchley Park had striven to provide the Royal Navy with timely and accurate intelligence. While the OIC gathered intelligence from numerous sources, the GC&CS concentrated on gleaning intelligence from enemy codes and ciphers. Information obtained from these sources was called Special Intelligence. By the beginning of 1941, the cryptanalysis section at Bletchley Park was decoding and reading much of the *Luftwaffe* and *Wehrmacht* cipher traffic, but little of the *Kriegsmarine*'s, although the former sources sometimes provided indirect information on German shipping movements.

The Germans encoded and decoded messages and signals electro-mechanically with a cryptographic '*Schlussel*' machine known as Enigma.

The *Kriegsmarine*'s version was more sophisticated and was known as the Enigma-M. The *Kriegsmarine* was also more security conscious and used different ciphers for different operational areas, commands, and for specific operations. Auxiliary cruisers and supply ships operating in overseas waters, for example, used a dedicated cipher called *Ausserheimisch* (nicknamed 'Pike' by GC&CS) which, incidentally, was never broken by the British. *Heimisch*, or 'Dolphin', was the cipher used by all surface ships operating in the Baltic and the North Sea. It was also used by ships operating from, or off, the occupied territories and by all operational U-boats until February 1942.[43] By March 1941, the cryptanalists at Bletchley Park were reading much of Dolphin, but with a month's lag time.[44]

Material found on board *München* included the May and June daily settings for the Enigma-M. On 9 May, convoy escorts depth-charged and crippled *U-110*. The U-boat was blown to the surface, where its crew, thinking the boat would quickly founder, abandoned ship. Unfortunately for the Germans, *U-110* stayed afloat long enough for a boarding party from the destroyer HMS *Bulldog* to recover the Enigma-M, the Dolphin handbook with the daily settings valid till the end of June and a host of related documents.

The captured material permitted the cryptanalists at Bletchley Park to read current Dolphin traffic as well as some older signals dating back to February. Some of this Special Intelligence was used in the hunt for the battleship *Bismarck* and in the sinking or capture of seven of the eight tankers and supply ships sent to assist *Bismarck* and *Prinz Eugen* during their breakout. Bletchley Park also supplied information on the location of patrolling U-boats, allowing, where possible, convoys to be routed around them. It also supplied information on U-boat resupply arrangements. Where time and resources permitted, a Royal Navy warship or Coastal Command aircraft could then be despatched to the rendezvous point, or likely area, if the exact location was not known.

On 25 June, with the daily settings for the Enigma-M due to expire, another 'pinch' was arranged. The armed trawler *Lauenberg* was captured, with the settings for July. From July until February 1942, when the Dolphin cipher was changed, Bletchley Park had little trouble overcoming the daily changes in the settings, although delays from four to forty-eight hours did occur.

Despite these spectacular breakthroughs with the Dolphin cipher, the GC&CS could not read Pike. As a result, the Admiralty's knowledge of the movements of the German raiders was sketchy. What little was known was collected from sources such as D/F intercepts, raider reports, and the statements of survivors. The information was then disseminated by the Naval Intelligence Division (NID) through the Weekly Intelligence Report (WIR).

The largest advance in raider intelligence, however, had been gained through the destruction of *Pinguin*. Information obtained from the survivors, combined with existing intelligence, permitted NID to issue a Raider Supplement with WIR No.64 of 30 May 1941.

The supplement provided a general description of the armed merchant raiders employed by the Germans, their tactics, and their operational areas and strategy, with details of each raider. Seven raiders were known to have been deployed but, as the real identities of six were not known, it was decided to identify each with a letter of the alphabet. All were reportedly armed with 5.9-inch guns as well as torpedo tubes, and all were believed to make use of paint, false names and deck houses, dummy funnels, ventilators and sampson posts when changing disguise.[45]

To assist in the identification of these raiders, photographs or silhouettes were provided, as well as the following notes on each vessel:

Raider A – Reported to resemble *Uckermark*. Sits low in the water. Slightly raked bow, counter stern. Squat oval funnel close abaft bridge. Two boats each side abaft funnel not visible in silhouette. Foremast well aft and mainmast well forward. Looks like a tramp. 8,000 to 10,000 tons.

Raider B – Raked bow, cruiser stern. Foremast abaft the well deck, funnel (probably telescopic) close abaft the bridge. Dummy bulwarks in the fore deck give an unbroken line from forecastle to bridge structure. Sampson posts immediately before and abaft midship superstructure. Cross-trees on both fore and main masts very high up. 4,000 to 5,000 tons. Length about 350 feet.

Raider C – Typical cargo liner. Raked bow, cruiser stern, two heavy masts and big funnel. Large bridge superstructure. Dummy

bulwarks in fore well deck give an unbroken line from forecastle head to bridge. Noticeable features are foremast stays, which are carried seven feet inboard to allow gun flaps to fold clear, and single sampson post on centre line at break of poop deck (this may be moveable). 8,000 to 9,000 tons.

Raider D – Modern fruit ship, raked bow, cruiser stern. Two masts and one squat funnel. Forecastle flush to bridge. The deck aft of the midship superstructure is noticeably lower than that forward of it. Reported to resemble *Ahrensberg*. About 4,000 to 5,000 tons.

Raider E – Real identity *Santa Cruz*. Well raked slightly clipper bows, cruiser stern, two masts. One funnel close abaft the bridge. Some passenger accommodation. Very fine lines forward. Dummy bulwarks in well deck give unbroken, noticeably straight, lines from bow to stern. 3,866 tons.

Raider F – No.33 was engaged and sunk by HMS *Cornwall* 500 miles north of the Seychelles on 8th May, 1941. In appearance and equipment she was very similar to the other Indian Ocean raider, Raider 'C'.

Raider G – Squat funnel in centre of rather high superstructure. Stern half-counter, half-cruiser type. Reported to resemble modified *Kulmerland*. Estimated 10,000 tons.

As far as strategy went, it was considered that the raider captains followed the same general policy, which was 'to be content with small gains, not to risk their ships by attacks on warships, even if of inferior strength, or on defended shore objectives, and to rely on the cumulative effect of the loss of two or three ships per month and the disorganization caused to trade by our counter-measures'.[46]

As for tactics, it was noted that attacks on merchantmen are always 'sudden and severe, the primary targets being the bridge, W/T room, and gun'. Their reactions if confronted by warships, however, were somewhat vague. Raider 'E' (*Thor*), it was noted, opened 'fast and accurate fire at

17,000 yards' when intercepted by HMS *Carnarvon Castle*. Raider 'F' (*Pinguin*), however, waited until the range had reduced to 12,000 yards before opening fire on HMS *Cornwall*.

On 26 September 1941, WIR No.81 gave this updated information:

Armed merchant raiders are very well equipped, capable of remaining at sea for 18 months if necessary, and of engaging anything weaker than a 6-in. cruiser with some prospects of success. They have, however, endeavoured to avoid being brought to action, and have contented themselves with exacting a heavy toll of unescorted merchant ships.

Only one raider has so far been sunk, that destroyed by HMS *Cornwall* in the Indian Ocean on 8th May, 1941. One other raider has been engaged three times by British armed merchant cruisers, but succeeded in escaping twice and in destroying her adversary, HMS *Voltaire*, on the third occasion.

Several prizes have been sent into French Biscay ports, and others have been thoroughly rifled before being sunk. Supply ships are sent out from time to time to supply the raiders with provisions, munitions and fuel, but fuel does not present the same problem as it did in the last war. The raiders do not rely on shore bases, but cruise about slowly in deserted areas of the oceans effecting repairs and changing their appearance. As they all carry aircraft for reconnaissance, they are able both to locate victims and avoid warships hunting them.

The following is a brief summary of their individual achievements.

Raider A – Official German No.36. Believed to be the *Neumark*, 7,820 tons. Left Germany in April 1940, and proceeded to the Western Pacific, where she sank or captured eleven ships between June and December, 1940. She is believed to have returned to Germany in August 1941, without having achieved much further success.

Raider B – Official German No. believed to be 45. Identity unknown. About 4,000 tons. Joined 'A' in the Pacific in October,

1940, without having previously carried out any attacks. Operated with 'A' until Christmas, 1940. Shelled Nauru 26th December, 1940. Present whereabouts unknown but has not had much success and may have returned to Germany.

Raider C – Official German No.16. Believed to be *Goldenfels*, 7,800 tons. Left Germany in March, 1940. Sank one ship in South Atlantic and then proceeded to Indian Ocean, where she sank or captured twelve ships in 1940, and three ships in January and February, 1941. Then returned to South Atlantic and sank three ships in April and May, 1941. Present whereabouts unknown, but may have returned to Germany.

Raider D – Official German No. believed to be 21. Believed to be *Parangua*, 6,100 tons. Sank or captured twelve ships in the North Atlantic between the West Indies and Cape Verdes from June to October, 1940. Returned to France, and may have sailed again during the first half of 1941. May have attacked five ships in the South Atlantic in May, June and July, 1941.

Raider E – Official German No.10. *Santa Cruz*, 3,866 tons. Sailed from Germany on 5th June, 1940, and sank or captured eight ships in the South Atlantic from July to October, 1940. Was engaged by HMS *Alcantara* in July and HMS *Carnarvon Castle* in December, but escaped. Sank or captured seven ships in the Freetown-Pernambuco area between January and April, 1941, and sank HMS *Voltaire*. Returned to Germany at end of May. Probably now ready to sail again.

Raider F – Official German No.33. *Kandelfels*, 7,800 tons. Left Germany early June, 1940, and after one attack in South Atlantic, sank, captured or mined twelve ships in the Indian Ocean and Australian waters from August to December, 1940. Captured three Norwegian Whale Refineries and eleven whale catchers in the Antarctic in January. Returned to Indian Ocean and sank three ships in April and May, before being herself sunk by HMS *Cornwall*.

Raider G – Official German No. believed to be 41. Believed to be *Steiermark*, 9,400 tons. Very little is known about this raider, but she may have sunk two or three ships in the North Atlantic in January and February, 1941, and was reported to be in the Indian Ocean in March.

As far as the Australia Station was concerned, WIR No.81 added that there 'has been no activity in the Indian Ocean since June, and possibly none since the beginning of May. It is probable, however, that a raider is in the area and will soon resume operations'. As for the Pacific Ocean two, but possibly three, ships were attacked west of Panama in the middle of August. The raider responsible was then thought to have 'proceeded towards New Zealand, as a ship was attacked 1,200 miles north-east of North Island on the 11th September. The movements of this raider since then are not known'.

The Naval Intelligence Division had a branch in Australia with its own Director of Naval Intelligence, Commander Long. In 1940, to pool and co-ordinate the intelligence services of the RAN, the RAAF and the Army, a Combined Operational Intelligence Centre (COIC) was established, Long being appointed director.[47]

The two offices issued regular intelligence summaries in much the same way that the Admiralty's Naval Intelligence Division issued the WIR. The Australian branch of the NID issued a monthly summary called the Australian Station Intelligence Summaries, and the COIC issued a weekly summary. The distribution list for this summary included HMAS *Sydney*.

Adding weight to the WIR No.81 deduction that a raider was probably operating in the Indian Ocean was an August 18 entry in the Australian Station Intelligence Summaries (ASIS). This entry noted 'that there were indications from W/T traffic of the presence of a German unit in the Indian Ocean on 17 and 21 July'. It was thought that the traffic was intercommunications between the raider and its supply ship, 'possibly arranging for the transfer of prisoners from *Mareeba* and *Velebit*'. (An earlier WIR had indicated that these two vessels may have been lost due to weather.)

Further evidence of a Pacific raider was highlighted in the COIC weekly summary No.19 (WS/19) of 22 September.[48] WS/19 noted that four ships (*Kota Nopan, Australind, Devon,* and *Silvaplana*) appeared to have been attacked between the latter part of August and 11 September. The raider

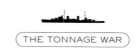
responsible for these attacks was considered to be Raider 'G', although it was also considered possible that a second raider was operating with it. Despite the detailed raider summary provided in WIR No.81, the COIC summary referred to Raider 'G' as No.46 instead of No.41.

WS/19 also included an appendix of raider intelligence. This was modestly entitled 'A review of intelligence of enemy raider activity over the past few months with a view to ascertaining what raider or raiders are at present operating in the Pacific'. The review was comprehensive and included known raiders, suspected and known losses due to raider activity, suspicious sightings, reports from POW's and D/F bearings. All reports, from the North and South Atlantic, the Indian and the Pacific Oceans, were studied. The review concluded that:

> All the positive evidence points to Raider G (No.46) being both the Indian Ocean and the Pacific Ocean Raider. On negative grounds only, Raider D could have been the raider. Similarly on negative grounds Raider E could have been the raider, but this is improbable (especially as regards the Indian Ocean sinkings) in view of her obvious need of refit after a long period at sea. Finally, assuming the accuracy of the suggestion that she has been operating in the Sth. Atlantic, Raider B could have reached Easter Is. by 3/9 at 15 knots for 16 days, a most unlikely performance.
>
> It would appear therefore that Raider G is the Indian Ocean and the Pacific Ocean Raider.

The review also concluded that if a second raider was operating in the Pacific it was probably Raider 'D'. Unfortunately, the review's conclusions were incorrect. Worse, the belief that Raider 'G' was now operating in the Pacific was possibly to have tragic consequences.

Kormoran (Raider 'G') had indeed been responsible for the attacks in the Indian Ocean but did not transfer its area of operations to the Pacific. The 'Pacific raider' was in fact two other vessels. *Komet* (Raider 'B') had been responsible for the attacks on *Australind*, *Kota Nopan* and *Devon*, and *Atlantis* (Raider 'C') had been responsible for the attack on *Silvaplana*.

The incorrect number given in WS/19 for Raider 'G' was rectified in WS/21 of 6 October. In this summary, Raider 'G' was designated No.41

and identified as *Steiermark*, a diesel-electric vessel similar in silhouette to *Osorno* and *Wuppertal*.

Although WS/21 contained no additional information on possible raider activity in the Indian Ocean, there were a number of D/F fixes reported which suggested that the Pacific raider was operating in the south-west Pacific, possibly in the Tasman Sea.

A fortnight later, WS/23 reported that *S.G. Embiricos* had failed to arrive at its destination, and that this, coupled with the fact that another vessel was overdue, raised the possibility that a raider was again operating in the Indian Ocean. The report concluded that 'such a raider could now have reached the western section of the Australia Station'. WS/23 also indicated that there was still evidence of a raider operating in the Pacific. In addition, further D/F bearings and sightings suggested that a second raider, or possibly a supply ship, was operating with it, the latter scenario being supported by reports of enemy merchant ships having departed from Japanese ports during August and September.

The possibility that enemy merchant ships operating out of Japan were acting as raider supply ships was taken very seriously and prompted the inclusion of an appendix to WS/23. It provided a great deal of information about each vessel, its likely role, and whether it was armed or stiffened for armaments. The vessels listed were *Regensburg, Havenstein, Ursula Rickmers, Spreewald, Burgenland, Anneliese Essberger, Elsa Essberger, Münsterland,* and *Ramses*.

A notable omission from this list was *Kulmerland*, which actually was a raider supply ship. *Kulmerland* had sailed from Kobe on 3 September to resupply *Kormoran*. The ship's omission may have been due to the fact that WIR No.64 of 30 May had reported it probable that '*Kulmerland*, the Pacific raider's supply ship, last located at Emirau, 23rd December, 1940 has returned to Bordeaux after a rendezvous with *Scheer* in the South Atlantic in early March'. Although this was incorrect, it appears that as a result of this report, *Kulmerland* was struck from the list of enemy vessels in Japanese ports. Interestingly, *Burgenland* (*Kulmerland*'s sister ship) was listed, and was reported as having sailed from Kobe 'about 10' September.

WS/23 also provided more information on Raider 'G'. The Admiralty indicated that this vessel displaced 9,400 tons and was 524 feet in length. Its hallmark features were a flush deck from the break of the forecastle to

the stern, raked bow, probably half cruiser half counter stern, two masts, fairly fat round funnel close abaft a square bridge superstructure, four pairs of tall, typically German samson posts two forward two aft, though these were probably removed or cut down. The raider was described as being similar to *Antilla*. Furthermore, Raider 'G' was again suggested as being the Pacific raider.

The question of an Indian Ocean raider was again raised in ws/24 of 27 October. This reported that it was now considered likely that *Mareeba* and *Velebit* were raider victims and that the raider responsible could now be on the Australia Station. As for the Pacific, there was confirmation of the presence of at least two enemy units. One unit, probably a raider, was operating in the mid Pacific, and a second unit, either a raider or a supply ship, was operating in the western Pacific.

On 10 November ws/26 was issued. It contained two reports of possible unidentified aircraft sightings in Western Australia. One was over Geraldton on the night of 3 November and the other was over Pearce aerodrome on the night of 6–7 November. Although both reports received low reliability gradings, the comment on the Geraldton report is interesting because there had been two previous reports of aircraft in the vicinity.

> On the assumption that an aircraft was responsible for the latest sighting and that this aircraft was raider-based, the Indian Ocean raider could have reached the area at 12 knots from the position given by OLIVIA on 20/10. One of the Pacific Ocean units would also have had time to reach the vicinity of Geraldton.

In essence, if Raider 'G' was the western Pacific raider mentioned in ws/24, ws/26 indicated that it could have been in the vicinity of Geraldton on 3 November.[49]

Given the time factor, however, it is doubtful if *Sydney* received a copy of ws/26 before sailing from Fremantle on 11 November. If this was so, all previous intelligence indicated that Raider 'G' was still in the Pacific. But regardless of where Captain Burnett thought it was operating, he still had to consider the possibility that the Indian Ocean raider had reached the Australia Station and was operating in the waters off the Western Australian coast.

Although Burnett may not have received WS/26, he should have received a copy of Admiralty general message 771A, issued by the Admiralty on 4 November 1941. AGM771A contained the latest anti-scuttling instructions and would have served to remind Burnett of the importance of saving merchant tonnage. This general message was reissued, with slight amendments, on 27 November as CAFO 2302 'Enemy Merchant Ships-Anti-Scuttling Instructions'.

CAFO 2302, which incorporated AGM771A and CAFO 1069/41, contained this information:

1. Commanding officers are given full discretion to take such steps as the circumstances require and to use force to save the enemy ship and to ensure that occupants of ships' boats obey their orders promptly.

2. Crews are not, however, to be left in open boats on the high seas, or to drown in their ship.

3. Normally:

   (a) The main object should be to get the boarding party on board the enemy ship as quickly as possible.

   (b) Scuttling can best be hindered or prevented by rapid action designed to disorganize the scuttling arrangements and to prevent the crew taking to boats.

4. The following significance has been given by broadcast to Group WBA in the International Code, which is to be used in preference to individual signals:

   'Stop—do not lower boats—do not use radio—do not scuttle—if you disobey I open fire'.

5. If the ship is definitely identified as enemy, fire may be opened immediately after sending of WBA. The primary object is to induce a state of irresolution in the enemy's mind.

6. Aircraft sighting a suspected enemy merchant ship should report and shadow, endeavouring to remain unobserved. No repeat no

attempt should be made to divert or stop unless surface vessels are unable to make contact, in which case objects of aircraft should be:

(a) Prevent crew scuttling and taking to boats.

(b) Divert ship to most suitable British or Allied warship or port.

If a ship is identified as enemy, aircraft may take such action as is necessary to disorganize scuttling arrangements, e.g., machine gun the bridge and the boats at the davit head.[50]

As can be seen, Burnett, like all other commanding officers, was placed in an awkward and potentially dangerous position. The Admiralty wanted the disguised merchant raiders intercepted and destroyed, but it also wanted enemy merchant ships captured. Clearly, the two objectives were in conflict.

With raider identification instructions (CAFO 143) indicating that boarding may be necessary to confirm suspicions, and anti-scuttling instructions stating that 'the main object should be to get the boarding party on board the enemy ship as quickly as possible', it was inevitable that there would be a tragedy. Sooner or later, an Allied warship would corner a disguised raider, attempt to get an anti-scuttling party on board, and be bloodily repulsed.

Until 19 November 1941, however, the Germans had actually prevented this occurring. Before this date, the German raiders had not allowed a British warship to approach closer than 10,500 yards, but on that fateful day Detmers kept his nerve and successfully drew *Sydney* to within 1,500 yards.

Curiously, within seventy-two hours of the *Sydney/Kormoran* action, another potential disaster developed in the South Atlantic. On 29 October the raider *Atlantis* rounded Cape Horn and entered the South Atlantic. The raider had been at large for eighteen months, steamed over 100,000 miles, had sunk or captured twenty-two ships and was now homeward bound. Hopes of a fast trip home, however, were dashed when Kapitän zur See Bernhard Rogge received orders to rendezvous with *U-68*.

Concerned about the number of times supply ships had been surprised while refuelling U-boats, and despite assurances that the naval

codes could not be broken, Rogge consulted with *U-68*'s skipper and proposed that they steam off to a position well away from the rendezvous point. Kapitänleutnant Merten agreed, and the refuelling of *U-68* was conducted in a more remote location. Rogge then received instructions to refuel *U-126* later in the month at the rendezvous position known as Lily 10.

On the morning of 22 November *Atlantis* and *U-126* met as scheduled. Against Rogge's better judgement the refuelling took place at the rendezvous because a defect had developed in *Atlantis*'s port engine.

Rogge's fears about being surprised at the rendezvous were well founded. Due to the advance arrangements made for *U-126*'s refuelling, the cryptanalysts at Bletchley Park had been given sufficient time to decipher the instructions issued to *U-126* and to pass on this Special Intelligence to the OIC. As a result, the heavy cruiser *Devonshire* was ordered to the likely rendezvous area to conduct a search for enemy raiders and supply ships. Sensibly, *Devonshire* was also warned that U-boats could be encountered.[51]

At 0816 on 22 November, lookouts on *Atlantis* sighted a three-funnelled cruiser.

Captain R.D. Oliver, RN, commanding *Devonshire*, had sent his Walrus on a dawn reconnaissance and on its return was informed that a merchant ship lay stopped in position 4° 20' South 18° 50' West. Speed was increased to 25 knots and course altered to intercept. At 0809 the masts of the vessel were sighted. Eleven minutes later, the Walrus was catapulted. The aircrew, supplied with photographs of known German raiders, had instructions to identify the ship.

As soon as the fuel hose and securing lines were cast off, Rogge turned away in order to place *U-126* between *Atlantis* and the enemy cruiser. *U-126* immediately dived, and the boat that had been ferrying supplies was left to its own devices. The Walrus, on sighting the boat, the abandoned fuel hose, and a small pool of oil, signalled 'SSS' to *Devonshire*. Warned by this U-boat sighting report, Oliver manoeuvred *Devonshire* at 26 knots to avoid torpedo attack and approached no closer than 12,000 yards.

At 0837, Oliver fired two warning salvoes in an attempt to prompt a response. Oliver was hoping that the vessel would either return the fire or scuttle. His main fear was a repetition of the *Cornwall/Pinguin* action. If the vessel was a supply ship carrying prisoners, it was hoped that it would scuttle, thereby avoiding unnecessary loss of life.[52]

Rogge, knowing the cruiser's 8-inch guns out-ranged him, knew his only hope lay in buying time, in which U-126 could manoeuvre into a favourable attack position. Accordingly, *Atlantis* was stopped while the W/T office began transmitting 'RRR RRR RRR' *Polyphemus* 4.20 S., 18.35 W. 0940 GMT'. Unfortunately for Rogge, U-126 had mistaken *Devonshire*'s warning shots for aircraft bombs. Concerned about its own survival, U-126 dived and left *Atlantis* to its fate.

The raider report had the desired effect, however, as Oliver was forced to consider the possibility that *Polyphemus* was genuine. According to information held by *Devonshire*, the real *Polyphemus* could have reached the area. Signals were exchanged, but Oliver failed to receive any satisfactory answers. As a result of the reported presence of a U-boat, Oliver could not close to investigate. His only option, therefore, was to break W/T silence to consult his C-IN-C.

While waiting for a reply, Oliver ordered the Walrus to report on the vessel's stern. The aircrew reported that the vessel had a cruiser stern, similar to *Atlantis*. When the C-IN-C advised that *Polyphemus* was not genuine, Oliver opened fire.

The first salvo was short, the second a straddle. From the third salvo onwards, *Atlantis* was hit repeatedly. Rogge, not wishing to disclose his vessel's true identity, withheld fire and prepared to abandon ship under cover of smoke. Oliver, unable to sight the target through the smoke, was forced to cease fire and manoeuvre into a more favourable position. During the lull Rogge gave the order to scuttle and abandon ship. *Devonshire*, however, soon began to register hits again. Shortly after 1000, the raider's secondary magazine blew up. *Atlantis* sank quickly by the stern.

Oliver, his work done, left the survivors to their fate. Because of the danger posed by the U-boat there was no question of stopping to rescue them. Although he had been unable to confirm the vessel's identity, the large number of survivors indicated that something more than a supply ship had been destroyed.

The Admiralty subsequently established that HMS *Devonshire* sank the raider *Atlantis* on 22 November 1941. The action was then seen as a classic

example of how to deal with a suspect vessel. But it could easily have become another embarrassing encounter for the Royal Navy. Special Intelligence had played a key role in the intercept, and the warning that a U-boat was present prevented Oliver making the same tragic mistake that Burnett made. With the knowledge that a U-boat was in the vicinity, Oliver knew he could not close with the vessel in order to make a positive identification or to prevent it from scuttling.

THE ADMIRALTY GOES INTO DAMAGE CONTROL

On 16 December 1941, obviously prompted by the loss of *Sydney*, the Admiralty issued a warning on the dangers of closing with enemy raiders.

Admiralty Message 1618A warned that 'enemy raiders will always disguise themselves and use appropriate name in any signal whether by an RRRR message on 500 kc/s or reply to a challenge'. It also considered that commanding officers were perhaps underestimating the offensive power of the raiders, the message noting that 'enemy raiders are often powerfully armed with guns and torpedoes and if fitted with modern RDF may be able to open fire even at long ranges with great accuracy'. In what appeared to be veiled criticism of Burnett's handling of *Sydney*, the Admiralty claimed that 'in no repetition no case so far has disguise adopted been such as should have deceived commanding officers had they trusted the negative intelligence that information of ship's move-ments had not been reported to them'.

Clearly, commanding officers were expected to trust the positive information that was contained on the VAI. Interestingly, though, there was no recommendation that W/T silence should be broken to confirm suspicions if a vessel was not on the VAI.

Furthermore, while the Admiralty had used the *Cornwall*, *Sydney* and *Devonshire* incidents as examples, Message 1618A failed to acknowledge the different circumstances of the *Devonshire* action.

Manwaring (*Cornwall*) and Burnett (*Sydney*) made their intercepts in the Indian Ocean where, in 1941, there was no threat of U-boat attack. Although the available intelligence warned them that they could be dealing with a raider, Manwaring and Burnett were obliged to fully

investigate the vessels they encountered. According to the instructions issued by the Admiralty, this involved close inspection and boarding if necessary. Oliver (*Devonshire*) on the other hand, was warned that U-boats could be encountered. This warning, and the subsequent evidence that a U-boat was present, prevented him closing to make a positive identification. Oliver therefore had no option but to break W/T silence to ascertain if *Polyphemus* was genuine.

Message 1618A also failed to clarify the Admiralty's position on the importance of capturing enemy merchant ships. Incredulously, this did not occur until 11 August 1942, when the Admiralty issued message 0734A, which was noted as being a continuation of message 1618A.[53]

Message 0734A was significant in that it not only clarified the merchant tonnage question and the requirement to maintain W/T silence, but also defined how suspicious vessels should be investigated.

On the question of identification, message 0734A said that 'if a ship can not immediately be definitely identified by information available and use of challenge procedure she should be regarded as suspect. Wireless silence may have to be broken to obtain confirmation of suspicion from shore authorities'. The recommended subsequent action on the identification of a suspect ship was to 'stop her and warn her that she will be fired on if she moves engines'. The 'ship should not be boarded but should be made to send a boat with all ship's papers, master and some of crew for interrogation'. It was also recommended that exposure to torpedo attack should be avoided and that the 'utmost vigilance should be observed at all times in presence of any suspected raider and fire opened immediately if any suspicious activity is observed'.

As for the merchant tonnage question, message 0734A stated that 'though it is preferable from point of view of British shipping tonnage to capture enemy merchant ships or supply ships rather than sink them, unless CO is satisfied that no risk is attached to process of capture he should sink an enemy ship rather than attempt to capture her'.

Clearly, by August 1942, the lesson had been learned. Following *Sydney*'s loss, no British warship attempted to capture an enemy merchant ship. Although the need to save merchant tonnage had not diminished, in fact quite the opposite, no one appeared willing to jeopardize their command for the sake of a capture.

An interesting example of how the circumstances had changed, but more importantly how the new Admiralty instructions were being adhered to was the *Adelaide/Ramses* incident.

At 1416 on 28 November 1942, the light cruiser HMAS *Adelaide*, forming part of the escort for convoy OW 1, sighted a ship off its port bow. The convoy at this time was approximately 800 miles north-west of Shark Bay. *Adelaide*, in company with the Dutch cruiser *Jacob van Heemskerck*, immediately increased speed to investigate, leaving the convoy under the protection of the Australian corvettes *Cessnock* and *Toowoomba*. Six minutes later, the suspect vessel was seen to alter course away. At 1446, it transmitted a 'RRRR' report on the commercial wavelength, identifying itself as the *Tartyang*. When no ship of this name could be found in the books carried by *Adelaide*, Captain J.C.D. Esdaile, RAN, broke W/T silence to confirm the vessel's authenticity with the Naval Officer in Charge, Fremantle. Unfortunately, no reply was received. Esdaile noted in his report that he assumed the signal did not get through. When the range reduced to 15,000 yards Esdaile ordered action stations.

At 1519 the vessel transmitted another 'RRRR' report, this time in the name of the *Taiyang*. Esdaile and his Navigating Officer, Lieutenant J.W. Penney, RANR, then began the task of trying to confirm the vessel's identity. It was noted that while the vessel was not unlike the description given for *Taiyang*, the shapes of the stern and bridge were different, as were the number of samson posts. The vessel also failed to respond to the secret challenge, and failed to answer a W/T message transmitted to it. Penney, however, produced a pack of 'German Armoured (*sic*) Merchant Vessels and Merchant Ships' identification cards and discovered that the vessel bore a strong resemblance to the German *Ramses*.

Shortly after 1530, with the range now down to 12,000 yards, the vessel transmitted 'YYY 23.9 S 23.9 S 99.25 99.25 PUL'. At the same time it began lowering boats. Ten minutes later an explosion was observed on the after part of the ship. This explosion produced a dense cloud of smoke, which quickly enveloped the ship, leaving only the masts and the top of the funnel visible.

Esdaile considered this to be a hostile act, and at 1544 opened fire from a range of 10,600 yards. This ceased at 1552 when the vessel suddenly sank. *Heemskerck*, which had joined in the firing, was ordered to

rejoin the convoy while *Adelaide* moved in to pick up survivors. The survivors comprised seventy-eight Germans, ten Norwegian prisoners, a pig and a dog.

From the Germans it was learned that the vessel was *Ramses*. They had departed from the Japanese port of Yokohama on 10 October and were attempting to run the blockade. When the captain realized that escape was impossible, he ordered *Ramses* to be scuttled.

Esdaile subsequently reported that:

> In deciding to open fire, it was visualized that one of two things had happened:
>
> (a) The ship was an armed raider, had sent away a 'panic' party in boats, had started a smoke screen to hide preparations on board, and was preparing a surprise in the event of ADELAIDE closing to investigate to within effective gun and torpedo range.
>
> (b) The ship was unarmed, had blown scuttling charges, and abandoned ship.
>
> The answer in both cases was considered to be to open fire:
>
> (a) for obvious reasons and
>
> (b) to hasten the end and enable me to get back to the convoy which by this time was hull down.[54]

Clearly, Esdaile had acted in accordance with the instructions contained in Admiralty message 0734A.

From this study of the tonnage war, it is clear that on 19 November 1941 Burnett may also have acted in accordance with Admiralty instructions, specifically those relating to the capture of enemy merchant ships.

Yet despite the circumstantial evidence, the question remains. What really prompted Burnett to close to within 1,500 yards of the supposed *Straat Malakka*? Did he believe he was dealing with a friendly merchantman, or did he suspect he was dealing with a raider supply ship? If it was the latter, was he attempting a capture in accordance with Admiralty instructions?

Captain Joseph Burnett, RAN,
on the bridge of *Sydney*.
Australian War Memorial negative no. 128096

THE INTERCEPTION

G. HERMON Gill's account of the loss of HMAS *Sydney* raised unpalatable questions about Burnett's handling of *Sydney* on 19 November.

Gill wondered why Burnett did not use his aircraft, or why he failed to keep his distance and use *Sydney*'s superior speed and armament. He also wondered why Burnett 'did not confirm his suspicions by asking Navy Office by wireless if *Straat Malakka* was in the area'. He raised these questions in 1957 and wrote that they were 'questions that can never be answered'.[1]

Gill, however, was perhaps being negative or even defeatist in his attitude, for a study of the *Kormoran* survivors' statements must answer some of these questions.

Gill, an officer closely involved in the events subsequent to *Sydney*'s loss, accepted the German claims as being accurate. When introducing his account of *Sydney*'s last action, he wrote that the story had been 'pieced together through exhaustive interrogation of *Kormoran*'s survivors. No room was left to doubt as to its accuracy'.

Notwithstanding Gill's views, there are doubts about the accuracy of the German claims. Some believe that the Germans gave false information to avoid possible charges of war crimes.

These doubts and beliefs stem primarily from the sometimes puzzling and contradictory statements made by the Germans. A study of their statements, however, reveals that they were also puzzled by certain aspects of the encounter. Specifically, none could understand why *Sydney* closed to such a short range.

Another detail that emerges is that many survivors, because of their battle station, only had a limited view of the intercept and action. Others, stationed below decks, saw nothing at all. Most only learned the full story once they abandoned ship and began exchanging information in the lifeboats and rafts. Consequently, as a result of each man adding to, omitting, exaggerating or understating what he saw or heard, nearly every aspect of the encounter has differing versions of what supposedly happened.

Clearly, only a small proportion of *Kormoran*'s crew was capable of providing a complete account of what actually happened. Perhaps only the bridge personnel, the weapons officers and the rangefinder operators, who, because of their duties, were fortunate enough to be able to witness the entire engagement from beginning to end. In this group are Detmers (captain), Skeries (gunnery officer), Brinkman (anti-aircraft officer), Greter (torpedo officer), von Gösseln (battle watch officer), Messerschmidt (mines officer), Meyer (navigating officer), Ahlbach (yeoman of signals), Otto Jürgensen (quartermaster), and Hans Peiler (rangefinger operator). Unfortunately, some of these 'key' witnesses refused to discuss the engagement with the interrogating officers, as was their right as prisoners of war.

The prize officers, who took up a battle station at the stern of the ship before the start of the action, could possibly be added to this group. Bunjes was one of these officers, and he gave a great deal of information on the intercept and action phases. What his battle station duties were is not clear. As he said he 'had no special job, just to be ready for an emergency'.[2] Because of his vague description of his battle station, it is difficult to verify his credentials. Although Bunjes may have been in a position to witness the events he described, it is conceivable that he offered information that was based on hearsay.[3]

To get the least corrupted account of *Sydney*'s approach to *Kormoran*, it is necessary to focus on the claims made by the men best placed to witness it. In particular, the claims made by Detmers, for he, above all others, was ideally placed to see and understand all that happened. Besides being a key witness, Detmers, as commanding officer, also bore ultimate responsibility for the loss of *Kormoran*. More importantly, in terms of accountability, Detmers would also have been responsible for ensuring that an 'after action report', detailing how *Kormoran* had been lost, was prepared. Regardless of what the Australian authorities were told, an accurate report on the loss of *Kormoran* should have been prepared (or memorized) for the German authorities.[4]

Before trying to understand how *Sydney* was lost, we must look at why *Kormoran* was lost, and why it was where it was on 19 November 1941.

The simple answer to this question can be found in Detmers's operational orders.[5] Detmers's primary task was the 'execution of cruiser warfare in foreign waters'. By German definition, cruiser warfare meant the destruction or capture of enemy merchant ships.

It was anticipated that by waging war against merchant shipping in distant waters the enemy would be compelled to redeploy his forces to counter the threat. The unexpected appearance of commerce raiders in remote areas of the globe was expected to force the enemy to convoy its ships in these otherwise 'safe' areas and to increase protection for this shipping. This would hinder trade and draw warships away from the more crucial theatres.

Although not as successful as some other raiders in disrupting trade and forcing the redeployment of enemy forces, Detmers nevertheless managed to sink or capture eleven ships in eleven months.[6] And although he was not satisfied with this figure, his orders stated that the 'long term restriction and harassing of the enemy is more important to the success of the operation than a high record of sinkings accompanied by a rapid deterioration of the auxiliary cruiser'. In other words, the success of the cruise would not depend on the number of vessels sunk, but on the number of months Detmers could remain at sea.

To assist Detmers, fuel and provisions were supplied to the raider as required, one such resupply being carried out less than four weeks before *Kormoran* was sunk.

On 16 October 1941, Detmers rendezvoused with the supply ship *Kulmerland* about 1,000 miles west of Fremantle in position 32° 30' South 97° East. *Kulmerland* was detached on 26 October, having supplied *Kormoran* with 3,328 tons of fuel-oil and enough supplies to keep the raider going until June 1942.

According to Detmers's post-war account, following the resupply he took *Kormoran* towards the coast of Western Australia. He said that his intention was to lay mines. A signal from Germany, which reported a westbound convoy in the vicinity of Cape Leeuwin, however, altered these plans.

Although he did not reveal his intentions (to lay mines) to his captors during the war, Detmers's claim is consistent with his operational orders. In the minelaying section, Detmers was advised that Cape Otway, Adelaide and Fremantle were considered choice targets for *Kormoran's* mines.

The warning of the westbound convoy, escorted by HMS *Cornwall* (actually HMAS *Canberra*), forced Detmers to avoid contact by steaming north. He claimed that he proposed to scour the neighbourhood around Shark Bay and if no vessels were found he would lay mines. *Kormoran's* war diary reveals that Detmers had considered mining Geraldton or Carnarvon in August, but owing to the sparse traffic entering these ports, he decided against it.

Further support for Detmers's claim can be found in the interrogation notes for *Kormoran's* assistant navigator, Otto Jürgensen. During the interrogations at Harvey, Jürgensen revealed that they 'had tried to lay mines near [the] Western Australian coast, but *Sydney* interrupted them'.[7]

Curiously, however, in a 1998 interview with Australian journalist David Kennedy, *Kormoran's* former mines officer, Heinz Messerschmidt, claimed that the minelaying story was 'rubbish'. For safety reasons, mines were not armed until required. Arming involved the insertion of the fuses and the fitting of the long strikers, or horns. It was a laborious and time-consuming task. Messerschmidt indicated that twenty-four hours' notice was required before the mines could be deployed and he said to Kennedy that he received no such notice from Detmers.

Despite Detmers's stated intentions, many remain unconvinced and, because there is doubt, a number of theories about Detmers's 'real motives' have emerged over the years. These range from a secret rendezvous with a Japanese submarine to a deliberate attack on *Aquitania* or *Sydney* or both.

Although there was never any real evidence to support the claim of Japanese involvement, this theory has gained a great deal of popularity. But it should be understood that the Japanese submarine theory is just that—a theory.[8]

Similarly, there is no evidence to show that Detmers was hoping to 'ambush' *Sydney*, although the claim that he was planning to attack *Aquitania* does warrant consideration. This claim was first made by *Kormoran* survivors picked up by *Aquitania*, so it has a 'ring of truth' about it. A comment by one of the survivors, however, indicates that the original *Aquitania* claim may have been nothing more than a sardonic remark. On asking a steward the name of the vessel that had rescued him, and given the name *Aquitania*, the survivor called the steward a liar, as that ship 'had been sunk nearly a year ago'.[9]

It is known that Detmers was receiving some intelligence on shipping movements in the Indian Ocean, but it is doubtful that such information would have been sufficiently accurate to enable him to attempt an attack on *Aquitania*. Even if Detmers was aware of *Aquitania*'s proposed route and timetable, there was no guarantee that such a valuable vessel would be sailing without escort. The only warships capable of escorting a vessel the size and speed of *Aquitania* were cruisers, and an armed clash with a cruiser was to be avoided at all costs. It is also relevant that Detmers's orders stated that passenger liners were also to be avoided. Besides the fact that Britain had armed many such vessels (AMCs), liners were considered 'a considerable burden for auxiliary cruisers owing to the strength of the crew and the number of the passengers'.[10]

Considering Detmers's orders, it is doubtful that he was attempting an attack on *Aquitania*. Given the raider tactic of prowling recognized shipping lanes in the hope of sighting a victim, it is more likely that Detmers was simply searching for enemy shipping when intercepted.

Although *Kormoran*'s course when sighted (025°) would have taken the raider to the east of the Sunda Strait–Fremantle shipping lane, with sunset approaching, this would have been a sound tactical move. Once the sun had set, the raider would have been difficult to detect against the

darkening eastern horizon, and potential victims would have been beautifully silhouetted against the lighter western skyline. When *Sydney* appeared on the horizon, however, the hunter became the hunted.

To understand how *Sydney* was lost, it is necessary to establish what actually happened after *Kormoran* was sighted on that fateful day, principally how *Sydney* approached the disguised raider.

In general, the prisoners indicated that *Sydney* drew steadily nearer from a position off their starboard quarter while the exchange of signals took place. By the time the exchange was complete, *Sydney* had reduced the range to less than a mile and had taken up station on their starboard beam. In other words, *Sydney* had sighted them, given chase, and had not varied the angle of approach until within a mile of the supposed *Straat Malakka*.

Despite this rather direct and incautious style of approach, the authorities did not question the German claims. It was this very acceptance of the prisoners' description of *Sydney*'s approach that raised the questions about Burnett's handling of *Sydney*. But if we accept the prisoners' claims and at the same time question Burnett's handling of *Sydney*, the Navy's readiness to accept a number of anomalies in the German account must also be questioned.

Despite the general acceptance of the German account of the action, the Australian naval authorities did have cause to doubt the authenticity of some of the prisoners' earlier claims. This attitude was allayed somewhat, however, when Detmers's and Ahlbach's statements were examined because both men surrendered information that could not have been fabricated.

When asked about the exchange of signals, Detmers said that shortly after the initial sighting the cruiser began signalling the letters 'NNP'. Ahlbach stated that the cruiser signalled the letters 'NNF' or 'NNP' by 'searchlight' (signal lamp) when still some 7 miles away.

Neither of these signals made sense to the Germans. The interrogating officers consulted their signal books. It appeared that *Sydney* had actually signalled 'NNJ'. This signal, which was apparently seldom used in the early war years, meant 'You should make your signal letters'. According to Detmers and Ahlbach, *Sydney* made this signal for nearly half an hour without receiving a reply.[11]

Although this could be considered a long time, it was not unreasonable given the circumstances. At this stage of the intercept *Sydney* was simply trying to identify a merchantman that had correctly turned away on sighting an unidentified vessel. As the merchantman was refusing to acknowledge his signal, Burnett had to reduce the range to make a visual identification. Given the distance and the relative speeds of the two vessels, this would take time.[12] Although Burnett could have speeded up proceedings by demanding that the vessel stop, he may have thought it was pointless. If the vessel were not going to acknowledge the 'NNJ' signal, it probably would not acknowledge a stop signal either. Burnett had little option but to persevere with the 'NNJ' signal while he closed the range.

When the range reduced sufficiently, Burnett decided to try a flag hoist. According to Ahlbach, when they did not answer the three-letter signal, the cruiser made the two-letter signal 'Hoist your signal letters' ('VH'). Although this signal was understood, Detmers instructed Ahlbach to keep the answering pendant code flag at the dip. This signified that the cruiser's signals could not be clearly distinguished. Detmers claimed that after waiting a suitable time, he instructed Ahlbach to raise the answering pendant to the top and hoist 'PKQI', the signal letters for *Straat Malakka*.[13]

To convince the warship that *Straat Malakka* was genuine, Ahlbach fumbled with the flags before eventually hoisting them to the triatic stay between the foremast and funnel. As *Sydney* was closing from their starboard quarter (10° off their stern according to Ahlbach), these flags could not be clearly seen. This prompted another signal to hoist the flags clear so that they could be distinguished. Ahlbach complied by lengthening the halyard and drawing it to starboard.

It was this apparent inefficiency in signalling that led the interrogating officers to conclude that it was a *'ruse-de-guerre'*. In other words, it was assumed that the Germans had deliberately drawn out the exchange of signals to lure *Sydney* closer. After the war, Detmers said that this had been his strategy. Ahlbach's wartime statements, however, do not support this view. On 9 December 1941, Ahlbach told the interrogating officers that he had drawn the halyard to starboard so that the cruiser could see the signal flags because they 'did not wish to lure the cruiser nearer', implying that at this stage Detmers was still hoping to avoid a confrontation.

Kormoran, resupplying a U-boat in the mid-Atlantic in
March 1941. *Sydney* would have been presented with
a similar view of *Kormoran* during the exchange of
signals. The difficulties of trying to identify a vessel by
its hallmark features from a position astern are obvious.
Bibliothek für Zeitgeschichte, Stuttgart

Regardless of the strategy, Burnett now knew that he was apparently
closing the Dutch motorship *Straat Malakka*. Consultation of Lloyd's
Register would have shown that it was a new ship, constructed in 1939
and registered in Batavia. Consultation of the VAI, however, would have
shown that *Straat Malakka* was not expected to be in the area. Unknown
to Detmers, and probably Burnett, the real *Straat Malakka* was on the
other side of the Indian Ocean, having left the port of Beira on the east
coast of Africa the same day.

As *Straat Malakka* would not have been on the VAI, it would be logical
to assume that Burnett would have wanted more information. According
to Detmers's post-war account, *Sydney* asked where they were bound. He
claimed he replied, 'Batavia'. Ahlbach's wartime statements supported
this claim. Ahlbach said that the cruiser asked by light and flags where
they were bound, and they replied Batavia.[14]

It is not clear if Burnett then asked for the port of departure, but Detmers said that he was asked the nature of his cargo. To this he replied, 'Piece-goods'.

What interested the interrogating officers was not the exchange of signals, but the confusion caused by one signal. Ahlbach said that after the cruiser had asked them for their destination it made another two-flag hoist. Although he could not remember the actual signal, he clearly remembered his bewilderment after consulting the code book to establish its meaning. He said it meant 'Have you suffered damage from cyclone, typhoon or tempest?'

The 1931 International Code of Signals contained two references to cyclones and typhoons. 'GY' ('Cyclone, hurricane, typhoon is approaching. You should put to sea at once.') and 'IK' ('You should prepare for a cyclone, hurricane or typhoon.')

Neither of these two signals made sense to the interrogating officers either. That was until the secret call for *Straat Malakka* was discovered to be 'IIKP'. It was then realized that *Sydney* had made the signal 'IK', this being the secret challenge.

The procedure was for a warship (or aircraft) to challenge a suspect vessel by signalling the two inner letters of that vessel's secret call sign. The vessel was then expected to reply by signalling the two outer letters of its secret call sign. Unfortunately for Detmers, he did not know *Straat Malakka*'s secret call sign, and could not reply correctly.[15]

Because *Sydney* had signalled 'IK', and Ahlbach had mistaken it for a storm warning, the authorities accepted this as proof that the prisoners were telling the truth.

The only puzzling aspect of the 'IK' signal was that it was supposedly followed by the signal 'Hoist your secret call', although Ahlbach claimed that the cruiser flashed the signal 'Show your secret sign'. That either of these signals was made is unusual, as there appears to have been no provision for such a signal in the challenge procedure.

Even more confusing was Detmers's wartime claim (1 December 1941) that the cruiser ordered him to stop. This order was apparently made before the plain-language demand for the secret call. Detmers's claim, however, was not supported by Ahlbach, who said that the cruiser did not signal stop. Although there is no ready answer for these conflicting views,

it would be reasonable to assume that Ahlbach, whose job it was to read *Sydney*'s signals, would have been more likely to read them correctly.

It is noteworthy that the demand for the secret call was made shortly before fire was opened. During this final stage of the exchange of signals, Detmers would have been under a great deal of stress. Although there was still a chance that the cruiser would signal 'Proceed' and depart, he had to assume that action was inevitable. In which case, he would have been trying to decide when the critical point had been reached, the point where he would declare identity and open fire.

In the International Code the single letter signal 'I' meant 'I am directing my course to port'. The signal 'K' meant 'Stop instantly', a signal that Detmers would have recognised in any situation. It is therefore possible that Detmers mistakenly interpreted the 'K' in the 'IK' signal as a demand to stop. If this was so, once Detmers thought he had been ordered to stop, it is doubtful that he would have bothered to read any subsequent signals. The order to stop at this late stage would have indicated that the critical point had been reached. It meant that action was imminent, as the cruiser would open fire if he refused to stop, and stopping was out of the question, because he would need manoeuvring speed once fire was opened.

Detmers did not repeat his 'stop' claim in his post-war account. It is possible, therefore, that Detmers was mistaken, and that he made this claim on 1 December before he had a chance to discuss the subject with his fellow officers.

As the interrogating officers understood it, by the time the exchange of signals was complete, *Sydney* had closed to within a mile of the disguised raider. Then, when Burnett asked for the secret call, Detmers decamouflaged and opened fire.

In accepting the prisoners' claims, the Australian authorities appear to have accepted that Burnett took no precautions and literally steamed straight into Detmers's arms. Strangely, no one appears to have questioned why Burnett acted in the way that was alleged. Even Commander Dechaineux, when he concluded that Burnett had been deceived, failed to consider what might have prompted Burnett to close, although his initial consideration that the inefficiency of merchant ships in challenge and reply procedure contributed to *Sydney*'s loss provides a clue to his thoughts.

There are a number of theories on why Burnett closed, but the most obvious reason, and one that is indirectly supported by the prisoners' statements, is that he had cause to doubt the merchantman's claimed identity.[16]

If Burnett was confident that *Straat Malakka* was genuine, there was no need to close. If he suspected that the merchantman was not genuine, however, he had only two basic courses of action to follow. He could attempt to positively identify the vessel, or he could allow it to proceed. Clearly, the latter was not an option at all.

The question, therefore, is not what prompted Burnett to close, but what caused him to be suspicious.

Gill contended that if Burnett was suspicious, he should have used his aircraft, or broken w/t silence to consult with shore authorities. He also argued that Burnett should have stood off and forced the issue with his main armament. This is what Farncomb had done earlier in 1941 when he encountered *Coburg* and *Ketty Brövig*. Unfortunately, Farncomb expended an enormous amount of 8-inch shell in resolving the issue, earning unfavourable comment at Navy Office. Significantly, Burnett was among those who reviewed Farncomb's report of the action and passed comment on the ammunition expenditure.[17]

Although it has been claimed that this criticism of Farncomb may have influenced Burnett's handling of *Sydney* on 19 November, the argument does not take into account the different circumstances of the two incidents. Farncomb was involved in a search for enemy vessels. During the search he encountered two suspicious ships, which refused to reply to his signals, and fled before his distinctively British cruiser. Burnett, on the other hand, was returning to Fremantle after routine escort duty. He encountered a vessel which also ran, but answered his signals, albeit reluctantly.

Put simply, Burnett's circumstances did not warrant the use of gunfire.

Within an hour of first sighting, Burnett obtained all the information he could expect to obtain from the supposed *Straat Malakka*. He had done so without the use of his aircraft, without breaking w/t silence and without endangering his command.

According to the German claims, Burnett established that the name of the vessel was *Straat Malakka* and that it was carrying 'piece-goods' (general cargo) to Batavia. It is possible that he also established that the last port of call was Fremantle. If Detmers and Ahlbach are to be believed, Burnett obtained this information while *Sydney* was still in a relatively safe position of 8,000 to 9,000 metres off their starboard quarter.[18]

Although the vessel's name, cargo, port of destination, and possibly last port of call was not much to work with, this basic information was all that Burnett needed. Once he established the vessel's name, he could check the VAI to see if it should be in the area. He could also consult the shipping recognition books to see if the features of the vessel before him corresponded with the description given in his books.

If the supposed *Straat Malakka* had been on the VAI, it could have been considered genuine. If its overall dimensions, tonnage and hallmark features corresponded with those given for *Straat Malakka*, it could have been permitted to proceed.

As the real *Straat Malakka* was off the east coast of Africa, it would not have been on Burnett's VAI and Burnett should have been suspicious, particularly so if Detmers claimed that his last port of call was Fremantle because this was also *Sydney*'s last port of call.

The claimed destination of Batavia should also have created suspicion. When *Sydney* was first sighted, *Kormoran* was steering a course of 025°, which was not the course one would steer if one were making for Batavia. Evidence that Burnett saw *Kormoran* on the original course came from the prisoners.

During Detmers's interrogation on 2 December, the notetaker recorded that 'when raider saw cruiser their yard arms were well over the horizon, so look-out of cruiser must have seen the raider haul across', implying that *Sydney* saw *Kormoran* alter course. Two days later, *Kormoran*'s navigating officer, Meyer, said that their course had been 024° and that they did not alter course 'until it was certain that the ship was a cruiser of the "Perth" class'. Further support comes from *Sydney*'s early smoke development, indicating that Burnett's lookouts had already made a sighting and steam was being raised to increase speed.

Detmers's turn westwards should also have aroused suspicion. It is more likely that a genuine Dutchman, fleeing from what he believed was an enemy warship, would have steered towards the coast and possible help.

Just before 1800, a critical point had been reached. Burnett was confronted with a suspicious vessel that could not be permitted to proceed until its identity had been established. At this stage there was no real need to use the Walrus, and breaking W/T silence to consult shore authorities would probably only provide Burnett with the information he already had, namely, that the *Straat Malakka* should not be in the area. In which case he would have broken W/T silence for no purpose, and he would still have to establish the vessel's true identity.

Realistically, there was only one option open to Burnett. He had to identify the vessel by visual inspection. Such an inspection should have been at the maximum range that conditions would permit, and preferably from a beam-on position. If he wished to speed up proceedings, he could also have ordered the vessel to stop.

If the supposed *Straat Malakka*'s silhouette and hallmark features appeared correct, a close inspection or boarding would be the next step. Once identity was confirmed, *Straat Malakka* could be permitted to proceed. If the hallmark features did not correspond with those given for *Straat Malakka*, then suspicion would deepen. At this point the vessel would have to be treated as a raider or raider supply ship.

It is quite possible that Burnett was on the verge of ordering the supposed *Straat Malakka* to stop, or was preparing to manoeuvre onto the vessel's beam to conduct a medium range identification check, when a new factor entered the equation. With questionable timing, Detmers transmitted a Q message. The time was approximately 1800.

THE Q SIGNAL

On 8 December 1941, W/T operator Hans Linke told his interrogators that two Q messages were transmitted shortly before the battle with the cruiser. He claimed that a position of 26° South 111° East was given, followed by the time in Greenwich Mean Time, then the name *Straat Malakka*. Linke also said the signal had been transmitted on '200 watt power' and was meant to be picked up in the Dutch East Indies. As for the purpose of the Q signal, he said it was 'intended to distract attention from them'.

The following day, W/T operator Ernst Pachmann offered similar information. He too had been questioned on 8 December but had refused to answer questions about his part in the action. After a night in the cells, he decided to co-operate. He admitted that two Q messages had been transmitted about ten minutes before fire was opened, adding that they had tried to avoid a fight. In describing the message sent, Pachmann claimed that it was 'QQQQ 111E 26s 1100 GMT Straat Malakka' and emphasized that they gave the name instead of the international letters ('PKQI').

Linke's and Pachmann's statements give a good account of what was supposedly transmitted, but Detmers's offering was particularly vague. In his post-war account he said that the signal 'QQQ Straat Malakka' was transmitted. He gave no position and no time. This was at odds with the wartime statements of Linke and Pachmann.

That a Q signal was transmitted was confirmed by two independent sources: Geraldton Radio and the tug Uco. Unfortunately, neither party received the complete transmission. Curiously, the fragments received were not entirely consistent with what was claimed to have been transmitted.

Geraldton Radio reported that at 1805 on 19 November it received a weak unintelligible message that ended with '7C 11115E 1000 GMT'. As nothing else was received, it would appear that Geraldton picked up the final part of Kormoran's second transmission. The petty officer telegraphist in Uco picked up even less. At 1803, he heard a faint Q signal, apparently complete but unreadable. Two minutes later he heard 'QQQQ QQQQ' followed by an unintelligible group of figures but ending with '1000 GMT'.

Both reports indicate that the second transmission ended with the time and the letters 'GMT'. But if the statements made by Pachmann and Linke are to be accepted, the letters 'GMT' should have been followed by 'Straat Malakka'. Both recipients also recorded the time given in the signal as 1000z, although Pachmann claimed that the time sent was 1100z. As a result, there are two substantial inconsistencies in the statements made by Pachmann, which also throw doubt on Linke's statements.

It would also appear unusual that 'Straat Malakka' would be transmitted at the end of the signal. Normally, a vessel transmitting a Q signal

would identify itself before giving its position. The purpose of these signals was to let the authorities know that a particular ship was under threat. Often, a vessel under attack did not have time to transmit a complete report. The priority, therefore, was the transmission of the ship's name or signal letters.

Regardless of what was transmitted, the Q signal should have given Burnett further cause to be suspicious. If the Q signal was transmitted in the name of the *Straat Malakka*, it was somewhat late, to say the least. The merchantman had turned and run at 1700, but the Q signal was not transmitted until 1800. If the master of the supposed *Straat Malakka* was genuinely concerned for his ship's safety, the Q signal should have been transmitted as soon as *Sydney* was seen to alter course towards him. To wait an hour defied logic. Besides, by 1800, it should have been patently obvious to the merchantman that *Sydney* was a warship, not a disguised merchant raider.

The position given in the Q signal is also of interest. Linke claimed that the position given was 26° South 111° East. Although Pachmann supported this, he indicated that the longitude was given before the latitude. The signal received by Geraldton Radio gave a longitude of 111° 15' East, and a latitude of '7C'.

The author Michael Montgomery suggests that '7C' represents a latitude of 27° South.[19] If this assumption is correct, then the position given in the Q signal was 27° South 111° 15' East, a position some 30 nautical miles south-east of Detmers's claimed action position of 26° 32' South 111° East.[20]

As Linke indicated that the Q signal was meant to distract attention from them, it is conceivable that the position given in the Q signal was 27° South 111° 15' East, and that the Q signal was transmitted in the hope that it would draw *Sydney* away.

By 1800, when the signal was transmitted, Detmers had just about run out of options to avoid a confrontation. He knew that he could not out-run the cruiser, and at a range of around 9,000 metres, he could not out-shoot it. Although well within range of his 15-centimetre guns, an artillery duel with a cruiser at such a distance would be suicidal. If he was forced into action, Detmers's only real hope lay in drawing the cruiser nearer so that the small calibre weapons and torpedoes could be

employed. Either way, his chances of survival were slim. Detmers and his men knew about *Pinguin*'s loss and were under no illusions about what would happen to them if they were cornered by an enemy warship.

It is therefore quite possible that the Q signal was transmitted with the intention of deceiving Burnett into thinking that a raider was attacking another ship. The position of 27° South 111° 15' East would have been over the horizon in relation to *Sydney*'s position, and 30 miles represented an hour's steaming time for a Perth class cruiser. If the position given in the Q signal was over the horizon, Detmers may have been trying to 'lose' *Sydney* so that he could escape.

The only puzzling aspect of this scenario is that both Linke and Pachmann gave a Q signal position of 26° South 111° East. As both men were W/T operators and apparently knew a great deal about the sending of the signal, it would be logical to assume that they also knew what was actually transmitted. It is also possible that one of them was personally involved in transmitting the signal. Alternatively, neither man transmitted the signal.

During the interrogations at Harvey, Linke and Pachmann were billeted in Hut No.30 with fellow W/T operators Nolden, Marmann, and Jakubek. When these men were questioned, they refused to talk about the transmission of the Q signal, although it is likely that they discussed the subject among themselves in the hut. Linke and Pachmann, therefore, may have surrendered information that had been gleaned from the other men, which may not have been entirely accurate.

On the position of 26° South 111° East, it is noteworthy that a number of prisoners gave these co-ordinates as the battle position. This is curious, because many prisoners stressed that Detmers was secretive and rarely told them the ship's position. That many were able to give a position for the battle suggests that they were at least told where they were before they abandoned ship, this being a vital piece of information if the boats were expected to make a landfall. In this context, it will be remembered that Linke was in one of the boats that succeeded in reaching the coast and that Linke was able to tell the authorities in Carnarvon that *Kormoran* had been in position 26° South 111° East when they sighted a 'convoy of 5 to 7 ships', escorted by a Perth class cruiser. Linke, therefore, may not have known, or could not remember, the position given in the Q signal,

and gave the battle position instead. This could explain why Linke and Pachmann's description of the Q signal was at odds with what was received by *Uco* and at Geraldton.

There was another facet to the Q signal, namely, the inclusion of a transmission time. Providing a transmission time in a Q signal was not unusual, but giving the time with the letters 'GMT' was. Although Greenwich Mean Time was the acknowledged time to use in signals, denoting the time with the letters 'GMT' would have been considered odd.

Although Burnett would not have been aware of it, in October 1941, Germany updated its instructions for emergency signals from ships at sea. When being pursued by the enemy, German ships were to transmit British type 'RRRR' or 'QQQQ' messages on the international distress frequency. They were to include their secret German call sign, but with the addition of the letter 'G' at the front of the call sign. This would signify that the vessel was facing an emergency. It was anticipated that British land stations would repeat the signal and, by monitoring such stations, Germany would hear of the vessel's plight.[21]

Although *Kormoran* does not appear to have transmitted a secret call sign prefixed by the letter 'G', it is conceivable that the 'G' in 'GMT' was intended to let Germany know that *Schiff 41* was in trouble. By way of comparison, it is perhaps significant that when *Atlantis* was intercepted by *Devonshire* on 22 November the raider transmitted 'RRR RRR RRR *POLYPHEMUS* 4 20s 18 35w 0940 GMT'.

Linke's statement that the signal was meant to be picked up in the Dutch East Indies suggests that it may have been intended that the Dutch receive the signal and repeat it, although there is no evidence of the Dutch receiving the Q signal.

This is not surprising because, given the time of day, it is doubtful that a 600m/500kc signal transmitted at 200 watts would have reached the Dutch East Indies. It is also questionable whether the signal would have reached Perth. The only land station known to have acknowledged the Q signal was Geraldton, and although Detmers claimed (post-war) that Perth acknowledged his Q signal, there is no evidence to support this claim. Considering the request made by Geraldton, asking all ships if there was anything to report, it is not inconceivable that *Kormoran's* W/T operators heard Geraldton's call and mistook it for the Applecross W/T station in Perth.

The Q signal should have increased suspicion, but according to Detmers's post-war account, Burnett's only reaction was to ask for the secret call. There is evidence, however, to suggest that Burnett reacted differently. Curiously, it was Detmers who provided it.

On the night of 10–11 January 1945, Detmers and nineteen other prisoners escaped from Dhurringile. Detmers was recaptured near Shepparton on 18 January and when searched was found to be carrying a small notebook or diary. When it was discovered that Detmers had encoded entries in the notebook it was confiscated and sent to a secret cryptanalysis unit in Melbourne (Fleet Radio Unit, Melbourne or 'FRUMEL') for analysis. It was subsequently established that Detmers had used the Vigenère grid cipher to record two accounts of the action between *Sydney* and *Kormoran*.[23]

One of these accounts, in the form of a deck log, was given the title 'Action Report'. The other was in the form of an engine room log and titled as such. By 15 July 1945, both accounts had been decrypted and translated into English.[24]

DETMERS'S 'ACTION REPORT'

Wednesday 19.11 Course 25, Speed 11; 26.34 South, 111 East. [Wind] SSE 3 to 4, Sea 3 medium swell from SW. Very clear.

1555 Lookout JANSEN reports sailing ship in sight on port bow, bearing approx. 20 degrees true. Report corrected currently to 2 sailing ships, several vessels, 2 smoke clouds, apparently escort.

Alarm. Turned away to port on to 260. Full speed ahead.

1600 Cruiser made out, identified as PERTH class, on course. South. Course 250 into the sun. Approach of darkness not due before 1900. Producing large quantities of smoke ourselves. Engine room reports: No.4 engine out of order. Speed therefore approx. 14 knots.

1605 Cruiser turns towards; range over 150 hm [15,000 metres].

Approaches slowly making 'NNJ' repeatedly on searchlight. Hoist signal for STRAAT [*Straat Malakka*]. Appreciate situation and make decision.

1645   No. 4 engine running again on 8 cylinders. Speed 14 maintained; at 80 hm ceased measurement with 3 metre rangefinder, for reasons of disguise, continued ranging with 1.35 metre rangefinder. Continual signalling.

Cruiser approaches slowly on starboard quarter showing narrow silhouette.

1700   Report on 600 metres QQQ STRAAT EBFS. PERTH radio repeats and requests further report if necessary.

1715   Cruiser draws away on starboard beam 90 hm [9,000 metres] distant.

1725   Morse signal in (MAKS): HOIST YOUR SECRET CALL.

Further delay can only make situation worse. (Cruiser) stops engines, thus has not the least suspicion. Therefore

1730   Removal of disguise. Dutch flag struck, War flag flies clear of main mast. Time taken 6 seconds. Guns and torpedo given permission to fire.

Enemy drops slowly astern.

2 torpedoes inclination 80, speed 14, point of aim bow and stern. Also slow alteration to 260 so as not to interfere with guns. First salvo single shot short. Gun range 13. Second salvo. Third fourth fifth, up 400. About 4 seconds later scores hit on bridge and control position, followed immediately by full salvo from enemy, over no hits. Then approx. 2 salvoes at 5 second interval. Hit amidships, aircraft, bridge. Correction for deflection left between forward turrets. A/A MG's and starboard 3.7 effective against bridge, torpedo tubes and A/A armament.

Up to fifth salvo no reply, then 'C' turret well and fast. Hits in funnel and engine room. 'D' turret only two or three

salvoes, all of them over. 'A' and 'B' turrets no longer (firing). At about eighth or ninth salvo torpedo hit forward of 'A' and 'B' turrets. Torpedo passed short distance ahead.

Stern almost completely submerged. Course 260 maintained since torpedo tubes not manned because of A/A MG fire.

Enemy turns sharply towards. Course and speed maintained to get clear.

Top of 'B' turret flies overboard, further hits forward.

1735 approx. Enemy passes astern in unfavourable position for firing his torpedoes.

Thick smoke caused by fire in engine room conceals enemy from bridge.

A/A Control Officer continues with stern armament. Range approx. 40 hm.

Enemy's guns pointing to starboard. His A/A is not manned.

1745 approx. Turned away to port in order to destroy enemy completely. Shortly afterwards revolutions drop rapidly, no communication with engine room. Simultaneously four torpedo tracks. Hold course because questionable whether engines would make the turn and tracks deviate well astern. Course 240. (Torpedoes) pass short distance astern. Simultaneously engines break down. LENSCH reports engine room and all fire-extinguishing apparatus completely out of order. Order to try and get at least one engine working.

1750 approx. Gunnery control working again from forward position with whole battery at 60 hm. SYDNEY course south slow speed. On fire from bridge to after funnel. Constant further hits.

1800 approx. Single torpedo at 70 hm inclination 80, speed 5. Miss astern.

1825 Guns check. Last range 90 hm. Shots 104 hm. Relative bearing 225. Rounds fired approx. 500 base fuze, 50 nose fuze. Prepare to scuttle.

Lower all boats and life-saving equipment. Impossible to reach engine room; satisfied myself personally of this. No.2 electric installation working but useless. Enemy disappears from sight at approx. 160 hm. Course approx. 150. Glare visible until about 2200 then occasional flickerings.

2100 approx. All life-saving apparatus lowered and cast off. Still 124 men on board including almost all officers. Such guns as are still working can thus be manned. Only small quantity of smoke in mine hold.

Both boats from No.2 hatch.

2330 approx. Both lowered, one with 59 (men). Explosive charge in port forward oil tank.

2355 Smoke increasing heavily on mining deck.

2400 Paid off. Touched off charge, last boat cast off.

0035 Mines explode. Ship sinks rapidly stern first.

There are several contentious points in this version, which have come about through different translations of the original document.[25] And the times quoted are 'Golf' time.

As there are no indications to the contrary, it would appear that the Australian authorities were satisfied that Detmers's account was genuine, especially when it was realized that his account of the action confirmed what they had established in 1941 through interrogation. The reason why Detmers was carrying the coded reports is simple. As *Kormoran*'s senior officer, it was Detmers's responsibility to ensure that a full report on the loss of the raider reached the German naval authorities.

Admittedly, by January 1945, Detmers's chances of successfully delivering such a report to Germany were extremely remote. It is understood, however, that the report and the engine-room log were prepared early in 1942, when Germany's chances of winning the war were quite good.[26]

Although the whole action report is fascinating, of particular interest is Detmers's description of *Sydney*'s approach. Detmers indicated that at 1645G (1745H) *Sydney* was approaching slowly on *Kormoran*'s starboard quarter. Thirty minutes later the cruiser was drawing away onto the raider's starboard beam, 9,000 metres distant. Then at 1730G, when fire was opened, *Sydney* was slightly abaft the starboard beam at a range of 1,300 metres.

Although the claim that *Sydney* was 9,000 metres off *Kormoran*'s starboard beam at 1715G may have been a translation error, it is also possible that it was not. If it was not an error, it indicates that *Sydney*'s approach was not direct. And if *Sydney*'s approach was not direct, then the accepted view of *Sydney*'s loss may be fundamentally flawed.

Because the action report was encoded, it is assumed that it was never intended to be read by the Australian authorities and is therefore considered to be a genuine account of the action between *Kormoran* and *Sydney*. For this reason it is the preferred account to analyse. To simplify matters, all times quoted are local Western Australian ('Hotel') time.

THE INTERCEPTION

At 1655 *Kormoran*'s lookout sighted a vessel off the port bow. When the sighting was interpreted as several vessels with an escort, Detmers decided to turn away and increase to full speed. Although *Sydney* was the only other vessel present, the mirage effect distorted its features, making it look as if there were several vessels. When the sighting was identified as a Perth class cruiser, Detmers decided to alter course from 260° to 250°.

At 1705, *Sydney* altered course and gave chase. A short time later, the cruiser began flashing the letters 'NNJ'. In reply, Detmers hoisted the signal letters for the *Straat Malakka*. The next time given was forty minutes later. At 1745, or shortly after, the main rangefinder was withdrawn for the purpose of disguise. According to Detmers, the exchange of signals continued. As the signal letters for *Straat Malakka* had already been hoisted, this reference to a further exchange can only refer to *Sydney* asking for the port of destination, possibly the port of departure, and the nature of the cargo. *Sydney* was then recorded as approaching slowly on the starboard quarter and presenting a narrow silhouette.

While *Sydney* was still some distance astern, Detmers ordered a Q signal to be transmitted. The time for this was given as 1800, which is consistent with the times quoted by Geraldton and *Uco* for their receipt of a mutilated Q signal.

By 1815, *Sydney* was claimed to have drawn away from the starboard quarter and taken up station off the starboard beam at a distance of 9,000 metres. Then, in the space of fifteen minutes, *Sydney* closed to approximately 1,300 metres. While doing so, the cruiser apparently made the signal 'Hoist your secret call'. Unable to reply, Detmers declared identity and opened fire.[27]

In contrast to the accepted view of *Sydney*'s approach, the action report indicates that *Sydney* did not steam on a parallel course, at a range under a mile while the exchange of signals took place. Rather, it would appear that *Sydney* did not close with *Kormoran* until minutes before fire was opened.

Detmers maintained this sequence of events, albeit in a less precise format, in his post-war account. In this, he said that the exchange of signals in which he declared his ship to be *Straat Malakka*, occurred before 1735. A short time later, with *Sydney* between 'eight and nine thousand metres' away, and showing 'the narrowest possible silhouette', Detmers claimed that he was asked what cargo was being carried. After replying 'piece goods', he ordered the Q signal to be transmitted. He then informed his crew that they were about to go into action with a small (light) cruiser. He claimed that he made this announcement because the ship had been at action stations for over an hour and that his men could see and hear nothing.

After informing his crew, Detmers said that he then saw that the cruiser had an aircraft on the catapult. Although he did not indicate where *Sydney* was, Detmers implies that it had moved from its position astern, the narrow silhouette previously displayed perhaps preventing the Walrus being seen. Detmers then said that *Sydney* was 'something over three thousand metres' away and closing. *Sydney* then altered course 'a point or two to starboard', broadening its silhouette. At the same time the cruiser gave the signal 'Give your secret call'. *Sydney* was claimed to have repeated this signal while steaming broadside on, at a range of 'about a thousand metres'. On receipt of this second signal, Detmers gave the order to decamouflage and open fire.

Essentially, what Detmers said was that *Sydney* was closing from a range greater than 3,000 metres shortly before fire was opened. Again, this implies that *Sydney* was not steaming parallel at a range under a mile while the exchange of signals took place. Although Detmers did not state where *Sydney* was before closing from a range beyond 3,000 metres, it would be logical to assume that the cruiser was closing from the action report position of 9,000 metres (90 hm) off the beam.

A statement made by Detmers during his 7 January 1942 interrogation perhaps supports such a scenario. In this he claimed that when he 'first saw *Sydney* he did not know what ship she was. When she turned broadside on, I realized she was a first class cruiser, and I quite expected to be sunk as I could not escape her'.

In the accepted version of the intercept, *Sydney* alters course, approaches from the starboard quarter, then steams alongside *Kormoran*. As *Sydney* draws parallel, it presents its beam to the Germans. At no time does *Sydney* 'turn broadside on'. In Detmers's action report, however, *Sydney* does turn broadside on immediately after the Q signal is transmitted.

If Detmers was correct, how could most of his crew get it so wrong?

The answer would appear to lie in Detmers's post-war account. In this, he said:

> My men had been at action stations for over an hour now and it seemed a long time to wait, particularly when they could see and hear nothing; and as I expected action to be opened at any moment I now spoke to all stations over the intercom informing them that we were about to go into action with a small cruiser which we should be well able to dispose of.[28]

From this statement, it would appear that many of those who claimed that *Sydney* was steaming parallel for some time before fire was opened probably did not actually see *Sydney* until after *Kormoran* decamouflaged. It is conceivable that most of the claims were based on assumption and guesswork. Obviously, many, particularly the gunners, would have seen *Sydney* steaming parallel at close range when *Kormoran* decamouflaged,

but before this moment they probably did not have much of an idea where the cruiser was.

Although it would be reasonable to assume that some members of *Kormoran*'s crew would have caught glimpses of *Sydney* as it approached, most would have seen and heard nothing until the raider declared identity. So, if most of the crew could see nothing, there is little to substantiate the claim that *Sydney* was steaming parallel, at a range under a mile, while the exchange of signals took place.

The timing of Detmers's announcement to his crew is also interesting. He indicated that he did this after the Q signal was transmitted. In other words, shortly after 1800. At 1815, according to the action report, *Sydney* was observed to draw away onto the starboard beam, 9,000 metres distant. Considering the timing, it is probable that it was *Sydney*'s manoeuvre that prompted Detmers to inform his crew that they were about to go into action.

Drawing away onto the beam would have exposed *Sydney*'s after turrets and opened up A-arcs, thereby permitting all four of *Sydney*'s turrets to be trained on the suspect vessel. Such a manoeuvre may had led Detmers to believe the cruiser was preparing to open fire. Support for such a hypothesis can be found in the 'Engine Room Log'. At 1815 the log recorded: 'damage control centre shifted from starboard gangway to port gangway, as being probably away from the firing'.

Detmers perhaps informed his crew that they were about to go into action with a cruiser that was on their starboard beam. If so, after being informed that the cruiser was on their beam, and then finding it still there when they decamouflaged, many crew members may have assumed that the cruiser had been steaming alongside all the time. If this is what actually occurred, it is probable that this incorrect assumption was passed on to the interrogating officers in much the same way as Linke's 'convoy' had been.

The authorities had been able to check the convoy story with the shipping plots to see if the claim was genuine, but there would have been no way that the authorities could confirm or deny the claims about *Sydney*'s approach. As most of *Kormoran*'s bridge personnel and the weapons officers chose to reveal little or nothing of *Sydney*'s approach, the authorities would have had little option but to accept the claims of the other men.

Detmers, however, offers an alternative scenario. His action report stated, and his book implied, that Burnett only took *Sydney* to within a mile of the supposed *Straat Malakka* minutes before fire was opened. Although there was no logical reason for Burnett to have taken *Sydney* within a mile of a suspicious merchantman, then nonchalantly steam alongside while exchanging signals, there are several logical reasons why he would have drawn away to a position 9,000 metres off the supposed *Straat Malakka*'s beam.

THE MANOEUVRE TO STARBOARD

1. The most simple, but least likely reason for the manoeuvre to starboard was that Burnett, after receiving the Q signal, if it *was* being transmitted in the name of the *Straat Malakka*, wanted to reassure the merchantman that *Sydney* was friendly. The easiest way to do this was to provide the merchantman with a broadside silhouette of *Sydney*. If this was the reason for the manoeuvre, however, it does not explain Burnett's decision to close.

2. By moving to a position abeam of the supposed *Straat Malakka*, Burnett would have been presented with a broadside view of the merchantman. Through the rangefinders, binoculars and telescopes, the silhouette of the supposed Dutchman could be studied and compared with the information contained in the shipping recognition books.[29]

3. When the Q signal was transmitted, *Sydney*'s D/F operators would have obtained a bearing on the transmission. If the Q signal was not transmitted in the name of *Straat Malakka*, and contained a position which was over the horizon, Burnett may have manoeuvred to starboard in order to obtain a second bearing on the transmission. Plotting the two bearings on a chart would have provided a point of intersection. This point would have represented the transmission source. Such a simple exercise would have helped determine if the transmission was emanating from the supposed *Straat Malakka*.

4. If the Q signal was not transmitted in the name of the *Straat Malakka* and contained a position which was over the horizon, Burnett may have decided to launch the Walrus to investigate. The manoeuvre to starboard may have been for the purpose of increasing speed to permit a catapult

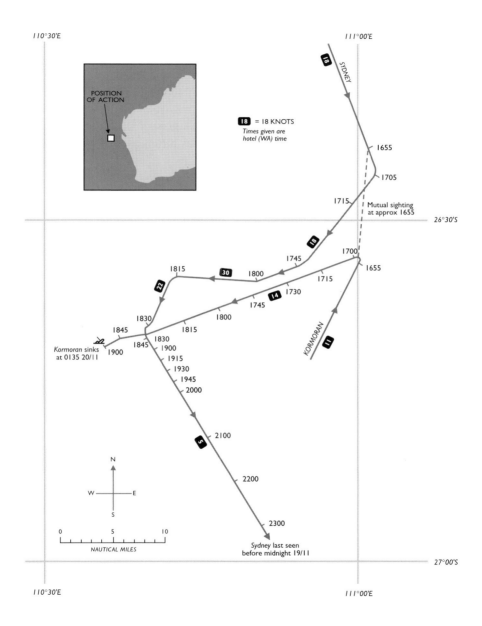

110°30'E

111°00'E

18 SYDNEY

POSITION
OF ACTION

18 = 18 KNOTS
Times given are
hotel (WA) time

1655

1705

1715

Mutual sighting
at approx 1655

26°30'S

1700

1655

1745

18

1745

1715

1815

30

1800

22

1730

14

1745

1800

1830

1815

KORMORAN

11

1845

1830

Kormoran sinks
at 0135 20/11

1845

1900

1900

1915

1930

1945

2000

N

2100

5

W — E

S

2200

0   5   10

2300

NAUTICAL MILES

Sydney last seen
before midnight 19/11

27°00'S

110°30'E

111°00'E

Track chart of action between
Sydney and *Kormoran*.

launch of his aircraft. Such a scenario would appear to be supported by the German claims that *Sydney*'s aircraft was seen to be prepared for launching.

5. Bearing in mind that Burnett should have been suspicious before the transmission of the Q signal, the manoeuvre to starboard might have been for an entirely different purpose. Before the Q signal, *Sydney* was allegedly some 8,000 to 9,000 metres astern (starboard quarter) of the suspect vessel. This was well inside the known gun range of the German raiders. Altering course to bring all four 6-inch turrets to bear on the vessel, may have been an attempt to draw a response from a potential raider.

Points 3, 4 and 5 may have had some bearing on the manoeuvre to starboard, but the most simple and logical reason for the manoeuvre was that Burnett wanted to make a visual inspection of the supposed Dutchman.

The identification of merchant ships was an important part of naval practice during the Second World War and, because merchant ships were sometimes difficult to identify, a methodical and detailed system was devised to simplify the process. This system relied on the recognition of a vessel's hallmark features. These consisted of the hull form, the layout of the superstructure and the number and location of masts, samson posts and funnels. Given favourable light and weather conditions, these features permitted vessels to be identified by type, length and approximate tonnage from a considerable distance. The illustration of a wartime observation report shows how these features were identified and recorded (see diagram on p. 201).

It was acknowledged that a vessel's features, and consequently its length and tonnage, could not be estimated with any degree of accuracy unless a broadside view was obtained. The tonnage of a vessel was estimated from its length, and the most accurate method of establishing the length of a vessel was with the use of the main rangefinders and an instrument called the Weymouth Cooke Sextant Rangefinder, the latter being supplied to HM ships as a means of obtaining the range of an object when either the height or the length of an object was known; and the height or length of an object when the range was known.

This instrument was calibrated for ranges from 1,200 to 18,000 yards, and it, or a similar instrument, could have been used in conjunction with

ENEMY (OR SUSPECTED) MERCHANT SHIPS — OBSERVATION REPORT

						REPORT
1	TIME	:- 3·30 A.M/P.M. (NAVAL PERSONNEL USE SERVICE PROCEDURE) LOCAL TIME				
2	POSITION	:- "CLOSE IN" / "WELL OUT" "OFF MORNA POINT".				
3	COURSE & BEARING	:- OR ALTERNATIVELY MERELY INDICATE — "NORTH", "SOUTH", "NE, SW", ETC.				
4	SPEED & ANY SUBSEQUENT ALTERATION OF COURSE	:- SPEED 12 KNOTS (IF ANY ALTERATION OF COURSE, REPORT)				
5	TYPE OF BOW	STRAIGHT BOW	CLIPPER BOW	RAKED BOW	MAIERFORM BOW	
6	TYPE OF STERN	COUNTER	HEAVY COUNTER	CRUISER	SEMI-CRUISER	
7	HULL TYPE / COLOUR OF TOPSIDES / BOOT TOP (IF POSSIBLE)	FLUSH DECK BLACK TOPSIDES.		FLUSH DECK RAISED F'CSLE BLACK TOPSIDES. F'CSLE WHITE		
		TWO WELL DECKS... TOPSIDES BLACK		RAISED F'CSLE, LONG POOP, ONE WELL. TOPSIDES BLACK.		
8	SUPERSTRUCTURE DISTINCT UPPERWORKS ABOVE DECKLINE / POSITION OF HOUSES / COLOUR	PASSENGER HOUSES AMIDSHIPS & AFT COLOUR BUFF		CARGO HOUSES AMIDSHIPS & AFT COLOUR GREY		
		PASSENGER HOUSES NEARLY CONTINUOUS COLOUR WHITE		CARGO OR TANKER ISLAND BRIDGE HOUSE AFT COLOUR BROWN		
9	MASTS NUMBER TYPE POSITION COLOUR	FOUR MASTS TWO FRD / TWO AFT FUNNEL COLOUR BUFF	TWO MASTS ONE FRD / ONE AFT FUNNEL COLOUR BROWN	TWO GOAL POST MASTS WITH F'CSLE T'PN M'STS BOTH FRD FUNNEL COLOUR WHITE		
10	FUNNELS NUMBER SIZE RAKE	ONE FUNNEL RAKED CONE TOP LARGE	ONE FUNNEL UPRIGHT LARGE	ONE FUNNEL RAKED SQUAT	ONE FUNNEL UPRIGHT EARLY M/V TYPE	
11	FUNNELS COLOUR MARKINGS POSITION	BUFF AMIDSHIPS	RED WITH BLACK TOP WAIST	BLACK WITH WHITE BAND AFT		
12	SAMSON POSTS NUMBER TYPE COLOUR	GOAL POST / ORDINARY SAMSON SAMSON POSTS	5 SETS SAMSON POSTS COLOUR BUFF 1 F'CSLE 4 FRD FUNNEL 2 FRD BRIDGE 5 AFT 3 AFT			
13	GUNS	:- "NO GUNS", "1 GUN AFT", (AS THE CASE MAY BE) REPORT ONLY GUNS SEEN				
14	SIZE OF VESSEL	:- "LARGE", "FAIR SIZE", (IF POSSIBLE, GIVE APPROX. TONNAGE)				
15	MARKINGS	:- "DANISH FLAG AMIDSHIPS", OR ANY DISTINCTIVE FEATURE.				
16	OBSERVERS	:- "OBSERVED BY LIGHTHOUSE KEEPER".				
17	REASON OF SUSPICION	:- "SPLASHES OBSERVED AFT AS THOUGH MINELAYING".				
18	REPORTED BY	:- GIVE NAME ETC."				

Enemy Merchant Ships —
Observation Report.
Courtesy Royal Australian Navy

the main rangefinders to establish the length of the supposed *Straat Malakka*.³⁰

Once Burnett moved onto the supposed *Straat Malakka*'s beam, regardless of the range, it should have been obvious that the vessel was not what it claimed to be. Even at 9,000 metres it would have been obvious that the merchantman's features were not the same as the real *Straat Malakka*'s.

The *Straat Malakka* was listed as having a length of 455 feet and a gross tonnage of 6439 tons. Hallmark features included a raked stem, counter stern, single funnel amidships, two masts and four sets of samson posts. It should have been obvious to Burnett and the men engaged in trying to positively identify the vessel before them that it was a much larger ship. It was over 50 feet longer than the *Straat Malakka*, and its tonnage was well in excess of 6,439 tons. Most noticeably, the vessel on their port beam had a cruiser stern. From a beam position Burnett would have been able to confirm that the vessel he had intercepted was not the *Straat Malakka*.

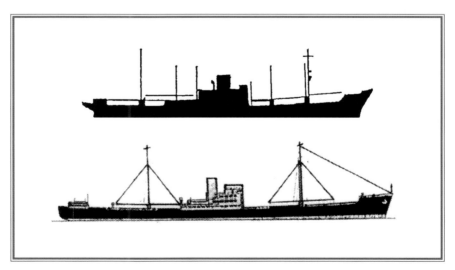

Top: Silhouette of *Straat Malakka* as provided
in Talbot-Booth's *What Ship is That?*
Bottom: Silhouette of Raider 'G', as supplied
by the Admiralty in October 1941
National Archives (Vic) MP 1580/1

Therein lies the mystery. If Detmers was correct when he recorded *Sydney* as being 9,000 metres off his starboard beam at 1815, Burnett must have closed with full knowledge that the vessel was not *Straat Malakka*. The same is true if Detmers's action report is not correct. If, as the prisoners claimed, *Sydney* closed from a position off *Kormoran's* starboard quarter, it should have been obvious to Burnett well before fire was opened that the vessel did not have a counter stern. So in either case, Burnett should have been suspicious and ready to open fire as soon as *Kormoran* began to decamouflage. But according to all accounts, *Sydney* was caught off guard. *Sydney* was not prepared to open fire instantly and suffered accordingly.

Despite all the theories, accusations and apologies that have emerged over the years, it must be remembered that Burnett was not a fool. He would not have jeopardized his command without due consideration and deliberation. He would not have closed if he thought the supposed *Straat Malakka* was a raider. So before passing judgement on the man, it is important to look at the information that was available to him, which might have influenced his decision to close with what was clearly a suspicious vessel.

It is obvious that there was really only one factor that Burnett had to consider, namely, was the vessel claiming to be the *Straat Malakka* a disguised merchant raider?

If Burnett considered that the vessel was a raider, there was no question of closing. But if he considered that it was not a raider, he had to identify it, and the only way that this could be accomplished was by close inspection or boarding.

Unfortunately for Burnett, there was no safe and reliable method of identifying raiders. CAFO 143 of January 1941 indicated that in most cases boarding would be necessary. Although reliable, this was far from safe, and after *Cornwall's* clash with Raider 'F' it is doubtful that anyone would have attempted to board a potential raider. Burnett was, therefore, in a difficult position. Without any positive indication that the vessel before him was a raider, he would have been forced to rely on the negative indications.

Previous encounters between German raiders and units of the Royal Navy had revealed that the Germans would not hesitate to open fire

when intercepted. The pattern that had emerged by November 1941 was that raiders would open fire at extreme range and attempt to escape. The closest that anyone had managed to get was about 10,500 yards, this being the estimated range that *Cornwall* had closed to before *Pinguin* declared identity and opened fire. That the vessel claiming to be the *Straat Malakka* had not opened fire when the range reduced, and especially when *Sydney*'s main armament was trained on it, perhaps indicated that the vessel was not a raider.

Another consideration would have been that *Kormoran* had a very clean profile. The raider had no suspicious deck cargoes or structures that could conceivably conceal guns. Although Detmers had had a dummy wooden gun erected on the poop deck to complete *Kormoran*'s disguise as an Allied merchantman, a gun in such a position should not have aroused suspicion.

So, the negative evidence, although flimsy, suggested that the supposed *Straat Malakka* was not a raider.

But while the physical evidence suggested that the vessel was not a raider, the available intelligence suggested that a raider could be operating in the waters off the Western Australian coast.

The only raider identified as having operated in the Indian Ocean since the sinking of Raider 'F' (*Pinguin*), was Raider 'G' (*Steiermark*, alias *Kormoran*). A description of Raider 'G' had been given in WS/23, and although the features described would not have been dissimilar to the vessel before Burnett, there was a slight difference in the sterns. WS/23 indicated that Raider 'G' had a half cruiser, half counter stern, while the vessel before Burnett had a true cruiser stern.

This apparent semi-cruiser stern of Raider 'G' was highlighted in a photograph that was distributed to British warships in October 1941. Although *Kormoran* had a cruiser stern, the photograph was deceptive, and indicated that the raider had a semi-cruiser stern. Confusingly, a silhouette of Raider 'G' issued at the same time showed the raider with a cruiser stern. While it is assumed that copies of the photograph and silhouette were issued to *Sydney* in October, this is yet to be confirmed.

Unfortunately, the Naval Intelligence Division erroneously believed that Raider 'G' had left the Indian Ocean in August and moved into the Pacific. Although WS/26, issued on 10 November, indicated that Raider 'G'

The photograph of *Steiermark* (*Kormoran*)
issued to British warships in October 1941.
Courtesy WA Newspapers

Beam view of *Kormoran*. The sleek lines
disguise the ship's sinister purpose.
Bibliothek für Zeitgeschichte, Stuttgart

might have returned to the Indian Ocean, it is not known if Burnett received this intelligence before he sailed. If not, it is probable that Burnett was led to believe that Raider 'G' was still in the Pacific. Nevertheless, Burnett still had to consider the possibility that another raider was operating in the Indian Ocean.

On 3 October 1941, *Sydney* was returning to Fremantle after escorting convoy US12B to the Sunda Strait. At 1810, when in the approximate position of 10° 10' South 104° 50' East, lookouts sighted an unidentified object. Burnett ordered action stations and an increase in speed while course was altered to investigate. The object, however, was soon identified as a floating target. At 1830, *Sydney* secured from action stations and reverted to cruising stations. Four minutes later the ship was stopped and the port cutter lowered to recover a crudely made battle practice target. The target, constructed primarily from baulks of Oregon Pine, Borneo hardwood and 44-gallon drums, was recovered with the ship's crane, lowered into the waist and dismantled.

The ship's officers were perplexed by the find, although it was thought that it might have drifted from Christmas Island, some 40 miles away. In his report to RACAS, however, Burnett concluded that 'It is considered that there is just a possibility that it may have been a target dropped by a raider'.[31]

Two days later, probably as a direct result of the target find, Burnett addressed the ship's company. He informed them that there was a raider in the area and that every man was to be on his toes and at the highest pitch of training.[32]

As if to reinforce the message, a report was received on the evening of 6 October that an unidentified vessel had been sighted off Rottnest Island. Fearing that the vessel may have been an enemy minelayer attempting to lay mines, Burnett broke W/T silence to inform SWACH that *Sydney* was proceeding to arrive at the entrance to the searched channel (through Fremantle's protective minefield) by 0400 on 7 October. Burnett's intention was to prevent *Queen Mary*, also on independent passage, entering the searched channel until it had been thoroughly swept. To this end, he requested that the troopship be ordered by signal not to enter the channel until it received further orders. Burnett later reported that he had considered conducting a search for the raider but due to the

uncertainty of the available information and *Sydney*'s fuel situation he abandoned the idea.[33]

Although a 'Board of Investigation' into the suspicious sighting off Rottnest led Burnett to report that in his opinion no unknown ship had been present, it is clear that he initially considered a raider was responsible.

THE USE OF THE WALRUS

Gill indicated that if Burnett was suspicious of the supposed *Straat Malakka* he should have used his aircraft.

During the early war years, many cruisers carried at least one amphibious aircraft. Most of the British cruisers so equipped carried Walrus or Seagull V type aircraft, principally for reconnaissance and gunnery spotting duties. In the reconnaissance role, their task was to find and fix.[34] If the aircrew sighted a vessel while on patrol, they were to attempt to identify it, accurately plot its position, course and speed, and relay this information to their parent ship. Depending on the circumstances, this could be done either by W/T, visual signal, or by landing and reporting verbally.

When trying to identify merchant vessels, the aircrew were expected to employ the recognized challenge procedure, and unless a vessel acted, or looked suspicious, the aircrew would generally accept the information received. Normally, this did not create a problem, but as the following examples show, when an enemy ship was located, the aircrew often found it difficult to pierce the enemy's disguise.

On 6 June 1941, while on anti-submarine patrol in the South Atlantic, a Swordfish from the aircraft carrier HMS *Eagle* sighted a merchant ship. On being challenged, the vessel identified itself as the Norwegian *Kristiania Fjord*. The steamer then altered course and increased speed, arousing suspicion. It was assumed that the vessel was enemy, and as it was only 30 miles from *Eagle*, it was decided to despatch more aircraft and attempt to force the vessel to close with the carrier for closer examination. Despite having machine-gun fire directed across its bows, the vessel could not be induced to alter course. Two 250-lb bombs dropped within 20 feet of the ship also failed to influence the merchantman, and after a further two

hours of shadowing the aircraft had to abandon their mission due to lack of fuel and return to *Eagle*.

A strike force was then despatched to intercept the yet to be positively identified vessel. When they located what they thought was *Kristiania Fjord*, they found it stopped, on fire and being abandoned. Again, the vessel was ordered to proceed towards the carrier, presumably so that an attempt to salvage could be made, but again there was no response. With three boats already cast off, the aircraft had little option but to attack with bombs. They left the ship well ablaze and settling by the stern.

The vessel's true identity was only established when it transmitted an SOS in the name of the German ship *Elbe*.

A more successful intercept followed a few days later, although again, the vessel's true identity could not be established from the air. On 15 June another of *Eagle*'s Swordfish sighted a merchantman flying the Dutch flag. When ordered to stop, the vessel was abandoned. Some well-placed machine-gun fire, however, convinced the crew to reboard their ship. The aircraft remained on station until the cruiser *Dunedin* arrived with an anti-scuttling party. The vessel was found to be the German tanker *Lothringen*.[35]

In both cases, the aircrew concerned could not make a positive identification. The same difficulties were experienced when the raiders *Pinguin* and *Atlantis* were intercepted. Neither of the disguises adopted by these vessels could be pierced from the air, despite the fact that the aircrew of *Devonshire*'s Walrus were supplied with photographs of *Atlantis*.

The other interesting point about *Lothringen*'s intercept was that even in mid 1941 it was still possible, and desirable, to capture enemy vessels.

Whether Burnett understood the limitations of trying to identify merchant ships from the air is a matter of conjecture, although Detmers was puzzled why *Sydney*'s aircraft was not launched because, according to him, 'the wind and weather conditions simply called for it'. Perhaps Ahl had a greater understanding of the situation. He said *Sydney* had no real need to launch the aircraft because the cruiser could see they could not escape.[36]

Despite Detmers's fear that his camouflage would not stand up to close scrutiny from the air, Ahl perhaps knew there was little the aircrew could achieve once they were aloft, apart from preventing *Kormoran* escaping.

Obviously, Burnett must have considered using the Walrus, as Detmers indicated that its engine was started. This appears to have occurred around 1800, about the time of the Q signal transmission and an hour after the first sighting.

The timing may have been coincidental, but it is possible that the Q signal prompted Burnett to use the aircraft. If the Q signal contained a false position, Burnett may have decided to use the Walrus to investigate the report while he kept *Sydney* on station. Once the D/F operators confirmed that the transmission was emanating from the suspect vessel, however, he may have decided there was no longer a need to launch the aircraft. An alternative scenario is that Burnett may have waited until the exchange of signals was complete before deciding on the question of employing the Walrus.

Despite being readied for flight, the Walrus was not launched. Shortly before Detmers declared identity, the Walrus' engine was observed to be shut down. The time of this occurrence appears to be 1825, as the action report stated that '(cruiser) stops engines' at this time. Although some have interpreted the entry as '*Sydney* stops engines', this would appear to be incorrect. More recent research has revealed that Detmers was referring to the aircraft's engine being stopped at 1825.[37]

This is not an unrealistic assumption because, by 1825, *Sydney* would have been very close to *Kormoran*, and the need to launch the aircraft would have long since passed. Burnett may therefore have ordered the Walrus to be shut down and the catapult swung inboard.

There is another possible explanation for Burnett's decision not to launch the Walrus. Given the weather conditions, the aircraft could have been catapulted without difficulty, but the state of the seas may have made its recovery dangerous or even impossible. The pilot could have been instructed to land at Carnarvon or Geraldton for recovery the following day, but Burnett may have wanted to keep the aircraft on board for a dawn reconnaissance. If Burnett considered that he had caught a raider supply ship, and the raider was in the vicinity, he may have thought it more prudent to retain the Walrus so that it could be used in a search for the raider.

There is one final point about Burnett's decision not to launch the Walrus. If he had the slightest doubt that he was dealing with a raider, he

would, or should, have launched it, if not to help in the identification process, then certainly to remove a fire risk in the event of action. Previous battle experience had shown that these aircraft were particularly vulnerable to splinter damage and a fully fuelled aircraft was a serious fire hazard.

It will never be known how or why Burnett decided that the suspect vessel was not a raider, but it is clear that he must have reached this conclusion.

In ruling out the possibility that the vessel before him was a raider, Burnett may have considered that it was a raider supply ship. Such a consideration would explain Burnett's readiness to close. It would also explain his apparent reluctance to open fire and, when he did open fire, that fire was directed high.[38] Additionally, it may explain why he chose not to use his aircraft, and why he apparently chose to maintain W/T silence.

PRESERVING W/T SILENCE

The claim that *Sydney* did not transmit any W/T signals is also interesting. Although Burnett may have been justified in breaking W/T silence to consult shore authorities on the whereabouts of the *Straat Malakka*, such an act may have been considered pointless. If Burnett was convinced that the vessel was not what it claimed to be, he may have thought it more desirable to maintain W/T silence rather than break it for the sole purpose of confirming what he already suspected. In other words, given the circumstances, he may have considered it more important to preserve W/T silence.

If Burnett thought he was dealing with a raider supply ship, and the raider was in the vicinity, he may have wanted to capture the vessel silently, as the silent capture of the supply ship could have led to the destruction of the raider.

That such a consideration is valid can be seen in the actions of the Naval Board after they learned of *Kormoran*'s loss. The Naval Board tried to suppress news of *Kormoran*'s destruction for as long as possible, because they considered that by not announcing the raider's loss they might have been able to locate and destroy its supply ship.

If this was Burnett's reason for maintaining W/T silence, however, the reason may have become invalid once Detmers transmitted the Q signal,

and certainly so when Detmers decamouflaged. Once Burnett realized he had inadvertently closed with a raider, he should have ordered that an enemy sighting report or action report be transmitted. At this point, however, Burnett's immediate concern would have been how to deal with the raider. Consequently, there may have been some delay in ordering an enemy sighting report. Then, within minutes of fire being opened, it was probably too late. According to the information obtained from the *Aquitania* prisoners, *Sydney*'s foremast was shot away shortly after fire was opened. With the foremast gone, *Sydney* would not have been able to transmit because all the transmitting aerials were attached to this mast.[39]

Significantly, Detmers found himself in the same predicament. During his interrogation on 2 December, he said that there had been a chance to radio Germany at the beginning of the action, but his 'attention was taken by the fight'. When he later ordered his signal officer to send a report, the order could not be carried out as 'the radio was too badly smashed'.

KULMERLAND?

Although it is perhaps pointless trying to pinpoint which particular vessel Burnett thought he was dealing with, as he may not have known himself, there was one raider supply ship that was known to have operated in Australasian waters. This was *Kulmerland*, and its construction and general appearance were not dissimilar to those of *Kormoran*, particularly its stern features.

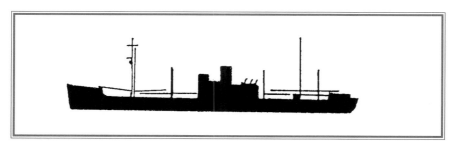

Silhouette of *Kulmerland* as provided in
Talbot-Booth's *What Ship is That?*

Kulmerland was identified as the supply ship that had operated with the Pacific raiders in November 1940. Although the raiders were not identified, *Kulmerland* was—disguised as the Japanese freighter *Tokyo Maru*. Furthermore, WIR No.45 (17 January 1941) named *Kulmerland* as the vessel responsible for laying the mines that claimed two ships in the Bass Strait, one off the coast of New South Wales and one in the Spencer Gulf.[40]

In November 1941, Malaya and Singapore were being reinforced to counter the growing Japanese threat in the Pacific, and the increasing number of vessels plying the waters along the Western Australian coast would have justified the deployment of a minelayer. That the Germans, after mining the eastern and south-eastern seaboard in November 1940 would, with Teutonic thoroughness, return to mine the western seaboard twelve months later, could have been considered a very real possibility. When one considers Detmers's claim that he had taken *Kormoran* into Western Australian waters for the express purpose of laying mines, the minelayer fear was well founded.

It is conceivable that Burnett may have thought that the supposed *Straat Malakka* was actually *Kulmerland*, even though the latter's length and displacement may not have been large enough to convince a trained observer.

It will never be known which ship Burnett believed he had intercepted. All that needs to be understood is that, if Burnett thought he had cornered an enemy supply ship, he would have attempted to capture it in accordance with Admiralty instructions. Evidence of Burnett's awareness of his responsibilities can be found in *Sydney*'s logbooks. These reveal that the anti-scuttling parties were regularly exercised, the last known exercise being conducted on 24 October 1941.

PREPARING TO BOARD?

If Burnett was attempting to capture what he believed was a raider supply ship or minelayer, there should have been visible indications that he was preparing to lower a sea-boat with an anti-scuttling party.

Curiously, there is very little evidence of this. The only prisoner to suggest that *Kormoran* was going to be boarded was Lensch, who claimed

that the cruiser lowered a boat before fire was opened. Although the evidence is not strong, Lensch's claim is supported by Detmers's post-war account. In this, Detmers said that after fire was opened he noticed that a 'motor-cutter was hanging helplessly halfway over the side', implying that a cutter was being lowered. The boat to which both men referred was probably *Sydney*'s port cutter, as this would have been the only sea-boat visible before fire was opened.

There might be another explanation, however, for the apparent manning of the port cutter. As there were indications that Burnett was contemplating launching the Walrus, this cutter may have been manned in readiness for the catapult launch, it being normal procedure to have the sea-boat manned and ready for lowering in case the aircraft should accidentally ditch.

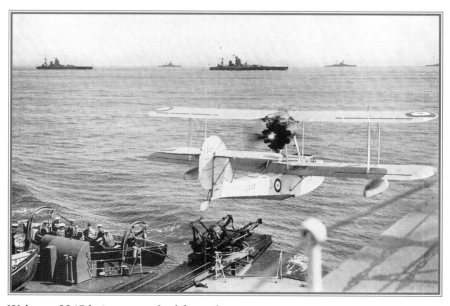

Walrus L-2245 being catapulted from the Town class cruiser HMS *Southampton*. The sea-boat is manned and ready to be lowered should the aircraft ditch on take off. Note the general service life-jackets worn by the boat's crew.

If Lensch was correct, however, when he said the boat was lowered, and Detmers's statement is interpreted as a boat partially lowered, this would suggest that it had been manned for a purpose other than the recovery of the aircrew. It would indicate that Burnett was attempting a capture and was despatching an anti-scuttling party. At the very least, it shows that Burnett was not satisfied with the merchantman's claimed identity and was going to despatch a boarding party.

There is a possible explanation why none of the other prisoners mentioned a boat being lowered, or being prepared for lowering. *Sydney*'s port cutter was positioned slightly abaft the bridge on the same level as the forecastle deck, and in such a position was highly visible. It was also in the line of fire. The sight of a boatload of helpless men being shot to pieces may have been a spectacle that most men preferred not to discuss. Firing at a warship could have been seen as an impersonal act. Firing on a boatload of men might have been seen as something else.

Although the cutter was probably not deliberately fired upon, disclosing the fact that a boatload of men had been shot up was not the sort of information a prisoner would willingly disclose to his captors.

One of the men who would have been in an ideal position to see *Sydney*'s port cutter was Jakob Fend. He served *Kormoran*'s starboard 3.7-centimetre gun and was apparently given the task of knocking out *Sydney*'s bridge or DCT or both. During a visit to his men on 8 January 1942, Detmers singled out Fend, awarded him the Iron Cross, First Class, and congratulated him on his marvellous shooting. Clearly, Fend would have been directly responsible for the deaths of many of *Sydney*'s key personnel. Yet when he had been interrogated on 5 December he told his captors he had served the port 3.7-centimetre gun and had not fired during the fight.

On the question of whether Detmers was ordered to stop, it should be understood that if Burnett was attempting a capture, the last thing he would have wanted was to see his quarry scuttling before he was in a position to close. In other words, if Burnett had his suspicions but had not yet ruled out the possibility that the vessel was a raider, he may have been reluctant to order the vessel to stop. If he did so, and the vessel scuttled, he would have been forced to stand off and watch his potential prize sink, lest it be a trap.

Therefore, in all likelihood, Burnett would have waited until he was sure that the vessel was not a raider. Once this doubt was removed, he would be free to close when he chose and to delay the order to stop until the last possible moment. In this way, he would be able to get as close as possible without disclosing his intentions, and the closer he could get before the vessel scuttled, the better the chances his anti-scuttling party would have of saving the vessel.

In other words, if Burnett believed that he was dealing with an unarmed supply ship or minelayer, he would not have given the order to stop until he was ready to board it.

Although Detmers's claim that *Sydney* ordered him to stop was not supported by Ahlbach, it is conceivable that an order to stop was signalled shortly before fire was opened. Once the distance between ships had reduced to under a mile, the order to stop would not have been long in coming, and Detmers would have known this. Therefore, if Burnett did signal the order to stop, it is possible that the signal prompted Detmers to declare identity and open fire. Although Detmers claimed that he waited until the bearing between ships was stationary before giving the order to decamouflage, it is conceivable that the order to stop was the catalyst.

Needless to say, if an order to stop was signalled, it was not obeyed. All evidence points to Detmers maintaining a constant speed of 14 knots during this critical phase of the intercept. This is not surprising. Skeries would have required a stable gun platform if he were to have any chance of accurately ranging then hitting the cruiser with his obsolete equipment. That Detmers was well aware of this requirement may be seen in the action report. In this he recorded 'slow alteration to 260 [degrees] so as not to interfere with guns'. Not only did Detmers maintain a steady 14 knots, but he endeavoured to keep *Kormoran* on a steady course. When he did alter course, apparently in order to assist Greter with his torpedo shot, he made the turn slowly so as not to upset the aim of his gun layers and trainers.

There is a theory that Detmers did stop, or at least reduced speed, so that he could fire an underwater torpedo before declaring identity. There are some indications that an underwater torpedo was fired at the start of the action, but it is doubtful that this occurred. The theory, however, has merit and will be looked at in due course.

SYDNEY'S FIRST SALVO

Most references to *Sydney*'s opening salvo indicate that it was aimed high, either passing directly over or slightly abaft the raider. The Germans thought that this was the result of poor shooting, but this explanation is far too simplistic. Lieutenant-Commander M.M. Singer, RN, was an experienced gunnery officer, and it is difficult to believe that he could have failed to hit a target of 8,736 tons at the claimed range of 1,300 metres. But if Singer did miss, it is not inconceivable that he was instructed to, remembering that a 'frightening near miss' was recognised as an effective method of discouraging an enemy vessel from scuttling while an attempt to capture was being made. Alternatively, Singer might have been instructed to aim for the vessel's bridge.

The destruction of the bridge was another tactic that had been devised when an attempt to capture was being made, the theory being that if the bridge were destroyed, the order to scuttle might not be issued. Although it was preferable to capture enemy vessels undamaged, sacrificing the bridge and the bridge personnel was justifiable if the vessel could be captured with its cargo intact. Despite the fact that *Kormoran*'s bridge was not destroyed by *Sydney*'s opening salvo, there is sufficient evidence to suggest that this may have been the intended target.

Regardless of whether the first salvo hit or missed, it would have been fired with the knowledge that the vessel was a raider. According to the prisoners' statements, *Sydney* opened fire at the same time, or shortly after, they fired their first salvo, although Detmers, in his first interrogation, said that *Sydney* might have fired first by half a second. Either way, *Sydney* opened fire after *Kormoran* began to decamouflage.

Normally, the point of aim was the base of the centre of mass. In real terms, this meant the waterline immediately below *Kormoran*'s bridge. If Singer's guns had been aimed at this point, that is where the first and subsequent salvoes should have struck. Singer and his gunnery team would not have wasted precious seconds elevating the guns to the point where the first salvo could miss. In other words, it is probable that *Sydney*'s guns were elevated to bridge height before Detmers declared his identity.[41]

Although many claimed that *Sydney*'s first salvo was high, two prisoners claimed that it struck amidships. Bunjes said that the cruiser's first

salvo hit 'amidships in the engine room near the funnel', and Foerster said that 'after the first salvo there was no fire fighting equipment left in the raider', implying that *Sydney*'s first salvo hit the raider in the engine room. Unfortunately, both of these claims are difficult to substantiate. Foerster was below deck and would not have been able to see *Sydney* fire its first salvo, and Bunjes may not have been in a position to see either.

Detmers and Jürgensen, on the other hand, were in a position to see. Although Jürgensen claimed that the first hit was through *Kormoran*'s funnel, Detmers claimed in his action report that *Sydney*'s first salvo went over, scoring no hits. Detmers also claimed that after a short delay 'C' ('X') turret began firing 'well and fast', scoring hits in the funnel and engine room.

Given Detmers's and Jürgensen's claims it would appear that Foerster and Bunjes were mistaken, perhaps describing hits from a subsequent salvo.

The important consideration, however, is that the first salvo would have been fired with the knowledge that the merchantman was a raider. In which case, it seems incredible that Singer would have fired what was described as a full salvo if he knew his shells were not going to hit. Conversely, if he knew his guns were aimed at the raider's bridge, he probably would not have hesitated to open fire. The destruction of the bridge would have destroyed the command structure and seriously impaired the raider's offensive capability. *Kormoran*'s gunnery officer understood this, and that is why he made *Sydney*'s bridge a priority target.

In all likelihood, *Sydney*'s first salvo was aimed at *Kormoran*'s bridge. How Singer managed to miss is a question that cannot be satisfactorily answered, although Detmers's action report claim that *Sydney* dropped astern as he decamouflaged may provide a clue. Whether this alleged slowing of *Sydney* was part of a preplanned manoeuvre, or was simply an attempt to get astern of a decamouflaging raider will never be known. If it was the latter, and Singer was not forewarned that *Sydney* was about to reduce speed, the reduction in speed may have been sufficient to cause the first salvo to miss a relatively small target like the bridge.

In this context, the hit on the funnel is interesting. In his post-war account, Detmers claimed that a shell 'ripped through our funnel at about bridge height'. Von Gösseln said under interrogation that although the

bridge was not hit the funnel directly behind the bridge was. The claims were supported by Brettschneider, who wrote in his diary that the hit on the funnel caused casualties on the bridge and destroyed a lifeboat on the boatdeck.

Detmers implied that the shell that struck the funnel came from *Sydney*'s second salvo, accrediting the hit to 'x' turret. 'Y' turret, he claimed, fired 'two or three salvoes, all of them over'.

There is evidence, however, to suggest that Detmers may have been mistaken about 'Y' turret's fire. W/T operator Willy Tümmers, who appears to have been stationed in the W/T office behind the bridge during the action, claimed that three shells struck the bridge. One hit, he said, caused deaths and casualties directly in front of the radio room, and 'finished the radio'. This implies that a four-gun salvo, possibly fired by 'x' and 'Y' turrets, tore through *Kormoran* at bridge height, one shell striking the funnel while the other three passed between the bridge and the W/T office before exploding in the sea.

Alternatively, the shells responsible for the four hits may have come from *Sydney*'s opening salvo. Seeing the shells explode behind *Kormoran* may have given Detmers the impression that they had gone *over* when they had gone *through* his ship.

Regardless of where the shell, or shells, struck, or from which salvo they came, it is significant that the damage was at bridge height.

Another anomaly concerning *Sydney*'s first salvo is that a well-trained 6-inch turret crew was expected to be capable of achieving a rate of fire of eight rounds per minute per gun. Given that *Sydney*'s turrets were already trained on *Kormoran*, and that it took about twenty seconds for Skeries to bring his 15-centimetre guns into action, Singer should have been able to fire two or three salvoes before Skeries could get a single shot away. With fifteen to twenty seconds in which to respond to the threat, Singer and his gunnery team appear to have done nothing. Clearly, something delayed the firing of *Sydney*'s first salvo.

If gyro firing was employed, it is conceivable that some time would have been lost due to the motion of the ship, although it is doubtful that fifteen to twenty seconds would have been lost due to open gyro-firing circuits. An alternative explanation is that *Sydney*'s guns were not on target, but aimed off for a near miss, in accordance with anti-scuttling

procedures. If so, Singer would have lost precious seconds training onto the target before firing his first salvo.

There is of course another, less palatable, explanation for the delay in the firing of *Sydney*'s first salvo. That is that Burnett closed with his guns in the unloaded condition. Unlikely as this sounds, this may have occurred if Burnett was conducting an exercise with what he believed was the genuine *Straat Malakka*. Burnett, however, had cause to be highly suspicious of the vessel. It is, therefore, extremely doubtful that he would have been conducting a drill or exercise. It is also unlikely that Burnett would have closed with a suspicious vessel with his guns in the unloaded state.

The most logical explanation for the delay in firing the first salvo is that Singer had his guns aimed off.

WAS SYDNEY AT ACTION STATIONS?

In recent years, it has been suggested that *Sydney* was not at action stations when it closed with the supposed *Straat Malakka*. The claim is based on the post-war statements of some of the *Kormoran* survivors, who have said that *Sydney*'s anti-aircraft guns were not manned and that 'pantrymen' or galley hands could be seen on the upper deck.

Although Detmers stated in his action report that *Sydney*'s anti-aircraft guns were not manned, the Australian naval authorities accepted that *Sydney* had been at action stations. Even Gill, after reviewing the available information before writing the official history, concluded that *Sydney* had been at action stations when it closed with *Kormoran*.

There is, however, evidence to suggest that the claims may be true.

In his post-war account, Detmers stated that through 'glasses' he had been able to see that *Sydney*'s four turrets and the port torpedo-tubes were directed at them, but 'as far as I could make out, her eight [*sic*] 4-inch anti-aircraft guns were not manned'. He also claimed that shortly before fire was opened, 'pantrymen in their white coats' could be seen 'lining the rails' to look at them.

Detmers's statement that the 4-inch guns appeared not to be manned and that 'pantrymen' could be seen on the upper deck implies that all was not well in *Sydney*. If *Sydney* had been at action stations, the 4-inch guns

should have been manned and 'pantrymen' should not have been visible on the upper deck. On the other hand, the claim that all four 6-inch turrets were trained on *Kormoran* suggests that *Sydney* was at action stations.

Sydney's logbooks reveal that under Burnett's command only two of the four degrees of readiness were assumed when at sea. The ship was either at the fourth degree (cruising stations), or the first degree (action stations).[42]

When at the first degree of readiness, all hands would close up at their action station and all weapons would be manned. At the fourth degree of readiness, only a portion of the ship's armament would be manned. Normally, this entailed only 'B' and 'X' turrets being manned. The claim that all four turrets were trained on *Kormoran* as *Sydney* closed, indicates that *Sydney* was at action stations.

What then of Detmers's claim that the anti-aircraft guns were not manned and that 'pantrymen in their white coats' could be seen lining the rail?

If *Sydney* was at action stations, the 4-inch guns should have been manned, while 'pantrymen' should not have been visible on the upper deck. Mess stewards, cooks and bakers all had action stations that should have seen them below decks in such places as the shell handing rooms or manning the shell hoists.

This raises the question, was it possible for *Sydney* to be at action stations but have the 4-inch guns unmanned and so-called pantrymen lining the rail? The short answer is yes.

If Detmers is to be believed, and his action report accepted, between 1815 and 1830 the following was occurring:

Sydney was closing from a position approximately 9,000 metres off the beam with all four 6-inch turrets trained on *Kormoran*. Given the angle of approach, 'X' and 'Y' turrets would have been trained on extreme forward bearings.

The Walrus, having been prepared for flying off, was now being shut down. This would have resulted in a number of men working on the upper deck in the vicinity of the catapult.

If a sea-boat's crew had been mustered in preparation for a catapult launch, and was no longer required, these men may have remained in the vicinity of the cutter to which they had been detailed. Conversely, they might have been returning to their action stations.

As Burnett appears to have been attempting a capture, one of the anti-scuttling parties might have been assembling near the port cutter.

Normally, when a warship is at action stations, there is no requirement to have a sea-boat manned. But in *Sydney*'s case, there were two scenarios in which men would have been taken away from their action stations in order to man a sea-boat, namely a catapult launch, and the requirement to assemble an anti-scuttling party.

This could explain why it appeared that the 4-inch guns were not manned.

For long-range anti-aircraft defence, *Sydney* was equipped with four 4-inch guns on single mountings. These mountings were not fitted with shields. Because the 4-inch guns crews had no gunshields to shelter behind, they were not only exposed to the elements and the blast of their own guns firing, but also the muzzle blast and concussion of the aft 6-inch turrets if they were fired on extreme forward bearings.

The effect of blast and concussion had been noted during gunnery trials and on active service and was quite fearsome. When 'x' and 'Y' turrets were fired on extreme forward bearings the blast and concussion was capable of causing local damage to the ship, blast damage to the aircraft, and injury to exposed personnel. Even men in the enclosed aft control position suffered.

The severity of this blast and concussion was well described by W.H. Ross in *Stormy Petrel*.

> I recall one cabin in the superstructure close by 'x' turret in particular. It caught the full blast of both after turrets as they fired on a forward bearing … the scuttle and deadlight were neatly blown off … and the sliding door lifted bodily from its slots and blasted to the other side of the passage way. Water pipes in the vicinity had been burst by the concussion.[43]

Another example can be found in Geoffrey Brooke's *Alarm Starboard*. During his wartime service, Brooke served in a number of RN warships, including the 6-inch cruiser HMS *Bermuda*. In this ship he commanded 'x' turret. After seeing his previous ship, *Prince of Wales*, and *Repulse* sunk by torpedo bombers, he was keen to develop a method whereby he could

Sydney's 'x' and 'y' turrets firing
on an after bearing.
V. Gibson

employ his turret against attacking aircraft. He found that with the aid of an extension on the voicepipe to the turret trainer, and a bell-push connected to a bell in front of each gun layer, he could sit on the rim of the manhole in the turret roof and direct and fire his guns in a manner not unlike a tank commander.

Unfortunately, sitting on the roof exposed him to the blast and concussion of his three 6-inch guns every time he fired a broadside. To help overcome these effects, he wore concussion earpads, and after ringing for the guns to be fired would double up and close his eyes. Even though he was some 30 to 35 feet behind the muzzles, he would still be engulfed in the scorching blast. Despite his precautionary measures, Brooke noted that normal hearing would not return for several days.[44]

According to one of *Sydney*'s former 4-inch gunners, when the aft 6-inch turrets were fired on extreme forward bearings, the exposed 4-inch guns crews were subjected to the same effects. Given the opportunity, the gunners would take cover, either sheltering on the opposite side of the 4-inch gundeck or lying flat on the deck.[45]

That lying on the deck was not an unnatural posture for ratings in exposed positions can again be found in *Stormy Petrel*. During the Cape Spada action, Ross recorded that only one casualty was sustained in *Sydney*; an able seaman who was slightly wounded while lying prone on the deck.[46]

One of the three survivors from *Hood*, Able Seaman Tilburn, had taken up a similar posture during the action with *Bismarck* and *Prinz Eugen*. At the inquiry into the loss of *Hood*, Tilburn was asked what he saw. Diplomatically, he replied that he was 'lying down most of the time — on the boatdeck before the port forward UP [unrotated projectile rocket launcher] mounting — so his view was restricted'.[47]

It is also recorded that Burnett, shortly after taking command of *Sydney*, recommended that shields be fitted to the 4-inch and 0.5-inch mountings for the protection of the crews. He was partially successful in that shields were manufactured and fitted to the 0.5-inch machine-gun mountings, but no modifications were made to the 4-inch guns before *Sydney* was lost. His attempt to obtain shields for the 4-inch guns suggests that he was aware of the exposed conditions that the gunners had to work under.

It is therefore possible that *Sydney*'s 4-inch gunners were at their action station, but might have been lying down in case the aft 6-inch turrets started firing on forward bearings. In such a position the plating attached to the guard-rail around the 4-inch gundeck would have screened them from view and given observers the impression that the guns were unmanned.

If there had been any threat from the air, these men would undoubtedly have stood at their posts and suffered the effects of blast and concussion as a case of necessity. As there was no threat from the air, and none from the apparently unarmed merchantman that could not be adequately dealt with by the 6-inch guns, the torpedo tubes and the forward 0.5-inch machine guns, the port 4-inch gunners might have been permitted to stand down and seek shelter.

Another consideration was blast damage to the aircraft. Normally, if the 4-inch guns were to be employed, the Walrus was flown off the ship. If this was not practicable or possible, the wings would be folded and braced to avoid blast damage. Such precautions were not taken when a repel aircraft exercise was conducted by *Perth* in July 1940. Six rounds were fired from the 4-inch guns and the resulting muzzle blast crumpled a wing of the aircraft.

As *Sydney*'s Walrus was observed to be prepared for flight, it would be logical to assume that the 4-inch guns would not have been used until the aircraft was either flown off or shut down and protected against blast damage. If so, and because of the requirement to have a sea-boat manned in preparation for a catapult launch, the redundant gun crews might have been called upon to man the sea-boat. This would not only explain why the port 4-inch guns appeared not to be manned, but it may also explain why 'pantrymen in white coats' were seen on the upper deck.

While Detmers described men in white coats as 'pantrymen', others have claimed that they saw men in aprons on the upper deck.[48] In reality, what Detmers may have seen were gunners or ratings in white shirts and shorts. From a distance, even through binoculars, such clothing could have been mistaken for white, knee-length coats. Similarly, the men in aprons may have been ammunition handlers. Photographs of the 4-inch gun crews conducting practice shoots during 1941 clearly show loading numbers wearing protective aprons.

Sydney's 4-inch gunners conducting a practice
shoot in Australian waters in 1941. Note the
ammunition handlers wearing protective aprons.
T. Fisher

Sydney's port cutter would have been clearly visible to anyone on board *Kormoran* in a position to see. As Lensch and Detmers indicated that this boat was being lowered, or had been lowered when fire was opened, it would be logical to assume that the boat crew (anti-scuttling party) and lowerers would also have been clearly visible before fire was opened.

Two of the prisoners recovered by *Aquitania* claimed that the faces of the men near the torpedo tubes and the aircraft were distinguishable, but no one mentioned having seen men in the vicinity of the port cutter. As 'pantrymen' and 'kitchen hands' would not have been manning the torpedo tubes or making up numbers in the catapult crew, it is conceivable that they might have been 'lining the rail' in the vicinity of the port cutter or the port waist. In other words, the 'pantrymen' and 'kitchen hands' seen on the upper deck may actually have been 4-inch gunners who had initially been called on to man the sea-boat for the catapult launch of the Walrus.

As anti-scuttling parties were generally made up of specialists, a crew assembled to man the sea-boat for the launch of the aircraft would not have been used for anti-scuttling purposes.[49] Instead, they may have been detailed to help lower the cutter with the anti-scuttling party. If so, these men would have had the opportunity to stand at the rail and observe the supposed merchantman while the anti-scuttling party was being assembled.

The German claims, therefore, may be correct. *Sydney* could have been at action stations with what *appeared* to be pantrymen and galley hands on the upper deck.

It should be understood that this, and all previous possible scenarios or explanations are just that—possibilities. No one can categorically state how or why *Sydney* was lost. Similarly, no one alive knows why Burnett elected to take his command so close to an otherwise suspicious vessel. The best that a latter day researcher or historian can do is to offer realistic possibilities and probabilities based on the operating procedures and practices and Admiralty instructions that were in force at the time of *Sydney*'s loss.

When viewed as an isolated incident, there is little to be found in the German statements to indicate why Burnett acted the way he did, but when viewed within the wider perspective of the conduct of the war at sea up to November 1941, one can see a possible motive for Burnett's actions.

At this stage of the war, if an enemy supply ship or blockade runner was encountered at sea, the intercepting warship was under instructions to prevent that vessel being scuttled. From his previous appointment as Deputy Chief of Naval Staff, Burnett would have been acutely aware of the critical need to make up for lost merchant tonnage.[50] If Burnett believed the supposed *Straat Malakka* was a raider supply ship, he was duty-bound to attempt to capture it. Perhaps not surprisingly, the German statements support such a scenario.

Burnett, like all commanding officers, was placed in a very awkward position when confronted with a suspicious vessel that could prove to be a raider in disguise. The German strategy of covertly arming selected merchant ships meant that any of the enemy supply ships or blockade runners encountered could be a raider. The Admiralty nevertheless continued to instruct its commanding officers to attempt to capture enemy merchant ships. It was clearly only a matter of time before someone caught a tiger by the tail.

Captain Bevan of *Leander* and Captain Manwaring of *Cornwall* had both been extremely lucky in their encounters with enemy raiders, and it was unfortunate that the Admiralty did not recognize this and act on the warnings that these two encounters provided. It was not until after *Sydney* had been lost that the Admiralty was moved to issue the appropriate warnings.[51]

In July–August 1943, when a review of the policy of capturing enemy merchant ships was being conducted, the Admiralty reaffirmed its January 1941 (CAFO 143) view that raiders would be difficult to identify. In the new draft CAFO, the Admiralty conceded that:

> The primary difficulty confronting HM Ships is that of identification; hesitation engendered by doubt has been clearly apparent in many encounters that have taken place.
>
> There can be no positive recognition unless the enemy blunders into some act that discloses his real character; he is well aware of the efficiency of his disguise and he will employ every artifice to maintain the pretence until all hope of escape has faded.[52]

In a rare insight into the Admiralty's thoughts on the loss of *Sydney*, the 1943 review also found that 'the advantages to be gained by saving tonnage are generally outweighed by the danger to the intercepting ship—a point forcibly illustrated by the fate of the SIDNEY [*sic*]'.

So although the Admiralty did not publicly admit it, it concluded that it had been inevitable that a warship would be severely damaged or sunk while attempting to capture an enemy merchant ship which was actually a raider in disguise.

On 19 November 1941 fate decreed that HMAS *Sydney* would be that ship.

—6—

THE ACTION

> Will tell nothing of the KORMORAN. Even though the KORMORAN is
> sunk, there may be other ships built on similar lines. It would help
> the English still to describe the KORMORAN. It would help them
> identify other ships. Although a prisoner he has rights and knows
> what they are.[1]

Such were the views of Petty Officer Erich Trottmann who, like many of
his fellow prisoners, refused to provide the interrogating officers with any
potentially valuable information on *Kormoran* or its action with *Sydney*.
Some provided fragments of what they saw or heard. A few, like Bunjes,
Skeries and Hildenbrand, were willing to divulge a good deal more.

Trying to establish whether the fragments are fact, or distorted views
of fact, is almost impossible, and trying to place them in chronological
order is equally difficult. The statements made by Bunjes, Skeries, and
Hildenbrand, however, coupled with Detmers's statements and his action
report, allow a reasonably accurate outline of the action to be formed.

The fragments can then be placed against this overall view to verify their authenticity and to see when they occurred. In this way, the pieces of the puzzle can be drawn together to obtain a more comprehensive and more accurate account of the action.

THE ACTION

During his formal interrogation on 1 December 1941, Bunjes claimed that *Kormoran* opened fire in response to the cruiser's demand for the secret call. He said they 'opened the covering plates of the guns and fired the first shots', at a range of 1,200 metres, in 'less than a minute'. After *Kormoran* had 'fired four or five salvoes the cruiser turned and seemed to attempt to ram'. It passed astern, however, then came under fire from *Kormoran*'s port guns. At this stage the cruiser was 'enveloped in smoke, on fire, and down by the bow'.

The cruiser's first salvo hit *Kormoran* 'amidships in the engine room near the funnel'. Bunjes added that they were hit three or four times, though some salvoes went over. At about 1840 a fire started and 'something was wrong in the engine room', causing *Kormoran* to stop. The action lasted about twenty minutes.

Disturbingly, the information supplied by Bunjes at Swanbourne on 1 December was beginning to differ from that which he had surrendered to *Yandra*'s officers only days before. In a report dated 30 November, Lieutenant Taplin included the following narrative, which was compiled from information supplied by Bunjes.

At 'Action' the German flag was broken out and all guns which would bear were fired, the Raider firing first, her first salvo striking the Cruiser at about 'B' Turret and bridge structure and about 'Y' Turret. Seconds after the Cruiser fired but missed 'over'. All Raider's salvoes appeared to hit while Cruiser took considerable time to find gun hitting range. Soon after engaging, both ships turned to Port, the Raider slightly and the Cruiser hard over passing astern of the Raider about 1 mile distant. This manoeuvre appeared to the Raider crew to be an attempt to ram. The action continued on opening course, the Raider firing four gun salvoes, and also when Cruiser was on her port quarter, fired a torpedo which struck the Cruiser forward causing a large fire and reducing her speed considerably. The Raider was first hit by the Cruiser at about the 4th or 5th salvo, which struck her engine room, completely wrecking it and causing uncontrollable fire. Torpedoes were seen to be fired by the Cruiser but these did not hit Raider.

The engagement terminated at about 1840 [1940H], the Cruiser ceasing first, lying stopped directly astern about 10,000 metres distant and badly on fire. The Raider was then also burning fiercely and 'abandon ship' was ordered.

Despite his willingness to talk, Bunjes may not have been in a position to witness all of the events he described. If this was so, it may explain his changing claims. If he did not witness a particular event he would have been forced to rely on the claims of others, principally, the men with whom he shared the lifeboat. After landing at Fremantle, however, Bunjes joined the officer group. From the officers, Bunjes undoubtably heard different accounts of events that he did not witness.[2]

One man who was obviously well placed to witness the events he described was Skeries. Being the gunnery officer, he was able to provide a more detailed account of Kormoran's fire. Skeries was interrogated at Harvey on 4 December and provided this account:

Directed artillery in last fight; took up position for firing 4 p.m. [1700H] (above bridge); took range; fight began 5.30–5.45 — Cruiser came nearer (1,300 metres) — first salvo fell short (1 shot) — next shot ranged at 1,600 metres — too high: Cruiser was 1,500 metres away. Shot about 8 salvoes — 2nd hit bridge near funnel, 3rd forward tower — 4th Machine room; 5th shot the Cruiser's aeroplane (burnt) — motor ran then shut off — shots fired systematically — lucky shot that aeroplane was hit.

Altogether 450 shots with 15 cm. guns; used also the A A guns shot torpedo tubes of cruiser and the 1" guns — easily visible. After 8–10 salvoes — 3rd turret had shot two or three times, 4th turret shot — does not know where Cruiser's shots landed. Torpedo

struck forward between two first turrets. Torpedo officer sent torpedo not Sk [Skeries], passed the forward of Cruiser (which was nearly motionless) to avoid shots from the stern turrets (3 and 4). As they were passing … 1st and 2nd [turrets] could not fire (put out of action by 3rd and 4th salvos [*sic*]—2nd blown up by 10th salvo).

Cruiser turned; KORMORAN turned and fired again—Cruiser burning amidships and steamed off very slowly—last shot range—10 km (6 ¼ miles).

Bow dipping, Cruiser listed slightly, shots from 1" guns of Cruiser mostly short.

Skeries added that *Kormoran* was hit by the cruiser's 3rd and 4th turrets and that he lost sight of his opponent at midnight. *Sydney* was then '225 degrees bearing from last shot'.[3]

Seaman Ernst Hildenbrand also supplied a good description of the action, and as he had served the starboard aft 15-centimetre gun (No. 5 gun), he had been assured of a good view. Hildenbrand claimed they opened fire 'some time before the cruiser' and that their 'first salvo hit the cruiser'. After the second salvo, the cruiser caught fire. Many hits were observed, 'setting fire at first, bow, then bridge', although there was no damage aft. He added that they had fired as quickly as possible and that his gun fired fifty shells during the forty-minute action.

Hildenbrand indicated that *Sydney* had come up on the starboard side to within approximately 1,200 metres, although he claimed that his gun had fired at a range of 1,100 metres. He also said that they were instructed to aim always for the waterline. When hit, *Sydney* had 'continued at fair speed, then stopped and dropped astern, broadside on to take up position slightly astern on the port side'. Hildenbrand added that he did not know whether his ship had been hit while the cruiser was on their starboard side, but claimed that it had fired for five to six minutes while on their port side and that 'three or four big shells' hit and damaged *Kormoran*.

Detmers provided a basically similar but less detailed version of events during his interrogation on 1 December.

Range was somewhat more than 1 mile. First salvo of the Cruiser was over the Raider—Raider's first salvo hit the conning tower of

the Cruiser. There was then some delay. Raider fired two torpedoes, one of which missed and one hit, about 20 metres from the
bow. The fore turrets then stopped firing. The third turret of the
Cruiser hit the raider. He [Detmers] thought the Cruiser was going
to ram him, but it passed astern of the Raider and then fired four
torpedoes. Raider turned towards the torpedoes, and they passed
ahead and astern of him. Cruiser then turned away behind a smoke
screen—when seen later the second funnel was burning. Raider
badly on fire, and fire fighting apparatus was badly damaged. At
midnight he sank his ship, having at 11 o'clock given orders to
leave ship. Had earlier sent all away except a hundred. There were
some boats in a hatch which took three hours to get out because
of low power, then the rest left.

Thinks both ships opened fire at same moment—perhaps
Cruiser half a second earlier. All guns and torpedo tubes of the
Cruiser were trained on Raider as she approached. As the Cruiser
approached, aircraft was warming up on catapult, and she tried to
launch it but the aeroplane was hit. At the end of the action the
range was from 9 to 10 kilometres.

Detmers was interrogated again on 2 December but was apparently
not questioned about the action. When questioned by the military on
7 January 1942, however, he made these claims:

> I opened fire at approximately 1,100 metres and my first broadside
> badly damaged SYDNEY, carrying away most of her superstructure.
> I again fired a broadside, which did further extensive damage. I
> then torpedoed her, one of my torpedoes struck her near the for-
> ward funnel. Her bows immediately dipped and she turned and
> tried to ram me. I avoided this by turning quickly and let her have
> a further broadside. As she swung past me closely, she could,
> apparently, fire no more, and she was blazing fiercely, particularly
> near the after funnel. The action then broke off.[4]

Although differing in minor aspects, the sequence of events described
by these four men was basically the same, namely, that *Sydney* closed to

a range between 1,100 and 1,500 metres before fire was opened. Within a minute of the declaration of identity, the first shots were exchanged, both ships opening fire at about the same time. Although Bunjes and Detmers differed in their opinions about where *Sydney's* first salvo fell, Hildenbrand and Detmers both claimed that *Kormoran's* first salvo hit. Then, after a brief exchange of fire, *Sydney* was hit by a torpedo.

Sydney, almost stopped in its tracks by the explosion of the torpedo, recovered, then turned and passed astern of the raider. (Skeries thought that it was *Kormoran* that had executed the turn, but he confirmed that a turn did occur.) From a position astern, and broadside on, *Sydney* fired four torpedoes before retiring behind its smoke. *Kormoran* then turned to port and, as *Sydney* entered the arcs of the raider's port battery, these guns started firing. The action ended when the range had opened to about 10,000 metres.

During the action, *Sydney* managed to put several shells into *Kormoran*, one salvo starting an uncontrollable fire that ultimately forced the abandonment of the raider. Although Bunjes, Skeries and Detmers claimed that *Kormoran* had been hit while *Sydney* was on their starboard side, Hildenbrand said that *Sydney* had hit the raider after it crossed to their port side.

This basic sequence of events compares favourably with Detmers's action report. The same sequence of events was given by the survivors picked up by *Aquitania*. Because the *Aquitania* group were landed at Sydney, effectively isolating them from the other groups of survivors, their claims are useful in assessing the consistency of the claims made by individuals in the other groups.

Despite the fact that many of the twenty-six men who composed the *Aquitania* group served below decks, Captain Farncomb managed to obtain a fairly comprehensive account of the action. On 1 December 1941, Farncomb submitted the results of a second interrogation. In introducing his narrative of the action, he said: 'Most of the prisoners were prepared to discuss the action, although some were surly. One, Fritz Treber, was particularly loquacious on the subject. He also seemed fairly intelligent. From his account—corroborated in general by other prisoners—a comparatively clear outline of the action with HMAS SYDNEY can be deduced.'

Farncomb added that Treber was serving one of the 15-centimetre guns during the action and had a clear view of what occurred.

SYDNEY was sighted hull down about 1600 (H?) on 19th November, 1941 and shortly afterwards identified as a cruiser. No.41's hands were at once sent to Action Stations. The initial course of the raider was not stated, but the Quartermaster on watch agreed that the action was fought on a Westerly course. SYDNEY approached on No.41's starboard quarter with main armament trained (on this point Treber was definite) and signalling continuously by lamp. No.41 made no reply. On SYDNEY's closing to a range estimated by several men as about 1000–1500 metres, the latter the maximum, No.41, about 1700, opened fire, hoisting the German ensign at the same time. SYDNEY opened fire about 15 seconds later, possibly after No.41's second salvo, although there was some doubt on this latter point.

SYDNEY was hit on the bridge by the first salvo, the bridge was wrecked and a fire started; her foremast was shot down shortly afterwards and one of the first rounds hit the port torpedo tubes and started a bad fire which destroyed the aircraft. Two prisoners stated that the faces of men near the tubes and aircraft were distinguishable, that tubes and catapult were trained outboard and that the aircraft's propeller was revolving; she was apparently about to fly off.

No.41 fired three torpedoes (according to one report) of which one hit forward. At the same time SYDNEY was being frequently hit near the waterline and about the upper deck. No.41 fired in all about 100 rounds. After receiving considerable damage, SYDNEY began to drop astern, firing at a slow rate and burning forward and aft: flames also coming from the funnels.

By this time No.41 had been hit five or six times. One hit in an oil fuel tank started a bad fire which could not be extinguished. There was another serious hit in the engine room which eventually put the main engines out of action, causing the ship to lose way and then stop. Her foremost gun was also hit. She had meanwhile forged ahead of SYDNEY and after receiving the hit in the engine room turned slowly to port.

Both ships ceased firing about this time (approximately 1720), both being on fire, with SYDNEY badly down by the bows, the foc'sle-head being only about six feet out of the water. It was stated that occasionally her propellers could be seen coming out of the swell.

After about 20 minutes' pause, SYDNEY fired another round which missed. No.41 replied with her port battery and claimed a hit. (I believe Treber's relative hitting claims are boastful exaggeration.) Firing then ceased (about 1745). SYDNEY was not seen to fire torpedoes.

At about 1815–1830, finding the fire out of control and her main engines disabled, No.41 abandoned ship into boats and rafts and scuttled. She blew up, though apparently not with a particularly severe explosion, about three hours later. Her crew abandoned ship on her port (or weather) side as flames and smoke prevented the starboard boats from being used. SYDNEY could now be seen about four miles away burning fiercely and 'glowing' in the gathering darkness. No rating claimed to have seen her sink, but most men stated that she was last seen about 2100…

No boats were seen to leave SYDNEY, but it was thought that they would have been destroyed. One boat was seen to be badly hit early in the action.[5]

Although the times quoted by Farncomb would appear to be inaccurate, the description of the action is consistent with the claims made by Bunjes, Skeries, Detmers and Hildenbrand.

THE 'FRAGMENTS'

Taking *Kormoran*'s bridge personnel first, Messerschmidt, who helped Skeries by spotting the fall of shot for line, said that the first salvo was fired at a range of 1,500 metres.

Von Gösseln estimated that the range at the opening of fire was 1,200 metres and that it was about 10,000 metres when *Kormoran* finished firing.[6] He admitted that 'the bridge was not hit, but the funnel directly behind the bridge was'. Von Gösseln also said that before the first salvo was fired the Dutch flag was hauled down and the German flag run up. He added that torpedoes were fired by both ships, but 'cannot give information about [the] torpedoes'.

Jürgensen provided more. He claimed that *Kormoran*'s first salvo was successful and that the cruiser's forward turrets were badly damaged. The cruiser replied 'almost immediately' and the first hit was through their funnel. He added that one of the guns on the starboard side was damaged, as was the engine room, causing the ship to stop. He then said '*Kormoran* fired two torpedoes', one of which hit the forepart of the cruiser. Jürgensen added that '*Sydney*'s two torpedoes missed', implying that both vessels fired torpedoes about the same time. *Sydney* then 'turned and appeared to have the intention of ramming, but did not do so'. Both ships 'continued to fight, and the length of the engagement was perhaps one hour'.

According to Jürgensen, they received the order to abandon ship approximately one hour before sundown. At this time *Sydney* was 10,000 metres away. After the men had been about an hour in the lifeboat, the fire on *Sydney* suddenly vanished, although no explosion was heard. He added that the cruiser did not appear to have thrown out a smoke screen, but that 'thick black smoke' had been emitted from the fire.

That the range at the start of the action was 1,500 metres was confirmed by the midships rangefinder operator, Hans Peiler, and corroborated by Brinkman, the anti-aircraft weapons officer. Brinkman claimed that his weapons began firing with the first salvoes and that the range was 1,500 to 1,600 metres. He added that his task was to shoot down the cruiser's aircraft should it be launched and flown over them, but as it was not, he was able to employ his whole battery against the cruiser's torpedo tubes and anti-aircraft guns. He also said that two torpedoes were fired at the cruiser while they were steaming parallel but with 'one further forward' (possibly referring to *Sydney* being slightly astern). Although two were fired, he said only one hit and that it struck the cruiser 'under [the] forward turret almost at right angles'.[7]

Brinkman also confirmed that *Sydney* fired torpedoes in the second phase of the fight, claiming that two were 'shot from starboard side of cruiser but [they] did not strike'. He added that the cruiser did not lay a smoke screen but that *Kormoran* created one 'accidentally'.

Pre-war photo of *Sydney* steaming alongside
Australia. Distance between ships is approximately
500 metres. *Kormoran*'s gunners would have been
presented with a similar but more distant view of
Sydney when they decamouflaged.
G. Truswell

The gunners and ammunition handlers surrendered information that, in
general, conformed with the other men's statements. Rudolph Heinrich,
who was a reserve gunner on the No.1 gun (starboard forward), claimed
that he saw the cruiser for about a minute during the interception phase,
but then nothing after being ordered below; adding weight to the belief
that once at action stations, very few would have been in a position to
observe *Sydney*'s final approach. Of equal interest is Heinrich's claim that
it took more than a minute to prepare the gun for firing, although he may
have been referring to the time taken to prepare for decamouflaging.

Actually serving the No.1 gun was Anton Schweier. Unfortunately, all
that he would divulge was that he was present when the first shot was
fired, perhaps indicating that it was his gun that fired the first shot.

The crew of the No.3 gun had a little more to say. Petty Officer Paul Kobelt was the layer of the No.3 gun. He said that he was wounded by a splinter from a hit on his gun, the shell striking the mounting before exploding in the sea behind them. Kobelt added that during the action his gun fired many times, both to starboard and to port. He also said that he did not know which gun was the first to fire as there had been an error in the transmission of the order to fire. Kobelt claimed that he had received the order to fire on the port side, but, on decamouflaging, found the cruiser on the starboard side. He therefore had to swing his gun around before it could be fired.[8]

Another man who was also wounded by splinters from the hit on the No.3 gun was Johann Wolfsgruber. He claimed that there were eight other men at his gun, one of whom was killed. Referring to the cruiser, he said that there was much return fire.

This aspect of heavy return fire was also commented on by Wilhelm Kurz, an ammunition handler on the No.4 gun. Although claiming that he saw thirty or forty hits on the cruiser, he said that the cruiser also scored hits, and that one 'burst of four' struck the 'machine room'. He added that one shell also struck the 'oil chamber', perhaps implying that the shell which tore open the fuel tank came from a different salvo.

Some men served the guns that were initially on the lee side of the firing (No.2 and No.6 guns). As a result, they did not take part in the action until *Sydney* passed astern of *Kormoran* and entered their arcs of fire. One of these men, Hans Dahm, acknowledged that his gun fired once the cruiser appeared on the port side. He added that his shots struck the cruiser.

Serving the No.6 gun was Adolph Dornis. He said that his gun fired only in the second phase of the action. He also said that the guns could be loaded down below and that they could be made ready in one minute.[9] Dornis also said he received a burn wound after coming into contact with the hot gun and from handling hot shell cases, although Karl Ackermann, who claimed to have been a loader on the same gun, denied that anyone in his crew was burnt. The claim that the guns became very hot, however, was corroborated by Karl Heinz, who said that because of the rapid salvo firing the gun barrels failed to recoil.

An entry in Hermann Rademacher's confiscated diary provides further evidence that the 15-centimetre guns became overheated, as he recorded

that they refused to fire. He also noted that the rate of fire had been so great that the ammunition could not be supplied quickly enough. In describing the action, Rademacher wrote that their first salvo hit aft, while the second hit the bridge. The range was given as 1,500 metres. Unfortunately, the authorities appear to have had trouble reading Rademacher's writing because they could not make out where the third salvo struck. It was noted, however, that the 3.7-centimetre gun scored a hit on the artillery stand (DCT) about the time the third salvo was fired. *Kormoran's* No.3 gun was then described as being hit, causing the death of one man. This was followed by the claim that the cruiser's aircraft was struck.

Rademacher also wrote that a torpedo hit *Sydney*, although the entry has it striking under the 'forward doors' (probably meaning forward turrets). He then described a quick succession of salvoes, during which *Sydney* attempted to release a torpedo. Although well ablaze, *Sydney* passed astern and fired four torpedoes. Besides the hit on the No.3 gun, *Sydney* was credited with shell hits in *Kormoran's* engine room and funnel.

Unfortunately, it is not recorded when Rademacher made these diary entries, or when the diary was confiscated. But it conformed, in general, with the statements made by others during the December interrogations. When Rademacher was interrogated at Harvey on 5 December, he claimed that he was a stoker and 'saw nothing that happened at sea'.

The claim that *Kormoran* was successful with one of its torpedoes comes up quite often in the interrogation statements, although it is curious that the torpedo gunners themselves chose to remain silent on the subject. There is, however, a statement made by Friedrich Schmitt, who served the starboard above-water torpedo tubes, which supports the claim. He said that he sent one torpedo and that there was 'not much firing after torpedo', implying that there was little firing after *Sydney* was torpedoed. He also said that he 'could see cruiser burning all over when he fired the tube torpedo', indicating that *Sydney* was well ablaze before the torpedoes were fired.

The 2-centimetre gunners and loaders, perhaps surprisingly, had even less to say about the action. While they would have been extremely busy in the initial stages of the engagement, they would have been in an ideal position to observe *Sydney* during the action. It is unfortunate that these men decided to keep their knowledge to themselves.

One of the few to talk was Heinz Zoppeck, a loader on the starboard midships 2-centimetre gun. He said that he did not fire as 'he received no orders'. Zoppeck was wounded in the buttocks by splinters from the 'first shot', was 'taken to hospital and remained there'. He said that he and another man were wounded by the same shot, which struck the funnel. The other man may have been Paul Heinz, as he claimed that he was wounded in the neck and shoulder by splinters from the first hit.

The only other 2-centimetre gunner who chose to talk was Hans Ziegler. He too was stationed amidships. Ziegler admitted that his gun fired early in the action but claimed that the cruiser was soon too far away and out of range.

Although few chose to discuss the action with the interrogating officers, a thread of consistency can be seen in the statements made by those who gave information. There are some aspects of the German claims, however, which warrant closer examination.

SIX SECONDS

According to his post-war account, Detmers claimed that when satisfied that the critical moment had come, he gave the order to decamouflage, the command being either 'Enttarnen' or 'Fallen Tarnung' ('Drop camouflage'). On receiving the order to decamouflage (via telephone), signalman Ehrhardt Otte hoisted the German flag to declare the ship's identity. Otte stated that the war flag was 'ready unfurled, and was plainly visible as soon as they began to hoist', although it took eight to ten seconds for the flag to reach the top of the 'big aft mast head'.

While the war flag was being hoisted, the armament was cleared for firing. The screens concealing the 15-centimetre guns and torpedo tubes were raised or lowered in accordance with their method of concealment. The 2-centimetre guns were raised hydraulically into position and the screen concealing the starboard 3.7-centimetre gun was dropped.

As soon as the war flag was visible, Detmers gave permission for fire to be opened ('Feuerlaubnis').

According to the prisoners' statements, there must have been a short pause before the first shot was fired. Although Otte said that the war flag

could be fully hoisted in eight to ten seconds, the training of the 15-centimetre guns took longer. Even allowing for the fastest crew (No.1 gun) to break their own record for laying and training, there would have been a delay of several seconds before the first 15-centimetre gun was ready for firing. This scenario is supported by Otte's statements. He claimed that when the first shot was fired, the flag would have been at the top, indicating that at least ten seconds elapsed between the order to de-camouflage and the firing of the first gun.

Strangely, although the 3.7-centimetre and 2-centimetre guns should have been able to open fire almost immediately, this does not appear to have occurred. All evidence points to these guns withholding their fire until the 15-centimetre guns opened up.

A great deal of uncertainty now exists about how soon after the declaration of identity the first shot was fired. This uncertainty stems primarily from Detmers's post-war claim that 'within six seconds of the order to decamouflage the first shot was fired from our leading gun'. Although this claim has been acknowledged and repeated in many subsequent accounts, it is most likely incorrect, as none of the statements made during the interrogations support it and even Detmers's action report claims otherwise. In this he recorded: 'Dutch flag struck, War flag flies clear of main mast. Time taken 6 seconds. Guns and torpedo given permission to fire'. Clearly, the 'six seconds' figure referred to the flying of the flag, not the firing of the first shot.

It would appear that Detmers's action report contained the correct information, and subsequent applications used the figure of six seconds out of context. By way of example, the report submitted by Dr Habben claimed that camouflage was removed 'in the record time of 6 seconds … the Man of War ensign and the Commander's pendant were hoisted and the Dutch flag lowered. The ensign had hardly broken before the first shot fell from the first gun'.[10]

In his undated report of the action, Bunjes wrote, 'At 1730 hrs, six seconds after we have revealed our identity, the first salvo is fired from our four 6-inch [15-centimetre] guns on the starboard side', implying that the first salvo was fired six seconds after identity was declared.

It would appear that as time passed, the original meaning of the figure of six seconds became lost. By the time Detmers wrote his post-war account, the figure came to represent the time taken to fire the first shot.

Alternatively, it may have taken six seconds to reveal identity (as opposed to Otte's estimated eight to ten seconds), and a further six seconds to fire the first 15-centimetre gun. As the guns would have been loaded before being decamouflaged, twelve seconds would not have been an unrealistic time for the covering plates on the bow and stern guns to be raised and the guns swung onto the target.

KORMORAN OPENS FIRE

The other question raised by the prisoners' statements is what actually constituted the first salvo. By definition, a salvo is the simultaneous discharge of a number of guns. Yet Skeries and Detmers implied (post-war) that the first 'salvo' consisted of a single shot.

That Skeries chose to use salvo firing in preference to each gun firing independently is beyond doubt. On *Kormoran*, this involved relaying range and bearing data to each gun position via telephone. All guns would then be fired on the sounding of a centrally controlled fire gong, the number of guns fired in a salvo being dependent on how many guns could bear on the target and whether they were ready to fire.

Why then would Skeries use a single gun in the first salvo when he had four guns available?

The answer would appear to lie in the method of concealment of the 15-centimetre guns. Because Nos 3 and 4 guns relied on hydraulically lowered hatch walls, they took slightly longer to decamouflage than the bow and stern guns, the latter being concealed behind counterweighted steel plates which opened upwards. Given the circumstances, it was critical that the first salvo was fired as quickly as possible. Therefore, Skeries may have rung the salvo gong while Nos 3 and 4 guns were still decamouflaging. This would have provided for a two-gun salvo comprising Nos 1 and 5 guns. If one of these two guns was not quite ready when the salvo gong rang, a ragged salvo would have resulted.

According to Skeries's statement, this is what appears to have occur-red: 'First salvo fell short (1 shot)—next shot ranged at 1,600 metres—

too high.' What Skeries appears to have been saying was that of the two shells fired, one fell short of the target, while the other was aimed too high.

This would suggest that Skeries had ordered the No.1 gun to be layed for 1,300 metres and the No.5 gun to be layed for 1,600 metres. As Skeries had to work without his main rangefinder, this makes sense. If he was uncertain of the range, he may have needed to 'bracket' the target with his first two shots to establish it. This is supported by his gunnery narrative, in which he said that he only established the range as 1,500 metres *after* he had fired two shots.[11]

Given the size of the target and the relatively close range, it should not have been necessary for Skeries to bracket the target with his first salvo. It must be remembered, however, that Skeries said his shots (or salvoes) were fired systematically. In other words, he had specific targets on *Sydney*. From his gunnery narrative it would appear that his initial target was *Sydney*'s bridge, followed by the forward turrets and then the forward engine room. It is conceivable that Skeries was trying to knock out *Sydney*'s bridge before changing targets to the forward turrets. To do this, he needed to find the correct range and find it quickly.

As his second salvo was claimed to have hit the bridge near the funnel, it would appear that his first salvo did consist of 'ranging shots'.

The claim that *Kormoran*'s first salvo was successful also fits in with this scenario. Even if the first shot (No.1 gun) was deliberately aimed low, given the relatively flat trajectory of high-velocity naval shells, it should have hit *Sydney* somewhere forward. Although many would have considered such a hit successful, if it hit below the line of the bridge, Skeries may have been justified in calling it 'short'.

Whether the shell fired by the No.5 gun hit *Sydney* is debatable. Skeries claimed that the second shot 'ranged at 1,600 metres'. It is not exactly clear what he meant by this, but the term 'ranged' can also mean that the shell failed to find the target. In other words, it may have passed over the target. Given that Hildenbrand estimated *Sydney* to be 1,200 metres away, this may have been what Skeries meant.[12]

Of equal interest is the composition of Skeries's second salvo. As Nos 3 and 4 guns could not be readied in time for the first salvo, the second salvo should have consisted of these two guns firing for the first time, and

Nos 1 and 5 firing for the second time. But according to the statement made by Kobelt, his gun (No.3), on being decamouflaged, was found to be pointing the wrong way. Whether this mistake emanated from the gunnery control position or was made at the gun position is not known, but it prevented the No.3 gun from firing in the second salvo. It would therefore appear that the third salvo was the first full (four gun) salvo.

Taking into account the error associated with the training of the No.3 gun and the fact that Zoppeck did not receive the order to fire, the overall picture of *Kormoran* is not the one of cool efficiency that Detmers portrayed in his post-war account. Indeed, the closer this story is studied, the more inconsistent it becomes.[13]

Returning to the first salvo, as soon as the No.1 gun fired, *Kormoran*'s lighter weapons began firing. With *Sydney* abaft the beam, the single 3.7-centimetre gun and all five of the 2-centimetre guns should have been able to bear on the target. This is supported by Brinkman's claim that he was able to use his whole battery against the cruiser's torpedo tubes and anti-aircraft guns.

Although the prisoners referred to the 2-centimetre guns as 'machine guns' they were actually automatic cannon, each capable of firing high-explosive shell at a cyclic rate of 280 rounds per minute.[14] They were given little credit, but these guns would have played a key role in neutralizing return fire from *Sydney*. Employed as they were, the men manning, or attempting to man, *Sydney*'s unprotected torpedo tubes and 4-inch guns would have been mown down by the hail of 2-centimetre shells. Those not hit and killed outright would have been showered with shrapnel as the shells exploded on impact with the ship's superstructure. Albert Ruf's statement that 'the men on the cruiser's aircraft were shot to pieces before it could take off' suggests that the 2-centimetre guns were also used against the crew of the Walrus.

The 3.7-centimetre gun was also used against a specific target, namely *Sydney*'s gunnery control towers above and abaft the bridge. Given the range, however, it is questionable whether the 0.68 kg high explosive armour piercing shell fired by the 3.7-centimetre gun had the ability to defeat the ⅜ to ½ inch plating of the DCT.[15]

Regardless of whether or not the 3.7-centimetre shells had the ability to penetrate its plating, it does appear that director firing stopped after

Sydney, conducting a 4-inch practice shoot on
8 May 1941. Note the wings of the aircraft,
folded to avoid blast damage. The Walrus and the
4-inch guns were both targeted by Brinkman's
2-centimetre battery on 19 November 1941.
T. Fisher

Sydney's opening salvo. And Jakob Fend, the starboard 3.7-centimetre gunner, was decorated by Detmers for his shooting, which suggests that Detmers may have considered Fend responsible for knocking out *Sydney*'s DCT.

According to Rademacher's diary, about a hundred shells were fired by the 3.7-centimetre gun. Although it is not stated, it is assumed that most, if not all, of these shells were fired by the starboard gun. It is also assumed that these were directed at *Sydney*'s bridge. Even allowing for shots that fell short or ranged over, it can be seen that a large number of shells would have exploded on or about the bridge and the DCT. Apart from the heavy toll these shells would have taken of the exposed bridge personnel, it is quite possible that a number of shells hit and damaged the DCT.

Although *Sydney* is alleged to have only fired one salvo under director control, Skeries's more primitive form of fire control was apparently not disrupted by *Sydney*'s shellfire, permitting him to employ salvo firing throughout the action. Although there is evidence of the 15-centimetre guns firing independently, this appears to have occurred when *Sydney* passed astern and came under fire from *Kormoran*'s two stern guns.

Given Skeries's statement that he fired 'systematically' and that he had specific targets on *Sydney*, it is not surprising that he opted to use salvo firing. Although independent fire would have permitted a much higher rate of fire, as each gun could have fired as fast as it could be loaded, Skeries would have had little control over his gunners and the targets they chose.

Although there were disadvantages in using salvo firing, Skeries may not have had much choice. At the start of the action, the close range, coupled with the rolling of the ship may have prevented the low-mounted Nos 3 and 4 guns using their sighting telescopes.[16] If so, these two guns may have been aimed using bearing and elevation figures supplied via telephone, then on hearing the salvo gong, fired blind. In other words, if these two guns could not sight the target, their shooting may have been quite erratic, their shells either dropping short or passing over the intended aiming point. Salvo firing, however, would have given these guns at least some chance of hitting the designated target, provided they were fired at the same moment as the bow and stern guns.

Such a scenario would appear to be supported by Skeries's claim that the cruiser's aircraft was struck by a lucky shot. This had occurred during

the fifth salvo, which was probably aimed at the waterline below the Walrus. As Skeries claimed that his fourth salvo was aimed at the 'machine room', it is possible that this was also the target for the fifth salvo. Skeries probably used the word *Maschinen-raum* to describe the aiming point for his fourth salvo, *Maschinen-raum* being German for engine house or engine room.

Although *Sydney* had two engine rooms, Skeries probably selected the hull between the funnels as his aiming point. This area encompassed the forward engine room, which also happened to be positioned directly below the aircraft and catapult. As Hildenbrand said that they were instructed to aim for the waterline, it would be logical to assume that the aiming point for the fourth and fifth salvoes was the waterline between the funnels, and that a stray shell, possibly fired from No.3 or No.4 gun (firing without the aid of sights), missed the intended aiming point and accidentally struck the Walrus.

It is difficult to ascertain where every salvo was aimed, but it would appear that most of those fired before *Sydney* passed astern were aimed at the forward turrets, bridge, and the midships region. What can be established is this:

First salvo – Consisted of two shots aimed at the bridge. The first shell fired (No.1 gun) struck *Sydney* forward but hit below the point of aim. The second shell fired (No.5 gun) either missed or hit above the point of aim.

Second salvo – Consisted of three shots aimed at the bridge. One or more shells struck the 'bridge near funnel' (Skeries), 'carrying away most of her superstructure' (Detmers). It is probable that *Sydney*'s foremast was brought down by this salvo.

Third salvo – The first full, four-gun salvo. As *Sydney*'s bridge had been struck and set on fire by the second salvo, it appears that the third salvo was aimed at the forward turrets. According to Skeries, 'A' and 'B' turrets were put out of action by his third and fourth salvoes.

Fourth salvo – Apparently aimed at the waterline in the vicinity of the forward engine room. It is possible, however, that one or more guns continued to fire on the previous bearing, as *Sydney's* forward turrets were apparently hit again.

Fifth salvo – Probably aimed at the waterline between *Sydney's* funnels. A stray shell struck the Walrus.

Sixth to eighth salvoes – Unknown, but possibly aimed at the midships region either on the waterline or the upper deck. One shell was claimed to have started a fire in the vicinity of the torpedo tubes.

It is conceivable that Skeries was 'systematically' working his way along *Sydney*. If this was so, salvoes six, seven and eight may have been aimed at the after engine room and/or the 4-inch gundeck and the torpedo tubes.

Ninth salvo – Possibly still aimed at the midships region. About this time, it was claimed, a torpedo struck *Sydney* below the forward turrets. According to Eldridge, a salvo struck *Sydney* amidships at about the same time as the torpedo hit.

Tenth salvo – It is not known where this salvo was aimed, but as *Sydney* altered course towards *Kormoran* a direct hit was observed on 'B' turret, the roof of which was blown overboard.

It is not known exactly how many salvoes were fired before *Sydney* passed astern, although Skeries implied that only about ten salvoes were fired by him before he lost sight of the cruiser. According to Farncomb's report of 29 December, which was apparently based on information supplied by Treber, about fifteen salvoes were fired.

Given the life or death circumstances of the first phase, ten to fifteen salvoes would appear to be a rather low rate of fire. We must, however, consider the timeframe. Detmers gave the order to decamouflage, or drop screens, at about 1830. It then took about fifteen seconds for the first salvo to be fired. Three to four minutes later *Sydney* was torpedoed, the torpedo striking during the eighth or ninth salvo. Then, at approximately 1835, *Sydney* passed astern. Skeries therefore had only four or five minutes in which to fire salvoes before *Sydney* passed out of the arcs of his starboard battery.

Although it should have been possible for Skeries to fire more than ten to fifteen salvoes in the available time, precious seconds would have been lost each time he changed targets. Shifting the point of aim on a target that was also dropping astern would have slowed the rate of fire considerably. Even so, given that the 15-centimetre guns could be fired at a rate of about eight rounds per minute, and that some survivors claimed that fifteen rounds per minute was achieved for a short period, this number of salvoes still appears to be low.[17]

Hildenbrand's claim that his gun fired fifty shells, however, upsets the equation. As his gun (No.5) could not bear on *Sydney* after the cruiser passed astern, these shells must have been fired in the first phase. This creates a serious discrepancy in the number of salvoes fired.

The answer perhaps lies in the fact that for a short period of time, Hildenbrand's gun was the only one capable of firing. Once *Sydney* passed out of the arcs of fire of gun Nos 1, 3 and 4, they were forced to stop firing. *Sydney*, however, remained in the fire arcs of the No.5 gun. Released from the requirement to fire salvoes, Hildenbrand and his companions probably fired as fast as the ammunition could be passed and the gun loaded, perhaps firing an additional thirty or forty rounds in the minutes that were available.

Such a rate of fire was possible, but it would have overheated the gun to the point where it would have become unserviceable. This too is supported by the survivors' claims. Several commented that the guns became overheated and would not go back in train after recoiling.[18]

Once *Sydney* was directly astern, the No.6 gun started firing, and for a short time supported the No.5 gun. Their fire, according to Detmers's action report, was directed or controlled by Brinkman. *Sydney* then crossed onto *Kormoran*'s port quarter and passed out of the arcs of fire of the No.5 gun.

While *Sydney* executed this manoeuvre, Detmers maintained his course and speed. In doing so, he opened the range to about 4,000 metres, but limited his offensive capability to two, then one 15-centimetre gun. Detmers, however, was also providing his enemy with the smallest possible target at which to fire torpedoes. This proved to be a sound decision because *Sydney* did fire torpedoes from a position astern of *Kormoran*.

A short time after *Sydney* crossed onto *Kormoran*'s port quarter, all firing ceased, ending what was termed the first phase of the action.

That a pause in the firing did occur is corroborated by a number of the prisoners, although why this came about is not clear. Detmers was obviously still keen to continue with the action because his next move was to alter course to port to open the arcs for his port battery. It is possible that the temporary lull was a forced one, perhaps caused by overheating of the No.6 gun or the target becoming obscured by smoke.

GRETER'S TORPEDOES

Like many aspects of the *Sydney/Kormoran* action, the question of when and how *Kormoran*'s torpedoes were fired has generated a great deal of speculation and supposition.

The most popular theory is that Detmers fired a surprise torpedo from his starboard underwater tube before the declaration of identity. Although this theory has merit, it is not supported by the evidence.[19]

To launch a torpedo from an underwater tube, *Kormoran* had to be almost stationary or actually stopped. These tubes, one on each side, were not fitted with extension sleeves, and as a result, if a torpedo was fired while the ship was under way, the water moving past the torpedo port would force the half-launched torpedo against the side of the tube. This would result in the torpedo becoming jammed in the tube or thrown off course.

To use his starboard underwater tube, Detmers would have had to stop the engines then wait until the ship was almost stationary before Greter could launch a torpedo with any chance of success. Such an occurrence is not supported anywhere in the prisoners' statements, Detmers's action report or the reconstructed engine-room log. This is not surprising. Stopping the engines would have given Detmers no manoeuvring speed in the impending action and given his enemy a stationary target at which to fire.

Tactically, there were other disadvantages in using the underwater torpedo tubes for a surprise attack, especially at such a range.

Underwater torpedoes were normally launched by compressed air. In submarines, the air used to start the torpedo was vented from the tube to a tank inside the submarine. Without such a vent, a large air bubble would appear on the surface, betraying the location of the submarine. As a surface vessel equipped with submerged torpedo tubes would normally be in full view of the enemy, there was no requirement to recover the compressed air. For this reason it is doubtful that *Kormoran* was equipped with vented torpedo tubes, in which case, the firing of an underwater torpedo would have resulted in a large tell-tale bubble being produced alongside *Kormoran* and in full view of *Sydney*.

According to Greter, however, his torpedoes could be launched from the submerged tubes without the use of compressed air. When the raider went to battle stations, the watertight torpedo tube covers were opened and the tubes flooded. The torpedoes could then be launched by compressed air or started in the tubes. In the latter case the torpedo would leave the tube under its own propulsion.[20]

Greter has said that the use of compressed air to launch a torpedo was of no importance, because his torpedoes left a trail of bubbles in their wake. As it would have taken well over a minute for the 27-knot torpedo to cover the required distance to the target, even a clandestinely launched torpedo could have been detected by its wake long before it reached *Sydney*.[21]

Additionally, there would have been no guarantee of success if Detmers had opted for a surprise torpedo attack. Although 1,100 to 1,500 metres was point-blank range for the 15-centimetre guns, it was a considerable distance over which to fire a single torpedo with any certainty of hitting the target. U-boat commanders knew the limitations of the weapon and preferred to close to within 600 metres of their victim before firing torpedoes.[22]

The greatest risk in using a torpedo to initiate action was the danger that the torpedo could malfunction. At the time it was well known that there were problems with the reliability of the German torpedo, and it is doubtful that Detmers would have taken a chance on his torpedoes running true and detonating properly.

The invasion of Norway in the spring of 1940 had proven disastrous for the German Navy. U-boat commanders had experienced torpedo failures from the start of the war, but the problem reached crisis point in Norway, where nearly every torpedo attack launched by U-boats and destroyers ended in failure. Most of the failures were experienced with the G-7 type torpedo and consisted primarily of faulty depth keeping. This made the torpedoes run deep and pass under their targets, or run surfaced, allowing them to be spotted by their intended victims and avoiding action to be taken.

The other problem was found to be the magnetic pistol, which was supposed to detonate the torpedo warhead under the steel hull of the target. This new type of pistol had numerous faults and insufficient trialling failed to identify all of them. Even the contact pistols, however, gave cause for anxiety. Because of their design, they needed a very broad strike angle to detonate the warhead. It was found that torpedoes hitting curved hull plates would not explode. After the battles for Narvik, German torpedoes were found on the beaches where they had run aground without exploding.

Another problem was premature detonation. The pistol had a safety device, much like a small propeller, that revolved as the torpedo travelled through the water. Over a predetermined distance, the propeller, or vane, would rotate a specified number of times and arm the pistol. Inexplicably, many torpedoes detonated at the end of their safety distance as soon as the pistol had armed.

Most of the faults were eventually traced to the torpedo-testing establishment at Eckernforde. In the subsequent court martial, the head of the establishment, and his two subordinates, were found guilty of negligence and each sentenced to six months' imprisonment.[23]

The problems, however, did not go away overnight. The failures continued to occur through 1941 and into 1942. That the raiders also suffered torpedo failures can be established by studying the records of their attacks. Nearly all raider captains experienced some problem with their torpedoes, but perhaps Krüder had the worst experience.

On 7 May 1941, *Pinguin* was almost struck by one of its own torpedoes, which had been fired at *British Emperor*. After hitting the water, the torpedo surfaced then veered to the left. With *Pinguin* still under way, the rogue torpedo began to describe a circle, which it was soon realized would place it on a collision course with the raider. Krüder ordered an

emergency turn, and the torpedo passed within twenty metres of *Pinguin's* bow.[24]

Detmers would have been well aware of these failures, if not from his meetings with U-boat skippers and raider colleagues, then certainly from his own experience. On 18 January 1941, he witnessed one of his own torpedoes, fired at *British Union*, detonate at the end of its safety distance and well short of the target.[25]

When all this is considered, it would appear unlikely that Detmers would have risked using a torpedo to initiate the action. But despite its shortcomings, the outcome of the battle would hinge on the torpedo. Although his guns could perhaps severely damage *Sydney*, it was only with torpedoes that Detmers could hope to cripple or perhaps even sink his opponent. The close range and relatively flat trajectory of the 15-centimetre shells would mean that *Sydney's* magazines, situated below the waterline, would be almost immune from a direct hit. *Kormoran*, on the other hand, was particularly vulnerable. The raider's magazines were not protected and, with the full complement of mines still aboard, *Kormoran* could be blown out of the water in a split second if just one shell were to penetrate the hull in the wrong place.

THE TORPEDO SHOT

Detmers's action report records that the initial attempt was for two torpedoes from the above water torpedo tubes. The aiming points for these torpedoes were *Sydney's* bow and stern. The target speed was estimated as 14 knots, and the inclination was calculated to be 80°. This calculation is interesting, for inclination is the term used to describe the angle on the target's bow. In this instance, it means that *Sydney* was not running parallel with *Kormoran* (because this would have provided an inclination of 90°) but was slightly bows on, by an angle of 10°. In other words, *Sydney* was still closing when the calculation for the shot was made.

Although the torpedoes were not fired immediately, the estimation of the target speed is interesting.

When torpedoes are fired at moving targets, a certain amount of 'lead' or 'aim off' must be applied. If the torpedo is aimed directly at a moving target, by the time the torpedo reaches the aiming point, the target will no longer be there. In other words, the torpedo has to be aimed at a point somewhere in front of the target, taking into account the speed of the target and the running time of the torpedo. If the calculation is correct, and the target does not alter course or increase or decrease speed, the torpedo should strike the target at the calculated point.

To hit *Sydney* Greter had to calculate the distance the cruiser would travel in the time it would take for his torpedoes to run the distance between the two ships. He then had to fire his torpedoes in advance of *Sydney*, the amount of 'lead' or 'aim off' being equal to the distance *Sydney* was expected to travel in the torpedo running time.

If *Sydney* was steaming at 14 knots and was 1,500 metres away, the amount of 'lead' required was nearly 770 metres. The torpedoes, travelling at 27 knots, would take nearly two minutes to reach the target. As *Sydney* was approximately 170 metres long, this distance represents an aiming point over four ship's lengths in front of the target. Not a particularly good shot to have to make.

This 'lead' or 'aim off' is important when considering whether or not the starboard underwater tube was used to initiate the action. In the unlikely event that it was, *Sydney* was in the safest possible position. Given that *Sydney* was claimed to be abaft *Kormoran*'s starboard beam, and the underwater torpedo-tubes were angled back 35° abaft the beam, a torpedo fired from the starboard underwater tube could not have hit *Sydney*. Although the torpedo-tube may have been pointing directly at the cruiser, by the time the torpedo had run the required distance to target, *Sydney* would have steamed out of the danger area.

Greter's choice of a bow and stern shot for his above-water torpedo-tubes is interesting because it indicates that he was trying to cover the possibility of the target increasing or decreasing speed or altering course after his torpedoes were fired. If *Sydney* maintained course and speed, he could perhaps expect two hits—one on the bow, and one on the stern. If not, he could expect at least one hit somewhere between the bow and the stern.

The other aspect of Greter's calculations that must be considered are the above-water torpedo tubes. According to Detmers's post-war account, the First World War vintage tubes were fitted with a cogwheel

and ratchet training mechanism, the tubes having to be manhandled into the correct position before being locked in place by the ratchet. Aiming then involved turning the ship towards the target. In other words, once the tubes were loaded and locked into position, it was quicker to turn the ship onto the target than to retrain the torpedo tubes.

According to the evidence, Greter did not launch his torpedoes immediately Detmers gave permission to fire. The delay was possibly due to the time required to prepare the tubes for firing, but the action report entry—'Enemy drops slowly astern'—could also explain it. If *Sydney* was reducing speed when Detmers declared identity, the reduction in speed might have upset Greter's shot calculations. Although the spread, using *Sydney*'s bow and stern as impact points, should have compensated for any change in the target speed. Detmers's decision to alter course from 250° to 260°, however, was clearly for the purpose of assisting Greter, and supports the claim that *Sydney* did reduce speed.

It is difficult to determine exactly when Greter fired his torpedoes, but he appears to have done so about the raider's third or fourth salvo. They obviously were not fired before the first salvo because Detmers said he made the alteration in course with little helm movement so as not to interfere with the guns, implying that the guns were already firing; and altering course before opening fire would have aroused suspicion.

The statement made by one of the torpedo men is a further indication that the torpedoes were not used until after the first salvo. Friedrich Schmitt claimed that the cruiser was 'burning all over' when his torpedo was fired, suggesting that *Sydney* had already been hit by shellfire when the torpedoes were launched.

Given the running time of the torpedoes, several more 15-centimetre salvoes would have been fired before the torpedoes reached the target. Again, this is consistent with the action report, which noted that a torpedo struck *Sydney* in the vicinity of the forward turrets at about the eighth or ninth salvo.

Curiously, the action report suggests that, before the torpedoes were fired, the deflection (the angle from *Kormoran*'s bow) was corrected left to a point under the forward turrets. To correct the angle of deflection left indicates that the initial calculated point of impact was abaft *Sydney*'s forward turrets, possibly amidships.

The fact that only one torpedo struck and that the other was observed (presumably by its wake) to pass a short distance ahead provides further indication that *Sydney* was still reducing, or had reduced, speed.

But there is another sequence of events that has recently come to light. In 1986, in an informal discussion with Lieutenant Alistair Templeton RANR (retired), Greter recalled that there were two firings. The first, from the forward tube missed, apparently passing ahead. The second shot, however, fired after the ship had been 'wiggled' to get the proper firing angle, hit *Sydney* approximately under 'A' turret.[26]

The reaction of *Sydney* after being torpedoed is equally interesting and has led some to believe that the cruiser was not at action stations.

What the *Kormoran* survivors said was that the explosion caused *Sydney*'s bows to bite deep into the water. A huge cloud of black smoke then enveloped the ship. When this cleared, *Sydney* was seen to be down by the bows. Clearly, a great deal of water had been shipped forward as a result of the explosion.

This has created the belief that *Sydney* did not have all water-tight doors and hatches closed, a condition that was not possible if the ship had been at action stations. Torpedo explosions, however, are capable of blowing a large hole in the side of a ship, and the blast effect, coupled with the huge volume of water that rushes in, tends to destroy all bulkheads and water-tight doors in the vicinity of the explosion. In other words, *Sydney*'s bows-down condition after being torpedoed was not unusual. It is consistent with similar cases where British cruisers were torpedoed forward, and despite the fact that the highest level of water-tight integrity was being maintained, immediately shipped a large volume of water forward.

The reason for *Sydney*'s manoeuvre to port immediately after being torpedoed has also generated debate, although the timing suggests that the two events were probably linked. Many of the *Kormoran*'s crew who witnessed *Sydney*'s bows swing towards them thought the cruiser was intending to ram. The evidence, however, does not support such a scenario. The relative positions of the two ships and their respective speeds clearly prevented the two from meeting in such a fashion. After being torpedoed, *Sydney*'s speed was reduced to an estimated 5 to 7 knots while *Kormoran*, despite being hit in the engine room, was apparently able

to maintain 14 knots for a short period of time. Although *Sydney* did eventually cross *Kormoran*'s track, by the time that it did so, the raider had increased the range and was in no danger of being rammed.

It is possible that *Sydney*'s turn to port was caused by drag, failure of the steering gear, or damage or loss of steam to the port engines. It is just as conceivable that it was a deliberate and controlled turn. Specifically, the turn may have been ordered in response to the firing of Greter's torpedoes, or the sighting of their tracks. Turning bows-on to oncoming torpedoes was standard procedure, and a turn to port would have allowed *Sydney* to meet the threat and 'comb' the torpedo tracks. Given *Sydney*'s reduced speed and the short range, however, it is probable that the ship could not be turned fast enough to avoid being hit.

An important consideration, however, is that up to the time the torpedo struck, *Sydney*'s after turrets were apparently still returning fire. Turning the ship to port effectively put these turrets out of action, as they would not have been able to bear on *Kormoran*. With 'A' and 'B' turrets knocked out, and the port torpedo tubes and 4-inch guns untenable, 'X' and 'Y' turrets were *Sydney*'s only means of hitting back. If the turn to port was made in response to the sighting of torpedo tracks, it was ill conceived.[27]

A turn to starboard, on the other hand, would have opened the range while still permitting 'X' and 'Y' turrets to fire, although such a turn would also have allowed the raider's starboard battery to continue firing. Turning to port enabled *Sydney* to move in behind the raider and, in theory, out of the arcs of fire of the raider's weapons. The turn to port, therefore, may have been made in order to prevent further damage to *Sydney*. With this in mind, it is possible that the turn to port was ordered before Greter fired his torpedoes.

SYDNEY PASSES ASTERN

The manoeuvring of *Sydney* to a position astern of *Kormoran* apparently brought a brief halt to the action. At about 1850, Skeries started salvo firing again with his port battery, in what the Germans termed the 'second phase' of the action. It was also about this time that *Sydney* fired four torpedoes before turning behind its smoke.

It is possible that the act of firing torpedoes influenced Detmers's decision to continue with the fight, although he recorded in his action report that he had already given the order for a change of course to 240° when the torpedo tracks were sighted. With his engines failing, the desire to open the arcs for his port guns outweighed his desire to take avoiding action against the approaching torpedoes. Detmers was not satisfied with crippling and beating off his opponent. He was determined to sink the cruiser that had put an end to his raiding activities. Detmers recorded that he 'turned away to port in order to destroy enemy completely'.

There is very little information available on the effectiveness of the fire from *Kormoran*'s port battery, apart from the action report entry, which claimed constant further hits. Although there is no doubt that the bulk of the alleged 550 shells fired during the action would have been fired in the second phase, when *Kormoran*'s gunners previous performances over similar ranges are studied, most of the shells would have fallen harmlessly into the sea.[28]

The composition of the total number of shells fired gives another clue to how many were fired in the first phase.

Detmers claimed that in total approximately 550 rounds of 15-centimetre shell were fired, but Skeries gave a lower figure of 450 rounds. But both said that only 50 rounds of nose-fuze shell were fired, the remainder being base-fuzed.

The close range at which the action was fought, coupled with the need to cause the maximum amount of damage, probably influenced Skeries to use the nose-fuzed shells in the opening salvoes. At close range, these shells, exploding on impact, would have had little difficulty in defeating the armour belt protecting *Sydney*'s machinery spaces. And their effect on the thin plating of the superstructure and the light armour of the 6-inch turrets would have been nothing short of devastating. *Sydney*'s upper works and turrets would have been torn apart by the exploding shells, and the resulting splinters would have torn through everything in their path.

An excellent example of the destructive power of a 15-centimetre nose-fuze shell was the hole blown in *Sydney*'s forward funnel during the Cape Spada action. According to the after action report, the shell 'exploded on the port side of the forward funnel 10 feet below the cravat.

A hole 3 feet square was blown in the inner and outer funnel casings on the port side, and many splinters passed through the funnel and emerged on the starboard side'.[29] Because the shell, fired by *Giovanni delle Bande Nere*, exploded on impact, it is reasonable to assume that it was of the nose-fuze type. This is based on the assumption that an armour piercing (base-fuze) shell would have passed through the port side of the funnel before exploding on the starboard side.

That nose-fuzed shells were employed in the first phase of the *Sydney/Kormoran* action is supported by Detmers's statement that the first broadside carried away most of *Sydney*'s superstructure, his choice of words suggesting the use of shells that exploded on impact. Armour-piercing shells, as their name implies, were designed to penetrate deep into the vitals of a ship before exploding, often showing little outward sign of having hit the target.

The number of nose-fuzed shells fired is also significant. Assuming only ten to fifteen salvoes were fired by Skeries during the first phase, and that every salvo was not a four-gun salvo, the actual number of shells fired would be close to fifty.

Of course, there is the question of how many shells, and of what type, were fired by the stern guns during the latter part of the first phase. As these guns, particularly the No.5 gun, would have been firing as fast as they could be loaded, it is conceivable that they fired whatever came to hand, perhaps firing a mixture of nose-fuzed and base-fuzed shells. It is equally possible, however, that these guns were instructed to fire base-fuzed shells to ensure the cruiser's armour belt would be penetrated as the range increased.

Overall, it is probable that between 80 and 100 shells were fired by *Kormoran*'s 15-centimetre guns during the first phase of the action and, of this total, approximately 50 shells were of the nose-fuzed type. The remaining 350 to 450 shells would have been fired in the second phase. This ratio has particular significance when it comes to analysing the German hitting claims and the extent of the damage sustained by *Sydney*.

Wilhelm Kurz, an ammunition handler on the No.4 gun, claimed he saw thirty to forty hits on the cruiser. Considering that most of the hits would have been scored in the first phase when the range was relatively short, and that a 50 per cent hit/miss ratio would be a reasonable

The hole blown in *Sydney*'s forward funnel by
a 6-inch shell during the Cape Spada action.
R. Buckingham

yardstick, Kurz's claim could be conservative. This view is supported by the claims made by an unidentified prisoner interviewed by Sergeant E. Caminer on 16 January 1942. Caminer reported that the young POW described the action in great detail and said that after *Sydney* crossed astern 'she seemed unable to swing her guns around so as to focus them properly onto the *Kormoran*'. This prisoner estimated that *Sydney* 'received fifty hits on the waterline alone, besides being effectively torpedoed'.[30]

Taking into account fatigue and exhaustion among the gunners and ammunition handlers, and the mechanical problems associated with the overheated guns, it would be fair to say that the percentage of hits in the second phase would be considerably lower. A figure of a hundred hits for the entire action is perhaps a reasonable estimate. Considering that even fifty hits represents over two tons of high explosive shells, it is not difficult to see how badly damaged *Sydney* would have been by 15-centimetre shellfire alone.

A THIRD TORPEDO

The action report recorded that at about 1900 a single torpedo was fired from *Kormoran*'s port underwater tube. The range was estimated as 7,000 metres, the target speed 5 knots. The inclination was calculated to be 80°, although one action report translation provides an inclination of 110°. The first angle of inclination is curious because it suggests that *Sydney* had swung around. The second, however, shows that *Sydney* was still steaming away.

Regardless of the inclination, 7,000 metres represented an almost impossible range for a single torpedo to be fired over with any hope of success. Not surprisingly, it was claimed to have missed astern.

SYDNEY'S FIRE

If the extent of the damage supposedly inflicted on *Sydney* is at times vague and nondescript, the damage sustained by *Kormoran* is more so. Obviously, *Sydney* damaged *Kormoran* to such an extent that Detmers was forced to scuttle his command but, apart from acknowledging about three or four hits, Detmers appears to have attempted to play down the extent of this damage. His action report only mentioned hits in the funnel and engine room, although his post-war account elaborated, adding that *Sydney*'s 'X' turret (which he claimed was responsible for these hits), fired with considerable accuracy. 'Y' turret, he claimed, fired two or three salvoes without effect. The interrogation notes, however, reveal that *Sydney* scored other hits.

The first hit received by *Kormoran* appears to have been on the funnel. Paul Heinz, a member of a 2-centimetre gun crew, claimed that he was wounded by splinters from the first hit. Zoppeck, possibly serving the same gun, was wounded at the same time. Zoppeck claimed that he was wounded by splinters from the shell that struck the funnel. If both men were wounded by splinters from the same shell, their statements suggest that the shell that struck the funnel was the first hit received. This view finds support in the statements made by Jürgensen and Bretschneider.

Although Bunjes claimed *Sydney*'s first salvo struck them amidships in the engine room, other evidence points to *Kormoran*'s engine room being hit well after the opening salvoes. The action report indicates that it wasn't until the raider's fifth salvo that the funnel and engine room were hit, although the engine room log recorded several hits in the main engine room at approximately 1835, five minutes after the declaration of identity.

According to the engine-room log, one shell tore open the bulkhead of the forward fuel tank, causing a thick jet of burning fuel-oil to pour into the engine room, rapidly filling it with 'opaque smoke'. Another shell passed straight through the engine room, piercing the firemain on both sides of the ship and putting the main fire-extinguishing system out of action. The portable foam extinguisher plant, which had been transferred by the damage control party to the port side of the engine room about fifteen minutes before the action started, was put out of action at about the same time. It is not clear if this was the result of splinter damage, a direct hit, or mechanical breakdown.

With both fire-fighting appliances knocked out, the oil fire could not be adequately fought and quickly became uncontrollable. An explosion on the starboard side damaged the transformers, destroying the excitation for the main generators. Although the engines themselves were not hit,

with the excitation destroyed, there was insufficient current available to drive the propulsion motors. With the engines effectively useless, permission was sought, and received, to abandon the engine room. The personnel were evacuated, although the engines were left running at high speed under the supervision of the control-room staff. An attempt was made to fight the engine-room fire from the propulsion motor room, but this failed when pressure could not be raised in the damaged firemain.

At approximately 1845 Lensch reported to the bridge to inform Detmers that the engine room and all the fire-fighting equipment were out of action. At about the same time the engines failed completely. Detmers ordered that an attempt be made to get at least one engine working again. When this order was relayed to the engineer officer, Kapitänleutnant Stehr, who had remained in the glass-enclosed control position at the rear of the engine room, he replied that the order could not be carried out. This officer and all but one of the control position personnel died a short time later when they were engulfed in flames while trying to escape from their smoke-filled enclosure.

Foerster, it will be recalled, claimed that there was no fire-fighting equipment left after the first salvo. It would appear that Foerster was telling the truth, but was incorrect when he said that the damage was caused by *Sydney*'s first salvo.

Foerster added that after the fire-fighting equipment was destroyed he tried to rig 'emergency gear'. Despite his efforts, the fire in the engine room became uncontrollable and began to threaten the magazines. As he was unable to contain the fire, he was forced to flood the magazines. Foerster indicated that in addition to the hit that destroyed the fire-fighting equipment, there was another, which stopped the raider. According to Foerster, the action lasted 'about twenty minutes'.

Kurz said that it was a salvo of four shells that struck the engine room. His claim that one shell (or salvo) also struck the oil chamber perhaps refers to the hit that opened up the bulkhead of the fuel tank in the engine room.

Hellmut Conzendorf's statement was equally vague. He said that his battle station was the auxiliary boiler room, and that he was wounded when the adjacent room was hit. Although he did not indicate which room was hit, it is conceivable that the shell he was referring to may have been the one described by Hans Böhm as striking abaft the engine room.

Böhm was stationed in the engine room during the action, and he supplied information that was consistent with Foerster's statements and the engine-room log. He said that the raider was hit in the engine-room oil tanks. About ten minutes after the action started, the engine room caught fire and had to be abandoned because of the smoke. He also said that the fire could not be fought because the fire-fighting installation was put out of action by a shell, which passed right through the ship. Böhm added that the engine room was abandoned with the engines left running at high speed.

Clearly, several shells, possibly a full (four-gun) salvo from 'X' and 'Y' turrets, struck *Kormoran*'s engine room a few minutes after fire was opened.

The hit or explosion that knocked out the transformers apparently also destroyed the power supply to the ship. Ernst Karl, who was the electrician in charge of the ship's lighting, said that the electricity supply was damaged and could not be repaired. The statement made by telegraphist

'First Salvo' by Ross Shardlow.

Helmut Funke suggested that it was a shell that caused this damage. Stationed below decks in the No.2 (reserve) radio room, Funke claimed that no messages were sent because the electricity supply 'was stopped by a direct hit'.

The other well-documented hit was the shell which struck the No.3 gun. Unfortunately, there is little to indicate exactly when this gun was hit, or which turret was deemed responsible, although it is perhaps relevant that 'X' turret was acknowledged by Detmers as firing with considerable accuracy. It is conceivable, however, that 'Y' turret could have been responsible, even though its fire was described as high. The only indication that a shell or salvo was fired high would have been the resulting splash in the sea on the lee side of the ship. The shell that struck the No.3 gun was claimed to have skimmed the deck, struck the mounting (killing one man and wounding others), and then exploded in the sea behind the ship. It is possible that this shell may have been fired by 'Y' turret, but was mistakenly thought to have gone over the ship.

The other possibility is that either 'A' or 'B' turret, or both, fired a second salvo and scored the hit on the No.3 gun. Despite the claim that these turrets only fired once (in *Sydney*'s opening salvo), a statement made by Detmers on 1 December 1941 suggests that the forward turrets were still in action after the first salvo. Detmers said that they 'fired two torpedoes, one of which missed and one hit, about 20 metres from the bow. The fore turrets then stopped firing'. Detmers's choice of words is interesting in that he implies that 'A' and 'B' turrets were still firing immediately before the torpedo hit. If Detmers was correct, and the forward turrets were still firing up to this point in the action, it is conceivable that they attempted to knock out the raider's forward guns or the torpedo tubes or both, the latter being in close proximity to the No.3 gun.

If 'A' and 'B' turrets were knocked out by Skeries's opening salvoes, there was another claim that may provide the answer to which turret was responsible for the damage to the No.3 gun. Bretschneider wrote in his diary that after 'X' and 'Y' turrets resumed firing, *Kormoran* received a hit on the poop deck, which started a fire.[31]

The sequence of events given by Bretschneider suggests that the hit on the poop deck was received after the engine room was struck and before

Sydney was torpedoed. Although Detmers said that 'x' turret was responsible for all the damage to *Kormoran*, it would appear improbable that one turret would have fired at the raider's engine room, changed targets to engage the No.3 gun, then changed targets again to fire at the stern. In all likelihood, 'Y' turret was responsible for one or more of these hits.

A possible scenario is that after the raider had been hit amidships, an attempt was made to knock out the guns. 'x' turret perhaps engaged *Kormoran*'s No.3 gun and 'Y' turret engaged the No.5 gun, the latter being mounted under the raider's poop deck.

Although there is insufficient information available to establish with any certainty exactly how *Sydney* fought its last battle, taking all available information into account, the most likely sequence is as follows:

First salvo – Consisted of a full, eight-gun salvo fired under director control, and fired either simultaneously as, or possibly shortly after *Kormoran*'s first salvo. This salvo was probably aimed at the raider's bridge.

Although Detmers thought this salvo missed, there is evidence to suggest that four shells may have hit. If the latter view is correct, one shell struck *Kormoran*'s funnel, while three passed through the bridge structure without exploding (Tümmers). With the possible exception of the shell that struck the funnel, all shells exploded in the sea behind *Kormoran*, giving the impression that the salvo missed.[32]

The possibility that the shell that struck the funnel exploded is supported by the widespread splinter effect, which destroyed one of the port lifeboats and wounded at least two ratings on the midships 2-centimetre guns abaft of the funnel.

Second salvo – Fired after some delay, on or about *Kormoran*'s fifth salvo. The delay was probably due to damage to the DCT.

This salvo may have been responsible for the hits behind the bridge and on the funnel. Alternatively, they struck *Kormoran* amidships in the vicinity of the engine room. It is assumed that this salvo comprised the four guns of 'x' and 'Y' turrets, firing in group or local control. One shell tore open the engine room fuel tank and

apparently exited the ship without exploding. A second shell also passed straight through the ship without exploding, but pierced the firemain on both sides of the engine room. A third shell detonated on the starboard side of the engine room, destroying the transformers. The fourth shell apparently exploded abaft the engine room.

'A' or 'B' turrets or both may have also fired in the second salvo, although it is extremely difficult to determine what effect (if any) their fire may have had.

Third and subsequent salvoes – The firing and placement of the third and subsequent salvoes are difficult to identify, but appear to have been fired by 'X' and 'Y' turrets in local control.

Although further shells may have been fired into *Kormoran*'s engine room, it is clear that some fire was directed at the raider's guns, 'X' turret possibly engaging the forward guns, while 'Y' turret engaged the after guns.

Despite the lack of direct evidence, it is also possible that *Sydney*'s 4-inch guns took some part in the action. Hildenbrand claimed that the cruiser fired for five to six minutes when it was on their port side, and that three or four big shells hit them. As all evidence points to 'X' and 'Y' turrets remaining trained to port after *Sydney* passed astern, Hildenbrand's claim implies that the starboard 4-inch guns engaged *Kormoran* for five to six minutes. Such a scenario would appear to be supported by Jürgensen. He said that after the cruiser turned, both ships continued to fight, suggesting that the starboard 4-inch guns were fired.

There is also evidence of the 0.5-inch machine guns being used during the action, as there are references to *Sydney* using 'pom-poms'. As *Sydney* was not equipped with 2-pounder pom-poms or 20-millimetre Oerlikons, it can only be assumed that the prisoners were referring to the 0.5-inch machine guns.

This assumption would appear to be supported by Skeries, who said that there was '1-inch' fire from *Sydney*, which was 'mostly short'. If this was actually 0.5-inch fire, it is not surprising that it was short. The 0.5-inch machine guns were designed for close-range anti-aircraft work, and 1,100 metres would have been close to the limit of their effective range. The possibility that some hits were obtained, however, is implied by the use of the words 'mostly short'.[33]

SYDNEY'S TORPEDOES

Like the gunfire, the firing of *Sydney*'s torpedoes contains an element of uncertainty. Although there is little doubt that four torpedoes were fired from the starboard tubes shortly after *Sydney* crossed astern of *Kormoran*, there is a question mark over whether any were fired from the port tubes earlier in the action.

Statements made by Detmers and Jürgensen indicate that *Sydney* may have fired two torpedoes from the port torpedo tubes early in the first phase of the action. There is no indication, however, about where these torpedoes went, if they were fired, and there is certainly no evidence of any hitting *Kormoran* during this period of the action. There is also the question of, if two, then why not four?

The latter can perhaps be answered by a study of *Sydney*'s torpedo tubes. The cruiser's torpedoes were launched by air impulse, the (cordite) impulse chambers being mounted on the top rear of each tube. In such a position they were particularly vulnerable to the close range 15-centimetre shell and 2-centimetre cannon fire to which the ship was subjected. Damage to any of these impulse chambers would have prevented the affected tube discharging its torpedo. Such damage may have prevented two of the four tubes being fired.

A more likely scenario, however, is that casualties among the torpedomen prevented any of the port torpedoes being fired.

There is another curious aspect about *Sydney*'s port torpedo tubes. In 1986, when discussing the subject with *Kormoran* survivors, Templeton was told that *Sydney*'s port torpedo tubes were swung inboard before the action started. Templeton considered that, if this was so, it suggested that the tubes had only been trained as an exercise and that Burnett was conducting a drill when he decided to close with the supposed Dutchman. There may, however, be another explanation.

If Burnett were attempting to capture what he thought was an enemy supply ship, he would not have wanted to torpedo it. Once he was sure

in his own mind that the vessel he was closing with was not a threat to his command, he might have ordered the torpedo tubes to be swung inboard. If this is what occurred, it is relevant that the torpedomen would have remained at their action station and observed proceedings, probably standing at the breech end of the tubes. As the tubes normally pointed towards the stern of the ship when in the fore and aft position, this would have placed the torpedomen at the forward end of the torpedo space. Such a position would have been quite visible to observers on *Kormoran* and may have added weight to the German belief that because men could be seen on deck, the cruiser was not at action stations. Such a position, forward of the tubes and under the 4-inch gun deck, would have afforded the torpedomen a fair measure of protection from the blast of the after 6-inch guns should they fire on an extreme forward bearing.

The other consideration is that if the port tubes were swung back inboard, they may have been made safe by the insertion of the striker pin retaining forks into the breech blocks. The time taken for the removal of these forks and the retraining of the tubes once fire was opened may account for the delay in their firing, if they were fired at all.

THE TURN TO PORT

One aspect of *Sydney's* actions that requires revisiting is the cruiser's turn to port immediately after being torpedoed. Up to this point, 'x' and 'y' turrets were apparently firing with some effect and might have succeeded in completely destroying *Kormoran* if they had been fortunate enough to put just one shell into a magazine or the raider's mine deck. The turn to port, however, closed A-arcs, preventing these turrets bearing on the target.

Although the turn was perhaps made as a result of the raider's torpedoes being sighted, other possibilities exist. One reason was that with the port torpedo tubes damaged or untenable, *Sydney* needed to turn in order to bring the starboard tubes into action, possibly from a position that was beyond the effective range of *Kormoran's* 2-centimetre guns. The need to bring the starboard tubes to bear was vital, and the probability that this was the reason for the turn is borne out by the fact that *Sydney* did deliver a torpedo attack from a position astern of *Kormoran*.

Another possibility is that there was a loss of power to 'x' and 'y' turrets. Although the turrets could be worked without power, it was a laborious and time-consuming operation. That there was a loss of power would appear to be supported by the claim that after turning to port *Sydney* was unable to swing the after turrets around. It is also conceivable that 'x' and 'y' turrets received damage that left them jammed on a port bearing.[34] This could have occurred through shell damage or the shock of the torpedo explosion.

A side effect of being torpedoed was that the explosion would send a shock wave through the ship, causing it to whip along its entire length.[35] In severe cases, this 'whipping' could cause additional damage. This occurred when the 6-inch cruiser *Birmingham* was torpedoed.

On 28 November 1943, HMS *Birmingham* was hit by a torpedo that struck the ship in the vicinity of the Asdic compartment, just forward of 'A' turret. The explosion caused, among other damage, the roller paths of 'A' turret to distort, jamming the turret. The explosion also caused the ship to whip along its length with the result that the roller paths of 'Y' turret also became distorted, jamming this turret as well.[36]

As the torpedo which struck *Sydney* was claimed to have detonated immediately below the forward turrets, there is a possibility that 'x' and 'y' turrets became jammed to port as a result of their roller paths becoming distorted due to whipping.

FIRING CEASES

Whatever the cause, with 'A' and 'B' turrets knocked out, 'x' and 'y' turrets jammed to port, the 4-inch guns apparently silenced, and the starboard torpedoes expended, *Sydney* was incapable of continuing with the action. There was little option but to disengage and withdraw under cover of smoke.

In a matter of minutes, the pride of the Royal Australian Navy had been reduced to a blazing wreck. *Sydney* had taken one torpedo forward and countless 15-centimetre shells on and above the waterline. The bridge and forward superstructure had been blown apart and now burned fiercely while another fire raged amidships. Furthermore, given the punishment

received, it is likely that a large percentage of the key personnel now lay dead or dying.

At 1925, approximately fifty-five minutes after the action had begun, Detmers ordered all firing to cease. *Sydney*, having managed to make an estimated 5 to 7 knots, was now some 10,000 metres off *Kormoran's* port quarter. Although *Sydney* had managed to survive its encounter with *Kormoran*, the cruiser was in a very bad way.

EXIT SYDNEY

One final consideration about *Sydney's* departure from the scene of battle is the course taken.

The action report noted that the cruiser steamed away on a course of about 150°, while the last gun bearing was 225° (225° to 235° according to Kobelt).

Like the British, the Germans based their target bearings on the axis of the ship, but while the Royal Navy employed Green (starboard) and Red (port) bearings of 0° to 180°, the German Navy used a 360° system. In German gunnery terms, the bows of the ship represented 0° and directly aft represented 180°. A target directly off the starboard beam would provide a bearing of 90° and a target off the port beam would provide a bearing of 270°.

A gun bearing of 225°, therefore, placed *Sydney* off *Kormoran's* port quarter. Considering the fact that by the time the last shots were fired, *Kormoran* would have been drifting beam-on to the prevailing winds, a bearing of 225° is consistent with *Sydney's* last known course, which is also consistent with Greter's final torpedo shot.

This then is the German account of what had occurred on 19 November 1941. Although there are contradictions and anomalies in the German statements, there is nothing to suggest that their claims were a fabrication. In fact, quite the opposite. The complexity of the account suggests that those who volunteered to talk, spoke the truth, or perhaps just as importantly, spoke what they thought was the truth.

POSSIBLE & PROBABLE CAUSES

WHEN last seen by *Kormoran* survivors, *Sydney* was afloat but on fire. A few thought that the cruiser must have sunk; others believed it steamed over the horizon. Some became dismayed and even angry that the cruiser did not return to rescue them.[1]

The difference in views about *Sydney*'s disappearance, however, would appear to be directly related to the plight of each survivor. Many of those who abandoned ship in the first group, at around 2000, lost sight of *Sydney* almost immediately, because their vantage point was now at or near sea level. Lensch, for instance, said that 'from the moment he stepped on to the raft he did not see the glare of the fire on the cruiser'. Those who remained on board *Kormoran* had the advantage of height, and were able to keep *Sydney* in view for several more hours.

While *Sydney* had remained in view, the bows were deep in the water and occasionally the propellers could be seen. The ship was also observed to be well ablaze forward and amidships. But some survivors claimed that the cruiser was on fire amidships and astern.[2]

Some time between 2100 and 2200, the fires disappeared from view. Afterwards, *Sydney* was identifiable only as a glow on the horizon. Around midnight, the glow, which had been seen to increase in intensity intermittently, began to fade. After *Kormoran* sank, at approximately 0135 on 20 November, there was only darkness.

The fires in *Sydney* had been seen to flare up and then fade away, but there was no noise of an explosion, and many, including Detmers, were astonished when they later heard that the Australian cruiser had failed to return to port. Even *Kormoran*'s doctor thought that *Sydney* 'would be able to make land, owing to her watertight compartments and short distance from land'.[3]

It is obvious that *Sydney* had been badly damaged during the action, but according to many witnesses had survived the engagement. The question, therefore, is would the damage sustained during the action have been sufficient to cause *Sydney*'s loss some time after the battle?

Without a surviving eyewitness to *Sydney*'s sinking, and without the luxury of a visual inspection of its wreck, one can only speculate. There is sufficient evidence, however, for certain conclusions to be reached.

Firstly, there are the interrogation statements of the *Kormoran* survivors. Their statements, and the interrogation summary reports, give a record of the eyewitness accounts of the action and the damage said to have been inflicted on *Sydney*.

Secondly, there are known instances where other British cruisers suffered similar damage and were saved or without good fortune lost. With the knowledge of what sort of damage similarly constructed warships could absorb, and what they could not, it should be possible to assess the damage suffered by *Sydney* and determine why it did not survive.

Thirdly, there is the lack of debris, oil, survivors or bodies found during the subsequent sea and air search. Although one splinter-damaged Carley float and one Australian naval pattern life-belt were recovered from the area north of where the action took place, their recovery position would suggest that they were blown off *Sydney* during the action. Although patches of oil were found, none was considered to have emanated from *Sydney*. In other words, it would appear that *Sydney* did not produce any floating debris or a substantial oil patch when it sank.

Each of these three aspects will be looked at, beginning with the case studies of action damage to British cruisers, specifically, that sustained by cruisers of the Leander and Modified Leander class.

The Leander and Modified Leander class cruisers were essentially of identical construction, tonnage and armament. The principal difference between the two classes was in the layout of the machinery. The Leanders had their boiler rooms grouped together, whereas the Modified Leanders had their boiler rooms separated.

Before looking at the case studies, we need to gain a basic understanding of how a ship floats, how its stability can be affected by flooding, and the measures that can be taken to reduce the danger associated with the loss of stability. And to take a brief look at how British-designed cruisers were equipped to deal with fire, damage and flooding.

The Leander class cruiser HMS *Orion*.
Note the trunking of the three
boiler-room uptakes into a single
distinctive funnel.
E. McDonald

BASIC PRINCIPLES

A ship's ability to float depends on two factors: weight and buoyancy.[4]

A ship's displacement, or weight, is determined by the volume of water displaced by the ship's hull, the weight of the ship being equal to the weight of the water displaced.

The sum weight of a ship is said to exert a downward force through a central point known as the centre of gravity.

Buoyancy is the upward force exerted on the ship's hull by the water. This force is equal to the volume of water displaced and is measured through a central point known as the centre of buoyancy.

The buoyant volume of a ship is the volume of the entire watertight part of the hull. The portion of the buoyant volume below the waterline is called buoyancy, and the portion above the waterline is called the reserve of buoyancy. A ship flooded by a volume of water equal to, or greater than, its reserve of buoyancy will sink.

'Freeboard' is the term given to the height between the waterline and the highest continuous watertight deck. Ships with a high hull, such as the County class of cruisers, have more freeboard and a larger reserve of buoyancy than ships with a lower hull, such as the Leander class of cruisers.[5]

How a ship floats is determined by the opposing forces of gravity and buoyancy. If a ship is stable, or in equilibrium, the forces of gravity and buoyancy act through the same vertical line. If a ship heels to one side, the centre of buoyancy will shift to that side. How far the centre of buoyancy shifts is determined by the size and shape of the submerged part of the hull. The centre of gravity, however, will remain unaltered. When the two opposing forces are not in the same vertical line, a moment is produced which tries to rotate the ship. Under normal circumstances, this moment will tend to rotate the ship back to an upright condition. Without going into the mechanics of 'righting moments' and 'righting levers', the lower the centre of gravity, the greater the tendency for the ship to return to an upright condition.

Basically, a ship's stability is dependent on the size and shape of the submerged part of the hull and the position of the centre of gravity. A ship with a low centre of gravity, for example, has greater stability and will roll

The high freeboard of the County (Kent)
class cruisers is evident from this view of
HMAS *Canberra*. This photograph depicts the
Australian cruiser shortly before its loss on
9 August 1942. Captain F.E. Getting, RAN,
appointed commanding officer of *Canberra*
in June 1942, died as a result of wounds
received during the attack on his ship.
N. Atwell

and recover quickly. A ship with a high centre of gravity has poorer
stability and will roll and recover at a slower rate.

Although good stability would appear to be more desirable than poor
stability, a warship is essentially a floating gun platform and, from a
gunnery point of view, a gun platform that rolls and recovers at a rapid
rate is most undesirable. A balance must be struck. A warship needs to
have a slower rolling motion for its role as a gun platform, but it also
needs to be sufficiently stable so that safety is not compromised if the
vessel is damaged or becomes partly flooded.

Flooding introduces new factors. It can cause the loss of a ship by
reducing the reserve of buoyancy, causing it to sink, or by reducing its
stability, causing it to capsize.[6]

Considering the weight effect only, the added weight of floodwater
lowers the centre of gravity. If the volume of floodwater is such that the

reserve of bouyancy is not seriously reduced, the added weight will actually improve initial stability, providing of course that the floodwater has no free surface.

Naturally, too much floodwater has a detrimental effect. The added weight can cause the ship to settle lower in the water, thereby increasing draft and reducing freeboard. This in turn reduces the reserve of buoyancy. In other words, if too much water collects inside the hull, the buoyant volume can be reduced to the point where the ship cannot stay afloat. Put simply, the ship will lose buoyancy and sink.

If the floodwater has free surface (water that is free to move about within the flooded spaces), even a relatively small volume can threaten the safety of a ship by reducing its stability. As the ship rolls or lists, the floodwater will obey the laws of gravity and flow to the affected side. The weight of the floodwater will be transferred to the low side of the ship, shifting the centre of gravity to that side and reducing the moment that tries to return the ship to an upright condition.

When floodwater is confined to one side of the ship, it will cause the ship to list to that side. This is undesirable, because list reduces the stability of the ship by changing the size and shape of the submerged part of the hull. In addition, the floodwater increases the ship's displacement, altering the centre of gravity.

List also reduces the safety and fighting efficiency of a ship for these reasons: speed and manoeuvrability are reduced; the list may introduce blind arcs of fire for the ship's armament when firing at minimum elevation over the high side of the ship; the list may raise the armour belt on the high side clear of the water, exposing the thinner shell plates (if the list is towards the enemy, the armour belt may become submerged and such a list then exposes the upper deck to direct fire, in effect, turning direct fire into more dangerous plunging fire); the efficiency of certain machinery, such as pumps, is reduced; as the angle of list increases, it becomes more difficult for personnel to move about the ship and to carry out their duties.[7]

Fortunately, in many cases, list can be corrected. The quickest means of correcting it is to counter-flood wing compartments on the opposite side by admitting sea water to them. This has the disadvantage, however, of increasing draft and decreasing freeboard. The preferred method, therefore, is to transfer fuel-oil to the fuel tanks on the opposite side of the list. Unfortunately, this is a slow process and not practicable under action conditions when a list may have to be corrected rapidly.

Flooding forward or aft can also affect the trim of a ship, but because longitudinal stability is usually so great, the resultant loss in stability is usually of little consequence, although flooding which changes the fore and aft trim by as little as 5 degrees can have a profound effect on freeboard at the flooded end. This may result in the propellers breaking surface or the bows becoming awash.[8]

As with the correction of list, transferring fuel-oil from the tanks at one end of the ship to the other is the preferable form of remedial action. When speed is essential, however, counter-flooding is the only real option. In this case, the preferred compartments are the fore and aft peaks; though by virtue of their fixed arrangements, it is easier to flood the magazines and shell rooms. The reason for this is twofold: these compartments, for safety reasons, are fitted with remote and locally controlled spraying and flooding arrangements. As a result, they can be flooded quickly. And their location, below the waterline, and fore and aft of the ship, are ideally placed for the correction of trim and the maintenance of stability.

Unfortunately, in cases where extensive flooding has occurred and communications have been lost through damage or failure of power, the countermeasures could not be implemented in time to prevent the loss of the ship. One such case was the sinking of the Dido class cruiser HMS *Bonaventure*, which was torpedoed by the Italian submarine *Ambra* on 31 March 1941. *Bonaventure*, hit in both engine rooms, sank by the stern in six minutes.

DAMAGE CONTROL AND FIRE FIGHTING

Every ship carried within its complement a damage-control organization that was specially trained and equipped to deal with most shipboard contingencies. When circumstances demanded it, its personnel would close up at strategic stations within the ship to deal with damage as soon as it occurred. In addition, equipment for fire-fighting, repairing damage and stopping leaks was stowed at various positions throughout the ship to enable damage-control measures to be implemented quickly. Emergency battery-powered lighting was also provided, which automatically turned on should the main lighting system fail.[9]

Fire fighting relied primarily on the main service (firemain) system, whereby a network of piping supplied sea water under pressure to various points and hydrants throughout the ship. The system was divided into sections so that damage to one part would not put the whole of the system out of action. Canvas hoses would then be used to bypass the damaged sections of pipe. In addition, the pumps that supplied the system with water were located around the ship so as to prevent the complete failure of the system through a single hit or explosion.

These pumps were dual acting: they could be used for supplying water to the firemain, or for pumping out flooded compartments. The pumps were either steam-driven or electrically powered. Both types, however, relied on the production of steam from the ship's boilers, the latter type using electricity supplied by the turbo generators. Early war experience forced a rethink of this policy when some cruisers were lost owing to the inability of their crews to combat fire or flooding after a loss of steam through action damage. As a result, diesel generators were progressively fitted to provide an emergency supply of electricity for damage control in the event of a complete loss of steam.[10]

Fires in magazines or shell rooms could be dealt with quickly, as these compartments were fitted with spraying and flooding systems.

Boiler and engine rooms, because of the risk of oil fires, were also specially equipped. These rooms were fitted with a steam-smothering system that was operated from outside the compartment. When this system was used, the compartment would be evacuated and sealed before steam was admitted to smother the fire. Smaller fires could be dealt with by using hand extinguishers, or foam units, which could be fitted to fire hoses connected to the firemain. Foam tubes were also fitted above these compartments to enable foam to be directed down through the compartment to the bilges.

As well as fire-fighting apparatus, leak-stopping equipment was carried in various stowages throughout the ship. This ranged from tapered wooden plugs for plugging small and large holes, to shoring timbers, and

leak-stopping mats. This equipment could be used for plugging above the waterline holes and for shoring up damaged or weakened bulkheads, hull plates, decks and hatches. Large holes, such as those created by torpedo or mine explosions, were usually beyond the scope of the ship's damage-control organization. In such cases, the design, construction and watertight subdivision of the vessel usually determined whether the ship would survive or not. The ability to minimize flooding resulting from such large holes depended on the condition, or state, of the watertight doors and openings that allowed access from one subdivision to another.

The highest condition of watertightness was always assumed when the ship was at action stations. This condition could also be assumed when a ship was moving through waters that could be mined or where torpedo attack was likely.

CASE STUDIES

The following examples of action damage provide a broad range of the major damage sustained by the Leander and Modified Leander class cruisers during the Second World War. Some of this damage can be compared with that said to be suffered by *Sydney*. Where no direct com-parison can be made, damage to other classes of British cruisers will be looked at.

One aspect that should not be overlooked was luck. Fortune favoured some ships and men and allowed them to survive but, in other cases, fate decreed that they should not.

HMS EXETER

The first large surface action of the Second World War involving units of the Royal Navy was fought on 13 December 1939. Commodore Harwood's hunting group, comprising the heavy cruiser *Exeter* and the light cruisers *Ajax* and *Achilles*, had been seeking and on this day found and engaged the German pocket battleship *Admiral Graf Spee*. The action subsequently became known as the Battle of the River Plate. Despite heavy damage to his own force, Commodore H.H. Harwood, RN, managed to inflict sufficient damage on *Graf Spee* to force it into the neutral port of Montevideo.

HMS *Exeter* was the first ship to be hit and initially took the full brunt of the German fire. The cruiser received extensive damage from shellfire, and as *Exeter*'s method of construction was similar to *Sydney*'s, it will be looked at in detail. It also provides an excellent example of the level of punishment a British cruiser could absorb without sinking.[11]

Exeter came under fire from *Graf Spee* at approximately 0617, having gone to action stations only minutes before. The damage-control organization had also closed up, but no amount of peacetime training could have prepared them for what was to come.

As the heavy cruiser was the main threat to the Germans, *Exeter* initially received the full attention of both of *Graf Spee*'s 11-inch triple gun turrets. The Germans achieved a straddle with their third salvo, and one shell, bursting in the sea just short of *Exeter*, riddled the ship with splinters. The damage inflicted was superficial but widespread. The starboard torpedo tube crew was almost wiped out, and another two men were killed when splinters pierced the hull plates.

The holes in the hull caused local flooding, and the splinters severed electrical cables and started fires. Among the severed cables were the internal communications circuits and the gun ready lamps and fall of shot hooter circuits. When these were cut, both systems short-circuited. Both funnels, the searchlights, and the starboard aircraft were also riddled, the latter spraying petrol over the after superstructure.

A short time later, *Exeter* received a direct hit, which fortunately failed to explode. The base-fuzed shell pierced the deck just abaft 'B' turret, tore through the sick bay, then went out through the hull on the port side, causing more local flooding.

Graf Spee's gunnery officer, Fregattenkäpitan Ascher, had found the range and decided to switch to nose-fuze shells to inflict more damage on the lightly armoured cruiser.

His second direct hit landed on the front of 'B' turret. The explosion tore off the armour plate and sent a hail of splinters through the wheelhouse and bridge. 'B' turret was knocked out and most of the turret crew killed. The damage to the bridge, however, was more critical. All the bridge personnel, with the exception of Captain F.S. Bell, RN, the torpedo officer, and one other officer, were either killed or wounded. The wheel-house was wrecked and all communications with the lower steering posi-tion and the engine room were lost. With the bridge effectively isolated from the rest of the ship, Bell made his way aft in order to regain control from the after conning position.

Although 'A' and 'Y' turrets were still firing, near misses continued to shower *Exeter* with splinters. Besides slicing more holes in the hull, the splinters severed many of the stays supporting and bracing the pole masts. This caused the masts to sway violently, tearing down the W/T aerials.

When Bell reached the after conning position, he found that this too was isolated owing to the loss of internal communications. As a result, helm orders had to be relayed to the after steering position by way of a chain of men. To make matters worse, petrol from one of the Walrus aircraft was spraying all over the after conning position. To remove a serious fire risk, Bell had the two aircraft jettisoned.

Shortly after Bell regained control of *Exeter*, Ascher scored another two direct hits. The first, bursting on the sheet anchor, tore a 8×6 foot hole in the plating just above the waterline. Splinters from this shell, as well as near misses from the same salvo, tore through the forecastle, cutting through bulkheads and starting fires. The second hit also struck the fore-castle, blowing a 12×12 foot hole in the deck abaft the cable holder.

Despite the damage and flooding forward, *Exeter* was still steaming at full speed. Most of this flooding was caused by shell and splinter damage, although some was caused by water gushing from shattered sections of the firemain. Without water, some fire parties were reduced to fighting the fires with buckets of sand.

On the positive side, the smoke from the numerous fires gave the impression that *Exeter* was worse hit than it actually was. Consequently, Ascher switched targets and engaged *Ajax* and *Achilles*. *Graf Spee*'s main armament, however, was swung back to *Exeter* a short time later when it was realized the cruiser was manoeuvring to fire torpedoes.

Within minutes, an 11-inch shell struck *Exeter*'s forward superstruc-ture. The shell entered the navigating officer's cabin, left through the armament office (killing five telegraphists in the process), then exploded on the barrel of the s-1 4-inch gun. The gun was knocked out and several of the gun crew killed. Splinters from the shell set fire to an adjacent 4-inch ready-use ammunition locker, causing the contents to cook-off, sending shrapnel flying in all directions.

Another shell penetrated the ship's side, as well as three bulkheads, before exploding in the chief petty officer's flat above the 4-inch magazine. A large fire started and, due to damage to the firemain, could not be fought. As the fire was a threat to the 4-inch magazine and the adjacent 8-inch magazine, it was decided to flood both compartments. This proved impossible because the flooding valve spindles were found to have been shot away. Fortunately, water from the shattered firemain had already got into the magazines, removing the threat of explosion. Water also got into the lower steering position and the No.1 low-power room, cutting the electricity supply to the compass repeaters.

Splinters from the same hit penetrated the bulkhead protecting 'A' boiler room but miraculously did little damage, the boilers being saved by a stack of spare fire bricks. Others severed a number of electrical cables, including those supplying power to the transmitting station. With the TS out of action, the turrets were ordered into local control. The changeover had hardly been effected when 'A' turret was knocked out by a direct hit, the shell exploding on the barrel of the right hand gun and tearing open the front of the turret.

Meanwhile, the fire on the CPO's messdeck had become uncontrollable. It had also spread to the lower servery flat, trapping the men in the main switchboard and forward dynamo rooms. While damage repair parties struggled amid the smoke and debris to rescue those trapped, fire parties tried to hold back the flames, their efforts hampered by splinter damage to the firemain and the fire hoses. Adding to their difficulties, the 50-ton fire and bilge pump broke down several times, interrupting the supply of water to the firemain.

With the TS and the DCT both out of action, and both forward turrets knocked out, the gunnery officer made his way aft to help with the control of 'Y' turret. Despite the blast and concussion, Lieutenant-Commander R.B. Jennings, RN, took up position on the after searchlight platform so he could spot the fall of shot. Corrections were shouted to the turret officer through the manhole in the turret roof. This arrangement, however, was short lived. At 0729, water entering the hull shorted out the power to 'Y' turret.

With all three 8-inch turrets now out of action, all torpedoes expended, and with only one 4-inch gun still serviceable, Captain Bell decided to break off the action.

Exeter was down by the bows by about 3 feet, having shipped an estimated 650 tons of water, and was listing nearly 10 degrees to starboard. The whole ship was a shambles and the fires were throwing up clouds of smoke. The engines, however, were still intact but, more importantly, so were the boilers. With steam available for the pumps, the list was gradually reduced by pumping oil-fuel from the starboard tanks to the port tanks, although trim could not be restored because of the volume of floodwater forward.

Incapable of making any more than 18 knots due to weakened bulkheads, steered by means of a boat compass, and unable to make W/T contact with Commodore Harwood (on board *Ajax*), *Exeter* retired from the action. It was several hours before jury aerials were rigged and contact with Harwood re-established. When Harwood learned of the full extent of *Exeter*'s damage, he ordered Bell to make for the Falkland Islands.

Exeter reached Port Stanley on 16 December. Of the ship's complement of 630 officers and men, 5 officers and 56 ratings had been killed, and 3 officers and 17 ratings had been wounded. Three ratings subsequently died from their wounds.[12]

A preliminary report on *Exeter*'s condition proposed that the cruiser be left in the Falklands until the end of the war, such was the extent of the damage. *Exeter*, however, was made sea-worthy again and sailed to Britain for repairs.

HMS ORION

On 28 and 29 May 1941, the Leander class cruiser HMS *Orion* was involved in the evacuation of troops from Crete. At about 0530 on 29 May, *Orion* was attacked by Ju-87 Stuka dive bombers and almost hit by a bomb that landed in the sea on the starboard side abreast 'Y' turret. Hull plating in the vicinity was damaged, causing local flooding. The after

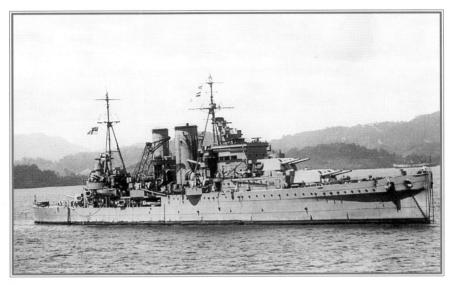

The rebuilt HMS *Exeter* off Sumatra in
February 1942. Note the new tripod masts
and the generous allocation of Carley floats.
T. Fisher

6-inch magazine also flooded, effectively putting 'x' and 'y' turrets out of action.

During another attack two hours later, the ship received a direct hit on 'A' turret. The 550-lb bomb completely destroyed the gun house, killing those inside and peppering the bridge with splinters and shrapnel. The gun barrels of 'B' turret caught the full blast of the explosion and were bent upwards, 6 inches out of true, rendering the guns useless. To make matters worse, Captain G.R.B. Back, RN, was mortally wounded by a machine-gun bullet during the attack, and died two hours later.

Orion was at the time the flagship of Rear-Admiral H.B. Rawlings, RN (Rear-Admiral 7th Cruiser Squadron). Although wounded himself, Rawlings took charge of the ship until Commander T.C.T. Wynne, RN, could take command.

At 1000, *Orion* received another crippling blow. A second bomb, possibly a 1,100-lb armour-piercing type, struck the bridge and penetrated into the heart of the ship before exploding on the armoured deck above the 4-inch magazine. The explosion wrecked the lower steering position, the transmitting station and the telephone exchange. It also killed a large number of key personnel as well as 150 soldiers of the 2nd Black Watch Regiment.

With the lower steering position wrecked and all internal communications gone *Orion* began steaming in circles, completely out of control. The cruiser's speed also became quite erratic, fluctuating between 12 and 25 knots. Sea water entering the oil-fuel tanks through damaged plates had contaminated the oil, causing steaming difficulties. While parties worked to put out the numerous fires, Wynne attempted to regain control of the ship. Human chains were formed to relay orders to the engine rooms and the after steering position, and about fifteen minutes later some control was established. About an hour after being hit, however, *Orion* took on a heavy list to starboard. Despite the transfer of oil to the port oil-fuel tanks this list could not be corrected.

Shepherded by the squadron, the crippled cruiser reached Alexandria at about 2000 that evening, limping in on one propeller and with only 10 tons of oil-fuel remaining. *Orion* returned to port with 260 dead and 280 wounded.[13]

HMS NEPTUNE

An incident significant for the loss of life was the mining of the Leander class cruiser HMS *Neptune*. On the night of 18–19 December 1941, *Neptune*, in company with HM cruisers *Aurora* and *Penelope*, and HM destroyers *Kandahar*, *Lance*, *Lively* and *Havock*, ran into an uncharted minefield off the coast of Tripoli.

The squadron, designated Force K, was steaming in line ahead when *Neptune* (the lead ship) detonated a mine. The time was 0106. *Aurora* and *Penelope*, the next ships in line, immediately sheered off to starboard, but *Aurora* detonated a second mine as it did so. Within minutes *Penelope* exploded a third mine with its paravanes.

Captain O'Conor, commanding Force K and commanding officer of *Neptune*, attempted to extricate his ship from the minefield by going astern.

Unfortunately, *Neptune* detonated another two mines while doing so. The explosion wrecked the propellers and rudder, completely immobilizing the cruiser. With his ship crippled and listing to port, O'Conor ordered a destroyer to come alongside.

Kandahar was ordered to close *Neptune* while *Aurora* and *Penelope* led the remaining destroyers north. O'Conor, then realizing that his ship might drift clear of the minefield, ordered *Kandahar* to wait.

Aurora, having shipped a considerable volume of water forward, was down by the bows and had developed a severe list to port. As *Aurora*'s speed was also seriously reduced, it was decided to detach the cruiser so that it could return to port before daylight. At about 0200, *Aurora*, escorted by *Lance* and *Havock*, departed for Malta.

Penelope, only lightly damaged but with a slight list to port, made preparations to take *Neptune* in tow. At 0207, *Penelope* ordered *Lively* to close with *Neptune*. *Penelope* would close and take *Neptune* in tow when signalled. Progress was slow, but at 0309 *Penelope* was instructed to approach. Nine minutes later *Kandahar* detonated a mine that blew its stern off. O'Conor immediately signalled *Penelope* to keep away, *Kandahar* making a similar signal to *Lively*.

Shortly after 0400, *Neptune* drifted onto another mine, which exploded under the bridge. Five minutes later the cruiser capsized and sank.

At 0411, *Kandahar*, realizing that the situation was hopeless, signalled *Penelope* that it should go. *Lively* requested permission to enter the minefield and rescue *Neptune*'s survivors, but the request was denied. Reluctantly, *Penelope* and *Lively* set course for Malta.[14]

Fortunately, *Kandahar* remained afloat and was able to make W/T contact with Malta. As a result the destroyer HMS *Jaguar* was despatched that afternoon with orders to rescue *Kandahar*'s crew, it having been ascertained that by the time *Jaguar* reached the scene *Kandahar* should have drifted out of the minefield.

Kandahar was located at 0400 on 20 December, but heavy seas prevented *Jaguar* going alongside. Although they had to swim across to *Jaguar*, 8 officers and 157 men were saved. There was no sign of survivors from *Neptune*.

In 1943, after an exchange of POW's, a sole survivor from *Neptune*, Leading Seaman J. Walton, was discovered. Walton was able to report that when ordered to abandon ship only two Carley floats were available. He managed to reach one of the floats, as did Captain O'Conor and fourteen other men. They saw no other survivors. Over the next four days all but Walton died of exposure, and he had been close to death when an Italian torpedo boat discovered the float on 24 December.

Only one man from *Neptune*'s entire complement of 764 officers and men had survived the cruiser's sinking.[15]

HMAS PERTH

In the early evening of 28 February 1942, HMAS *Perth*, in company with the American heavy cruiser USS *Houston*, sailed from the northern Javanese port of Tanjong Priok. *Houston* and *Perth*, the latter under the command of Captain H.M.L. Waller, RAN, had been ordered to make for the southern Javanese port of Tjilatjap, via the Sunda Strait. *Perth* was in the van, with *Houston* stationed 1,000 yards astern.

Reports indicated that the Sunda Strait was free of enemy shipping, and Waller expected to pass through unmolested. As Japanese submarines were known to be operating in the area, the two cruisers adopted a zigzag course, but proceeded at 22 knots to conserve fuel. At 2300, speed was increased to 28 knots.

Six minutes later, having almost reached the entrance to the strait, a vessel was sighted about five miles ahead, close to St Nicholas Point. The stranger was challenged by signal lamp, but its reply could not be understood. The challenge was repeated, but the other ship turned away, revealing the silhouette of a Japanese destroyer.

Perth immediately went to action stations while its course was altered to open A-arcs. Waller gave the order to open fire. As *Perth* swung to starboard, it was realized they had run into the middle of a Japanese invasion force. With enemy vessels to port and starboard, Waller ordered divided control of the guns so that they could engage the targets on both beams. *Houston* tried to conform with *Perth*'s movements, but the two cruisers soon became separated.

Waller ordered frequent alterations in course as targets presented themselves, while at the same time presenting his enemy with a more

difficult target. So skilful was Waller's handling of *Perth* that after nearly an hour of action the Japanese had not been able to score a decisive hit. Although the Australian cruiser was struck several times, its speed and fighting ability were not impaired. The first hit was received about twenty minutes after the action started, a shell of unknown calibre striking the forward funnel and causing superficial damage. A short time later, another shell struck the flag deck. At 2350, a third shell struck forward on the starboard side near the waterline and penetrated into a vacant messdeck before exploding.

During the running battle, *Perth* steamed in a wide circle in an attempt to protect *Houston*'s stern, its single after turret having been knocked out during an air attack in the Flores Sea some weeks before. By midnight, *Perth* had almost completed the circle and, with the 6-inch and 4-inch magazines almost empty and all torpedoes expended, Waller decided to make a run for the strait. Just as *Perth* settled onto the new course, disaster struck. A torpedo detonated on the starboard side in the vicinity of the forward boiler room. It appears that the explosion destroyed the bulkhead between the forward boiler and forward engine rooms, as both immediately flooded. Fortunately, the after boiler and engine rooms were not affected and continued to operate at full power. Speed, however, was cut dramatically. *Perth* listed to starboard then slowly righted itself.

On the bridge, Waller was heard to exclaim, 'Christ, that's torn it!' He then gave the order to prepare to abandon ship. The torpedo explosion also destroyed damage control headquarters, wiping out the men stationed there. But there was little they could have done if they had survived, because a short time later a second torpedo struck.

The second torpedo hit forward on the starboard side, directly below 'A' and 'B' turrets. At about the same time, the Walrus and the recovery crane were struck by shells, as was the 4-inch gundeck. As *Perth* began to list to starboard Waller gave the order to abandon ship.

Perth was now an easy target and was struck repeatedly. Miraculously, the electrical system remained undamaged, permitting the order to abandon ship to be broadcast throughout the ship. Within minutes of the order being issued, a third torpedo struck aft on the starboard side, damaging the propeller shafts and flooding the after 6-inch magazine and shell rooms. This was quickly followed by a fourth torpedo, which hit

forward on the port side. All electrical power then failed, but the loss of power was now of little consequence. At approximately 0025, *Perth* righted itself, then heeled over to port and sank by the bows.

Of *Perth*'s complement of 682 officers and men, 353 (including Waller) died. The survivors were captured by the Japanese and spent the remainder of the war as POWs. Only 229 men survived the ordeal.[16]

HMNZS LEANDER

HMNZS *Leander*'s active participation in the war ended abruptly on the night of 12-13 July 1943. With US cruisers *Honolulu* and *St Louis*, the New Zealand cruiser formed part of Task Group 36.1, which had been ordered to intercept a small force of Japanese warships making a 'Tokyo Express' run into the Kula Gulf off New Georgia. Just after 0100, the opposing warships clashed head-on, exchanging gunfire and torpedoes.

Shortly after fire was opened, *Honolulu*, leading *Leander* and *St Louis*, suddenly altered course to port. Unfortunately, the signal to turn to port 180 degrees was made on TBS and *Leander* and five of the six accompanying destroyers failed to hear the signal.[17] *Leander* was making almost 30 knots when Captain C.A.L. Mansergh, RN, ordered 'Stop—Full Astern' to avoid ramming *Honolulu*.

St Louis followed *Honolulu*, and Mansergh was attempting to conform, when at approximately 0125 a 24-inch torpedo struck *Leander* on the port side abreast 'A' boiler room.

The explosion blew a 30 × 20 foot hole in the hull plating and caused extensive structural damage. The blast wrecked 'A' boiler room and killed all personnel stationed there. Flooding extended from 'A' boiler room to the transmitting station, low-power room, forward dynamo room and the main switchboard, causing all electrical power to be lost. 'B' boiler room had to be evacuated when the supply air fans stopped, but 'C' boiler room escaped damage and remained tenable, although minor flooding occurred.

In addition, five oil-fuel tanks were destroyed and two others ruptured. The loaded port quad torpedo tube set, 50 feet aft of the impact point, was lifted bodily by the force of the explosion and displaced from its mounting.

Damage control parties quickly went to work, and some power and lighting was restored. Steam was also raised again in 'c' boiler room and, by cross connecting, the two boilers were able to supply steam to two of the engines.

With a heavy list to port *Leander*, escorted by the destroyer USS *Radford*, slowly made its way to Tulagi. There the cruiser was temporarily repaired and fitted with a cement patch, allowing *Leander* to sail to Auckland. A complete repair and refit was thought necessary and on 30 November the ship sailed for the United States. Because of the extensive amount of work required, *Leander* was not ready for service again until September 1945.[18]

HMAS HOBART

The more fortunate of the Modified Leanders, and the sole survivor of the class, was HMAS *Hobart*. At 1845 on the evening of 20 July 1943, however, the Australian cruiser almost became another war loss.

Hobart, under the command of Captain H.A. Showers, RAN, was returning to Espiritu Santo after an uneventful patrol west of the New Hebrides. *Hobart* was stationed three cables astern of HMAS *Australia*, with the US destroyers *Nicholas*, *Radford* and *O'Bannon* providing an anti-submarine screen. Like its consorts, *Hobart* was carrying out British Zig Zag No.38 and making revolutions for 23 knots. Despite these precautions, *Hobart* was struck aft on the port side by a 21-inch torpedo fired by the Japanese submarine *I-11*.

To quote from the Minutes of the subsequent Board of Enquiry: 'A mass of water, smoke and debris, was thrown high into the air, ratings on the Upper Deck in the vicinity finding it necessary to take cover. All lights in the ship went out and the ship took a list of some three degrees to port.'[19]

The shallow running torpedo struck just abaft 'Y' turret, blowing a 60 × 30 foot hole in the ship's side and almost severing the stern. All port side shell plating from the keel to the lower deck was demolished, and the starboard plating cracked and buckled. Transverse and longitudinal bulk-heads in the vicinity of the explosion were also destroyed or distorted. A

number of hold and platform deck tanks, storerooms and compartments, including the steering-gear compartment, immediately flooded. 'Y' shell room was completely demolished, and the after 6-inch magazine partly flooded.

Approximately 500 square feet of the lower deck was destroyed, with quarterdeck damage extending 40 feet either side of the explosion. The quarterdeck itself burst, venting the explosion to atmosphere, with deck plates and beams being pushed 6 feet 6 inches above normal height. 'Y' turret, weighing 60 tons, was lifted bodily by the force of the explosion and left jammed on a port bearing.

The damage to the electrical system was less visible. Both port and starboard after feeder cables were extensively damaged, and this damage,

Hobart's shattered stern, almost severed
by the torpedo, which struck the
cruiser on 20 July 1943.
AWM 300797

or the shock of the explosion, opened the supply breakers. This resulted in a loss of power throughout the ship and failure of the lighting. The main armament was thus forced to go into manual operation. The loss of power also caused the supply and exhaust fans in the engine rooms and all fire and bilge pumps to stop. The latter was a major concern and it was subsequently recommended that two of the eight fire and bilge pumps be steam driven.

Below the waterline, the port inner propeller was blown off, causing the after port engine to race. Working in darkness, ERA Johnston immediately shut off the supply of steam to prevent damage to the turbine.

On the bridge, as soon as it was realized that the ship had been torpedoed, orders were rung down to stop the engines. 'Close all watertight doors' and 'Action stations' was sounded and piped. Unfortunately, the loss of power prevented these orders being heard.

Once the engines were stopped, *Hobart* swung to port and quickly lost way. While the destroyers began searching for the offending submarine, the damage-control organization went to work. Power was soon restored, and the difficult task of assessing the damage started. To help correct the list, it was decided to pump oil from the port to the starboard tanks.[20]

When it was established that the forward boiler and engine rooms were undamaged and the outer propellers intact, *Hobart* got under way again. As the ship would not answer the rudder, all telemotor leads having been severed by the explosion, *Hobart* had to be steered with main engines.

Daylight revealed the full extent of the damage. Despite the calm conditions, the stern was seen to be moving perceptively, and it was feared that unless it could be steadied the stern might break off and damage the remaining propellers. It was decided to pass a wire around the stern. This had the desired effect, and *Hobart* continued towards Espiritu Santo at a steady 8 knots. Escorted by the US destroyers *Nicholas*, *Radford* and *Saufley* and helped by the tugs *Apache*, *Sioux* and *Vireo*, *Hobart* reached Espiritu Santo at 0228 on 22 July.

Shortly after arrival, *Hobart*'s forward and aft draught was measured. Draught immediately before being torpedoed was assessed as 17 feet 2 inches forward and 20 feet 9 inches aft. On arrival at Espiritu Santo, and despite oil being pumped from the after tanks to the forward tanks to help improve trim, *Hobart* drew 15 feet 4 inches forward and 24 feet aft.[21]

Hobart suffered seven killed, seven missing and sixteen wounded.

✧   ✧   ✧

The soundness of the design of the Leander and Modified Leander class can be seen from these case studies. *Leander* and *Hobart* were both struck by single torpedoes and, despite severe structural damage and flooding, survived. *Neptune* and *Perth* both suffered multiple underwater explosions and sank, but in neither case did the structural integrity of the hull fail. Both of these ships were observed to capsize and sink from loss of stability. *Neptune* detonated three mines and stayed afloat for approximately three hours before detonating a fourth mine and sinking in minutes. *Perth* was struck by two torpedoes before Captain Waller gave the order to abandon ship. *Perth* then sank inside of thirty minutes, helped on its way by two more torpedoes.

After the first torpedo struck *Perth*, Waller gave the order to 'prepare to abandon ship'. Waller did not consider that *Perth* was in imminent danger of sinking, otherwise he would have ordered abandon ship immediately.

The first torpedo to hit *Perth* opened up the forward boiler and engine rooms, immediately flooding both compartments. This caused the ship to list to starboard. Because of the large hole in the ship's side, once these compartments were fully flooded, they were in effect in direct communication with the sea. As a result, *Perth* righted itself and the list disappeared. Despite an increase in draught and an estimated 23 per cent reduction in reserve of buoyancy, *Perth* was still relatively stable and in no immediate danger of sinking.[22]

Waller's order to prepare to abandon ship, therefore, may have been based on the fact that *Perth* had lost speed and manoeuvrability and was now a much easier target.

Unfortunately, the *Leander*, *Hobart* and *Perth* case studies do not provide a good comparison for a single torpedo hit forward. The Dido class cruiser *Phoebe*, however, does.[23]

HMS *Phoebe* was torpedoed on 23 October 1942 by *U-161*. A single 21-inch (53-centimetre) torpedo struck the cruiser on the port side immediately below 'Q' turret (forward of the bridge) and blew a 40 × 30 foot hole

in the shell plating abreast 'Q' magazine. Immediate and progressive flooding occurred, encompassing 'B' and 'Q' magazine and shell rooms, the pom-pom and torpedo warhead magazines, Nos 1 and 2 low-power rooms, Nos 1 and 2 transmitting stations, the main switchboard and five oil-fuel tanks. An initial list of 6 degrees to port was corrected by counter-flooding. Unfortunately, the ship then took on a starboard list of 4 degrees. Structural damage prevented 'A' turret being fired, and reduced *Phoebe*'s speed to 6 knots. *Phoebe* survived the attack but was out of service for eight months.[24]

It is interesting to compare *Phoebe*'s reduced speed of 6 knots with *Sydney*'s claimed 5 to 7 knot speed after being torpedoed. The torpedo that struck *Phoebe* carried a 280-kilogram warhead. The torpedo that struck *Sydney* is believed to have carried a 195-kilogram warhead.

Clearly, the single most decisive blow suffered by *Sydney* was the torpedo hit under the forward turrets. When compared with the single hits to *Leander*, *Hobart* and *Phoebe* and the first hit received by *Perth*, it is reasonable to assume that *Sydney* should have survived the hit.[25]

The general description of *Sydney* as it steamed away from *Kormoran* was that the ship was down by the bows, listing slightly (Skeries) and that occasionally the propellers could be seen coming out of the swell. The after turrets were pointing away from *Kormoran*, and there were two large fires burning. These fires, located on the forward superstructure and abaft the forward funnel, were apparently uncontrollable and were still burning when *Sydney* steamed over the horizon.

Clearly, the bows-down condition was the result of flooding associated with the torpedo hit. Although it was claimed that *Sydney*'s propellers could occasionally be seen, this is not unusual for a ship that is trimmed by the bow. In an average load condition, the tips of *Sydney*'s propeller blades were only 4 to 5 feet below the surface. Therefore, even a slight change in trim forward would have permitted the propellers to break surface in moderate seas.

Admiralty issued damage control diagrams for *Sydney* indirectly support the German claims. These reveal that *Sydney* would have survived a torpedo hit on the port side under the forward superstructure but would have trimmed 4 feet by the bow, lost 8 per cent of the reserve of buoyancy, and heeled 7 degrees to port.[26]

These figures relate to a torpedo hit under the forward superstructure, but a hit under the forward turrets, approximately 30 feet further forward, would not have produced significantly different results. *Sydney* should have retained sufficient reserve of buoyancy to remain afloat.

A heel or list of 7 degrees to port, however, would have been sufficient to raise the armour belt on the starboard side to the point where the shell plates were exposed in the swell. In other words, once *Sydney* passed astern and presented its starboard beam to *Kormoran*'s guns, the boiler and engine rooms were left virtually unprotected. At the waterline, only the 1-inch thick shell plates would have protected the boilers and engines.

There is no doubt that *Sydney*'s trim and reserve of buoyancy would have been affected by the flooding of the forepart of the ship, but the resulting loss of trim and buoyancy should not have been sufficient to cause the loss of the ship. Therefore, there must have been other factors that either contributed to, or were the direct cause of, *Sydney*'s sinking.

The most obvious 'other' factor would have been a large on-board explosion such as a magazine blowing up, and in *Sydney* there were a number of areas where a potentially fatal explosion could have occurred. These were the forward 6-inch magazine and shell rooms, the after 6-inch magazine and shell rooms, the 4-inch magazine, the port torpedo tubes, and the depth charges on the stern.

If an explosion occurred in any of these areas, the resulting damage, in conjunction with the pre-existing torpedo and shellfire damage, would or should have been sufficient to cause the loss of the ship. To establish if an explosion could have occurred in any of these areas, we need to return to the German account of the action.

Besides the torpedo hit forward, *Sydney* was claimed to have been extensively damaged by 15-centimetre, 3.7-centimetre and 2-centimetre shellfire, the forward superstructure being set on fire and the forward turrets badly damaged in the opening salvoes. Several 15-centimetre salvoes were then directed at *Sydney*'s 'machine room'. Although it is believed that these salvoes were aimed at the machinery spaces between *Sydney*'s funnels, it is not clear where the shells actually landed or how much damage was inflicted. One shell, however, is known to have struck the Walrus. This hit, it is believed, also started a large fire amidships. A minute or so later, a single torpedo struck under the forward turrets.

Sydney then turned and passed astern of *Kormoran*. As the Australian cruiser passed astern, presenting its starboard beam, the raider's after 15-centimetre guns engaged the ship with rapid fire. If Hildenbrand's statements are interpreted correctly, much of this fire was aimed at *Sydney*'s waterline.

Clearly, there had been no direct hits on *Sydney*'s magazines, shell rooms, torpedo warheads or depth charges, because the resulting explosion would have been observed. The fires burning on the forward superstructure and amidships, however, may have reached a magazine or the torpedo warheads some time after *Sydney* had disappeared from view.

SYDNEY'S FIRES

Shortly after the action began, fire broke out on *Sydney*'s bridge and forward superstructure. This fire burned for the duration of the action and was still burning when the ship steamed over the horizon. It is assumed that efforts were made to extinguish this fire, but it is quite likely that, as in the case of *Exeter*, much of the available fire-fighting equipment was damaged or destroyed by shellfire.

Immediately below the forward superstructure was the 4-inch magazine. It was situated below the waterline and was fitted with flooding and drenching arrangements. If the fire managed to reach this magazine before it could be flooded, the resulting explosion, coupled with the existing damage, would have sunk the ship.

The 4-inch magazine should not have been directly threatened by the fire burning several decks above, but the possibility that the fire eventually reached this magazine cannot be ruled out. And although the magazine should have been deliberately flooded if threatened, this may not have been possible. *Sydney*, like *Exeter*, may have had the flooding valve spindles or gearing rods shot away or damaged. To save weight during *Sydney*'s construction, aluminium alloy valve handle wheels were fitted. These, if subjected to sufficient heat, would melt, making the valves useless.[27]

For the same reasons, the forward 6-inch magazine and shell rooms, located forward of the 4-inch magazine, may have been touched off by heat or flame. As Greter's torpedo breached the hull in their immediate vicinity, however, it is more likely that these compartments were flooded by torpedo-related damage. The possibility that the forward 6-inch magazine and shell rooms eventually exploded from fire or heat is therefore much more remote.

The amidships fire also started early in the action, and it too was still burning when *Sydney* steamed over the horizon. This fire was probably fuelled by petrol from the Walrus. Its fuel tanks, if full, contained 122 gallons of petrol. Most of the ship's boats were on either side of the aircraft catapult and immediately forward and abreast the forward funnel. They were predominantly made of timber and, as a result, would have provided further fuel for the fire.

As with the fire on the forward superstructure, the midships fire would have been extremely difficult to extinguish. Fanned by the breeze and fed by petrol, timber and other combustibles, this fire would have quickly become uncontrollable and could easily have spread aft to the torpedo tubes and the 4-inch gundeck.

Support for such a scenario can be found in Detmers's interrogation statements. On 1 December 1941, he claimed that after the cruiser passed astern its second funnel was seen to be burning. Then on 7 January 1942 he claimed that as *Sydney* swung past he could see that the ship was 'blazing fiercely, particularly near the after funnel'.

If Detmers was correct, within minutes of the Walrus being hit, the midships fire had spread aft to encompass the after funnel. Although it is unlikely that the after funnel itself caught fire, it is quite possible that the forward edge of the 4-inch gundeck became engulfed in flames. Fire in this area would have given the impression that the after funnel was on fire. Such a fire, if not controlled, could have spread to the 4-inch ready use ammunition lockers, causing the contents to explode. Although it is doubtful that exploding ammunition lockers would have contributed to the demise of the ship, they may have led to the German belief that further hits were being registered.

Immediately below the 4-inch gundeck were the torpedo tubes, and although the starboard tubes were empty, it is understood that the port tubes still contained torpedoes. If the amidships fire reached the port tubes, the heat could have caused the torpedo warheads to explode. It is

considered that the detonation of one or more 750-lb warheads would have destroyed a sizeable section of the hull. This, combined with the existing damage, would probably have been sufficient to sink the ship.

Interestingly, the question of torpedo warheads detonating from heat or fire had been raised during the inquiry into the loss of HMS *Hood*. According to the evidence produced, 'the effect of fire round a warhead would possibly lead to an explosion but it would have to be a fire of fierceness and duration and the result would be comparatively mild'.[28] It was also noted that the explosion of two warheads would produce an all round, almost instantaneous flash, coupled with a loud noise.

That a torpedo warhead would explode if subjected to sufficient heat was shown by an accident that occurred on board the destroyer HMS *Khartoum* on 22 June 1940. *Khartoum* suffered the misfortune of having the compressed air vessel in one of its torpedoes explode, causing the warhead to be driven into the after superstructure. The warhead demolished the oil-fired galley and started a fire, which could not be brought under control. The after 4.7-inch magazine was located immediately below the fire. As there was a very real danger that the warhead would explode and trigger the magazine, it was decided to beach the ship. All hands were then mustered forward. A short time later, the warhead exploded, detonating the magazine and blowing off the stern.[29]

If *Sydney*'s midships fire spread aft and engulfed the port torpedo tubes, it is possible that sufficient heat was generated to cause a torpedo warhead to explode. This may have occurred well after *Sydney* had disappeared from view.

It is conceivable that the midships fire spread aft, but it is doubtful that it would have threatened *Sydney*'s after 6-inch magazine or shell rooms. It is possible, however, that a base-fuze shell fired in the second phase of the action may have penetrated the quarterdeck and started a fire that eventually caused a shell room or the magazine to explode. Such a fire may not have been visible to observers on *Kormoran*, and its smoke may have been difficult to spot amid the large quantities of smoke generated by the bridge and midships fires.

There is no direct evidence of such a hit being registered, or an internal fire being started in the after part of the ship, but such an occurrence cannot be ruled out. It is equally possible that the after magazine and shell rooms were flooded by this time. If *Sydney* was down by the bows to the extent that the propellers were breaking surface, it may have been necessary to flood the after 6-inch magazine and shell rooms in order to restore trim.

The possibility that this occurred is perhaps supported by the lack of return fire from *Sydney*'s after turrets. Given that, even without power, the after turrets could be worked by hand and the guns fired by battery, it seems odd that no return fire was observed. If the after 6-inch magazine and shell rooms were flooded to restore trim, however, 'x' and 'Y' turrets would have been left with nothing to fire.

The possibility that *Sydney*'s depth charges exploded, blowing off part of the stern, must also be considered, although, again, such a scenario is not supported by the evidence, because no explosion or fire was observed on *Sydney*'s quarterdeck.

That the depth charges were a danger to the ship in a surface action was shown by Captain Bell's actions during the Battle of the River Plate. Before engaging *Graf Spee*, Bell ordered *Exeter*'s depth charges to be jettisoned lest they be hit and explode.[30]

In summary:

The uncontrolled fire on *Sydney*'s forward superstructure may have eventually reached the 4-inch magazine, causing it to explode.

The uncontrolled fire on *Sydney*'s forward superstructure may have eventually reached the forward 6-inch magazine and shell rooms, causing one or more of these compartments to explode. But given the flooding normally associated with torpedo damage, it is probable that these compartments were flooded early in the action, thus removing any subsequent risk of explosion.

The uncontrolled fire amidships may have eventually reached the port torpedo tubes, causing one or more torpedo warheads to explode.

The possibility that the after 6-inch magazine or shell rooms or both exploded is unlikely but cannot be ruled out.

The possibility that *Sydney*'s depth charges exploded is unlikely but cannot be ruled out.

From this summary, it can be seen that if *Sydney* sank as a result of its own munitions exploding, the most likely cause was the detonation of the 4-inch magazine. It is also possible that fire or heat caused one or more torpedo warheads in the port torpedo tubes to explode.[31]

Although none of the prisoners reported hearing any explosions, it is conceivable that an explosion aboard *Sydney* may not have been audible to the crew of the *Kormoran*. Distance, the noise from the raider's own uncontrolled fires, or the explosion of *Kormoran*'s munitions and mines might have 'drowned out' any sounds from *Sydney*.

Clearly, only a visual inspection of *Sydney*'s wreck will determine whether or not the ship was sunk by the detonation of its own munitions.

THE LACK OF OIL AND DEBRIS

Another factor that needs to be taken into consideration is the apparent lack of oil and debris from *Sydney*. A Carley float and an RAN-pattern life-belt were discovered north of where the action was said to have been fought, but no other traces of *Sydney* were found.

Normally, when a warship sinks as a result of battle damage, a 'debris field' of oil and floating wreckage is left on the surface. Although this 'field' of oil and debris will drift and disperse according to the prevailing winds and waves, its general location and composition can sometimes indicate where a vessel was lost and possibly how it was lost.

On 21 January 1940, for example, HMS *Exmouth* was torpedoed by U-22 off the Moray Firth. The destroyer had been providing escort for *Cyprian Prince*, which could not stop to give help because of the risk of being torpedoed itself. The merchantman arrived at Kirkwall thirteen hours later and immediately notified the authorities of the incident and the destroyer's last position. When rescue ships reached the area, they found a lifebuoy and a number of orange crates. These few items provided the evidence that *Exmouth* had sunk in the vicinity. Unfortunately, of the ship's complement of 175 officers and men, there was no trace. *Exmouth* had been lost with all hands.

When *Hood* was destroyed by a magazine explosion, HMS *Electra* was sent to pick up survivors. After approximately two hours steaming, the destroyer located a large patch of oil, a small amount of debris and drift-wood, and three survivors. Witnesses had seen *Hood* break in half when its after 15-inch magazine exploded, and the debris field confirmed the violent nature of the ship's destruction. Long tubes sealed at both ends were seen among the debris. These were assumed to be the crushing tubes from *Hood*'s underwater protection bulges. The fact that these had come to the surface indicated that the 42,100-ton battle cruiser had been literally torn apart by the explosion which sank it. Further evidence of *Hood*'s catastrophic end came in the form of a desk drawer full of ratings' documents, which would normally have been kept in an office deep inside the ship.

In most cases where the hull is breached, oil-fuel tanks are ruptured and a certain amount of oil released. Magazine explosions are no exception. In fact, because magazines are usually 'protected' by oil-fuel tanks, magazine explosions are more likely to release large quantities of oil. Therefore, if *Sydney* sank as a result of a magazine explosion, it is likely that a consider-able quantity of oil-fuel would have been released, assuming of course the oil-fuel tanks in the vicinity of the hull breach were not empty.[32]

Similarly, if *Sydney* sank as a result of torpedo warheads in the port torpedo tubes exploding, several tons of lubricating oil should have been released. It is assumed that such an explosion would not have broken the ship in two, but it would have destroyed a large portion of the ship's structure in the immediate vicinity. Although much of the blast would have been directed up and out, it is assumed that the bulkhead between the after boiler and engine rooms would have been destroyed and the hull plating, including the armour belt, severely distorted or destroyed. This localized damage would almost certainly have included the rupturing of the lubricating oil tanks in the after boiler room and possibly the adjacent oil-fuel tanks.

If the search for *Sydney* was comprehensive but still failed to find any debris or patches of oil, it is conceivable that the ship did not sink as a result of a magazine explosion or the detonation of torpedo warheads.

This raises the possibility that *Sydney* sank as a result of a loss of buoyancy or stability. For this to occur, the ship merely had to flood to a point where the reserve of buoyancy was seriously reduced or *Sydney* became so unstable that it capsized.

LOSS OF STABILITY OR RESERVE OF BUOYANCY?

According to Skeries, *Sydney* was listing slightly and trimmed by the bow when it steamed away. Although the flooding associated with the torpedo hit should not have seriously reduced *Sydney*'s reserve of buoyancy, the list would have had a profound affect on the ship's stability. Clearly, any further flooding on the side of the list may have caused *Sydney* to capsize and sink. Equally, the flooding of a large compartment, such as a boiler room, could have reduced the reserve of buoyancy to the point where *Sydney* could no longer stay afloat.

Although it is difficult to establish how much hull damage *Sydney* sustained, Hildenbrand's statements make it clear that a certain amount of fire was directed at the waterline. As in the case of *Exeter*, shell or splinter damage on or near the waterline would have allowed seawater to enter the hull. Such flooding may have been widespread and not necessarily confined to one side of the ship. Over a period of time, this flooding, if not checked, might have led to a reduction in the reserve of buoyancy or stability or both, and, inevitably, the loss of the ship.

Consequently, seemingly insignificant damage on or near the waterline could have been an important contributing factor in *Sydney*'s sinking.

It is also conceivable that internal fires led to buckling of the hull plating. This would have permitted seawater to enter and flood the affected compartments.

As several of Skeries's salvoes were aimed at *Sydney*'s machinery spaces, a possible scenario is that one or more 15-centimetre shells penetrated the armour belt on the port side and started a fire in a boiler or engine room. Alternatively, *Kormoran*'s stern gunners might have put several shells into the machinery spaces on the starboard side. Internal fires, not always readily visible to outside observers, can often be detected by the smoke produced.

Jürgensen described the smoke from the midships fire as thick and black. The smoke was so dense that when *Sydney* turned behind it the ship became obscured. Some thought that the cruiser had deliberately laid a smokescreen, but others thought that the smoke was merely the result of the fires. Either of these opinions may be correct.

The fact that the smoke was thick and black, however, suggests the presence of oil-fuel in the fire. Although *Sydney* may have been laying a smokescreen to cover its withdrawal, it is also possible that oil was actually fuelling the fire. Some oil would have been released from the fuel tanks ruptured by the torpedo hit and hurled into the air and onto the ship, but the intensity and duration of the amidships fire, and the smoke produced, suggests that a larger quantity of oil was fuelling the fire.

Significantly, the quantity of oil required was available in *Sydney*'s boiler and engine rooms, and an oil fire in either compartment would have produced an effect consistent with the German claims. Thick black smoke would have been generated and emitted from the fan trunks and vents at the base of the forward funnel and the area between the funnels and would have given the appearance of being generated by the upper deck fire.

A boiler or engine room fire could have started as a result of 15-centimetre shells either entering these compartments, or exploding against the armour belt. Given the close range, the 15-centimetre shells would have had little difficulty penetrating *Sydney*'s armour belt and wreaking havoc within the machinery spaces.[33]

A breach in the hull or the bulkheads surrounding the forward boiler room would have caused a sudden loss of air pressure in the room and could have resulted in the boilers flashing-back. If a flashback did occur, it is very likely that the boiler room personnel would have been severely burnt or killed. Without men to combat it, an uncontrolled oil fire would have resulted.[34]

Evidence of fire in the machinery spaces can be found in Captain Farncomb's 1 December report on the information obtained from the *Aquitania* prisoners on 30 November 1941. The prisoners claimed that when they abandoned ship *Sydney* was about four miles away, 'burning fiercely and "glowing" in the gathering darkness'.[35]

It is not known why the word 'glowing' was chosen, but it could be interpreted literally. An uncontrolled oil fire in *Sydney*'s machinery spaces would have generated an enormous amount of heat, and this heat would have caused the hull plates in the vicinity of the fire to 'glow' red hot.

The only effective way of combating an uncontrolled fire in a boiler or engine room is to seal off the compartment and attempt to smother the

fire. In many instances, however, it was a case of evacuating the compart-
ment and hoping that the fire would burn itself out. In *Sydney*'s case, such
actions might have had disastrous consequences. If the forward boiler or
forward engine rooms or both were abandoned due to fire caused by a
hull breach, the damage repair parties would not have been able to enter
the affected compartment(s). As a result, uncontrolled flooding could
have occurred. Flooding of either compartment, in conjunction with the
existing flooding forward, would have seriously reduced the reserve of
buoyancy.

ELECTRICITY AND STEAM

One final consideration is the effect of damage to *Sydney*'s electrical
system. From the case studies it can be seen that *Sydney* probably lost all
power when it was torpedoed, either the shock effect or a short-circuit
from floodwater causing the supply breakers to open. It is also probable
that much of the electrical system was extensively damaged by shellfire.

Although *Sydney*'s primary gun control circuits were vulnerable to
gunfire and bomb damage, the entire gunnery control system was reliant
on electricity. If power were lost, the main armament would have been
forced to go into hand working in group or local control. That this did
occur is supported by the prisoners' statements and the description of
Sydney's fire. Why 'x' and 'y' turrets could not be trained manually after
Sydney passed astern is unknown, although whipping or local damage
may have left the turrets jammed to port.

If *Sydney* had an Achilles heel, it was not the gunnery control circuits,
but its reliance on electricity. Every key component of the ship relied on
electricity, and the nerve centre of the ship's electrical system was the
main switchboard room. Unfortunately, because of design and weight
limitations, this room was put above the waterline and was not protected
by the armour belt. As a result, it was extremely vulnerable to shellfire,
bomb and torpedo damage. And given that the main switchboard room
was located on the port side of the ship, directly below the forward
superstructure, it is quite possible that it was damaged or destroyed early
in the action.

If the main switchboard room were destroyed, all electrically powered instruments, pumps and motors would have failed.

It is highly likely that the forward boiler room and possibly the forward engine room caught fire and had to be abandoned, but it is obvious that at least one boiler room and one engine room remained operational, otherwise *Sydney* would not have been able to steam away. This meant that *Sydney* had at least one turbo generator being supplied with steam, and possibly one or both diesel generators still working. Through the use of direct leads, power could have been restored to key components such as the surviving fire and bilge pumps. With one boiler room and one engine room still functioning, at least three steam bilge ejectors would have been available for limited control of flooding.

In other words, while *Sydney* was still producing steam, there was some hope that the ship could be saved. How much hope depended on the amount of floodwater *Sydney* had already taken in and whether the surviving pumps and ejectors had the capacity to check or reduce any additional floodwater.

How long *Sydney* managed to stay afloat is open to conjecture, but it is difficult to believe the cruiser would have survived the night.

—8—
WITH ALL HANDS

DESPITE the extensive air and sea search for *Sydney* and possible survivors, very little was discovered. The real tragedy, however, was that no trace of the crew was ever found. Although it is not known when or how *Sydney* sank, it would be logical to assume that some members of the ship's complement would have survived the sinking.

So what became of them? Why did 318 men from *Kormoran's* complement of 399 officers and men survive, yet not a single man from *Sydney's* complement was ever found, alive or dead.[1]

THE HAND OF FATE

Sydney was badly damaged during its encounter with *Kormoran*. Along with this damage, there would have been heavy casualties. Although it is difficult to quantify, it is conceivable that up to a third of the ship's complement were killed or wounded during the action.[2] And given that

Sydney may have sunk quickly and without warning, many of those who had survived the action might not have survived the sinking.

Given the nature of the damage, especially around the boat deck, the survivors may have had few, if any, of the ship's lifesaving appliances available to them. Without boats, Carley floats and adequate provisions, the life expectancy of any such survivors would have been short. When other wartime losses are studied, it can be seen that many would have died within hours of entering the water.

Kormoran's survivors, on the other hand, were comparatively well equipped for their struggle with the sea. All of the German and Chinese survivors were accommodated in the ship's boats and inflatable rubber dinghies. These craft kept the survivors relatively dry and, to a certain extent, protected them from the elements. In addition, the boats and dinghies were provisioned with food and water. On top of this, their morale and discipline were good. These men had survived an encounter with an enemy cruiser and had, to all intents and purposes, defeated their opponent. Buoyed by their success in battle, these men had the will-power, and the means, to survive.

Clearly, the *Kormoran* survivors had many advantages over *Sydney*'s survivors, not the least being the *Kormoran*'s large number of serviceable boats and dinghies.

Sydney's boats, with the exception of the two cutters, were stowed amidships abreast the forward funnel and on skids abreast the round-house, which supported the aircraft catapult. All of these boats, including the cutters, were made from timber and were particularly vulnerable to shell and splinter damage. As a good deal of *Kormoran*'s 15-centimetre and 2-centimetre fire was directed at *Sydney*'s upper decks, it would be logical to assume that most of the boats were damaged by shellfire or consumed in the resulting midships fire. It is also conceivable that the ship's crane, which provided the only means of hoisting the boats over the side and into the water, could have been damaged by shellfire or destroyed by the fire.

The only boats not dependent on the ship's crane were the two 32-foot cutters. As for these boats, it is almost certain that the port cutter was damaged by shellfire early in the action, though one prisoner's claim that he 'only remembered seeing two lifeboats on the *Sydney* and these had been shot to pieces' perhaps shows that both cutters were destroyed.[3]

It is possible that one or more of *Sydney*'s boats survived the action and the fires, but it is doubtful that any survived the sinking. If *Sydney* sank because of a loss of reserve of buoyancy or a magazine explosion, there would have been little or no time to get the boats away.

Without boats, the survivors would have been forced to rely on the limited number of Carley floats that the ship carried, and these were only designed to support life for a short period of time. The Carley float was essentially a large oval-shaped life preserver, which offered the occupants no shelter from the elements and often contained little in the way of provisions. Furthermore, because the internal structure consisted only of a slatted wooden grating suspended by rope netting, the craft floated in a semi-immersed condition whereby the occupants were always wet.

A boat, or even a rigidly constructed raft, such as those used by the merchant navy, could keep the survivor alive for a reasonable length of time, but the Carley float generally only prolonged life for five days at most. One wartime study, however, showed that the Carley float could only be expected to keep a man alive for three and a half days.[4]

These estimates can be seen to be only too accurate when the story of *Neptune*'s survivors is recalled. Of the sixteen who managed to reach a Carley float, all but one died of exposure within four days.

Carley floats were not designed to carry provisions. War experience, however, highlighted the value of at least having a supply of fresh water aboard. This was especially so in the Mediterranean, and contemporary photographs show small containers or barricoes of water lashed inside the floats. It is not known if this practice was continued once vessels left this particularly hostile theatre of operations, but in July 1941 the Admiralty advised, in CAFO 3291, that action was being taken to provide emergency rations for all life floats.

The rations were to consist of water and concentrated food packed into square airtight tins. It was intended that the provisions would be stowed inside a new type of double grating. Until new gratings could be made and fitted it was recommended that the tins be secured to the existing single grating. A follow-up CAFO, dated 20 November 1941, said that stocks of emergency rations 'are not at present adequate to meet requirements of HM ships on foreign stations'.[5]

It is not known if *Sydney*'s Carley floats carried an emergency supply of fresh water. Without water, the life expectancy of *Sydney*'s survivors would have been reduced to about five days, although there were recorded cases of men surviving for longer periods. The official history of the RAN and RAAF medical services during the Second World War noted that 'the survival time for a healthy, initially well-hydrated man without water in a warm to hot climate is up to ten days'.[6]

In many cases, however, the singular or multiple effects of injury, burns, shock and exposure tended to dramatically reduce survival time.

There were a great number of variables that could influence how long a man could survive in a temperate climate. The greatest killer was thirst. Without sufficient fresh water to quench their thirst, many men succumbed to the temptation to drink sea water. In most cases these men were subsequently overcome by delirium, madness then death through accelerated dehydration.

For personal use, every officer and rating was issued with an inflatable life-belt. This consisted of a rubber tube, which was covered with fabric and secured over the shoulders and around the body by tapes. It was inflated by means of a short flexible mouthpiece, although it was recommended that this not be done until the wearer was actually in the water. Contemporary photographs show that this recommendation was not strictly adhered to or enforced.

The life-belts were often worn around the waist in the deflated condition while at action stations, although some men preferred to roll it up and tie it to their belt, or carry it in a small 'action bag' which could be slung over the shoulder.

The US Navy also used this type of life preserver but found that the practice of constantly wearing them around the waist in the deflated condition prematurely wore out the rubber. The Americans also used a kapok life jacket that was much more practical, because its design kept the wearer's head and shoulders upright in the water. This feature permitted the wearer to conserve energy and even to obtain sleep. The life-belt, on the other hand, did not provide the necessary support and if one were to doze off while wearing one there was a very real danger of the wearer unconsciously flipping over onto his face and drowning.[7]

W.H. Ross wrote of his personal experience with these life-belts in his book *Lucky Ross*, saying that he had no confidence in them at all. Apparently, the only practical use for an inflatable life-belt was in using it as a pillow.

Perhaps providing an insight into how reliable these life-belts were considered to be was the official practice of having sea-boat's crews supplied with the general-purpose life jacket. These were a reversible canvas jacket onto which pockets containing slabs of cork or kapok were sewn. One was provided for each member of the sea-boat's crew.

In the likelihood that none of *Sydney*'s boats survived the action and the fires, the survivors, being dependent on the limited number of Carley floats and their inadequate life-belts, stood little chance. Those who had only their life-belt for support would probably have drowned or died of exposure within forty-eight hours.

In the event that some or all of the still serviceable Carley floats were released before the ship sank, those survivors who managed to reach the floats would probably have survived for several more days. Some may have survived for as long as five or six days, but it is highly unlikely that anyone would have been left alive after ten days.[8]

Apart from trying to cope with the effects of wounds, burns, shock, exposure, fatigue and thirst, there was another element that would have taken its toll of survivors, namely, sharks and other marine life. That sharks were present was confirmed by the statements made by *Kormoran* survivors and in letters written while prisoners of war.[9]

HMS DUNEDIN

On 24 November 1941 HMS *Dunedin* was torpedoed by *U-124* while on patrol in the mid Atlantic. *U-124*, under the command of Kapitänleutnant Mohr, was en route to the position where the raider *Atlantis* had been sunk two days previously in order to help rescue survivors. When in the vicinity of St Paul's Rocks, Mohr sighted the British cruiser and decided to attack.

The first of the two torpedoes to strike *Dunedin* apparently detonated the forward magazine, and the other hit under the after superstructure.[10]

The ship rolled onto its beam ends, righted itself, then sank stern first with heavy loss of life. *Dunedin* sank so quickly that none of the ship's boats could be lowered, nor was a W/T message transmitted. Those that survived the sinking had only their life-belts and a small number of Carley floats available for life support. To make matters worse, the sea was alive with sharks and barracuda, and in the following days many of the survivors were attacked.

By good fortune, the steamer *Nishmaha* discovered the survivors three days later. The master of the *Nishmaha*, O.H. Olsen, described many of the men as being close to death, while some he said were unconscious, delirious or hysterical and lacerated with all kinds of wounds.[11]

Of the seventy-two rescued on 27 November, five subsequently died from their ordeal. It is not known exactly how many men had been on board *Dunedin*, or how many survived the ship's sinking, but as the peacetime complement was recorded as 452 officers and men, it is assumed that the wartime complement was well in excess of this figure.

USS INDIANAPOLIS

At approximately 0005 on 30 July 1945, the heavy cruiser USS *Indianapolis* was struck by two torpedoes fired by the Japanese submarine *I-58*. The American cruiser sank within fifteen minutes of being hit and of the 1,196 officers and men on board, it was estimated that approximately 800 survived the sinking. As there was insufficient time to launch boats, these men went into the water in whatever they happened to be wearing. Some had kapok life jackets, some wore inflatable life-belts, others jumped into the water with no form of life-saving apparel at all.

Indianapolis had been on independent passage and despite managing to transmit several reports of the torpedoing and requests for help, the transmissions were either not heard or not acted upon. The survivors therefore found themselves alone in a hostile sea. Exactly how hostile became evident when at approximately 0130 the first shark appeared in the midst of a group of about 400 men.

Owing to a number of factors, most of the survivors initially became concentrated into three drifting groups, the remainder being spread out

over several thousand yards. One small group consisted of Captain C.B.McVay and eight men. Between them they had three rafts and one floater net. These rafts were similar to the Carley float but were constructed of kapok and covered with canvas, while the floater net was basically a large rope net made buoyant with pieces of cork.

McVay's group managed to recover from the sea a number of useful items, including a ration can of food and a cask of water. Unfortunately, seawater had contaminated the contents of the cask. During their first day in the water, McVay's group was visited by an extremely large shark, which could not be driven off. It was to become a source of great anxiety in the days that followed.

The second group consisted of about 150 men under the command of Lieutenant Redmayne. This group also had three rafts as well as two floater nets. Most of the group wore kapok life jackets and, like McVay's group, managed to recover an assortment of items from the oil covered sea, including several ration cans and water casks.

The largest group consisted of about 400 men and was known as the 'swimmer' or 'life-preserver' group on account of the lack of life rafts among these men. Worse, this group did not have any food or water. An estimated fifty of the men in this group died within hours of the sinking from injuries, shock, or drowning. Where possible the life jackets were removed from the dead so as to be of some use to those without, the corpses left to sink or drift away.

Sections of this large 'swimmer' group drifted apart during the hours before dawn. By daybreak, three sub-groups had formed. The largest contained about 200 men, the smallest about 50, and the third sub-group comprised about 100 men. It was towards these sub-groups that the sharks were attracted because of the high death rate and the abundance of bodies on which to feed. For most of the first day, the sharks were content taking stragglers and corpses. Later in the day and early evening, however, the numbers of sharks rose and the number of attacks increased.

On the second day, McVay's group increased to ten when another man and raft were sighted.

Redmayne's group, on the other hand, became smaller when several wounded men died during the night. Further bad news greeted the survivors when some of the water casks were found to contain undrinkable

salt- or oil-contaminated water. Sharks appeared in growing numbers, but no attacks were made. There were problems with discipline, however, when some men refused to obey orders and began to devour food that was supposed to be rationed. This food was predominantly Spam, which was salted and only increased the men's thirst.

The swimmer sub-groups also found their numbers depleted by dawn on the second day. The heat of the previous day combined with the unquenchable thirst that all were experiencing had driven some to suicide by drowning. Others were killed when fights broke out or became delirious after drinking salt water and swam away from the group. Conditions worsened during the day as more and more men succumbed to the temptation to drink salt water. These men consequently became delirious or hysterical or both and began thrashing about and exhausting themselves. Once exhausted they either drowned or went into a coma, usually with the same result. Others drowned when their inflatable life-belts became deflated or were punctured during the fights. The very clear water, which allowed the men to look down into the depths and see the sharks feasting on their drowned shipmates, increased the strain on everyone.

Already bad conditions deteriorated even further during the second night as the kapok life jackets became increasingly waterlogged. Although the life jacket remained buoyant, the wearer sank lower in the water, and increasing numbers of men became disheartened and discarded them. Most of these men subsequently drowned.

The third day dawned with McVay and his group intact and relatively well off, although they were still being menaced by their unwanted visitor. Unfortunately, the sharks accompanying the Redmayne group were not so quiet. They had begun attacking swimmers as they drifted or swam away from the main body.

The pattern of the previous day continued as the heat drove increasing numbers of men to drink salt water with predictable results. The mutinous behaviour of a small group of survivors on a floater net who began to steal food and water from the rafts heightened the difficulties faced by Redmayne and his fellow officers in trying to maintain order and discipline. By this stage, the effects of fatigue and exposure were striking down even the fittest men. In the evening Redmayne became delirious.

During the night the ship's doctor, Lieutenant-Commander Haynes, who had been providing comfort and inspiration to the men in the swimmer sub-groups, also became delirious. The leader of Haynes's sub-group was Marine Captain Parke, who was fighting a losing battle in trying to keep his men under control. His sub-group disbanded later in the day when Parke died. Most became easy prey for the marauding sharks.

A new sub-group formed under Ensign Moynelo and into this group Haynes was taken and cared for. Haynes found many men coming to him for help and advice even though he was in urgent need of help himself. Later in the afternoon, either realizing the urgency of the situation or overcome by insanity, Moynelo and about twenty-five others decided to swim for help. They were never seen again.

By the end of the third day, most men realized that it was only a matter of time before they too died and, as if to reinforce the fact, the sharks returned during the night and put many out of their misery. At dawn one man was found to have been cut in half by a nocturnal visitor.

As the fourth day dawned, the chances of being rescued before the sea and the sharks claimed them all must have seemed extremely remote. At about 1100, however, the pilot of a Ventura bomber on anti-submarine patrol happened to look down and saw a thin line of oil on the surface of the sea. The aircraft was being flown at 3,000 feet and it had only been by chance that Lieutenant Gwinn looked down to see the oil which he assumed was being trailed by a submarine.[12]

The Ventura was brought down to 900 feet to follow the trail to its source, and a short time later Gwinn sighted a 25-mile wide patch of oil dotted with what looked like heads. Gwinn dropped down even further to 300 feet in an attempt to identify the men in the water. With no knowledge of *Indianapolis*'s loss, Gwinn ordered his radio operator to report the sighting of thirty survivors and their position, while he turned the aircraft north. Six miles away, he found another group of about forty men and four miles further on he sighted another large group of survivors.

Down below, the survivors greeted the aircraft with a mixture of hope and despair. Each day aircraft had flown over and, despite signalling with mirrors and flares, the aircraft had continued on, totally oblivious to the plight of the men below. Gwinn's aircraft, although flying lower, gave no indication that it had sighted the survivors either. Then it turned, made a

low pass over what remained of the swimmer group, and began dropping survival equipment including two rafts.

Although *Indianapolis* should have arrived at Leyte Gulf on 31 July, and was now two days overdue, no one gave its non-arrival much thought. That is until Gwinn's amended report gave an indication that a large vessel had been sunk. With no reports of Japanese vessels being sunk in the area, the authorities requested all ships to report their positions. While the navy began confirming the locations of its ships, a relief aircraft was organized and despatched to relieve Gwinn, who had been ordered to remain on station. To provide help, a Catalina was scrambled.

When the Catalina arrived on the scene at about 1600, the pilot, Lieutenant Marks, seeing that sharks were active, decided to land and begin the rescue of the swimmer group. By nightfall his aircraft had recovered fifty-six survivors, including Haynes. A second Catalina arrived before dark and it too landed to begin picking up survivors. The crew of this aircraft saw many men in the water, but they soon discovered that all but one were dead.

By this stage it was ascertained that *Indianapolis* had not reported in, but it was still not understood that the estimated 150 men in the water were possibly all that remained of its crew.

At 2150, the destroyer escort USS *Cecil J. Doyle*, which had been diverted to the scene, sighted a star shell. *Doyle* illuminated the night sky with a searchlight and about two hours later made contact with Marks's overloaded and drifting Catalina. Shortly after midnight, the first of *Indianapolis*'s survivors stepped aboard *Doyle*. Within minutes an urgent message was transmitted to the Commander of the Western Carolines reporting the loss of the cruiser and the rescue of survivors.

Meanwhile, McVay's group drifted despondently far to the north.

By dawn, four more vessels had arrived and had begun rescue operations. At midday *Doyle*, with ninety-three survivors aboard, departed, having been relieved by the transport *Ringness*. No sooner had *Ringness* arrived than it was directed by search aircraft to pick up survivors from two rafts drifting to the north of the search area. This was McVay's group.

Captain McVay was the last survivor to be recovered from the sea, four and a half days after entering it. Of *Indianapolis*'s original complement of 1,196 officers and men, only 320 were found alive, although four later

died. In total, 880 officers and men died as a result of the sinking and the
aftermath.

The losses of *Dunedin* and *Indianapolis* had remarkable parallels with
that of *Sydney*. All three vessels were on independent passage when they
were lost, and in each instance their loss went unnoticed by the relevant
authorities. Each vessel sank in waters where sharks were active, and in
each case loss of life was heavy. The only clear difference between the
three cases was that the *Dunedin* and *Indianapolis* survivors were sighted
three and a half days after entering the water.

If the *Dunedin* and *Indianapolis* survivors had been rescued earlier, many
more men would have survived. Clearly, the longer these men stayed in
the water the less their chance of survival. Although it is difficult to
establish an accurate timeframe, it is conceivable that few, if any, would
have remained alive after six days. Given time, sharks and other marine
life would have removed all trace of the corpses.

Establishing how long it would have taken for the corpses to be
consumed or to simply decompose and disintegrate is also difficult to
determine. A study of an extract from the action report of the USS *Helm*,
which had been involved in the search for *Indianapolis*'s survivors, however, may give some indication.

> All bodies were in extremely bad condition and had been dead for an
> estimated 4 or 5 days. Some had life jackets and life belts, most had
> nothing. Most of the bodies were completely naked, and others just
> had drawers or dungaree trousers on—only three of the 28 bodies
> recovered had shirts on. Bodies were horribly bloated and decom-
> posed—recognition of faces would have been impossible. About half
> of the bodies were shark-bitten, some to such a degree that they more
> nearly resembled skeletons. From one to four sharks were in the
> immediate area of the ship at all times. At one time, two sharks were
> attacking a body not more than fifty yards from the ship, and continued
> to do so until driven off by rifle fire. For the most part it was impossible
> to get fingerprints from the bodies as the skin had come off the hands
> or the hands lacerated by sharks. Skin was removed from the hands of
> bodies containing no identification when possible, and the Medical
> Officer will dehydrate the skin and attempt to make legible prints …[13]

Another vessel examined twenty-nine corpses and found that due to decomposition or mutilation by sharks, only eleven could be identified. As the search operation concluded on 8 August, nine days after *Indianapolis* sank, it is assumed that very little remained by this time. Many floating corpses had to be weighted down and sunk, as advanced decomposition prevented them being taken on board.

Normally, decomposition (putrefaction) of a body is retarded by immersion in water, but in the case of the *Indianapolis* corpses the process appears to have been accelerated. This was most likely a result of the relative warmth of the water.

The process of decomposition normally starts in the abdomen because of the action and growth of anaerobic gas-forming organisms in the intestines. These organisms cause the abdomen to bloat and swell with gases. A victim of drowning will not float until this process has occurred. In cool water this may not occur until the sixth to the tenth day. Warm water will accelerate the process.

That the process had been accelerated in the case of the *Indianapolis* corpses is shown by the report that the skin had come off the hands of some, and the apparent ease with which the skin from the hands of others was removed to obtain fingerprints. This shows that decomposition was well established and that the cutis, or true skin beneath the epidermis, had become sodden and was beginning to peel or had already done so. This process does not normally occur until about the second week after death. Warm weather, however, can halve the time. Eventually, decomposition and sodden disintegration of the tissues breaks down the flesh, turning it into slime and causing the skeletal frame to collapse.[14]

In the case of *Sydney*, there were no survivors to help explain the loss of the ship, and no corpses. Clearly the greatest single factor working against *Sydney*'s survivors was time. Once in the water their chances of survival were totally dependent on help arriving fast. Within three days, many would have been dead as a result of wounds, shock, exposure or drowning. Within five to six days, only the fittest and mentally strongest would have been left alive. After ten days, it is extremely doubtful that anyone would have been left alive.

Yet one question remains. What happened to the corpses?

Even if *Sydney* sank with all hands and not a single man survived the sinking, the corpses of crew members not trapped within the ship should have come to the surface after six to ten days, if not before. If some of the crew managed to survive the sinking but not their time in the water, their corpses should also have come to the surface after decomposition had started; again, a period of six to ten days or possibly fewer if the water temperature was sufficiently high to accelerate the process.

Given that the *Kormoran* survivors described the days as warm to hot but the nights as cold, it is likely that the water was not sufficiently warm enough to accelerate decomposition. If this was the case, the corpses of *Sydney* crew members who died or drowned during the sinking or in the days following may not have begun to float until the eighth or tenth day after death. As the search for survivors was abandoned on 29 November, it is possible that the corpses may only have begun to come to the surface as the search operations were being concluded.

That a number of *Kormoran* survivors drowned while abandoning ship but no German corpses were found during the search supports such a hypothesis. One corpse was recovered from a small float, but there is no evidence of any corpses being found floating in the water.

Another consideration is that the search may not have been comprehensive enough and that floating corpses might have been overlooked. Alternatively, sharks and other marine life might have removed all trace of the corpses before searching ships and aircraft reached the scene.

There is, however, a possibility that corpses were found but either not reported, or the findings kept quiet or even covered up. Suggesting that this view may have some validity was a statement made by Commander Long in October 1945. In replying to Rycroft's request to release information to the public Long wrote: 'There has now been accumulated a mass of confirmatory information which leaves no doubt that there were no survivors from HMAS *Sydney*.'[15]

Long's choice of words is curious. By stating that there was a mass of confirmatory information that left no doubt that there were no survivors, Long implied that there was evidence to show that no one had been found alive. In other words, it is possible that some members of *Sydney*'s complement were found in circumstances that suggested that no one else

could be expected to be found alive. In short, corpses in an advanced state of decomposition.

If this was so, it was perhaps considered that little would be gained by sharing this information with the Australian public. Grieving families might have been comforted by the knowledge that their loved ones had been found, and a proper burial service conducted, but the realities may have dictated an alternative course of action.

If corpses were found during the search, or even after it was concluded, their condition may have been such that recovery was considered impracticable. Given the probable state of any corpses found, the finders might have considered it more prudent to leave them in the sea and let nature take its course.

The widely held belief that the lighthouse tender *Cape Otway* discovered a large number of corpses as it made its way along the coast shortly after the search was abandoned perhaps supports such a scenario. But there is no known documentation to support this claim. It is also relevant that Mr John Dunn, a former crew member of the *Cape Otway*, and on board at the time of the discovery, has said that no bodies were sighted.[16]

Clearly, it is important to treat all theories as theories, and to this end, any speculation about Long and withholding of information must remain speculation until or unless suitable documentation surfaces. While a more thorough search of archive files and private memoirs may provide this documentation and perhaps additional information on the results of the 1941 search, a reappraisal of the known documents and previous research may provide further clues to what happened to *Sydney*'s survivors.

DEBRIS

The only documented items found during the 1941 search for *Sydney* that could reasonably be expected to have originated from the ship were one life-belt and a single Carley float. Other items that might have come from *Sydney* but found after the search was abandoned included a Carley float that was discovered off Christmas Island in February 1942, a box marked 'HMAS SYDNEY' found in the vicinity of Green Islets (near Jurien Bay) in

June 1942, and a lifebuoy marked 'HMAS SYDNEY' which was recovered off Comboyuro Point, New South Wales in 1943.[17]

Further items not positively identified, but which may have come from *Sydney*, were found washed ashore north of Geraldton a short time after the battle.

The most well documented of these items is the Carley float recovered at sea on 28 November 1941 by HMAS *Heros*, and now on permanent display in the Australian War Memorial (AWM).

This float was recovered in position 24° 7' South, 110° 58' East, which placed it in the midst of *Kormoran*'s debris field. Given that *Sydney* was seen to disappear over the horizon after the battle, it is assumed that the cruiser created a debris field further to the south-east when it sank and that *Sydney*'s debris did not become intermingled with *Kormoran*'s. If so, this would indicate that the Carley float was probably blown off *Sydney* during the action and that it had drifted north at about the same rate as the debris from the raider, *Kormoran* being scuttled close to the position where the action was fought.

In 1993 the AWM examined the Carley float to establish whether the numerous holes in the float were caused by small arms fire. These holes have always been a source of speculation that the float might have contained survivors who were machine-gunned by the Germans. The analysis of the float and the pieces of munitions found inside the float led the investigation team to conclude that:

> The extensive damage to the float appears to have been caused by particles of shrapnel from at least one high-explosive shell detonating on or near the main structure of the ship and ricocheting into the float. There is no evidence of damage by small arms fire. Nor does the exterior of the float have any heat or burn marks to indicate that it was exposed to the fires reported to have broken out on *Sydney*.[18]

Their report also noted that 'the projectiles hit mainly from one side' and that 'the holes in the float, the projectiles removed from the float and the angles of trajectory and divergence of those projectiles is consistent with explosive shells detonating relatively near the float while the float was in a horizontal, stored position'.

The other item of interest from this float was the discovery of a large number '5' painted longitudinally on one side. While the research team stated that they could find no information or photographic evidence of *Sydney*'s floats being numbered, there is reason to believe that *Sydney*'s floats were numbered and that the number five denoted where this particular float was stowed.

On 1 November 1935, the newly commissioned *Sydney* arrived in Gibraltar to join the Mediterranean Fleet. Naturally, photographs were taken of the 'Rock'. Two have survived and can be viewed in the AWM photographic collection. Both show numbered Carley floats stowed on the 4-inch gundeck.

That the numbering of Carley floats was not just a peacetime practice can be established by studying wartime photographs of HMA Ships *Australia*, *Hobart* and *Shropshire*. These reveal British as well as American

The Rock of Gibraltar viewed from *Sydney*'s 4-inch gundeck. Note the Carley float stencilled with the number 4.
AWM P02308.005

pattern floats numbered sequentially. The numbering started from the forecastle and worked aft, with odd numbers on the starboard side and even numbers on the port side.

Sydney carried differing numbers of Carley floats throughout its life, and it is difficult to determine how many and of which pattern the ship carried at any given time. Photographs taken in mid to late 1941, however, indicate that Sydney carried the following number and pattern of floats:

> Two Pattern No.20 floats stowed horizontally on the port side of the boatdeck abreast the forward funnel.
>
> Four Pattern No.20 floats stowed vertically on the blast screen on the 4-inch gundeck; two on the starboard side and two on the port side.

These were supplemented by an unknown number of floats stowed horizontally on the quarterdeck. The last known photograph of Sydney's stern shows two Pattern No.18 floats with one Pattern No.20 float 'nested' in the starboard float.[19]

It is possible, though not supported by the available evidence, that the Pattern No.18 floats were removed before November 1941 and that two Pattern No.20 floats were shipped in their place. War experience had shown that the large Carley floats were unmanageable and that an increased number of smaller floats was more desirable.[20] That this requirement was acknowledged by the RAN was demonstrated on Sydney during 1941 by the removal of the Pattern No.18 floats from the blast screen on the 4-inch gundeck. They were replaced with four Pattern No.20 floats.

Whether Sydney carried Pattern No.18 floats, Pattern No.20 floats, or a combination of both on the stern during its final voyage is not known, but it is assumed that if Captain Burnett had adopted the practice of numbering the ship's floats, the floats stowed on the stern would have also been numbered. As the starboard 4-inch gundeck floats would have been numbered '1' and '3', the float stowed at the stern on the starboard side of the quarterdeck would have been painted or stencilled with the number '5'. If, as the September photograph suggests, a Pattern No.20 float was stowed inside a Pattern No.18 float, these floats would have

Sydney crewmembers pose in front of a Pattern
No.18 Carley float on the 4-inch gundeck. The
smaller Pattern No.20 Carley float was designed to
fit inside the No.18 float. Note the slatted wooden
platform, which made up the floor of the float.
R. Buckingham

been numbered '5' and '7', although it is not known which float would have carried which number.

On the port side of the ship, the two Pattern No.20 floats stowed abreast the forward funnel would have been numbered '2' and '4', and the two Pattern No.20 floats stowed on the 4-inch gundeck would have been numbered '6' and '8'. Any float stowed on the port side of the quarterdeck would therefore have been numbered '10'.

As the Pattern No.20 float recovered by HMAS *Heros* still has the number '5' painted on its side, it would be logical to assume that this float was stowed horizontally on the stern of *Sydney* on the starboard side. It is noteworthy that such a position is consistent with the findings of the scientific examination of the float.

Knowing where this particular float was probably stowed on *Sydney* raises other questions that are more difficult to answer. For example, how and when did the float become detached from the ship?

It has been suggested that as the float shows no sign of heat or burn marks it may have been blown off *Sydney* early in the action. The recovery of the float from a position close to, or within, the *Kormoran's* debris field would tend to support such a theory.

Carley floats were normally fastened to the deck or superstructure, but considering the damage to the float, the anchor ropes or wires may have been shot away and the float either physically blown overboard, or unshipped when *Sydney* was torpedoed.

That the neighbouring port float was not sighted or recovered raises another question that cannot satisfactorily be answered, although the port float might have sustained more damage than the starboard float and might have sunk if it too was blown overboard. The same may also apply if the recovered float had been stowed inside a Pattern No.18 float. The larger float may have absorbed more damage and, being a much heavier float, may have also sunk if it was blown off the ship.

Some have suggested that the recovered Carley float might have come from *Kormoran*, the raider perhaps having picked it up from one of its victims. This would explain the presence of the float in the same general area as the debris from the raider, but as *Kormoran's* logbooks do not mention any floats being captured or recovered it is doubtful if the Carley float came from the raider.

The material used in the float's construction shows that the float was almost certainly ex-*Sydney*. The AWM investigating team found that while the outer covering of cork and canvas conformed with standard Admiralty floats, the inside framework and buoyancy tanks were made of galvanized steel instead of Admiralty specified copper. The steel used carried the following manufacturer's brand:

LYSAGHT

ZINCANNEAL

AUSTRALIA

PANEL QUALITY

Taking into consideration the Australian manufactured galvanized steel used in the float's construction, it would be logical to assume that the float was manufactured in Australia from available materials. Furthermore, given that *Sydney* was lost in the vicinity of where the float was found, it would be equally logical to assume that the float originated from the Australian cruiser.

The other item recovered during the search that was assumed to be ex-*Sydney* was an RAN-type life-belt. This was recovered by *Wyrallah* on 27 November in position 24° 22' South, 110° 49' East and was found to be still inflated. It was noted that the securing tape was knotted but had snapped, suggesting that the wearer had inflated the belt before entering the water and that the belt had been torn off when the wearer jumped or fell into the sea. The only identifying mark found on this life-belt was 'OTRC 11/39', which was found stamped on the rubber tube.[21]

A second life-belt was reported as having been recovered by *Evagoras* on the same day. This was incorrect. A subsequent report dated 4 December 1941 said that investigations had revealed that *Evagoras* did not pick up a life-belt.[22]

At about the same time the search for *Sydney* was being conducted, other *Sydney*-related items were found on a beach near Fremantle. In June 1991, during a discussion with Fremantle Maritime Museum staff, Mr Tom Osborne recalled finding items of clothing in seaweed on the beach north of the cable station at Cottesloe. He believed he found these items shortly before the loss of *Sydney* was announced. The clothing apparently

consisted of navy shirts and an 'HMAS SYDNEY' hatband. Naval authorities were advised of the find and staff were brought in to sweep the beach, but nothing else was found.[23]

Mr Osborne was never given a satisfactory answer to why these items came to be on the beach, as the navy remained tight-lipped about the incident. It is conceivable, however, that the clothing belonged to one or both of the two stokers who were absent without leave from 31 October until 11 November. Sentenced to sixty days' detention, these two men remained in Fremantle while their shipmates steamed north with *Zealandia*.

THE CHRISTMAS ISLAND CORPSE

On or about 6 February 1942, another item that may have come from *Sydney* was recovered. Late in the afternoon or early evening, lookouts on Christmas Island sighted what was thought to be a Japanese submarine. Examined with binoculars, the object was identified as a Carley float, which appeared to be occupied. The Pilot boat was despatched to investigate and to tow the float back to the island's jetty. The sole occupant of the float was found to be deceased and partly decomposed.

The Harbour Master, Captain J.R. Smith, in a report dated 25 February 1942, said that he was of the opinion that the float was of naval pattern because it was grey in colour and the wooden decking was branded with the word 'PATENT'. He also noted that the roping attached to the float contained a red yarn running through the strands. The corpse was clad in a blue boilersuit, which had been bleached white by exposure. A shoe was found with the corpse, which the island doctor considered did not belong to the deceased.[24]

The report submitted by Smith said that it was a single canvas shoe and that it was branded either 'McCowan' or 'McEwan'. He also noted that the letters 'Pty' could be identified, followed by a crown or a broad arrow or both. The view that it was a canvas shoe had been supported in a 23 February 1942 report by Mr J.C. Baker, who was in charge of the island's radio station. Although Baker could not recall what markings were found on it, he said that it was probably branded 'CROWN BRAND PTY 4', but he was not entirely certain about the 'CROWN' or the '4'.

On examining the corpse, the doctor determined that the body was that of a white male. But as no personal effects or identity disc were found, the man's identity could not be established.[25] It was also noted that the eyes and nose were missing, probably the result of birds, and that fish had apparently eaten away all the flesh from the right arm.

The float itself was noted as having been damaged by gun or shellfire, with pieces of metal still embedded in the outer covering. What appeared to be a bullet hole was found in the wooden decking. One piece of metal found embedded in the 'kapok' filling immediately below a small round perforation in the outer covering was considered to be what remained of a bullet. Other pieces of metal found in the 'kapok' appear to have been identified as shrapnel.

It was the manufacturer's brand found on the inside framework, however, that provided more information on the origins of the float. Smith reported that the inside framework and the divisions between the buoyancy tanks were branded 'LYSAGHT DUA-ANNEAL ZINC. MADE IN AUSTRALIA INSIDE'.

Baker's recollection of the brand was slightly different. He recalled that the brand was 'MADE IN N.S.W. ANNEALED ZINC INSIDE'.

Significantly, Baker recalled that the float was marked with the number '2' on the outside covering, a detail that was overlooked or forgotten by Smith. The other observation recalled by both men was that barnacles up to 1 inch in length, and apparently ordinary marine growth up to 6 inches long, were found on the float, suggesting that it had been in the water for some time.

An official 'inquest' was said to have been conducted on Christmas Island a short time after the float and corpse were discovered and a copy of the report forwarded to the Australian authorities. This report could not be located in 1949 when the theory that the float may have originated from *Sydney* was being mooted. The DNI at the time, Captain G.C. Oldham, RAN, investigated the matter and, working from the shipping intelligence reports that contained Smith's and Baker's statements, concluded that the float was not from *Sydney*. Oldham admitted that 'the clothing found on the corpse could possibly have been that of an RAN rating', and the markings on the shoe 'definitely corresponded with supplies from our stocks' but because of the 'particulars given of the covering

of the Carley float' he considered that the float 'did not belong to an HMA Ship'.[26]

Despite Oldham's opinion that the float was not from *Sydney*, many people remain unconvinced. Most notable is the author Barbara Winter, who asserts that the float did come from *Sydney*. Fellow HMAS *Sydney* author Dr Tom Frame is more skeptical. Although, in the light of evidence submitted to the 1998 Commonwealth inquiry into the sinking of *Sydney*, it is understood that Dr Frame now considers it likely that the Christmas Island float did come from *Sydney*.[27]

A CASE FOR A CARLEY FLOAT

Although Captain Smith was of the opinion that the Carley float was of naval pattern, there is insufficient evidence to prove this assertion. The simple fact that it was painted grey does not mean that it came from a warship. Some merchant ships mounted one or more defensive guns, which were manned by navy gunners. When the ship carried insufficient lifeboats to accommodate these extra men, rafts or Carley floats were taken on board to provide some means of life support should the ship be sunk.[28]

That the Christmas Island float came from such a ship is possible, although there is no evidence of any ships carrying DEMS (Defensively Equipped Merchant Ships) gunners being lost in the region at the time or in the months preceding February 1942. *Eidsvold* was torpedoed off the island shortly before the float appeared, but the island authorities do not appear to have connected the float and corpse with the loss of the Norwegian vessel. Furthermore, *Eidsvold* was not a DEMS ship and would not have been issued with Carley floats. Other merchant ships were lost in the period in question, but merchant navy rafts were of a different pattern and construction, and were visually very different from a Carley float.[29]

The possibility that the Christmas Island float was a 'navy pattern' float becomes more of a probability when Smith's description of the roping attached to the float is studied. He described a red yarn running through the strands.

Admiralty rope, as used by the Royal Navy, was identified by a colour coded 'Rogue's yarn'. The 1937 Admiralty Manual of Seamanship, Volume 1, noted that all rope for naval use was made at the roperies at Chatham and Devonport in England, and that a 'Rogue's yarn' of coloured jute was incorporated in the yarns of the rope for identification purposes. Devonport produced rope with a red yarn, and Chatham produced rope with a yellow yarn. Trade manufactured rope was noted as being identified by a blue 'Rogue's yarn'.

Obviously, the use of Devonport rope on the Christmas Island float would suggest that it had come from a Royal Navy vessel, and the fact that the float was numbered would also support this view. The number '2' would indicate that it was the forward-most float on the port side of the vessel of origin. Although these two factors, if they had been considered, should have been sufficient to indicate that the float had come from an HM ship, the fact that the covering of the float consisted of 'kapok' instead of the standard cork apparently convinced Oldham otherwise.

But was Oldham justified in arriving at this conclusion?

The rope was clearly of Admiralty origin, the number on the float suggested it had come from an HM ship, and the clothing found on and with the deceased occupant suggested that the corpse could have been an RAN rating. In addition, the brand on the inside framework of the float revealed that the float had either been constructed in Australia or had been made from Australian-manufactured galvanized steel.

There is insufficient information available to help explain why kapok was said to be used as a covering material, but it is conceivable that wartime shortages led to its use as a substitute for cork.[30] Alternatively, it is possible that the Christmas Island float was covered with cork, but due to the effects of immersion or exposure, the cork may have become so degraded that Smith and Baker did not recognize it as cork.

Smith and Baker apparently relied solely on their memories when they made their reports. Significantly, both men gave differing views on the state of decomposition of the corpse, the brand on the footwear, the length of the barnacles, and perhaps of more significance, the manufacturer's brand on the steel panels of the float.

Neither of the brands remembered by Smith and Baker can be identified. Lysaght's were the only manufacturers of galvanized iron and

steel sheeting in Australia in the 1930s and 1940s, and their range of products did not include a 'Dua-Anneal Zinc' or 'Annealed Zinc' branded flat sheet. Early Lysaght sheet iron products were identified by the 'ORB' or 'QUEEN'S HEAD' brand. The former was applied to corrugated-iron products and the latter was applied to flat sheet products. In the mid to late 1930s, a new treatment process was developed by Lysaght's. The steel so treated was stamped with the brand name 'ZINCANNEAL'.[31] Significantly, this was the brand name found inside the AWM Carley float. It is highly probable that this was the brand name found inside the Christmas Island float.

Clearly, neither man could remember exactly what was branded on the steel panels. Given that Smith and Baker could not remember the brand name correctly, it is possible that they may have been wrong when they recalled that the covering material was kapok.

The condition of the corpse and the boilersuit it was clad in are also of interest. The island doctor could not, or did not, provide an estimate of how long the occupant had been deceased, but the faded condition of the boilersuit would suggest that the corpse had been exposed to the elements for some time. Establishing how long the float had been adrift and how long its occupant had been dead would help in establishing the origin of the float and the identity of the deceased.

Unfortunately, the lack of detailed information on the float itself and the absence of a medical or coroner's report on the corpse makes this difficult.[32]

Smith's claim that the barnacles were at least an inch long, however, would indicate that the float had been adrift for many weeks. It is not known which species of barnacle was found on the float, but it is assumed that they were either small goose-barnacles (*Lepas ansenfera*) or large goose-barnacles (*Lepas anatifera*), both species being common.[33]

The latter has a larger flexible stalk, which can grow to 8 or 9 inches, although some specimens have been found that are up to 12 inches long. They will generally attach themselves singularly or in clumps to anything floating in the sea by means of their stalk, the animal proper being encased in a shell that resembles a mussel in size and appearance. Growth rate is dependent on nutrient and, as the waters around Christmas Island are nutrient rich, their growth rate in these waters could be relatively fast.

The equally vague descriptions of the corpse reveal little apart from the fact that the body was decomposed. The eyes and nose were missing, but this could have been the result of birds or decomposition, the eyes normally liquefying within six to ten days, although this process may have been accelerated in the warm, moist environment.

It is assumed that the wooden grating of the float was made from the same material as that identified on the AWM float, namely, New Zealand kauri. This is a species of pine with good flotation qualities. It is also assumed that the weight of the corpse was not sufficient to force the decking underwater to its fullest extent, and that the decking more or less floated with the corpse perhaps immersed in a few inches of water. This would account for the observation that the corpse's right arm was devoid of flesh, apparently eaten away by fish. In such a position, the body would have been kept moist by sea water and warm by its exposure to the sun. The boilersuit would have also helped to warm the corpse and promote putrefaction. This process probably started within twenty-four hours of death and was well advanced within three or four days.

Given the free access of air around the corpse and the average long-term temperature range for Christmas Island in February (24.5° Celsius minimum to 28.1° Celsius maximum), it is also conceivable that mummi-fication occurred on those parts of the body not directly immersed in the sea. This could have occurred due to the rapid drying of tissue fluids. Formation of adipocere on the immersed parts of the body was equally possible, although this process would probably have taken several weeks to develop.

Adipocere is basically a post-mortem change in the body fats, which turns it into a firm wax-like substance. Extensive adipocere formation can retard skeletonization and help preserve the internal organs.

In short, the occupant of the Christmas Island float may have been deceased for as little as a week. Conversely, the corpse may have been several months old. Without a more accurate description of the state of the body and the extent of decomposition, it is impossible to arrive at a definite timeframe. It is possible that the corpse had decomposed within a week, but it is doubtful that the barnacles and marine growth found on the float would have grown to the size described in so short a time. Therefore, while the condition of the corpse and the extent of marine

growth were probably consistent with the required eleven weeks of exposure if they had originated from *Sydney*, nothing can be proven.

The pertinent question, however, is given that 645 men from *Sydney*
were lost in November 1941, and a naval pattern Carley float containing
an unidentified corpse in naval pattern clothing materialized off Christmas Island in February 1942, why didn't Oldham pursue the matter to its
logical conclusion and have the corpse exhumed for examination?
Although buried in what is believed to be an unmarked grave in the local
cemetery, it should have been possible in 1949 to locate the gravesite with
the help of locals or surviving personnel who were present at the funeral.

Oldham's investigations suggested that the corpse could have been that
of an RAN rating, so there was clearly a possibility that the corpse was ex-
Sydney. That Oldham ruled out this possibility because the covering of the
Carley float consisted of kapok instead of cork brings into question his
method of investigation and his subsequent conclusion. The fact that the
float was numbered, and carried Admiralty rope, would indicate a naval
origin, and as the only naval loss in the region at the time was *Sydney*, there
is basis for the belief that the Christmas Island float was ex-*Sydney*.

If this float did originate from *Sydney*, that it was numbered '2' would
suggest that it was the forward float on the port side, abreast the forward
funnel. This area was subjected to a great deal of 15-centimetre and 2-
centimetre shellfire, and possibly even 7.92-millimetre machine-gun fire.
As a result the two floats stowed there would almost certainly have been
damaged by shrapnel or machine-gun bullets or both. Such damage would
be comparable to what was identified on the Christmas Island float.

Because the area around *Sydney*'s forward funnel was observed to catch
fire shortly after the action started, and the Christmas Island float was not
burnt or scorched, it is conceivable that the float was blown off *Sydney*
early in the action. The presence of a shoe that did not fit the corpse in the
float would suggest that at least two men were also blown overboard at
about the same time. Perhaps supporting such a scenario is the fact that the
corpse found in the float wore no life-belt; nor was one found on the
decking of the float. Anyone wearing an inflated, or perhaps even a
deflated life-belt, when blown overboard, would most likely have had the
belt torn off on hitting the water. This was demonstrated by the recovery
of the inflated life-belt with knotted but snapped securing tapes.

Returning to the issue of the shoe, Dr Michael McCarthy of the Western Australian Maritime Museum has proposed that the alleged brand name may not have been a manufacturer's name at all, but the name of the wearer. Smith thought that the name on the footwear was either 'McCowan' or 'McEwan', but two members of *Sydney*'s crew had almost identical names: Able Seaman T.H. McGowan, and Able Seaman M.A. McKeown. Although the footwear was considered not to have belonged to the corpse, establishing the identity of the corpse may shed more light on whether McGowan or McKeown survived *Sydney*'s sinking and perhaps eventually found a grave on Christmas Island.

If this unfortunate chapter is to be closed, the relevant authorities must have the Christmas Island corpse located, exhumed, and examined. Enlistment and medical records, with DNA testing, may prove whether or not this man was a member of *Sydney*'s complement. Perhaps, then, at least one person's loved ones will know that their son, brother, husband, or father is no longer 'missing'.

SYDNEY DEBRIS?

With the entry of Japan into the war on 7 December 1941 and its rapid conquest of Singapore and the Dutch East Indies, the vast and mostly uninhabited coastline of Western Australia became extremely vulnerable to enemy attack. With very few resources and insufficient troops to cover the whole coast, a Special Mobile Force (SMF) was established so that it could be deployed rapidly to certain areas of the coast to oppose any enemy seaborne landing. In April 1942, the SMF was based in the Moora-Jurien Bay area, given the task of patrolling and defending the coast between the Moore River (north of Perth) and Dongara (south of Geraldton). On 5 May, a patrol discovered evidence of enemy activity at Jurien Bay, including the finding of a Japanese flag. Then, on 13 June, near Green Islets, another patrol found a Japanese life-belt and a box that was marked 'HMAS SYDNEY'.[34] Unfortunately, it is not clear whether this box was considered to have come from *Sydney* as a result of the November action or had been adrift for a considerably longer period of time.

Another item which could perhaps be traced to the ship was recovered near Comboyuro Point, New South Wales, on 19 March 1943.[35] This was a lifebuoy marked 'HMAS SYDNEY'. Again, it is not known whether the authorities considered that the lifebuoy had miraculously drifted around the coast from the other side of Australia, or whether there was a more logical explanation for its appearance sixteen months to the day after the ship had been lost. Some are of the opinion that the ship's name was painted over in wartime, but a battered lifebuoy recovered in the Indian Ocean in 1942 carried the name 'HMS CORNWALL' as well as the ship's crest. The heavy cruiser was sunk by Japanese aircraft south of Ceylon on 5 April 1942.

That possible evidence of wreckage from *Sydney* washed ashore shortly after the action has come to light thanks to the research of Mrs Glenys McDonald. In a paper submitted to the Western Australian Maritime Museum in 1993, McDonald recorded the findings of numerous inter- views she had conducted with members of the community who had lived in the Port Gregory region during the war. Port Gregory is situated about forty miles north of Geraldton.

Recovered from the beach at Shoal Point, north of Port Gregory, were four or five life-belts or life jackets, a 4-gallon tin of cabbage, a 4-gallon tin of methylated spirits, a 150 gallon square galvanized tank containing kapok, another smaller square steel container resembling an ammunition box, some bottles, a tyre on a damaged rim, and a fired flare attached to a piece of packing case said to have been marked 'HMAS SYDNEY'.[36]

The life-belts or life jackets, which were khaki in colour and stamped with a broad arrow, were described by one man as canvas bags filled with kapok. RAN-issue life-belts were blue and inflatable, but the general- purpose life jackets that *Sydney*'s sea-boats (cutters) were equipped with were khaki and made of canvas. These jackets had cork- or kapok-filled pockets sewn onto them and, to the uninitiated, may have resembled a bag of kapok.

Although it is impossible to confirm, it is conceivable that four or five general-purpose life jackets of the type *Sydney*'s cutters were equipped with were found on the beach at Shoal Point.

The tins of cabbage, methylated spirits, and the larger steel container of kapok cannot be positively identified, nor can the smaller ammunition container, which was said to contain jelly beans. The tyre, however, is interesting.

According to McDonald, one witness recalled that the tyre was '36 × 8 × 35 inches', and when fitted to a new rim was used on a Bedford or Chevrolet truck. Another witness described the tyre as being '700 × 20' with a lug-type pattern. The rim was bent in the middle and quite useless, but the tyre was new and was used on a 1937 model truck and later a Ford tractor.

Although the tyre itself cannot be directly linked to *Sydney*, there is a remote possibility that it may have come from its Walrus aircraft.

There were two types of wheel fitted to Walrus aircraft. A Dunlop type with roller bearings and a Palmer type with plain bearings. The Dunlop wheels had rims which measured 19.0 × 3.12 inches and were fitted with 19 × 8 inch tyres. The Palmer wheels had rims which measured 19.06 × 3.75 inches and were fitted with 895 × 200 millimetre tyres. [37]

The metric 895 × 200 mm represents 35.23 × 7.87 inches and this size compares favourably with the 36 × 8 × 35 inch size which was given by the first witness. Although the size of the tyre recovered is almost identical to that which was fitted to the Palmer wheeled Walrus aircraft, the tread pattern is unusual for this type of aircraft.

Contemporary photographs of Walrus and Seagull aircraft indicate that normally only smooth tyres were fitted. A surviving Walrus in the Fleet Air Arm Museum collection, however, is fitted with treaded tyres with a lug pattern on the edge of the tread.

It is conceivable that the tyre and rim found at Shoal Point came from a Walrus or Seagull type aircraft, but it is doubtful that a complete wheel and tyre from *Sydney*'s Walrus would have survived the destruction of the aircraft aboard ship. On the other hand, given the alleged damage to the rim of the recovered wheel, it is possible that it was blown off the aircraft and onto the deck when the Walrus was struck by a 15-centimetre shell.

If any or all of the items recovered at Shoal Point came from *Sydney*, they indicate that the ship may have stayed afloat for a considerably longer period than has hitherto been estimated. Given the prevailing conditions at the time, if *Sydney* had sunk on the night of 19–20 November, the debris should have drifted north in the same manner as the debris from *Kormoran*. For *Sydney*'s debris to wash ashore in the region

of Port Gregory, the ship would have to have sunk considerably closer inshore.

Taking into account the damage sustained, however, it would appear unlikely that *Sydney* could have stayed afloat long enough to reach a position where its debris would wash ashore. It is also odd that no other debris was found either at sea or along the coast, as the RAAF flew over this area during their search operations, while the Army conducted sweeps along the beaches. Specifically, it would appear unusual that no oil-fuel washed ashore, although there were two reports of oil stains being sighted off the coast north of Geraldton. These sightings were made by Geraldton-based Anson aircraft on 26 and 27 November.

Unfortunately, the Shoal Point debris, like the Comboyuro Point life-buoy, can perhaps be linked to the loss of *Sydney*, but that is all. Until more information becomes available, or *Sydney*'s wreck is found in a position that would support the supposition that debris washed ashore, any speculation about the origins of the debris must remain just that—speculation.

—9—

AN HONOURABLE DEATH

N O study of the possible reasons for *Sydney*'s loss with all hands can be regarded as complete until one of the less palatable theories — that *Sydney*'s survivors were killed — has been addressed.

Because of the damaged condition of the Carley float recovered by *Heros*, many have formed the opinion that *Sydney*'s survivors were shot after they abandoned ship. This theory has gained a great deal of support in recent years, particularly since the release of Montgomery's *Who Sank the Sydney?* and Ramage had entertained similar thoughts in December 1941. But, like most theories about the loss of *Sydney*, there is little evidence to support the claim that survivors were killed in the water. The only 'real' evidence is the battle-damaged Carley float. Significantly, the 1993 AWM study of the float found no evidence of damage from small arms fire.

The most popular reason for the supposed shooting of *Sydney*'s survivors was that Detmers had opened fire under a white flag and wished to eliminate possible witnesses should he be forced to answer charges of war crimes. Another is that a Japanese submarine had been

involved in *Sydney*'s sinking and the survivors had been killed to conceal this alleged involvement.

There is no evidence to support the claim of Japanese involvement, but the question of a feigned surrender does warrant scrutiny. Some believe that Burnett would not have closed with the supposed *Straat Malakka* unless the vessel had displayed a white flag. But if Detmers had run up a white flag, he would, in essence, have been identifying his ship as enemy, the white flag indicating that he had ceased all hostile acts.[1]

As Burnett should have been suspicious of the vessel, the hoisting of a white flag would have confirmed that it was not what it claimed to be. In other words, a white flag would have indicated to Burnett that he was not dealing with a confused Dutchman but an enemy raider or raider supply ship.

If Burnett thought he was dealing with a raider, it is doubtful that he would have closed, but if he thought he had cornered a raider supply ship, he might have decided to close to attempt a capture. The white flag theory, therefore, is credible.

The white flag/surrender theory appears to have merit, but it should be understood that there is no evidence to support the claim. As there is no evidence, any theory that survivors were shot to conceal an illegal ruse must be treated with extreme caution.

On the other hand, there was another, legal, subterfuge that Detmers could have used that may also have prompted Burnett to close. Namely, the feigned scuttling and abandoning of the supposed *Straat Malakka*. Such an act might have convinced Burnett that his quarry was a raider supply ship and that it was scuttling to prevent capture. If Burnett thought that a potential prize was scuttling itself, it is likely he would have closed in order to despatch an anti-scuttling party.

Although this scenario is, again, only theory, *Kormoran* was fitted with smoke generators.[2] The use of one or more smoke generators in the final stages of the intercept may have been all that was required for Detmers to convince his opponent that the supposed *Straat Malakka* was scuttling. Significantly, two of the prisoners mentioned that smoke was created by their ship.

Walter Kriesel, one of the men recovered by *Trocas*, said that the 'wind caused smoke from [the] raider to drift towards [the] cruiser, producing

the effect of a smoke screen'. Brinkman said that a smokescreen was created 'accidentally' by *Kormoran*. These men may have been referring to the smoke produced by the engine room fire, but it is conceivable that the smoke was created artificially, Detmers perhaps using his generators to lure *Sydney* closer once he realized that combat was unavoidable.

Detmers would have been well aware of the Royal Navy's policy on the capture of enemy supply ships and blockade runners, and it is possible that he used this knowledge to his advantage.[3] By drawing *Sydney* to within boat-pulling range for the despatch of the anti-scuttling party, Detmers would have provided his weapons officers with the best possible chance of inflicting the maximum amount of damage in the available time.

If Detmers did use his smoke generators to lure *Sydney* closer, it is doubtful that he would have told his interrogators. By keeping the British ignorant of raider tactics, he was allowing others to use the ploy if they found themselves in similar circumstances.

Pretending to scuttle or abandon ship was not in breach of international law, but opening fire under the protection of a white flag was. It is therefore doubtful that Detmers would have risked using a white flag when he had another, legitimate, ruse at his disposal.

Many theories, however, die hard. Some believe that because Detmers's and von Gösseln's boats were recovered at sea they were responsible for the shooting of *Sydney* survivors. The reasoning is that two other boats managed to reach land, while these two remained at sea. Unfortunately, the proponents of this theory overlook the simple fact that the occupants of the two boats, which succeeded in reaching the coast, *wanted* to make a landfall.

In his post-war account, Detmers said that he had remained in the shipping lanes because he 'was hoping to fall in with a neutral steamer'. Whether he was hoping to be rescued by a neutral ship, or was intent on seizing a vessel by force of arms is not exactly clear, but it is obvious that he did not want his war to end so soon. As if to emphasize this point, he forbade his men to fire rocket signals when they sighted a large four-funnelled steamer (*Aquitania*). His reason was that he suspected it was an auxiliary cruiser. To be picked up by an armed merchant cruiser would mean internment for the duration of the war.

Why von Gösseln's boat failed to reach the coast is not as clear, although the fact that it was overloaded with seventy-two men (originally seventy-three) may have had some bearing on how it handled. With little freeboard and only a makeshift sail, it may not have been possible to maintain a course towards the coast. Given the wind and wave conditions after 20 November, von Gösseln and his men probably had their hands full just trying keep their boat afloat.[4]

Another problem with the theory that Detmers and von Gösseln stayed in the vicinity of the debris field to shoot *Sydney* survivors is the survival of the Chinese. Three of the four Chinese crewmen ex-*Eurylochus*, who had remained aboard *Kormoran* as laundrymen, survived the action. Two were accommodated in von Gösseln's boat and the third was found a place in Detmers's boat. If *Sydney* survivors had been shot, it is extremely doubtful that the Chinese 'witnesses' would have been permitted to live. Their survival, despite the shortages of water, food and space in the lifeboats, suggests that there was no sinister motive for Detmers and von Gösseln remaining in the shipping lanes. And when the Chinese were given the opportunity to tell the Australian authorities all they knew about the raider, there was no mention of atrocities or the shooting of prisoners.[5]

Detmers's fear of an enemy 'court martial', however, was real. In his post-war account, he said no less than three times that he thought he might find himself before a court of inquiry, although there is little to suggest that these concerns had anything to do with the supposed shooting of survivors. Initially, he thought that the cruiser may have remained afloat and wondered what its surviving crew would say about the conduct of the engagement. Then, when he learned of *Sydney*'s loss, he feared that he would have to explain how an auxiliary cruiser had defeated a first-class cruiser. His final reference to a possible 'court martial' was his appearance before a 'commission of inquiry', presided over by an admiral and two other officers.

This 'commission of inquiry' was actually the interrogation of *Kormoran*'s officers at Swanbourne on 1 and 2 December 1941. The officers conducting the interrogations were Rear-Admiral Crace, and Commanders Dechaineux and Ramage. Detmers claimed that after discussing the action he was questioned 'about the prisoners and how they had been treated, and whether everything possible had been done to save the lives of the

crews of the ships we had captured and sunk'. He thought that he would have difficulty explaining the presence of the Chinese aboard *Kormoran*, but said that he was able to prove that these men had stayed willingly. Significantly, Detmers's post-war claims about the line of questioning are supported by the surviving wartime interrogation notes.[6]

Thus, Detmers's concerns about possible charges against him were based on the conduct of the action and the handling of the prisoners from ships sunk or captured.

On the conduct of the action, it appears that Detmers's main fear was being accused of opening fire before declaring identity. Support for such a hypothesis can be found in the interrogation notes. Although it does not appear to have been a question put to the prisoners, several made a point of telling the interrogating officers that the German flag was flying before, during and after the action. Curiously, most of these men can be identified as having been in the same lifeboat as Detmers. This shows that he might have impressed on them the need to tell the enemy that they had opened fire under the German flag.

As no charges were ever laid against Detmers, it would appear that the authorities were satisfied that he had no case to answer.[7]

Detmers's actions at the end of the war perhaps demonstrate most clearly that he did observe the rules of engagement.

A FILM OF THE ACTION

On 15 March 1945, Detmers suffered a debilitating stroke that left him paralysed. He was transferred to Heidelberg Military Hospital in Melbourne where he underwent three and a half months of therapy. Although he learned to use his limbs again, he never regained the use of his right hand. While he was in hospital, the war in Europe ended.

Following Germany's surrender, Naval Intelligence decided to make further inquiries about the *Sydney/Kormoran* action. In particular, Commander Long wanted to ascertain the fate of some reels of film, which he believed might have been brought ashore.[8]

On 1 November, Detmers was released from hospital and transferred to Tatura POW camp. Detmers learned of these inquiries on his arrival. The

following day, the camp commandant was advised that Detmers had authorized the divulgence of certain information.

During the action with *Sydney* Dr List had taken approximately thirty shots of the various phases of the battle with a 30-millimetre Leica camera. This camera had been brought ashore by List and was subsequently buried in a 'cave or hole in the cliff face' at Red Bluff. Detmers decided to inform the authorities of the existence of this camera, because it was thought that the film was still in good condition. Obviously, Detmers believed that the photographs would corroborate his claims and would perhaps satisfy the Australian authorities that he and his men had told the truth.

Why the authorities were not told earlier of the existence of the camera is not known, although it is conceivable that the photographs depicted particulars of *Kormoran* that Detmers did not wish his enemy to see, at least not until the war was over.[9]

List was questioned on 3 November and told the interviewing officers that the film included pictures showing the approach of *Sydney* to *Kormoran*; the firing of salvoes by both vessels; damage to *Kormoran* from a direct hit; views of wounded personnel aboard *Kormoran*; and *Sydney* turning away in flames.

It was considered that List was telling the truth, and the potential value of the film worth the effort of trying to recover the camera. Consequently, List was flown to Western Australia and escorted to the site. Although he was able to pinpoint the location, the camera could not be found.

During the 3 November interview, List was also questioned about the fate of some reels of cinecamera film. On 16 October 1945, the Intelligence Officer, Murchison Prisoner of War Group, and Lieutenant-Commander Gill, had questioned Gerhard Keller about the fate of the film he had taken. He said that when he abandoned ship 'he left the films behind, having informed Dr List of this fact'. List confirmed that this film was left aboard *Kormoran*.

Walter Hrich had also been questioned in October, because it was understood that he too had filmed the action. He, like Keller and List, believed that the films were lost when *Kormoran* sank.

If the films of the action could have been saved (and sent home on a neutral vessel), their propaganda value would have been enormous. That they were left on board *Kormoran* seems incredible. Detmers appears to have thought so too. During a visit to his crew on 8 January 1942, Detmers approached a 'cook' and asked what had happened to the film he had taken. The man replied that it had been left on board. Detmers was quoted as saying, 'But you were one of the first men ordered to the boats and should have taken the film with you!'[10]

It is not known who Detmers spoke to on 8 January, but it would appear to be someone other than Hrich or Keller. Hrich was an officer and would not have been in the same compound as the other ranks, while Keller could not be described as a cook. According to the interrogation notes Keller was a photographer with 'UFA' before the war. He joined up on the outbreak of war and was attached to the Propaganda Ministry.

It is obvious, however, that Detmers had wanted the film of the action to be saved.

Was the film left on board *Kormoran*?

When *Centaur* left Carnarvon on 28 November 1941 with the *Kormoran* prisoners aboard, it also carried Lieutenant J.A. Robotham of the 5th Garrison Battalion. Robotham had served in France during the First World War but was captured by the Germans during their March 1918 offensive. As a POW, he had gained an understanding of German, which obviously led to his selection for the guard detachment aboard *Centaur*. In February 1943, Robotham was appointed Intelligence Officer, Murchison Prisoner of War Group, serving in this capacity until August 1944 when he was placed on the Reserve List.

Because of his position, Robotham was in close contact with the *Kormoran* prisoners for several years. From this contact he became convinced that they had buried something more than a camera north of Carnarvon.

After the war, Robotham returned to Western Australia, spending much of his time at Carnarvon and on Quobba Station. He believed the Germans had buried *Kormoran*'s logbook in a chest at the 17 mile well. Despite years of searching, Robotham failed to find the chest. It appears the reason he failed was that two Aboriginal boys he had befriended took delight in moving his survey pegs without his knowledge.[11]

To gain the help of the Aboriginal boys, brothers Boyo and Johnny Mitchell, Robotham told them the chest contained gold sovereigns, which he believed the raider carried as emergency currency.

Foreign currency was carried by the raiders, but it is extremely doubt-ful that *Kormoran* would have been carrying gold. *Atlantis* carried emergency money in the form of American banknotes. When *Atlantis* was being abandoned following its interception by HMS *Devonshire*, the administration officer issued the notes to Rogge's adjutant in case the survivors reached the coast or were picked up by a neutral ship.

It is also doubtful that *Kormoran*'s emergency money would have gone in the boat that landed at the 17-mile well. There were no officers in this boat, and the money, if it had been released from the custody of the administration officer, would not have gone in a lifeboat without an officer in command. If money did come ashore, it is more likely that it would have come ashore at Red Bluff, because the boat that landed there had several officers aboard. Significantly, this boat also contained *Kormoran*'s administration officer, Herbert Bretschneider.

As for *Kormoran*'s logbook, if it was taken off the ship, it is assumed that it would have gone into Detmers's boat and remained in his custody. Under no circumstances would this document have been taken ashore where it might have fallen into enemy hands. Detmers would have ensured that it was either destroyed or sunk in a weighted bag before he went into captivity.

So what could have been brought ashore at the 17-mile well? What was it that Robotham attached so much importance to that he spent much of his life looking for?

The answer perhaps lies in Detmers's 8 January 1942 exclamation: 'But you were one of the first men ordered to the boats and should have taken the film with you!'

Although there is no conclusive evidence, it would appear that the film of the action was not left aboard *Kormoran* but was given to a cook who was found a place in Petty Officer Köhn's boat. His boat was the first to be launched and, significantly, it was this boat that landed at the 17-mile well.

This unidentified cook perhaps misunderstood Detmers's question about the fate of the film and might have told Detmers and the accompanying camp commandant that the film was left aboard *Kormoran* because he thought this was what his captain wanted the enemy to hear. If so, Robotham may have spent years searching, wittingly or unwit-tingly, for the film of the action, which has never been found.

SIGNALS FROM SYDNEY?

Over the years a number of people have claimed that they heard or saw copies of signals allegedly transmitted by HMAS *Sydney*. Some of these claims can be traced to the Sydney PMG transmission on 4 December 1941, others would appear to be based on corruptions of the signals transmitted during the search for *Sydney*. But there is one claim that cannot be readily explained.

In 1981 the National Library in Canberra received the hand-written memoirs of Mr R.W. Mason, a former RAN writer. Mason had been stationed at HMAS *Harman* in November 1941 and in his memoirs claimed that signals were received from *Sydney* on the day the ship was lost.

On the evening of 19 November, after having dinner at home with his wife, Mason allegedly went to the station in order to report to the OIC, Acting Lieutenant-Commander Archibald McLachlan, RAN. Mason claimed that on arrival he discovered that there was a 'panic' on. He claimed that *Sydney* had reported that it had 'bailed up a queer customer in the Indian Ocean and was trying to identify her'. *Sydney* then reported it was 'about to open fire'. Nothing further was heard.[12]

Mason went on to say that next morning there was a conference between McLachlan, CPO Telegraphist Tiller and PO Telegraphist Hamilton. He claimed that the three 'closed ranks' and decided to keep the matter quiet to avoid an inquiry and court martial because the headset for the 'whole ship–shore channel' had been left unmanned during the 'panic'.

Little was made of Mason's claims until 1995 when Barbara Winter released *The Intrigue Master*. In her work on Commander Long and Naval Intelligence in Australia, Winter said that the story was 'odd'. According to Mason, *Sydney* transmitted before opening fire. Such a signal, however, would have been heard by *Kormoran*'s W/T operators, who were waiting to 'jam' any transmissions from the cruiser. As Winter pointed out, no signals were heard by *Kormoran*.[13]

In 1998, Mason's claims were again brought into question. During the parliamentary inquiry into the sinking of HMAS *Sydney* the Defence Sub-Committee received a number of submissions from people who had also served at *Harman* and who knew Mason. Nearly all refuted his claims.

Miss Marion Stevens, a former WRAN and stationed at *Harman* in November 1941 was particularly critical and said that nothing was received from *Sydney*. She also indicated that Mason could not have been home for his evening meal as his leave had been stopped by McLachlan. According to Stevens, Mason had to report nightly to CPO Telegraphist Ben Tiller.[14]

Mrs Daphne Wright, another former WRAN stationed at *Harman* also questioned the validity of Mason's claims. Wright said that to the best of her knowledge no one was aware of *Sydney*'s encounter with an enemy ship on 19 November as '*Sydney* did not break W/T silence'.[15]

A third WRAN, Mrs Judy Saunders, initially supported Mason's claims because she thought she could recall the incident, but in a supplementary submission she indicated that her 19 November dating of the incident 'could be inaccurate'.[16]

Further doubt about the accuracy of Mason's claims was raised by the submission of Mr Alan Cohn, a senior coder at *Harman* in November 1941. Cohn said that in his considered opinion, 'no message was received by *Harman* from HMAS *Sydney* at or after her action with the German ship *Kormoran*'.[17]

As a result of these submissions the Defence Sub-Committee concluded that 'doubt must exist regarding the accuracy of Mr Mason's recollections about the timing and indeed nature of the signal'.[18]

It is not known whether Mason's claims were fictitious or based on what he believed was fact, but it is clear that his memory of events was suspect. Given the German claim that there was 'no radio message from cruiser' (Tümmers), and the official RAN view that no signals were received from *Sydney* on or after 19 November, it would appear that Mason was mistaken in his beliefs.

If Burnett had chosen to break W/T silence to obtain further information on the *Straat Malakka* or to report that he had 'bailed up a queer customer', *Kormoran*'s W/T operators could not have failed to hear the transmission. Such a transmission should also have been received at Perth, by *Harman* or Coonawarra and perhaps by HMAS *Canberra*, the latter being at sea on 19 November and in the vicinity of Kangaroo Island, South Australia. That neither *Canberra* nor the W/T stations heard or received any transmissions from *Sydney* shows that Burnett maintained W/T silence before the opening of fire.[19]

Once it was realized that the supposed *Straat Malakka* was actually a raider, Burnett should have broken W/T silence to transmit an enemy sighting or action report. During the first few chaotic minutes of the action, however, *Sydney*'s bridge and forward superstructure came under heavy fire. Critically, within these minutes, *Sydney*'s foremast was toppled by a stray 15-centimetre shell. As no report was received from *Sydney* after the start of the action, it would appear that Burnett did not, or could not, authorize the transmission of an action report.

With the foremast shot away *Sydney* was mute, as the transmitting aerials for the main, second and auxiliary W/T offices were suspended from this mast. Once the aerials were brought down, nothing could be transmitted from the ship until jury aerials were rigged. The same probably applied to the emergency W/T set. Although an emergency set was carried, it is understood that the emergency aerial was not rigged until required. Thus, even if they had been authorized to transmit a report, *Sydney*'s W/T operators may not have been able to do so until new aerials were erected.

There is doubt, however, whether a message could have been transmitted even after new aerials were put up. Given the locations of the W/T offices, it is conceivable that all sustained damage or became flooded during the action.

The remote control office, because of its location on the lower bridge, was probably destroyed during the opening salvoes. Similarly, the second and auxiliary W/T offices may have been damaged or destroyed by shell-fire early in the action, or may have become flooded following the torpedo hit. As for the main W/T office, its location, on the lower deck and abaft the armour belt, made it particularly vulnerable to shell and splinter damage.

If not destroyed by shellfire, the Type 48 transmitter in the main W/T office may have been silenced by a loss of electricity. As power could have been restored and jury aerials rigged, it would appear probable that the transmitter was destroyed during the action.

As for the battery-powered emergency set, given the November 1940 (CAFO 2045) recommendation that it be stowed away from the main W/T office, it is probable that it was re-located to the remote control office and destroyed early in the action.

The absence of signals from HMAS *Sydney* on or after 19 November is therefore not inexplicable.

WAS THERE A BOARD OF INQUIRY?

Perhaps the most puzzling aspect of *Sydney*'s loss is the absence of a board of inquiry. In essence, a board of inquiry is an accident or incident investigation. If a warship is lost or damaged, an inquiry is convened to establish how and why the ship was lost or damaged. Very basically, the board's task is to gather and study all the available evidence, then in light of the evidence, compile a report of its findings or recommendations. The purpose of the exercise is not to punish but to prevent a similar incident reoccurring.

That this was accepted practice on the Australia Station during wartime is shown by the inquiries into the loss of HMAS *Canberra* on 9 August 1942 (inquiry held August/September 1942) and the damage sustained by HMAS *Hobart* on 20 July 1943 (inquiry held July 1943).

But apart from the reference to a 'Court of Inquiry' during the March 1942 Advisory War Council meeting, there is no evidence of a board of inquiry being held into the loss of HMAS *Sydney*.

It is conceivable, however, that as there were no survivors from *Sydney* it was deemed impracticable to convene a board of inquiry. Although there was no shortage of serving officers and men who had taken part in the search for *Sydney* and the subsequent interrogation of the prisoners, it may have been considered pointless to call these men as witnesses. Similarly, it may have been considered pointless, or even improper, to call enemy prisoners as witnesses, as they would have been required to give evidence under oath.

The question of whether or not a board of inquiry was conducted was raised during the 1998 parliamentary inquiry into the loss of the *Sydney*. As a December 1939 Admiralty Fleet Order (AFO 4131) said: 'Reports of Boards of Inquiry held to investigate losses of or damage to HM ships (other than small craft) by enemy action are to be rendered to the Admiralty in duplicate', it was considered that if a board of inquiry had been held, a copy should have been sent to the Admiralty. Despite

inquiries by the Defence Sub-Committee's historical advisor, Professor Peter Dennis, no record of a board of inquiry report relating to the loss of *Sydney* could be located in London.

Although it is considered likely that such a report (if it exists) would have been made available for public viewing at the British Public Record Office during the early 1970s after the expiry of the thirty-year rule, there is a historical precedent for some reports not being released.

On 11 April 1940 the light cruiser HMS *Penelope*, under the command of Captain G.D. Yates, RN, struck an uncharted rock off the coast of Norway. Despite severe structural damage, *Penelope* was eventually made seaworthy enough to make the journey back to Britain. A board of inquiry was then convened to establish why the cruiser had run aground. Forty years later, while researching the incident, former *Penelope* crew member Ed Gordon discovered that the findings of the board were not available. Correspondence with the Naval Law Division of the Ministry of Defence revealed that because of the 'sensitive nature of the report' the findings would not be made public until the year 2015.[20]

It is known, however, that *Penelope* grounded in only 6 feet of water and that after the inquiry Yates was lent to the RAN. It would appear that Yates earned the displeasure of their Lordships and was sent to the antipodes for his sins. As the report was described as sensitive, it is highly likely that a 75-year caveat was placed on its release in order to spare the feelings of the men involved.

A similar case can be found in the loss of HMS *Glorious*. The aircraft carrier and its attendant destroyers *Ardent* and *Acasta* were sunk by the German battle cruisers *Scharnhorst* and *Gneisenau* on 8 April 1940. A board of inquiry into the carrier's loss was subsequently convened, taking evidence from the small number of survivors recovered. It soon became clear that the Germans had caught *Glorious* totally unprepared for battle. No air patrols were being flown, and the crow's nest was not manned, even though conditions offered maximum visibility. None of *Glorious*'s Swordfish strike aircraft were armed. Captain G. D'Oyly-Hughes, RN, while still within striking distance of enemy aircraft based in Norway, had allowed his command to be taken by surprise by German surface vessels.

The full report of the board of inquiry into the loss of *Glorious*, like *Penelope*'s, has not been made available to the public.[21]

Obviously, when individuals or their actions were officially ques-
tioned or criticized and it was desired that those individuals or their next
of kin be spared any further ignominy, a caveat was placed on the release
of the relevant documentation. Given the circumstances of *Sydney*'s loss,
it is conceivable that if a board of inquiry had been held, the findings may
have been considered too sensitive for general viewing. In other words, it
may have been recommended that the report not be released for seventy-
five years. Yet according to the Defence Sub-Committee's 1999 report on
the loss of *Sydney*, the head of the Naval Historical Branch in the Ministry
of Defence (successor to the Admiralty) has said that no report relating to
the loss of *Sydney* is held by the Ministry of Defence.

There is a possibility, however, that such a report may have been
removed from Admiralty files and deposited at the Public Record Office,
still bearing a 75-year release date. Perhaps because of this possibility, the
Defence Sub-Committee recommended that 'a search be undertaken by
the Australian Government at the Public Record Office in London for any
records of a court or board of inquiry report into the loss of HMAS *Sydney*'.

Although it is doubtful that there ever was a board of inquiry, it is
logical to pursue the matter, for the findings of a wartime inquiry might
help explain why *Sydney* was lost.

SUMMARY OF EVIDENCE

HMAS *Sydney*, under the command of Captain J. Burnett, RAN, sailed from
the port of Fremantle on 11 November 1941. Burnett had been given the
task of escorting the troopship *Zealandia* to position 7° 56' South 104° 40'
East. There he was to rendezvous with HMS *Durban*, which would relieve
Sydney as escort. *Sydney* was then to return to Fremantle. Its ETA was PM
20 November. The rendezvous with *Durban* took place at midday on
17 November.

On Wednesday 19 November 1941, the German auxiliary cruiser HSK
Kormoran, under the command of Fregattenkapitän T.A. Detmers, was
heading in a northerly direction off the Western Australian coast. *Kormoran*,
still on its first war cruise, had been at sea for 352 days and had sunk or
captured 68,274 tons of Allied shipping.[22] At approximately 1655 local

time, another potential victim was sighted off the port bow. *Kormoran* was in the approximate position of 26° 34' South 111° East and was making 11 knots on a course of 25°.[23]

When it was discovered that the vessel off *Kormoran*'s port bow was a warship, Detmers ordered full speed and a new course of 260°. This heading would take *Kormoran* westwards, towards the sun and away from the enemy warship.

At approximately 1700, the warship (*Sydney*) was observed to alter course towards *Kormoran*. Detmers amended his course to 250°.

The range at this time was in excess of 15,000 metres, and reported smoke from *Sydney* suggests that Burnett had also ordered an increase in speed.

At approximately 1705, *Sydney* began flashing the letters 'NNJ' ('You should make your signal letters') to establish the unknown vessel's identity. This signal was made for some time before the use of the signal projector was discontinued. *Sydney* then used flags and made the signal 'Hoist your signal letters'. In response, Ahlbach hoisted the signal flags for the Dutch motorship *Straat Malakka*.

By this stage (1745), the range had been reduced to about 8,000 metres. Despite the reduced range, Ahlbach's flags could not be distinguished because they were obscured by *Kormoran*'s funnel. *Sydney* then supposedly made the signal 'Hoist your signal letters clear', and continued to do so until Ahlbach complied.

Burnett learned that the vessel was claiming to be the *Straat Malakka*. As the real *Straat Malakka* was on the east coast of Africa, it would not have been on Burnett's VAI.

At 1800, Detmers ordered a Q signal to be transmitted. *Sydney* was, at this time, still astern of *Kormoran* and presenting a narrow silhouette.

Sydney's precise movements after the transmission of the Q signal are not clear. It has long been assumed that *Sydney* closed from astern. To be more precise, it has been assumed that *Sydney* closed from a position off the raider's starboard quarter, drew level, then steamed alongside, about 1,500 metres distant, while the exchange of signals continued. Detmers's action report, however, provides a different view. It claims that shortly after the Q signal was transmitted *Sydney* drew away from its position on *Kormoran*'s starboard quarter and manoeuvred onto the raider's starboard beam, 9,000 metres distant. Then, in the space of about fifteen minutes, *Sydney* closed to within 1,500 metres of the disguised raider.

In isolation, there is little to support or negate either version. In the context of the accepted procedure for identifying vessels from their profiles, however, Detmers's action report account of *Sydney*'s approach is the more logical. Significantly, this alternative approach is now supported by one of *Kormoran*'s former W/T operators. In 1998, during an interview with the journalist David Kennedy, Hans Linke described *Sydney*'s approach as circular, and said that the cruiser steamed around them. 'She had a look at us from all sides, she wanted to know what sort of ship this is … and she steamed in a circle around us, a big circle. She gradually got nearer … She slowly approached us but kept at a distance all the time'. When queried whether the circle was closed, Linke said that it was more of a semi-circle. When asked if *Sydney* approached from astern, Linke said, 'No, she was parallel', indicating that *Sydney* had closed from a position off *Kormoran*'s beam.[24]

Although there is some doubt, it would appear that around 1800 *Sydney* altered course to starboard to take up a position 9,000 metres off the supposed *Straat Malakka*'s beam.

Before the transmission of the Q signal, *Sydney* flashed the message, with signal projector and flags, 'Where are you bound?' Ahlbach replied 'Batavia'. It appears that Burnett also inquired what cargo was being carried.

Sydney then made the flag signal 'IK', which was the secret challenge for the *Straat Malakka*. The vessel failed to respond.

By 1815, *Sydney* was approximately 9,000 metres off *Kormoran*'s starboard beam. The cruiser then altered course to port and closed. While closing, it is said that *Sydney* flashed the signal 'Hoist your secret call' or 'Show your secret sign'.

Sydney closed with main armament trained but with the 4-inch guns apparently unmanned. The port torpedo tubes, which had been swung out, were reportedly returned to their fore and aft position. The Walrus aircraft, which had been readied for flight, was shut down. Significantly, there is evidence to suggest that the port cutter was readied for use during the closing run, and may actually have been partially lowered in the final minutes.

Shortly before 1830, *Sydney* altered course to starboard, bringing it onto an almost parallel course with *Kormoran*, and speed was reduced to about 14 knots to match that of the suspect vessel.

At approximately 1830, Detmers decamouflaged, declared identity and opened fire. *Sydney* responded almost simultaneously.

Kormoran's first salvo appears to have been fired within fifteen to twenty seconds of the order to decamouflage being given. *Sydney* was struck forward by one or two 15-centimetre shells.

Sydney's first salvo was aimed high, and either missed completely, or passed through the after part of the raider's bridge and funnel, the shells exploding in the sea on the lee side.

After this initial exchange, *Kormoran* continued salvo firing at *Sydney*'s bridge, forward turrets and forward machinery spaces. The 15-centimetre guns were supported by the starboard 3.7-centimetre gun and the 2-centimetre battery. The former was directed against *Sydney*'s bridge and gunnery control towers and the latter were used against men on the upper deck, principally those attempting to man the torpedo tubes and the 4-inch guns.

Sydney, however, took considerable time to fire its second salvo. It appears that the main armament did not fire again until about the raider's fifth salvo.

At about the raider's fifth salvo, two torpedoes were launched from *Kormoran*'s above-water torpedo tubes. One torpedo was observed to strike *Sydney* below the forward turrets. The detonation occurred about the same time as shells from the raider's eighth or ninth salvo struck *Sydney* amidships.

On or about *Kormoran*'s fifth salvo, *Sydney*'s remaining serviceable turret resumed firing. At least one salvo, possibly two, struck *Kormoran* amidships, disabling the raider and starting an uncontrollable fire. A shell from another salvo pierced the shield on *Kormoran*'s No.3 gun before exploding in the sea, and another is believed to have struck aft in the vicinity of the poop deck. From the available information, *Sydney*'s rate of fire was slow, the raider supposedly firing three salvoes to every one from *Sydney*.

Following its torpedoing, *Sydney* altered course to port and passed astern of *Kormoran*. Shortly after 1835, from a position approximately

4,000 metres astern, *Sydney* fired four torpedoes. All four missed. Still under heavy fire, and apparently unable to bring the after turrets to bear, *Sydney* retired to the south-east under cover of smoke. The cruiser's speed was estimated at 5–7 knots.

At 1900, a single torpedo was fired from *Kormoran's* port underwater tube. No hit was observed. Twenty-five minutes later, Detmers gave the order to cease fire. Although *Sydney* had been struck by one torpedo and an unknown number of 15-centimetre shells, both on and above the waterline, the Australian ship had managed to steam out of effective range.

According to a number of witnesses, *Sydney* was down by the bows, extensively damaged by shellfire, and burning forward and amidships, although one witness believed that owing to its watertight compartments the cruiser was capable of reaching land.

Despite this belief, *Sydney* did not reach port. The cruiser was last seen, as a glow on the horizon, shortly before midnight on 19 November.

Sydney had maintained W/T silence before the action, and afterwards was apparently unable to transmit an action report or distress call. As a result, the authorities were unaware that *Sydney* had been in action. Although expected to return to Fremantle on the afternoon of 20 November, Navy Office waited until the evening of 23 November before ordering the ship to break W/T silence and report its ETA. With no report forthcoming, DNOWA contacted Western Area Headquarters (RAAF). At 0050 on 24 November, the AOC Western Area ordered an air search for *Sydney*.

This initial search, conducted on the morning of 24 November, proved fruitless. A second operation was therefore ordered for the following day. When it was learned that the tanker *Trocas* had recovered twenty-five German naval ratings in position 24° 6' South 111° 40' East, it was decided to escalate the search.

From 24 November until the end of search operations on 29 November, RAAF and Dutch aircrew engaged in the search for *Sydney* flew 118 sorties. They were supported 'on the ground' by six naval vessels and fifteen merchant ships.[25]

Although five boatloads of *Kormoran* survivors were sighted, the aircrews could find no trace of *Sydney* or its crew. A small amount of

Kormoran-related debris was discovered by search vessels, but the only items found that could be identified as having come from *Sydney* were a single life-belt and a single battle-damaged Carley float.

BURNETT'S DECISION TO CLOSE

It is difficult to determine why Burnett closed. It is assumed, however, that he knew that he was not dealing with the real *Straat Malakka*.

From a distance, the 8,736 ton *Kormoran* could have passed for the 6,439 ton *Straat Malakka*, but once the range was reduced the difference in tonnage should have been obvious.[26] It should also have been obvious that the hallmark features listed for the *Straat Malakka* did not correspond with the features of the vessel claiming to be it.

As a result, Burnett should have had serious doubts about the true identity of the vessel before him, which would not have been dispelled by the fact that the *Straat Malakka* was not on the list of vessels expected to be met.

Given that the vessel was running away from the relative safety of the coast and had transmitted a Q signal almost an hour after the chase began, Burnett should have had more than doubts about the vessel's identity. He should have been highly suspicious.

Although Burnett was under instructions to board suspicious vessels, he also had to consider the possibility that a suspect ship could be a raider in disguise. In which case, closing to board could prove to be an extremely dangerous undertaking. That Burnett did close would suggest that he had ruled out the possibility that the supposed *Straat Malakka* was a raider. It is also significant that the Walrus was still aboard when *Sydney* closed. If Burnett had the slightest doubt that he was closing with a raider, the aircraft should have been launched to provide early warning of hostile activity and to remove any fire risk. And all available weapons, such as the port 4-inch guns, should have been manned and readied for instant use, regardless of the danger to exposed men.

If Burnett was convinced that he was not dealing with a raider, he may have concluded that he had intercepted a raider supply ship. At this stage of the war, the capture of such vessels was highly desirable, both from the

saving of tonnage perspective and the possibility that the capture of a supply ship could lead to the destruction of a raider.

It will never be known for certain why Burnett decided to close, but the evidence points to him having closed in an attempt to capture. It shows that Burnett kept *Sydney* at the relatively safe distance of 8,000 to 9,000 metres while he attempted to identify the suspect vessel. He then closed and within about fifteen minutes took *Sydney* to within 1,500 metres of the supposed *Straat Malakka*. The speed of the approach, and the range to within which Burnett closed, are consistent with the anti-scuttling technique in use in 1941.

While closing, the signal 'Hoist your secret call' or 'Show your secret sign' was made. As this signal was not normally employed in the challenge procedure, it might have been sent as a distraction. As such, it might have been sent in order to help disorganize scuttling arrangements.

In the final minutes, *Sydney*'s port cutter was evidently readied for lowering. This suggests that Burnett was preparing to despatch a boarding or anti-scuttling party.

The claim that the torpedo tubes were swung back to their fore and aft position, while not supporting or negating the belief that Burnett was closing in an attempt to capture, at least shows that he did not wish to torpedo his quarry.

Perhaps the most significant clue to Burnett's intentions was the angle of elevation of *Sydney*'s main armament. *Sydney*'s opening salvo was high, far too high to be considered a gunnery error. That the salvo passed over or abaft *Kormoran*'s bridge suggests that the bridge was the point of aim. Again, the destruction of a vessel's bridge was a recognized anti-scuttling tactic.

Finally, Burnett's decision to maintain W/T silence, when he would have been justified in breaking it to consult with shore authorities on the whereabouts of the *Straat Malakka*, suggests that he had reasons for not breaking W/T silence. If Burnett believed he had intercepted a raider supply ship, and the raider was in the vicinity, the silent capture of the supply ship would have been essential if he thought there was a chance of destroying the raider as well.

WAS SYDNEY 'BATTLEWORTHY'?

It has been suggested that *Sydney* was not fully fit for battle when it put to sea on 11 November 1941. This belief has come about because of a suspected defect with 'A' turret and the shortcomings of *Sydney*'s 6-inch primary fire control system. The continued deferral of the ship's rearmament and the high turnover of men were not publicized and meant that many of *Sydney*'s more experienced ratings were transferred off the ship during 1941.

Although it is documented that a defect did develop in the training of 'A' turret during September 1941, Burnett's Letter of Proceedings for the month of October shows that the problem was rectified. And the statements made by the *Kormoran* survivors suggest that 'A' turret was trained on the raider during the interception phase and fired in the opening salvo. The claim that 'A' turret was unserviceable on 19 November would therefore appear to be incorrect.

The view that there was an inherent weakness in *Sydney*'s 6-inch primary fire-control system is harder to dismiss. In a 1938 report, Captain Waller highlighted the vulnerability of *Sydney*'s primary gun-control systems. Although Waller's main concern was the lack of protection for the cabling which linked the DCT and the HACS with their respective transmitting and calculating stations, he was also concerned about the ineffectiveness of the alternative control for the main armament. In short, he was concerned that if the DCT were knocked out or isolated, the ship's fighting efficiency would be significantly reduced.

Similar concerns were raised during the ship's design stage, when it had been recommended that a second DCT be mounted on the after superstructure, thus providing centralized fire control in the event of the bridge-mounted DCT being damaged or put out of action. Cost and weight limitations, however, prevented this recommendation being adopted.

The danger of not providing a second DCT was realized on 13 December 1939 when splinter damage to HMS *Achilles*'s DCT forced the main armament to go into secondary control. Fortunately for *Achilles*, the damage to the DCT was minor, and director firing was resumed after a short delay.

Sydney's fighting efficiency on 19 November, however, appears to have been critically impaired by damage to the DCT or the associated cabling or both. The evidence suggests that only one salvo (the first) was fired under director control. There was then an appreciable pause before main armament firing was resumed in secondary, group or local control. This pause allowed Skeries to destroy *Sydney*'s bridge and forward turrets without opposition, thereby significantly reducing *Sydney*'s offensive capability.

It is impossible to determine what actually caused the loss of centralized fire control. Although damage to the DCT or the primary fire control cables would appear the most likely cause, the main switchboard room was equally vulnerable to shell and splinter damage. In other words, the primary gun-control system could have been knocked out by a loss of power brought about by damage to the switchboard room.

Of course it is conceivable that power was lost without the switchboard room having been hit. Shell or splinter damage to the forward feeder cables, or shock, could have caused the supply breakers to open, as they had on *Hobart* when it was torpedoed.

That there was a loss of power is supported by the reported slow rate of fire of 'x' and 'y' turrets. Without power, the turrets would have been forced to go into hand working, resulting in a serious reduction in the rate of fire. It is significant that 'x' and 'y' turrets were observed to be still trained to port when *Sydney* passed astern of *Kormoran*, suggesting that the turret training motors were without power.

Loss of power would also have affected the ammunition supply arrangements. Under such circumstances, the shells fired would most likely have been the ready-use shells stored inside the gunhouse. These were CPBC type, and an emergency supply was stowed in racks in each turret. The cordite, however, would have had to be brought up from the magazine via the cordite hoist (worked by hand-operating gear).

Given the close range and *Kormoran*'s thin hull plates, CPBC shells would probably have passed straight through the raider without detonating. Such a scenario is supported by the prisoners' claims that many of the cruiser's shells passed through their ship without exploding.

Although *Sydney* obviously had problems with its main armament, the cruiser appears to have had even more problems with its secondary armament. According to Detmers, *Sydney*'s 4-inch guns failed to fire a

single shot during the action. This claim, if correct, is not altogether surprising.

Brinkman's 2-centimetre gunners had been given the task of preventing the cruiser's anti-aircraft guns being brought into action. Basically, this involved raking the 4-inch gundeck with automatic cannon fire to prevent the guns being manned. As *Sydney*'s 4-inch guns were not fitted with shields, this task was relatively easy.

This lack of protection for the 4-inch gun crews was a concern to Burnett, because in June 1941 he proposed that shields be fitted to the 4-inch guns. Unfortunately, the matter was still pending on 19 November. As a result, *Sydney*'s gunners could not man their guns without exposing themselves to the hail of 2-centimetre shell. The claim that the 4-inch guns did not fire at all during the action is testimony to the deadly effectiveness of the 2-centimetre fire.[27]

The only other design weakness, if it can be called that, which may have had some bearing on the loss of the ship, were the fire and bilge pumps. All relied on electricity. In addition, six of the eight pumps were located on the port side of the ship, directly below the main suction line. The failure of power, and possible shellfire damage to the pumps or the main suction or both, would have seriously hampered efforts to fight the fires and limit flooding.

Another shortcoming was the large volume of flammable material aboard the ship. *Sydney* had been built in peacetime to peacetime standards, and as a result was liberally equipped with timber fittings and furniture. And by November 1941, *Sydney* had been in commission six years. Painting, a regular maintenance task, normally involved applying a new coat over the existing paintwork. *Sydney* thus had six years of flammable oil-based paint on many of its internal and external surfaces. By 1940, the layers of paint on the barrels of the 6-inch guns, for example, had become so thick that after *Sydney*'s action with the Italian destroyer *Espero* (28 June 1940) it was found to have peeled off and 'hung in long reddish-grey streamers almost to the deck'.[28]

As the war progressed the navy realized that deck coverings, timber furniture and layers of oil-based paint constituted a serious fire hazard, and took the necessary steps to reduce the risk. But in November 1941 the lesson had yet to be learned.[29]

SYDNEY'S CREW

Clearly, *Sydney* had its faults and failings, but what of the crew? What of the men who fought and died aboard the ship?

Burnett's competence to command is often raised as a key issue, but rarely is the competence of his crew questioned.

Many of *Sydney*'s more experienced sailors had left the ship by November 1941 and, in many cases, these men were replaced by 'hostilities only' ratings with little or no naval experience. Could such men, perhaps leaderless after the opening salvoes, have played no small part in the loss of their ship?

Although there was a large turnover in the ship's crew during 1941, there is nothing to suggest that this change in men dramatically reduced *Sydney*'s fighting efficiency. In fact, given the level and intensity of training in the months preceding the action with *Kormoran*, *Sydney* was possibly better prepared for battle in November 1941 than it had been in May 1940 when it sailed to the Mediterranean.

As there is no evidence to the contrary, it must be assumed that the men under Burnett's command would not have acted or performed any differently from the men who had been under Collins's command in 1940.

On the question of Burnett's competence, by 19 November 1941 he had been in command of *Sydney* for six months, sufficient time for him to become fully acquainted with his ship and his command team. Although Burnett lacked battle experience, the command team, virtually unchanged from the Mediterranean days, was very experienced and extremely capable.

Collins had been in command of *Sydney* for 183 days when he received orders to sail to Colombo and on to the Mediterranean. Burnett had been in command of *Sydney* for 190 days when he encountered *Kormoran*.

WAS SYDNEY AT ACTION STATIONS WHEN IT CLOSED WITH KORMORAN?

The only evidence that *Sydney* was in a state other than action stations when it closed with *Kormoran* is the German claim that the cruiser's anti-aircraft guns appeared to be unmanned. The witnesses, however,

also claimed that the main armament was trained on them, suggesting that *Sydney was* at action stations.

Despite the contradictory nature of these claims, it was possible for *Sydney* to have main armament manned but with the anti-aircraft guns unmanned. This state of readiness (third degree of readiness) was known as defence stations. *Sydney*'s logs for the months preceding November 1941 reveal, however, that Burnett did not employ this degree of readiness. At sea, *Sydney* would normally be at the fourth degree of readiness (cruising stations). This allowed for two turrets, one forward and one aft, to be manned while the remainder of the crew went about their normal duties. If circumstances required a higher degree of readiness, *Sydney* would go straight to action stations.

Given the claim that all four of *Sydney*'s 6-inch turrets were trained on *Kormoran*, it is clear that *Sydney* was at a degree of readiness higher than cruising stations. Further, given Burnett's penchant for having *Sydney* at either cruising stations or action stations, it must be assumed that *Sydney* was at action stations when it closed with *Kormoran*.

THE ACTIONS OF NAVY OFFICE

In all probability, *Sydney* sank around midnight on Wednesday 19 November or in the early hours of the following day. The cruiser was not due to arrive at Fremantle until the afternoon of 20 November. Late arrivals, however, were not uncommon and W/T silence the norm. *Sydney*'s non-arrival on Thursday, therefore, should not have created any undue concern.

On the morning of Friday 21 November DNOWA sent a message to Navy Office, advising that *Sydney* had not arrived. Although the signal was addressed to the ACNB, it is believed that it went no further than DCNS, Captain Getting.[30]

Getting was not a member of the Naval Board, but as he was the First Naval Member's deputy, he may have considered the signal did not warrant the board's attention. Given the circumstances, this was probably the correct course of action. After all, Navy Office supposedly had the big picture. *Sydney* was returning to Fremantle after escorting *Zealandia* to the Sunda Strait. Except for Vichy French submarines engaged in escorting their own

vessels through the Sunda Strait, there was nothing in the waters off the Western Australian coast that constituted a threat to *Sydney*. Although there was evidence of raider activity in the Indian Ocean, intelligence reports indicated that the raiders avoided confrontations with warships.

In other words, Getting and his fellow staff officers at Navy Office apparently assumed that if *Sydney* were in trouble it would break W/T silence and report. While Burnett continued to maintain W/T silence, there was obviously nothing wrong and nothing to report. This attitude, or misconception, probably cost the lives of *Sydney*'s survivors.

It was not until the evening of 23 November that *Sydney* was ordered to break W/T silence and report its ETA in Fremantle. When *Sydney* failed to report, Farquhar-Smith requested an air search. *Sydney*'s survivors, if there were any left, had been in the water for almost four days.

Although there appears to have been no official questioning of the delay in taking action once it was reported that *Sydney* was overdue, there is evidence of veiled criticism in reports prepared by the British and Australian Naval Liaison Officers at Batavia.

On 29 November 1941, Acting Captain J.B. Heath, RN, submitted a five-page report to C-IN-C China, on 'action taken by CZM in respect of search for HMAS *Sydney*'. Heath said that 'surprise was expressed at the delay of four days before ACNB made their 0645Z/24 [request for air search] although no doubt good reason existed for this which was unknown to CZM'.[31]

The RAN Liaison Officer at Batavia, Acting Commander V.E. Kennedy, RAN, compiled a similar, but perhaps more tactful, report for the Naval Board. Kennedy wrote that 'regret was expressed that almost four days had elapsed before informing CZM that *Sydney* was overdue'.[32]

Clearly, the feeling in Batavia was that Navy Office should have requested an air search much earlier than 24 November.

It is difficult not to concur.

THE SEARCH FOR SYDNEY

The initial search objective was to locate *Sydney*. In real terms, this meant the aircrews engaged in the search were given the task of looking for an object 555 feet long. To cover the defined search area with the

available resources, it is understood that the aircraft were flown at a height that would offer maximum visibility while still allowing *Sydney* to be seen.[33]

Unfortunately, it is extremely doubtful that *Sydney* was still afloat by 24 November and given the damage sustained and the fierce fire amidships it is also doubtful that any of its boats survived the action and the sinking. In all likelihood, *Sydney*'s survivors were forced to enter the water on the night of 19–20 November with only their life-belts and perhaps a small number of Carley floats.

The life expectancy of men in such circumstances was generally quite low, with most survivors perishing in the first forty-eight hours. By Monday 24 November, when the first search was flown, it is probable that only those who had managed to reach a Carley float were still alive.[34]

If the Hudsons engaged in Monday's search actually reached the area where possible survivors were located, and there is some doubt about this, it is probable that the aircrews failed to notice them. The aircrews were asked to look for a ship, not 10 to 14 foot long Carley floats.

The air searches conducted on 25 November, however, were given the task of locating *Sydney* as well as its ship's boats. The aircrews now knew that they had to locate objects smaller than a ship. The sighting of one lifeboat at sea and two on the coast during the morning search is evidence that the search aircraft were flown at a height conducive to spotting boat-sized objects.

On the evening of 25 November, the Naval Board received a signal from the Admiralty that altered the search objective again. The Admiralty believed that *Sydney* had been torpedoed by the raider. The object of the search to seaward was now the location of ship's boats and rafts. This remained the objective until operations were concluded on 29 November.

If *Sydney*'s survivors were without Carley floats, the chances of them being seen would have been significantly reduced. In such circumstances, only the survivors' heads would have been visible.

The difficulties of sighting objects the size of human heads from the air is shown by the fact that all debris recovered on 27 and 28 November was discovered by search vessels. There is no evidence of any of the items recovered having been sighted by aircraft before their discovery by ships'

lookouts. And the Carley float recovered by *Heros* on 28 November was not sighted from the air, despite search aircraft having flown over it on 25, 26 and possibly 27 November. Clearly, possible *Sydney* survivors could also have been overlooked.

This is not to say that the aircrews were negligent in their duty. Poor visibility, navigational error and unserviceable aircraft all conspired to leave gaps in the search coverage, which allowed German lifeboats and even search vessels to go unsighted.

In all likelihood, the last of *Sydney*'s survivors saw search aircraft overhead, but the aircraft failed to see them.

THE FATE OF SYDNEY'S CREW

On 26 November 1941, the government decided to advise next of kin that *Sydney*'s crew were missing as a result of enemy action. After the search operations were concluded, the Navy advised next of kin that as no survivors had been found all crew 'are considered to have lost their lives in action …' The RAAF, however, took a different line. On 6 December 1941, they advised next of kin that: 'If, after full consideration of all the circumstances, the Air Board is compelled to conclude that there is no hope of [relationship and name] being found alive, a presumption of death will be made.'[35]

The RAAF, it appears, considered that some of its men may have been aloft in *Sydney*'s Walrus and may have survived the action. By June 1942, the RAAF no longer held this view, notifying the next of kin that all RAAF personnel aboard *Sydney* had died as a result of enemy action on 19 November 1941.

On 19 June 1942, however, the RAAF changed the date of death to 20 November. The Air Board had been advised that the Naval Board now 'presumed the death of naval personnel on board HMAS *Sydney* occurred on 20th November'.[36]

It is not exactly clear why the Naval Board decided to change the date of death. The only logical reason is that the Navy believed *Sydney* sank after midnight on 19 November and that they amended the date of death to 20 November as a result.

It would also be logical to assume that some would have survived the sinking, but how long these possible survivors may have lived, and how and where they may have eventually perished, cannot be determined.

The only evidence of possible survivors from *Sydney*'s sinking is the Carley float and corpse recovered off Christmas Island on 6 February 1942. There is a strong possibility that this Carley float and corpse originated from *Sydney*, but the evidence is inconclusive, and a positive link is yet to be made. There is also doubt whether this man, if he *was* a *Sydney* crew member, was a survivor from the sinking or was blown overboard during the action.

CONCLUSIONS

The primary cause of *Sydney*'s loss was Burnett's decision to close to within 1,500 metres of the disguised German raider *Kormoran*.

Although *Sydney* was superior to *Kormoran* in armament, armour and speed, Burnett lost nearly all these advantages when he closed and reduced speed. At 1,500 metres and steaming at 14 knots, *Sydney*'s only remaining advantage lay with its superior armament. *Sydney* was able to bring a broadside of eight 6-inch guns to bear against *Kormoran*'s four 15-centimetre guns.

This superior weight of broadside, however, was countered by Detmers's tactical advantage. Detmers knew he was engaging a warship, whereas Burnett was clearly ignorant of the fact that he had closed with a raider.

Contributing to the loss of *Sydney* was the failure of primary gun control shortly after the opening of fire. After the first salvo, Burnett's only remaining advantage was lost. Detmers's first salvo directly or indirectly crippled *Sydney*'s fire-control system, momentarily silencing the main armament. In the minute that followed, 'A' and 'B' turrets were knocked out and the 4-inch gundeck and torpedo space were raked with automatic cannon fire. In this minute, Detmers gained fire superiority.[37] With fire superiority, Detmers was able to comprehensively destroy *Sydney*.

It is difficult to determine the exact cause of the loss of primary gun control, although action damage to the DCT or associated cabling, or damage to the ship's electrical system, rate highly as probable causes.

It would appear that Burnett's decision to close was influenced by the Admiralty requirement to capture enemy merchant vessels.

In October 1939, to help make good merchant ship losses, the Admiralty issued instructions that enemy merchant ships were to be captured rather than sunk. These instructions were still in force in November 1941 despite the fact that Germany had in the meantime covertly armed a number of its merchant ships for employment as auxiliary cruisers. Although the Admiralty acknowledged that these raiders were powerfully armed and difficult to identify, it failed to comprehend that its anti-scuttling instructions could lead to a British warship being severely damaged while attempting a capture.

On 4 November 1941, the Admiralty advised: 'Commanding Officers are given full discretion to take such steps as circumstances require and to use force to save the enemy ship.' Admiralty general message 771A was issued fifteen days before Burnett encountered *Kormoran*.

The exact cause of *Sydney*'s sinking is difficult to determine. While a magazine explosion or a loss of reserve of buoyancy through extensive flooding is the most likely cause, the evidence is inconclusive. Therefore, the cause of *Sydney*'s sinking cannot be determined from the available evidence.

Similarly, it cannot be determined how *Sydney*'s entire complement of 645 officers and men perished. It would be logical to assume that many would have died during the action, but it is conceivable that some would have survived both the action and the sinking. How long these possible survivors may have lived, and how and where they may have eventually perished cannot be determined.

From the available information it would appear that Navy Office failed to make a proper appreciation of *Sydney*'s non-return to Fremantle on 20 November 1941.

The failure to comprehend that *Sydney* was possibly in difficulties delayed the transmission of the signal ordering it to break W/T silence and report its ETA in Fremantle. This in turn delayed the subsequent search and perhaps contributed to the loss of *Sydney* with all hands.

It is difficult to avoid concluding that the initial search for *Sydney* was at least forty-eight hours late in being ordered. Given that *Sydney* was reported overdue on the morning of 21 November, an initial search could have been ordered for the morning of 22 November. Although Navy Office assumed that *Sydney* would be twenty-four hours late because *Zealandia* had been twenty-four hours late reaching Singapore, this should have seen *Sydney* arrive in Fremantle on the afternoon of 21 November. Some effort to establish *Sydney*'s whereabouts could, or should, have been made on 22 November.

It is conceivable that such an effort may have resulted in the discovery of *Sydney* survivors.

AN HONOURABLE DEATH

The enduring tragedy of *Sydney*'s death is that its loss has been perceived as something shameful. For six decades, many have sought to blame Burnett. Others, unable to accept the German account, have sought alternative explanations for the demise of a fine ship and the 645 souls who served it.

Sydney's loss, however, was not shameful. Captain Joseph Burnett and the men under his command upheld the proud traditions of the ship and the Royal Australian Navy. Their actions on 19 November 1941 ensured the destruction of the raider *Kormoran*, and indirectly saved many other ships and countless lives. They not only rid the seas of a potentially very destructive raider, but also helped remove nearly 400 highly trained officers and men from Germany's war effort.

In the Garden Island Chapel in Sydney, there is a stained-glass window dedicated to the men who have served in three HMA Ships *Sydney*. It was erected in honour of those who served and to the eternal memory of those who perished. In the centre of the top half of the window is the ship's crest and surrounding the crest are the battle honours.

EMDEN 1914

CALABRIA 1940

CAPE SPADA 1940

MEDITERRANEAN 1940

KORMORAN 1941

KOREA 1951-52

Of the six, *Sydney II* was awarded no less than four.[38] Its final battle honour was 'KORMORAN 1941'. *Sydney*'s men did not die in shame. They fought with honour and died with honour. That is how they should be remembered.

One of the last known photographs of HMAS *Sydney*. Taken on 4 November 1941 when the cruiser entered King George Sound, Albany to land a mine disposal team.
L. Hockey

POSTSCRIPT

In August–September 2001 a Royal Australian Navy led team excavated a section of the European cemetery on Christmas Island, in an attempt to locate the remains of the unknown sailor buried there in 1942. No remains were found.

In November 2001 the Royal Australian Navy hosted a HMAS *Sydney* wreck location seminar. Four workshops (archival, oceanographic, oral and technical) were tasked with presenting the Chief of Navy, Vice-Admiral David Shackleton, with conclusions sufficient to allow him to make an evaluation on the appropriateness of a wreck search.

In June 2002 Vice-Admiral Shackleton announced that a suitable basis does not exist for an official search for the wreck of HMAS *Sydney*.

ROLL OF HONOUR
OFFICERS AND MEN LOST IN HMAS SYDNEY

Captain J. Burnett, RAN (VIC)
Commander E.W. Thruston, DCS, RN (NSW)
Commander (E) L.S. Dalton, DSO, RAN (NSW)
Commander (S) T.F. Maynard, RAN (VIC)
Surgeon Commander J.R. Hasker, RAN (VIC)
Chaplain the Reverend G. Stubbs, RAN (NSW)
Schoolmaster P.F. Skewes, RAN (QLD)
Lieutenant-Commander C.A.C. Montgomery, RN (NSW)
Lieutenant-Commander M.M. Singer, DSC, RN (WA)
Lieutenant-Commander A.M. Wilkinson, RAN (NSW)
Lieutenant-Commander (O) J.C. Bacon, RN (NSW)
Lieutenant-Commander (E) R.D. Handcock, RAN (NSW)
Surgeon Lieutenant-Commander F.H. Genge RAN (NSW)
Lieutenant T.G. Brown, RAN (VIC)
Lieutenant J.A. Cole, RANR (NSW)
Lieutenant T.E. Davis, RAN (NSW)
Lieutenant A.I. Keith, RANR (NSW)

Lieutenant E.E. Mayo, RAN (SA)
Lieutenant I.T.R. Treloar, RAN (VIC)

Lieutenant (E) W.T. Anderson, RANR (NSW)
Lieutenant (E) A.W. Wilson, RANR (NSW)
Lieutenant (S) R.E. Ridout, RANR (VIC)
Surgeon Lieutenant (D) M.C. Townsend, RAN (VIC)
Sub-Lieutenant A.E. Byrne, RANR (QLD)
Sub-Lieutenant A.V. Eagar, RANR (QLD)
Sub-Lieutenant E.R. Eddy, RAN (VIC)
Sub-Lieutenant B.A. Elder, RANR (NSW)
Flying Officer R.B. Barrey, RAAF (SA)
Sub-Lieutenant (E) A.J. King, RANVR (SA)
Sub-Lieutenant (E) F.H. Schoch, RANVR (WA)
Sub-Lieutenant (S) J.I. Clifton, RANR (WA)
Sub-Lieutenant (S) C.M. Mitchell, RANR (VIC)
Acting Sub-Lieutenant (S) D.W. McCabe, RAN (TAS)
Gunner F.L. McDonald, RN (ENGLAND)
Gunner (T) J.E. Peterson, RAN (VIC)
Acting Gunner J.K. Houston, RAN (SA)
Warrant (E) W.G. Batchelor, RAN (VIC)
Warrant (E) A.B. Biggs, RAN (NSW)
Warrant (E) F.W. Reville, RAN (NSW)
Warrant (H) J.A.E. Fuller, RAN (NSW)
Warrant (L) R.W. Nicholson, RAN (NSW)
Warrant (S) W.A. Owen, RAN (NSW)

Abernethy, R.B., Petty Officer Telegraphist (NSW)
Absolom, J.F., Acting Leading Stoker (TAS)
Addison, R.H., Acting Leading Seaman (NSW)
Agar, L.H., Chief Mechanician (VIC)
Allison, J.A.C., Able Seaman (NSW)
Anderson, C.J., Ordinary Seaman (SA)
Anderson, R.H., Able Seaman (WA)
Andrews, A.J., Able Seaman (WA)
Archbell, A.W., Acting Leading Seaman (VIC)
Armstrong, H.J., Ordinary Seaman (VIC)
Aumann, C., Acting Leading Stoker (VIC)
Avery, G.W., Able Seaman (NSW)
Aylott, W.L., Acting Petty Officer (NSW)

Ayton, L.G., Ordnance Artificer IV (VIC)
Bain, W.J., Able Seaman (TAS)
Baker, V.L., Ordinary Seaman (QLD)
Baker, W.A., Stoker (NSW)
Balding, H.R., Able Seaman (WA)
Barclay, V.N., Supply Assistant (VIC)
Barham, E.R., Sick Berth Petty Officer (VIC)
Barker, B.J.H., Able Seaman (WA)
Bartlett, M.E., Able Seaman (NSW)
Bath, W.J., Ordinary Seaman (NSW)
Batten, K.C., Stoker (NSW)
Baverstock, E.G., Able Seaman (WA)
Beattie, A., Leading Stoker (NSW)
Beattie, E.P., Stoker (NSW)
Beckett, R.J., Stoker (TAS)
Belcher, E.R., Wireman (VIC)
Bennie, G.R., Able Seaman (NSW)
Berwick, G.R., Wireman (VIC)
Bettany, J.H., Able Seaman (WA)
Betterman, D.R., Able Seaman (SA)
Bettinson, W.E., Leading Seaman (NSW)
Bevan, H.V., Able Seaman (WA)
Beverton, J.T., Stoker, (QLD)
Bibby, I.I., Engine Room Artificer I (NSW)
Biram, B.F., Petty Officer Cook (NSW)
Birch, J.W., Acting Leading Stoker (VIC)
Blackwood, J., Stoker (NSW)
Blake, J.S., Acting Leading Stoker (SA)
Blom, L.M., Stoker (WA)
Bodman, A.A., Able Seaman (WA)
Bone, G.F., Able Seaman (NSW)
Bonham, H.G.W., Engine Room Artificer IV (NSW)
Bonner, R., Mechanician I (NSW)
Bool, J., Ordinary Seaman (VIC)
Booth, E.A., Able Seaman (VIC)
Bowden, L., Stoker II (VIC)
Bowes, K.A.J., Stoker (NSW)
Box, R.A., Stoker II (TAS)
Boyd, D.W., Acting Leading Sick Berth Attendant (VIC)
Bradley, R., Ordinary Seaman (WA)

Brennan, E.N., Able Seaman (NSW)

Brind, M., Able Seaman (NSW)

Brodie, R.R., Acting Leading Seaman (TAS)

Brooks, D.L., Ordinary Seaman (SA)

Buchanan, A.R.M., Stoker Petty Officer (VIC)

Buck, C.C., Able Seaman (SA)

Buckingham, C.F.P., Able Seaman (WA)

Buckley, D.S., Ordinary Seaman (VIC)

Budden, K.E., Acting Yeoman of Signals, (NSW)

Bundy, F.P.K., Petty officer (NSW)

Bunting, J., Able Seaman (QLD)

Burgess, W.R., Signalman (NSW)

Burgoyne, M.A., Leading Steward (NSW)

Burke, K.T., Telegraphist (VIC)

Burke, L., Leading Cook (VIC)

Burke, W., Chief Engine Room Artificer, (NSW)

Burns, J.R., Acting Stoker Petty Officer (NSW)

Burnsyde, W.E., Stoker (WA)

Burrowes, D.J., Able Seaman (SA)

Burt, A.S., Wireman (VIC)

Butler, K.N.H., Supply Assistant (WA)

Butler, S.W., Able Seaman (NSW)

Cabban, V.R., Stoker II (NSW)

Cannon, L.J., Telegraphist (WA)

Carey, H.R.J., Able Seaman (VIC)

Carey, T.L., Chief Petty Officer Cook (VIC)

Carr, J.W.A., Able Seaman (NSW)

Carthy, G.T., Able Seaman (VIC)

Cartwright, A.M., Able Seaman (NSW)

Catley, R.R., Able Seaman (NSW)

Caudle, D.W., Ordinary Seaman (SA)

Challenger, C.W., Chief Stoker (VIC)

Chapman, N.O., Ordinary Seaman (WA)

Chapman, W.R., Stoker (NSW)

Charlton, C.L., Cook (TAS)

Christie, A.T.N., Stoker (TAS)

Christison, J.M., Ordinary Seaman (QLD)

Clark, D.M., Acting Leading Stoker (NSW)

Clark, T.W., Able Seaman (QLD)

Clarke, A.J., Leading Aircraftsman, RAAF (VIC)

Clarke, H., Acting Leading Stoker (WA)
Clayton, A.S., Stoker (WA)
Clement, W., Ordinary Seaman (VIC)
Clive, A.W., Stoker (WA)
Colbey, R.S., Ordinary Seaman (SA)
Cole, J.V., Ordinary Seaman (NSW)
Cole, S.A.W., Able Seaman (QLD)
Coleman, G.E., Wireman (NSW)
Colhoun, R.A., Stoker II (VIC)
Collie, C.B., Stoker II (QLD)
Collier, R.T., Acting Leading Seaman (VIC)
Collins, C.E., Able Seaman (NSW)
Collins, W.H., Able Seaman (NSW)
Conquit, W.C., Able Seaman (VIC)
Cookesley, C.W., Stoker (WA)
Coonan, B.R., Acting Leading Seaman (WA)
Cooper, A.L., Leading Stoker (VIC)
Cooper, A.D.W., Stoker II (VIC)
Cooper, B., Able Seaman (VIC)
Cooper, R., Stoker (WA)
Cooper, R.A., Able Seaman (NSW)
Coppin, G.W., Assistant Steward (SA)
Cork, W.J.M., Ordinary Seaman II (SA)
Cormick, T.G., Engine Room Artificer IV (VIC)
Courtis, R.J., Stoker (WA)
Cox, H.W., Acting Leading Stoker (NSW)
Cox, J.L., Signalman (TAS)
Cragg, G.L., Stoker (NSW)
Craike, B.W., Able Seaman (TAS)
Cranwell, H.A.G., Stoker (TAS)
Craske, B.J., Ordinary Seaman II (VIC)
Crawford, T.A., Acting Able Seaman (VIC)
Crocker, L.J., Petty Officer Cook (VIC)
Crowle, J.A.F., Stoker II (VIC)
Cummings, J., Able Seaman (NSW)
Cunnington, A.L.F., Ordnance Artificer IV (VIC)
Curtis, C.L.J., Wireman (VIC)
Curtis, R., Petty Officer (VIC)
Curwood, W.L., Wireman (VIC)
Daniel, K.H., Ordnance Artificer IV (VIC)

Darby, S.M., Able Seaman (WA)
Daunt, A.R., Stoker (NSW)
Davey, J.S., Petty Officer Cook (VIC)
Davies, S.J., Electrical Artificer (WA)
Davis, S.R., Leading Seaman (NSW)
Deacon, W.F., Able Seaman (VIC)
Deane, W.B., Ordinary Seaman (NSW)
Dee, T., Leading Steward (NSW)
De Forrest, M.C., Stoker (VIC)
De Gracie, J.P., Ordinary Seaman (WA)
Dempster, H.J., Stoker (VIC)
Devereux, E.G., Able Seaman (WA)
Dhu, L.E., Able Seaman (NSW)
Diews, B.A., Able Seaman (NSW)
Dimmock, D.C., Able Seaman (NSW)
Dix, G.K., Acting Leading Stoker (WA)
Dixon, T.C., Leading Stoker (WA)
Dobson, H.H., Able Seaman (WA)
Dodds, R., Leading Aircraftsman (NSW)
Doxey, A.H., Able Seaman (WA)
Doyle, E.F., Able Seaman (SA)
Drake, A.R., Able Seaman (VIC)
Drake, J.R., Stoker (VIC)
Duncan, E.R.T., Supply Assistant (VIC)
Dundon, S., Able Seaman (NSW)
Dunin, T., Steward (VIC)
Edenborough, A.G., Ordinary Seaman (NSW)
Edgoose, E.F., Ordinary Seaman (VIC)
Edwards, E.J., Able Seaman (QLD)
Edwards, F., Acting Stoker Petty Officer (NSW)
Evans, F.R., Petty Officer (NSW)
Ewens, R.U., Able Seaman (SA)
Fahey, W.R., Able Seaman (NSW)
Farrand, L.C., Ordinary Seaman (NSW)
Faulkner, A.J., Able Seaman (QLD)
Ferguson, D.W., Able Seaman (NSW)
Ferguson, K.C., Ordinary Seaman (QLD)
Fibbens, W.S., Telegraphist (NSW)
Finlay, G.L., Acting Ordnance Artificer IV (VIC)
Finlayson, H., Mechanician I (NSW)

Fisher, J.W., Leading Cook (NSW)
Fitzgerald, A.F., Blacksmith IV (VIC)
Fitzgerald, L.G., Acting Supply Petty Officer (NSW)
Fleming, W.S., Able Seaman (NSW)
Foote, R.E., Cook (SA)
Forbes, R.G.S., Ordinary Seaman (NSW)
Forsyth, G.E., Electrical Artificer IV (VIC)
Forth, H., Able Seaman (VIC)
Foster, N.D., Engine Room Artificer IV (NSW)
Foster, R.E., Leading Aircraftsman, RAAF (QLD)
Foulkes, R.E., Telegraphist (NSW)
Franklin, E.W., Leading Seaman (NSW)
Fraser, N.J., Ordinary Seaman (NSW)
Freer, W.E.A., Able Seaman (SA)
Friar, J.A., Engine Room Artificer III (NSW)
Frisch, E.D., Able Seaman (QLD)
Frith, W.R.O., Petty Officer, RN (ENGLAND)
Fry, R.A., Stoker (VIC)
Fryer, K.J., Ordinary Telegraphist (NSW)
Gamble, F.H., Petty Officer Telegraphist (VIC)
Gamble, R.F., Acting Petty Officer Telegraphist (NSW)
Gardiner, H.D., Ordinary Seaman (WA)
Garnett, W.H., Acting Leading Stoker, (NSW)
Garrett, B.F., Able Seaman (WA)
Gale, R., Leading Supply Assistant (NSW)
Gentles, H.S., Chief Stoker, (NSW)
Gilsenan, D.J., Steward (VIC)
Glackin, T.N., Stoker (QLD)
Glasby, H., Able Seaman (NSW)
Goodwin, N.F., Able Seaman (NSW)
Goodwin, W.J., Able Seaman (VIC)
Gothard, E., Acting Petty Officer Telegraphist (VIC)
Graco, H.M., Able Seaman (WA)
Graham, G.A., Ordinary Seaman (NSW)
Greaves, S., Able Seaman (QLD)
Green, A.E., Acting Stoker Petty Officer (QLD)
Green, J.R., Ordinary Seaman (TAS)
Green, T.L., Cook (NSW)
Greenwood, J.H., Ordinary Seaman (QLD)
Gregson, M.O., Ordinary Seaman (SINGAPORE)

Grinter, N.F., Acting Leading Stoker (VIC)
Gronberg, E.E., Stoker (WA)
Gwynne, D.A., Able Seaman (SA)
Haag, F.V., Stoker (VIC)
Hagan, A., Steward (NSW)
Hammond, L., Able Seaman (NSW)
Hare, R.W., Able Seaman (QLD)
Harricks, S.W., Able Seaman (NSW)
Hass, M.L.W., Able Seaman (QLD)
Harrington, A.F., Acting Leading Seaman (WA)
Harris, R.C., Able Seaman (VIC)
Harrison, L.A., Petty Officer Steward (NSW)
Hartmann, F.H., Regulating Petty Officer (VIC)
Haslam, A.C., Acting Leading Seaman (NSW)
Hattersley, J.O., Able Seaman (NSW)
Hawker, G.C., Steward (WA)
Hawkes, S.W., Able Seaman (WA)
Haynes, F.J., Stoker (NSW)
Haywood, G.J., Ordinary Seaman II (TAS)
Heaton, E., Acting Electrical Artificer IV (NSW)
Henderson, W.L.D., Stoker (WA)
Henrickson, J.O., Stoker (NSW)
Herington, H.F., Stoker II (NSW)
Heritage, R.G., Able Seaman (SA)
Herrod, H.F., Acting Leading Stoker (NSW)
Hewett, E.H., Able Seaman (VIC)
Hickey, R.A., Able Seaman (NSW)
Hill, D.H., Stoker (SA)
Hill, P., Able Seaman (WA)
Hill, R.H., Engine Room Artificer IV (SA)
Hobbs, G.J., Able Seaman (VIC)
Hogan, M.H., Ordinary Telegraphist (SA)
Holder, E.H., Telegraphist (NSW)
Holm, C.K.A., Able Seaman (VIC)
Homard, K., Aircraftsman I, RAAF (NSW)
Homer, A.W., Chief Stoker (NSW)
Honor, C.L., Telegraphist (SA)
Hooper, E.N., Ordinary Seaman (QLD)
Hopcraft, R.B., Shipwright III (NSW)
Hore, K.B., Able Seaman (NSW)

Horrigan, C., Able Seaman (VIC)
Howard, L.J., Able Seaman (WA)
Hudson, J.L., Signalman (QLD)
Hutchinson, R., Able Seaman (VIC)
Hutchinson, R.H., Able Seaman (NSW)
Hutchison, J.R., Stoker II (NSW)
Ingham, J.W., Acting Leading Stoker (WA)
James, M.C., Able Seaman (NSW)
Jarvis, W.J., Stoker II (VIC)
Jeffs, F.W., Ordinary Seaman (VIC)
Jennings, D.M., Able Seaman (NSW)
Jesnoewski, L.A., Ordinary Seaman (WA)
Johnson, P.A., Stoker II (TAS)
Johnston, D.E., Able Seaman (QLD)
Johnston, G., Writer (VIC)
Johnston, E.W., Able Seaman (NSW)
Johnstone, T.J.A., Able Seaman (VIC)
Jones, D.J., Acting Stoker Petty Officer (NSW)
Jones, D.E., Able Seaman (NSW)
Jones, I.D., Acting Engine Room Artificer IV (WA)
Jones, J.B., Engine Room Artificer IV (NSW)
Jones, P.T., Chief Petty Officer (VIC)
Jones, W.G., Chief Shipwright (NSW)
Jordan, E. J., Able Seaman (NSW)
Jordan, H.D., Able Seaman (NSW)
Joyce, W.R.J., Able Seaman (NSW)
Keane, W.J., DSM, Chief Ordnance Artificer (VIC)
Kearnon, R.A., Ordinary Seaman (NSW)
Keenan, F.B., Stoker (WA)
Kelly, J.V., Able Seaman (VIC)
Kelly, N.A., Stoker II (NSW)
Kennedy, R.J., Stoker II (NSW)
Kenney, A.H.L., Chief Petty Officer (SA)
Kent, L.S., Signalman (VIC)
Kettle, E.J., Able Seaman (NSW)
Kettyle, J.T., Leading Stoker (VIC)
Keys, R.F., Able Seaman (VIC)
Kirkham, E.J., Able Seaman (WA)
Kitchin, C.P., Stoker (SA)
Kleinig, A.A., Telegraphist (SA)

Knapman, W.B., Engine Room Artificer IV (SA)
Knapp D.J., Stoker II (VIC)
Knight, N.K., Steward (WA)
Kreig, A.D., Assistant Steward (SA)
Laffer, P.M., Ordinary Seaman (SA)
Lang, J., Able Seaman (QLD)
Lang, W.H., Stoker II (NSW)
Lawler, N.C., Ordinary Seaman (TAS)
Lawson, J.N., Supply Assistant (VIC)
Laxton, S.T., Sick Berth Attendant II (VIC)
Laycock, R.S., Stoker (VIC)
Lewis, A.H., Stoker Petty Officer (NSW)
Lewis, D.H., Bandsman (NSW)
Lewis, L.R., Acting Leading Seaman (NSW)
Lillywhite, H.E., Shipwright I (NSW)
Lockard, T.G., Acting Signalman (TAS)
Love, S.E., Stoker (SA)
Lowenstein, W., Stoker (TAS)
Lowry, F.W., Able Seaman (QLD)
Lynch, S.M., Able Seaman (TAS)
Lyne, R.V., Ordinary Seaman (VIC)
Mackinnon, M., Petty Officer (WA)
Males, T., Shipwright IV (TAS)
Mann, K.A., Ordinary Seaman (VIC)
Manning, M., Leading Cook (NSW)
Marley, S., Sergeant, RAAF (NSW)
Marson, A.R., Mechanician II (VIC)
Martin, A.D., Ordinary Seaman (SA)
Martin, J.H., Able Seaman (VIC)
Martin, L.F., Steward (VIC)
Martin, L.J.F., Ordinary Seaman (NSW)
Matheson, E.A.J., Ordinary Seaman (NSW)
Mathews, J.W., Able Seaman (VIC)
Maxwell, I.M., Ordinary Signalman (TAS)
Medlen, L.J., Sick Berth Attendant (SA)
Melandri, P.E.V., Bandsman (NSW)
Menzies, W., Able Seaman (NSW)
Miller, G.J., Cook (VIC)
Miller, J.D.H., Able Seaman (VIC)
Miller, K.R., Ordinary Seaman (VIC)

Miller, M.P., Steward (VIC)
Miller, R.A., Stoker (WA)
Milverton, P.F., Able Seaman (QLD)
Minns, L.C., Sick Berth Attendant (VIC)
Mitchell, F.J., Supply Assistant (VIC)
Mogler, R.C., Stoker (NSW)
Mordaunt, F.X., Petty Officer Writer (NSW)
Morisey, R., Able Seaman (WA)
Morphett, M.J., Cook (NSW)
Morris, E.P., Petty Officer (NSW)
Morris, R.K., Able Seaman (SA)
Moule, A., Stoker (NSW)
Mudford, L.F., Able Seaman (VIC)
Mulhall, J.D., Bandsman (NSW)
Murdoch, R.C., Able Seaman (SA)
Murray, M., Able Seaman, (WA)
Mutch, H.M., Able Seaman, RN
Myers, H.W., Stoker (VIC)
McAulay, A.C., Bandsman (NSW)
McAuslan, A.R., Chief Engine Room Artificer (VIC)
McBain, J.H., Chief Engine Room Artificer (NSW)
McCabe, E.V., Able Seaman (NSW)
McCallum, D., Canteen Assistant (SCOTLAND)
McClaren, A.A., Petty Officer (NSW)
McConnell, R.N., Stoker (NSW)
McCulloch, S., Able Seaman (NSW)
McCullough, S.J., Wireman (QLD)
McDonald, J.D., Able Seaman (NSW)
McDougall, W., Able Seaman (NSW)
McGregor, D.A., Cook (NSW)
McGowan, T.H., Able Seaman (VIC)
McHaffie, E.H., Painter I (VIC)
McKay, A.M., Leading Supply Assistant (NSW)
McKechnie, G.M., Ordinary Seaman (SA)
McKenzie, D.J., Able Seaman (VIC)
McKeown, M.J., Able Seaman (NSW)
McLean, W.E., Stoker Petty Officer (NSW)
McLeod, H.C., Acting Leading Stoker (VIC)
McLeod-Smith, A.F., Petty Officer (WA)
Nesbitt, J., Able Seaman (VIC)

Newman, C.A., Able Seaman (VIC)
Nicholls, M.G., Able Seaman (WA)
Nichols, F.R., Ordinary Seaman (TAS)
Nicol, T.E., Wireman (NSW)
Noble, C.T., Regulating Petty Officer (NSW)
Noell, A.J., Stoker (WA)
Norbery, S.W., Able Seaman (QLD)
Norman, C.G.J., Able Seaman (SA)
Norman, F.W., Leading Seaman (WA)
Norton, J.T.H., Leading Stoker (NSW)
Norton, M.A.H., Engine Room Artificer IV (NSW)
Norton, W.F.C., Able Seaman (NSW)
Nugent, C.J., Stoker ((VIC)
Nyal, L.J., Stoker II (WA)
Oakford, P.J., Ordinary Seaman (TAS)
O'Brien, E.B., Shipwright I (NSW)
Ogilvie, L., Able Seaman (VIC)
Oliver, A.H., Ordinary Seaman (TAS)
Opas, M., Canteen Manager (NSW)
Owens, E.H., Able Seaman (NSW)
Paling, D.R., Able Seaman (NSW)
Parkes, D.L., Able Seaman (NSW)
Parr, G.F., Chief Electrical Artificer (VIC)
Partington, L.W., Bandsman (NSW)
Pascoe, P.H., Stoker (WA)
Pastoors, W.C., Stoker II (NSW)
Patrick, C.W., Ordinary Seaman II (QLD)
Paul, S.R., Stoker (QLD)
Payne, J.R., Sick Berth Attendant (VIC)
Peak, J.M., Stoker (WA)
Pearce, E.V., Acting Engine Room Artificer IV (NSW)
Pelham, F.C., Bandsman (TAS)
Perger, F.J., Able Seaman (TAS)
Perryman, R.S., Able Seaman (WA)
Peters, M.W., Telegraphist (SA)
Peterson, P.W., Stoker (VIC)
Phillips, F.E., Able Seaman (NSW)
Pike, J.W., Able Seaman (NSW)
Pitt, W.H., Able Seaman (NSW)
Platt, R., Stoker II (VIC)

Pople, A.H.W., Band Corporal (NSW)
Potter, A.W., Ordinary Seaman (VIC)
Potter, C.A., Acting Supply Petty Officer (WA)
Powell, L.L., Able Seaman (NSW)
Prike, J.J., Able Seaman (WA)
Primmer, J.F.R., Able Seaman (QLD)
Pritchard, H.L., Ordnance Artificer IV (VIC)
Psaila, S., Canteen Assistant (NSW)
Pulham, E.G.M., Acting Leading Stoker (WA)
Purdon, E.T., Leading Seaman (NSW)
Purkiss, C.E., Wireman (NSW)
Putman, A.E., Ordinary Seaman (VIC)
Quilty, J.E., Acting Leading Seaman (VIC)
Quinn, G.F., Petty Officer Cook (NSW)
Ramsay, E.W., Able Seaman (WA)
Ranford, J.I., Ordinary Telegraphist (SA)
Ray, H.G., Able Seaman (QLD)
Redfearne, C.H., Stoker (WA)
Redmond, E.N., Ordinary Signalman (WA)
Reed, G.P., Writer (VIC)
Rees, R.J., Ordinary Seaman (TAS)
Reeves, E.L., Able Seaman (NSW)
Reeves, R.H., Ordinary Seaman (NSW)
Reid, G.R., Signalman (NSW)
Reilly, J.B., Acting Engine Room Artificer IV (VIC)
Remfry, E.J., Able Seaman (NSW)
Ricardo, J.L., Chief Petty Officer Butcher (NSW)
Rice, D.M., Stoker III (VIC)
Richards, H.N., Acting Engine Room Artificer IV (SA)
Richter, A.J., Acting Supply Petty Officer (NSW)
Riley, E.M., Ordinary Seaman (QLD)
Rippen, A.H.G., Telegraphist (WA)
Riters, E., Able Seaman (NSW)
Roberts, L.I., Stoker (WA)
Roberts, R.C., Assistant Cook (VIC)
Robertson, M.J., Leading Seaman (NSW)
Robertson, T.N., Acting Stoker Petty Officer (NSW)
Robertson, W.J., Leading Cook (VIC)
Rogers, C.A., Able Seaman (NSW)
Rogers, R.C., Signalman (TAS)

Rolfe, E.S., Able Seaman (NSW)
Rolley, E.D., Steward (QLD)
Rosevear, G., Able Seaman (NSW)
Rosevear, L., Able Seaman (TAS)
Ross, D., Petty Officer Steward (NSW)
Ross, J.T., Supply Petty Officer (NSW)
Rothbaum, L., Assistant Steward (WA)
Rowe, A.L., Able Seaman (WA)
Rowe, J.R.J., Telegraphist (WA)
Rowe, L.T., Stoker II (VIC)
Rowlands, H.E., Supply Chief Petty Officer (NSW)
Rudall, P.S., Ordinary Seaman (SA)
Salmon, J., Able Seaman (NSW)
Sampson, L.N., Supply Chief Petty Officer (NSW)
Sands, W.A.M., Chief Petty Officer (NSW)
Savage, L.R., Stoker (VIC)
Sawbridge, G.W., Bandsman (NSW)
Schache, W.H., Chief Petty Officer Cook (VIC)
Schmidt, A.H., Ordinary Seaman (SA)
Schultz, R.A., Stoker (NSW)
Scott, G.G., Acting Petty Officer (NSW)
Shadlow, E.H., Stoker II (NSW)
Shepherd, A.H., Acting Engine Room Artificer IV (WA)
Shepherd, D.J., Chief Petty Officer Telegraphist (NSW)
Shiers, A.E., Able Seaman (SA)
Shipstone, H.B., Petty Officer (QLD)
Short, H.K., Able Seaman (WA)
Sievey, R.T., Ordinary Seaman (NSW)
Silk, S.G., Chief Petty Officer (ENGLAND)
Simpson, B., Petty Officer Telegraphist (NSW)
Simpson, C.H., Able Seaman (VIC)
Simpson, R.A., Ordinary Telegraphist (SA)
Slater, A.G.H., Assistant Cook (VIC)
Smith, A.L., Chief Electrical Artificer (NSW)
Smith, A.J., Stoker II (TAS)
Smith, C.F., Able Seaman (WA)
Smith, D.W.C., Engine Room Artificer IV (SA)
Smith, E.E.F., Able Seaman (WA)
Smith, G.W., Stoker II(VIC)
Smith, R.G.S., Engine Room Artificer IV (VIC)

Smith, R.C., Supply Assistant (NSW)
Smith, R.S., Stoker (QLD)
Smith, W.F.A., Able Seaman (VIC)
Smith, W.H.R., Engine Room Artificer III (VIC)
Smith, W.R.D., Acting Petty Officer (NSW)
Soutar, W.N., Supply Assistant (NSW)
Spiller, H.J., Able Seaman (VIC)
Staff, R.F., Steward (VIC)
Stammers, R., Cook (WA)
Standish, G.F., Able Seaman (SA)
Stear, E.V.L., Bandmaster (VIC)
Steed, P.W., Ordinary Seaman (NSW)
Steele, R.M.M., Able Seaman (NSW)
Stenton, S.P.W., Stoker II (VIC)
Stephens, G., Acting Yeoman of Signals (NSW)
Stephenson, W.T.W., Stoker (TAS)
Sterling, L., Able Seaman (NSW)
Stevens, H.J., Bandsman (TAS)
Stevenson, R., Stoker III (NSW)
Stride, C.M., Stoker II (NSW)
Striethorst, R.C., Able Seaman (NSW)
Stripe, A.E., Able Seaman (SA)
Strugnell, J.W., Petty Officer (NSW)
Stuart, J.R.K., Stoker (NSW)
Stuart, W.F., Writer (VIC)
Stubbs, K., Stoker II (WA)
Sturla, J.R., Chief Stoker (NSW)
Sutton, D.O., Able Seaman (WA)
Sutton, K., Acting Stoker Petty Officer (VIC)
Tabor, F.A., Acting Leading Seaman (SA)
Tassel, H.W., Petty Officer (WA)
Tatters, G.N., Able Seaman (QLD)
Taylor, J., Telegraphist (WA)
Taylor, J.E., Able Seaman (QLD)
Taylor, J.M., Able Seaman (VIC)
Taylor, K., Ordinary Seaman (VIC)
Taylor, K.G., Able Seaman (WA)
Taylor, R.A., Leading Stoker (TAS)
Tennant, R.G., Engine Room Artificer III (NSW)
Thompson, H.E., Wireman (VIC)

Thompson, W.R., Stoker (NSW)
Thomson, A.J., Stoker (WA)
Trenbath, J.S., Stoker III (NSW)
Trenwith, H.G., Stoker Petty Officer (NSW)
Triggs, R., Master-at-Arms (QLD)
Tuffin, E.D., Able Seaman (WA)
Turk, H., Able Seaman (NSW)
Turner, G.A., Ordinary Seaman II (VIC)
Turner, H., Signalman (NSW)
Turner, K.J., Ordinary Seaman (VIC)
Turner, W.R., Able Seaman (WA)
Tyldsley, J., Chief Yeoman of Signals (NSW)
Tyler, C.D., Bandsman (VIC)
Unwin, J.E., Able Seaman (VIC)
Uren, T.W.J., Leading Steward (VIC)
Vassett, A.W., Electrical Artificer I (VIC)
Vogt, R.M., Able Seaman (SA)
Wait, H.T.C., Acting Supply Petty Officer (NSW)
Waldron. T.A., Stoker II (VIC)
Walker, A.J., Cook (NSW)
Walker, E.J., Yeoman of Signals (NSW)
Walker, K.J., Able Seaman (VIC)
Walker, W.A.G., Leading Signalman (WA)
Wallace, W.R., Stoker (NSW)
Walsh, G.S., Supply Assistant (SA)
Walsh, M.H.J., Able Seaman (VIC)
Ward, F.E.C., Able Seaman (WA)
Ward, J.J.R., Leading Stoker (NSW)
Ware, L.F., Joiner III (NSW)
Warren, V., Bandsman (VIC)
Waye, L.W., Acting Leading Stoker (SA)
Webb, A.C., Able Seaman (VIC)
Webb, O.E.R., Acting Petty Officer (NSW)
Weller, R.H., Acting Shipwright IV (TAS)
White, H.J.L., Signalman (VIC)
White, R.G., Able Seaman (NSW)
Whitfield, L.W., Chief Petty Officer Writer (NSW)
Whithear, A.G., Stoker (NSW)
Williams, A.D., Able Seaman (NSW)
Williams, D.L., Acting Petty Officer (NSW)

Williams, J.B., Stoker II (VIC)
Williams, J.H., Stoker II (WA)
Williamson, M.D., Leading Stoker (TAS)
Williamson, S.T.L., Acting Petty Officer (VIC)
Willis, G.B., Able Seaman (NSW)
Willis, P.J.C., Plumber I (NSW)
Willis, L.M., Cook (NSW)
Willis, R.V., Steward (QLD)
Wilson, C., Telegraphist (NSW)
Wilson, J.S., Able Seaman (SA)
Wilson, R.R., Sick Berth Attendant (SA)
Wilson, R.W.D., Ordinary Seaman (NSW)
Windham, R.B., Ordinary Telegraphist (SA)
Witton, B.L., Acting Leading Telegraphist (WA)
Wixted, R.J., Stoker II (NSW)
Wood, A.T., Able Seaman (WA)
Woodcroft, W.G., Leading Steward (VIC)
Woodhams, R.B.C., Stoker II (WA)
Woods, W.R., Acting Engine Room Artificer IV (WA)
Woodsford, A.C., Acting Leading Seaman (SA)
Woolmore, L.T., Ordnance Artificer II (VIC)
Worsley, W.C., Acting Electrical Artificer IV (NSW)
Wright, C.A., Able Seaman (TAS)
Wright, C.P., Signalman (TAS)
Wright, H.D., Assistant Steward (NSW)
Wyatt, E.W., Telegraphist (SA)
Yeoman, W.C., Stoker (NSW)
York, L.D., Able Seaman (NSW)
Young, J.R., Able Seaman (QLD)
Zammitt, S., Canteen Manager (NSW)

—APPENDIX II—

GERMAN ADMIRALTY ACCOUNT OF THE SINKING OF HMAS SYDNEY

IN 1943 *Kormoran's* surgeon, Doctor Siebelt Habben, was repatriated as part of an exchange of POW medical staff. On reaching Germany, he provided the German naval authorities with a detailed report on the *Kormoran/Sydney* action. The following is an extract from the text of that report.

Battle with the Cruiser SYDNEY—Sinking of both Ships

At about 1600 [1700H] hours on November 19th, 1941, in a position 26° 34' South and 111° East, the KORMORAN steering a course of 25° at moderate speed, sighted ahead a plume of smoke out of which quickly emerged a light cruiser bearing directly on KORMORAN. The auxiliary cruiser turned to port on a course of 260°, and hurried away from the cruiser at high speed, steaming at 18 knots. This course was against the sun, sea and wind. The cruiser took up the chase and drew near at a speed of 25 knots. There followed a long exchange of signals during which the auxiliary cruiser hoisted the Dutch flag. All signals sent by searchlight were answered by flag, as is the custom of merchant ships. The commander of the auxiliary cruiser quite consciously, and with great calmness, allowed the signal traffic to develop during which time he either hoisted the flags incompletely or else the flag 'not understood' in order to gain time and allow the cruiser to close within a very short distance. The Commander, in early deliberations, had envisaged in theory a situation such as this and he now put his plans into practice.

Towards 1730 [1830H], both ships were steaming at 14 knots on a course of 260°, the distance apart on the beam being 900 metres. SYDNEY was to starboard of KORMORAN. The enemy Commander apparently took the auxiliary cruiser to be completely harmless. The ship's aircraft, which previously had been swung out on its catapult, was swung back and stopped. The guns too, only seemed to be at half readiness. The only thing that was left out during the reciprocal exchange of signals was the giving of the secret call sign by the auxiliary cruiser. The answer was an order to remove camouflage, which was carried out in the record time of 6 seconds. At this order the Man of War ensign and the Commander's pendant were hoisted and the Dutch flag lowered. The ensign was hardly broken before the first shot fell from the first gun. This fell short but the second, a salvo from three guns, hit the enemy's bridge and control tower. SYDNEY fired her first salvo almost at the same time as KORMORAN second, but it fell far beyond the auxiliary cruiser. KORMORAN's third salvo hit the enemy's second turret, the roof of which was lifted up and prevented the first turret from swinging. This meant that the enemy had only his two after turrets available. The ship's aircraft, which had just been swung out and started up, was destroyed by a direct hit. After a corresponding time a torpedo fired from the KORMORAN's starboard above-water tube hit SYDNEY's bows just in front of the first turret. The torpedo tore a great hole in the ship's side. She sank deeply by the bows and for a moment it seemed as if she were going to break up. This reduced considerably the speed of the enemy. The 3.7-centimetre anti-tank gun under the bridge, and the 2-centimetre anti-aircraft guns added considerably to the fire of the heavy guns. They hindered the enemy from loading the torpedo tubes, which was continually being attempted, and from using light weapons and evidently caused many casualties amongst the personnel on the control positions of the cruiser.

The enemy only answered our fire with single shots from the 3rd and 4th turrets. A central fire control evidently no longer existed. These turrets succeeded in registering 3 hits on the KORMORAN which regrettably had serious consequences.

The first shell went through the funnel, exploded to leeward, the splinters penetrated the W/T room and killed two ratings.

The second destroyed the auxiliary cruiser's boiler room and a nearby oil-bunker. The ordinary and the foam fire extinguishers were put out of action through the resultant destruction.

The third demolished the transformers of the main engine installation.

The fourth shot, a dud, wounded several ratings on the third gun, who later died from their injuries.

The results from the hits were serious. A big fire broke out in the engine [room] with a great deal of smoke and many electrical discharges. Through the loss of the transformers the main engines stopped charging and the engines raced furiously. The first engineer, the electrical engineer and 14 engine room petty officers and ratings staked everything to fight the fire and to bring order into the machine installations again. They had to pay for this effort with their lives and never again came out of the engine room.

SYDNEY, who through reduction in speed had settled slightly astern, now tried to ram from astern the KORMORAN who was out of control. She was prevented in her intention by well placed fire, particularly from No.5 gun. SYDNEY turned round astern of the KORMORAN and steamed slowly, at about 5 or 6 knots, towards the south. In steaming away SYDNEY fired 4 torpedoes from the starboard tubes, all of which missed the target. The next [nearest] torpedo passed KORMORAN about 150 metres astern.

The enemy, whose turrets remained swung round to the port side, was heavily shelled by the auxiliary cruiser while she was making off. Salvo after salvo hit the ship particularly on the water line, which was peppered with holes. The auxiliary cruiser's guns were shooting at the rate of 4–5 salvoes per second [sic] and had, by the end of the engagement, fired 500 rounds of incendiary shells.

The auxiliary cruiser's artillery played the greatest part in wiping out the enemy.

Towards 1800 hours [1900H], as darkness fell, the enemy burning fiercely with a series of explosions on board, ran out of effective range of the cruiser's guns 104 hm on the port quarter of KORMORAN and disappeared slowly over the horizon. Towards 2300 [2400H] another final glare was seen. It can be assumed that this was the time the cruiser went down.

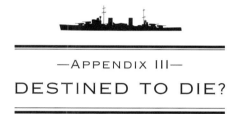

—APPENDIX III—

DESTINED TO DIE?

IN Greek mythology Phaeton, or Phaethon, was the son of Helios and Clymene. Helios (the Sun), was a servant of the Gods, and travelled across the sky in a chariot of fire drawn by four swift horses.

According to legend, when Phaethon reached adolescence he went to Helios seeking acknowledgement of his parentage. Helios told the boy that he was indeed his son, and to prove it allowed Phaethon to test him. Phaethon asked his father if he could drive his chariot. Helios, however, tried to dissuade the boy, as the horses needed a firm hand and the path was exact.

Some say that Helios reluctantly gave his permission. Others claim that Phaethon's sisters, the Heliades, gave Phaethon the chariot and the horses of the Sun without Helios' consent.

Against the wishes of his father, Phaethon set off on his journey across the heavens. But unaccustomed at being so high, he soon became frightened. Phaethon lost control of the horses, left his ordained path and almost crashed into the Earth. He scorched Africa and blackened the inhabitants, then rose too high and frightened the stars. When the stars complained, Zeus was forced to act.

Phaethon was struck by a thunderbolt and hurled from the chariot. He fell into the river Eridanus, or Po. Grief stricken, the Heliades stood on the banks of the river and wept. It is said that because they helped Phaethon take his father's chariot, they were turned into poplar trees, their tears becoming drops of amber. Phaethon's friend Cygnus, son of Neptune, grieved so much that Apollo changed him into a swan.

Phaethon was then set among the constellations as Auriga, the charioteer.

Perhaps in life as in legend, *Sydney* was destined to die amidst the elements of fire and water.

Chapter 1   HMAS *Sydney*

1   The Leander class comprised the cruisers *Leander, Orion, Achilles, Neptune* and *Ajax*. The Modified Leander class comprised the cruisers *Amphion, Apollo* and *Phaeton*. All three of the latter class were eventually transferred to the RAN and renamed *Perth, Hobart* and *Sydney* respectively.

   The principal difference between the two classes was in the layout of the machinery. The Leander class had six boilers arranged in three adjoining boiler rooms, the boiler uptakes being trunked into one large funnel. The Modified Leander class had four individually larger boilers arranged in two widely separated boiler rooms, thus requiring two funnels.

2   Raven, A. & Roberts, J., *British Cruisers of World War Two*, Arms and Armour Press, London, 1980, p. 156.

3   ibid., p. 434.

4   The standard 6-inch shell fired by *Sydney* was a base fuzed semi-armour piercing type known as the Common Pointed Ballistic Capped (CPBC). For shore bombardment, a High Explosive (HE) type, fitted with a more sensitive nose fuze, was employed.

   True salvo firing was employed when firing 6-inch HE as it was believed that if both guns were fired simultaneously one shell could detonate the other; either by the turbulence created by the passage of the other shell or by one shell striking the other while in flight.

5   Raven and Roberts, op. cit., p. 150.

6   When at sea, if submarine or U-boat attack was considered probable, it was not uncommon to have the depth charges armed and preset, ready for instant use. Although this saved valuable time should a contact be made, it had the drawback of endangering the lives of survivors if the ship was torpedoed and sunk.

7   Flashbacks occurred when there was an insufficient supply of air for the combustion process, the flame exiting the combustion chamber in search of oxygen.

   When *Sydney* was struck on the forward funnel by a 6-inch (152-millimetre) shell during the Cape Spada action, the explosion caused all sprayers on the forward boilers to flash back approximately two feet.

8   Newton, R.N., *Practical Construction of Warships*, Longmans, London, 1941, p.195.

9   Information obtained from the wartime notebooks of former Able Seaman T. P. Fisher.

10   The 'WA/T' system was the internal broadcasting or amplifying system.

11   National Archives (ACT), MP 551/1.

   Sydney's construction plans are extensive and comprise several bundles. Included in these bundles are some early Admiralty publications pertaining to the specifications of the then proposed Leander class of cruiser. These publications appear to have been issued as a set, which is now incomplete.

12   National Archives (VIC), MP 1714/1, CAFO 2045 W/T-Enemy Reports and Distress Messages (14.11.1940).

13 National Archives (VIC), MP 138/1, 603/263/624.

14 *Admiralty Handbook of Wireless Telegraphy*, BR 230, Volume 2 Wireless Telegraphy Theory, HMSO, London, 1940.

15 National Archives (VIC), MP 1049/5, 2026/3/511.

16 National Archives (VIC) MP 1049/5, 2026/3/294.

17 National Archives (VIC), MP 1049/5, 2026/3/429.

Chapter 2   The search

1 Four different time zones can be encountered in *Sydney/Kormoran* related documents. The British Admiralty worked on Greenwich Mean Time (GMT). As a result, nearly all naval signals relating to the loss of *Sydney* employed GMT. This time was (and still is) known as 'Zulu' time, and can be identified by the letter Z after the time or time/date group.

Eastern Australia (Victoria, New South Wales, Queensland, the ACT) kept 'Kilo' time, which is ten hours later than GMT, or simply, GMT plus ten hours. 'Kilo' time is identified by the letter K after the time or time/date group.

Western Australia kept 'Hotel' time, which is GMT plus eight hours. 'Hotel' time is identified by the letter H.

Kormoran, operating in the waters to the west of Western Australia, kept 'Golf' time, which is GMT plus seven hours.

Unless otherwise denoted, all times quoted in this chapter have been converted to Western Australian ('Hotel') time.

2 National Archives (VIC), MP 1587/1, 165P.

'HMAS SYDNEY 0426 11' referred to the signal sent at 1226 (0426Z) on 11 November, amending *Sydney*'s ETA.

3 Winter, Barbara, *HMAS SYDNEY*, Boolarong Publications, Brisbane, 1991 (reprint), p. 144.

4 National Archives (VIC), MP 1049/5, 2026/3/457.

5 National Archives (VIC), MP 1587/1, 164M.

6 Although many of the signals relating to the search for *Sydney* name the Naval Board as the addressee or the originator, most of these signals were sent to, or emanated from, Navy Office in Melbourne. Navy Office was the operational and administrative headquarters of the RAN. Although the Naval Board was accommodated within the office, day-to-day matters were generally handled by the staff officers at Navy Office.

The Naval Board was 'charged with the control and administration of all matters relating to the Naval Forces, upon the policy directed by the Minister, and [the Naval Board] shall have executive command of the Naval Forces'. (Hyslop, Robert, *Aye Aye, Minister*, AGPS, Canberra, 1990)

Naval operations, such as *Sydney*'s deployment, were the responsibility of the Chief of Naval Staff, and the administration and operation of naval vessels was the responsibility of the Rear Admiral Commanding the Australian Squadron.

In November 1941, the following members constituted the Australian Commonwealth Naval Board:

President – The Minister for the Navy, Norman Makin.

First Naval Member – Chief of Naval Staff, Vice-Admiral Sir Guy Royle, RN.

Second Naval Member – Commodore J.W. Durnford, RN.

Third Naval Member – Engineer Rear-Admiral P.E. McNeil, RAN.

Finance and Civil Member – Raymond Anthony.

Business Member – Hugh Brain.

Secretary to the Department of Navy (added 1940) – Alfred Nankervis.

The Secretary to the Naval Board was Honorary Paymaster Commander George Macandie, RAN.

7   In 1995 Group Captain C.A. Bourne (RAAF retired) made a statutory declaration that on the morning of Sunday 23 November he took part in a search to seaward for *Sydney*. Their orders were to search the normal southbound shipping lane as far as Latitude 34° 50' South then step aside 40 nautical miles westward and return on a parallel track to the datum on Rottnest Island. Although there is no record of this search in the SWACH or the Central War Room logbooks, an account of the search operations prepared by Third Officer Westhoven, WRANS, in 1945 for Lieutenant-Commander Rycroft, SO (I) Fremantle, mentions an air search from Rottnest on 23 November 1941.

8   SWACH, also known as ACH Fremantle, was a joint RAN/RAAF headquarters, responsible for the waters south-west of the Australia Station. Its role was to permit close co-operation between naval and air forces for trade defence and offensive action against enemy sea borne forces.

9   National Archives (WA), K 809/1, South Western Area Combined Headquarters logbook 2 July 1941-2 May 1942.

SWACH logbook entries relating to the search for *Sydney* start with 'Hotel' time but from 28 November are entered in 'Zulu' time.

10 Perth Radio was the civilian AWA radio station, located in the Perth suburb of Applecross. On the outbreak of war this station came under the control of the Royal Australian Navy and like all similar stations was provided with a direct link to the nearest Naval Intelligence, Coding and Operational centre. The principal RAN W/T station was HMAS *Harman*. Located in Canberra, it came into operation in December 1939. In February 1941 a second station (Naval W/T Station Coonawarra) was established at Darwin.

11 National Archives (VIC), MP 1587/1, 165P.

12 Catalina A24-11 departed from Port Moresby at dawn on 25 November and flew to Fremantle via Darwin. Catalina A24-14 was enroute from Rathmines to Port Moresby via Townsville when it received a signal diverting it to Fremantle via Darwin.

13 The seventh Hudson was deployed to Geraldton on the afternoon of 24 November.

14 National Archives (ACT), 1969/100/5, 105/30/AIR.

The search for *Sydney* highlighted many operational problems, not the least being the lack of suitable long-range patrol aircraft in Western Australia. The main difficulty, however, was inadequate communications. Once the search aircraft were deployed to Carnarvon, they were virtually isolated from the search co-ordinators at SWACH. Telephone communication between Geraldton and Carnarvon was so poor that all orders and signals had to be relayed through Pearce, which was in W/T contact with Carnarvon. Even this arrangement was not entirely satisfactory as a portable aircraft W/T set had to used at Carnarvon to maintain the link.

Another problem was the inadequate stock of 90 octane petrol at Carnarvon and Geraldton for protracted operations. As it was, the existing stocks, stored in 44-gallon drums, was found to be affected by condensation, much of the engine trouble being traced to water in the petrol.

15 National Archives (VIC), MP 1185/8, 2026/3/452.

16 The genesis for this belief may have been the intelligence summaries provided by the Combined Operational Intelligence Centre in Melbourne. The Australia Station Intelligence Summary (ASIS) for 19 February 1941 noted that four Vichy French submarines had entered the Indian Ocean the previous month. Two were to be based on Madagascar and the remaining two would be based in Indo-China. The COIC weekly summary for the week ending 22 September noted that four Vichy merchant ships had departed Saigon on 7 September. Three of these vessels, escorted by a sloop and a submarine, passed through the Sunda Strait unchallenged on 12 September, believed to be bound for Madagascar.

The weekly summary for 29 September reported that four Vichy merchant ships, escorted by the same sloop and submarine, would leave Madagascar on 10 October, presumably bound for Saigon via the Sunda Strait. The C-IN-C East Indies issued orders for the interception of this convoy.

The same weekly summary also noted that the Free French cruiser *Le Triomphant* and the sloop *Chevreuil* would leave Tahiti on 9 October escorting the sloop *Cap Des Palmes*, which was to sail to Singapore for conversion to an Armed Merchant Cruiser. The critical piece of intelligence was included in the weekly summary for the week ending 3 November 1941. Vichy French submarines based on Madagascar (also presumably engaged in escorting Vichy merchant ships through the Sunda Strait) had been given orders to fire on Free French warships on sight.

17 Frame, T., *HMAS SYDNEY*, Hodder & Stoughton, Sydney, 1993, p. 5.

18 National Archives (VIC), MP 1074/4, Inward Signals 24/11/1941.

19 National Archives (VIC), MP 1587/1, 165P.

20 Winter, op. cit., p. 155.

21 National Archives (WA), K 809/1.

22 ibid.

23 The 1845 entry in the SWACH log records the Catalina landing at Port Hedland,

apparently due to failing light. It is not clear when the Catalina landed at Geraldton for refuelling before operations on 27 November.

24 ACH Fremantle, Report of Operations 24th Nov. to 29th Nov. 1941. Copy held by the Western Australian Maritime Museum.

25 This was Detmers's boat and it had not been sighted by the lookouts on *Centaur*. The occupants of the boat had seen the vessel just on nightfall and although Detmers had been hoping to be rescued by a neutral vessel, the shortage of food and water prompted him to give up this notion and seek rescue. He therefore fired two red flares to attract the attention of the vessel and it was these two flares which led *Centaur* to the boat's location.

Because of his fear of having his ship seized by the Germans, Captain Dark had permitted only the more seriously ill or wounded to be taken aboard (nine Germans and one Chinese). The rest were given food and drink but were forced to remain in the boat.

26 Detmers, T.A., *The Raider Kormoran*, Tandem Books, London, 1975 (reprint), p. 197.

27 Report by Captain J.S.Airey. Copy held by the Western Australian Maritime Museum.

28 Extract from No.4 SFTS log. Copy held by the Western Australian Maritime Museum.

29 National Archives (WA), K997, 1/15/2.

30 National Archives (VIC), MP 1587/1, 164M.

31 Flying Officer Bourne (later Group Captain) in one of the Hudsons, saw a large warship which he could not positively identify in heavy sea mist. He and his fellow crew members had no idea that the *Tromp* was in the search area and subsequently reported that they had sighted an unidentified warship which was similar in appearance to a Japanese Mogami class cruiser.

32 National Archives (WA), K 809/1.

33 This vessel was later confirmed to be *Sunetta*. Its identification letters were actually PHUW.

34 National Archives (VIC), MP 1049/5, 2026/3/457.

Farquhar-Smith reported that one Catalina had reported sighting a patch of oil in position 23° 50' South 110° 09' East and that the aircraft had passed the information to *Wyrallah*.

Wyrallah, however, failed to locate the patch and considered that the aircrew of the Catalina may have mistaken a cloud shadow for oil.

The wording of the SWACH entry indicates that oil was sighted five miles south-east of the action position. Several action positions were identified in the days before the oil was sighted, but the accepted action positions appear to be those given by Detmers and Meyer.

These were 26° 32' South 111° East and 27° South 111° East respectively. Neither could be described as being remotely close to the position of the oil identified in the DNOWA report. This raises the possibility that two patches of oil were sighted: one in the vicinity of 23° 50' South 110° 09' South and the other much further south and in the vicinity of the action position.

35 National Archives (WA), K 809/1.
36 Vessel PDJR was established as being *Sunetta*. It is not clear if the aircrew had misread the vessel's identification letters or the wrong ones had been signalled.

   A summary of *Sunetta's* movements during the search prepared by the ship's master (contained in MP 1049/5, 2026/3/457), indicates that W/T messages were initially addressed to the ship using its international identification letters; a later message used its secret code letters. It is possible, that in a similar breach of security, *Sunetta* identified itself with its secret letters.
37 National Archives (WA), K 809/1.
38 National Archives (VIC), MP 1587/1, 165P.

Chapter 3   An open wound

1 During the Second World War Lieutenant-Commander George Hermon Gill, served within the Naval Intelligence Division as Publicity Censorship Liaison Officer. In November 1945, after a short period as Naval Historical Records Officer, he was demobilized and contracted to write the official history of the Royal Australian Navy's role in the war. The first volume, *Royal Australian Navy 1939-1942* was published in 1957. The second volume, *Royal Australian Navy 1942-1945* was published in 1968.
2 Montgomery, M., *Who Sank the Sydney?* Cassell, Melbourne, 1981.
3 National Archives (VIC), MP 1587/1, 164L.
   Most reports of *Aquitania's* discovery indicate that only one raft was found. The survivors recovered by *Aquitania* actually had two. One was a large inflatable rubber dinghy in which the twenty-six survivors were accommodated, while the other was a smaller inflatable dinghy, which was yellow in colour.
4 National Archives (VIC), MP 1185/8, 2026/3/452.
5 National Archives (VIC), MP 1587/1, 165P
6 The Naval Board's signal to the Admiralty was sent at 1634Z on 25 November. But it bore an incorrect Time Of Origin date; this being 1634Z/24. A follow up signal at 1909Z/25 compounded the error by referring to the earlier signal by this incorrect TOO date. That the 1634Z signal was transmitted at 1634Z on 25 November is confirmed by the contents of the signal. It contained a reference to six aircraft based at Geraldton carrying out a search on 26 November. The orders for this search were not issued until PM 25 November.
7 National Archives (ACT), A9240, Set 2 Vol 4. Background notes to War Cabinet Minute No. 1521.
8 National Archives (VIC), MP 1587/1, 165P.
9 Although it wasn't understood at the time, *Kormoran* was abandoned in two stages. At approximately 1930, Detmers, realizing his ship could not be saved, ordered

Kormoran to be abandoned then scuttled. Unfortunately, there was a shortage of readily usable boats. Of the four ship's boats stowed on the superstructure, one of the port boats had been destroyed in the action, and the two starboard boats could not be reached because of fire. This left one remaining port boat.

In addition to this boat, however, there were two boats stowed on the upper deck, two large lifeboats stowed in No.1 Hold, and an 11-ton minelayer stowed in No.6 Hold. As there was no power for the electric winches the minelayer could not be salved, and it would take several hours for the boats in No.1 hold to be extracted using block and tackle.

Therefore, as many men as possible were got off the ship in the three usable boats and a number of rubber dinghies and small metal floats. This group appears to have abandoned ship between 2000 and 2100. The second group abandoned ship once the two remaining boats were hauled from No.1 Hold and pushed overboard. They appear to have left the ship between 0030 and 0100.

10 National Archives (VIC), MP 1587/1, 165P.

11 National Archives (WA), K997/8, 1/15/2.

Ramage's report of the action was forwarded to the Admiralty at 0300K(1700Z/27) on 28/11. A subsequent reply from the Admiralty (2227Z/28) said that the information forwarded appeared to be correct and that the raider was probably No.41 or Raider 'G'.

12 National Archives (WA), K997/8, 1/15/2.

13 Despite Captain Dark's cautious attitude, he permitted the sick or wounded survivors to board *Centaur* on the night of 26 November.

14 There is an element of doubt about when Rycroft boarded *Centaur*. In his post-war account, Detmers claimed that he was questioned the following morning. The signal containing Detmers's statements, however, carries a time/date of 1315Z/27, indicating it was sent or received at 2115H on 27 November.

15 National Archives (VIC), MP 1587/1, 165P.

16 National Archives (WA), K997, 1/15/2.

17 Captain Farncomb appears to have been given the task of interrogating the *Aquitania* prisoners while *Canberra* was undergoing a refit.

18 National Archives (VIC), MP 1587/1, 164M.

19 This claim that the prisoners had been instructed to give incorrect answers would appear to refer to Rycroft's experiences with the prisoners aboard *Centaur*. In which case, he was probably correct. Most of the prisoners embarked in *Centaur* had been quartered in the Carnarvon gaol courtyard where Bretschneider had been active. It is quite possible that this officer issued such instructions on the morning of 26 November.

20 National Archives (VIC), MP 1587/1, 164M.

Of the four Chinese, three survived. One appears to have been killed during the action or drowned while abandoning ship. Two were accommodated in the lifeboat recovered by *Yandra*, and the fourth was accommodated in Detmers's boat.

The nominal roll of *Kormoran* survivors only lists the two Chinese recovered by *Yandra*.

21 National Archives (ACT), A9240, Set 2 Vol. 4.

22 *Kulmerland* rendezvoused with *Kormoran* on 16 October and, after supplying the raider with fuel and supplies, embarked *Kormoran*'s prisoners. *Kulmerland* departed on 26 October, rendezvoused with the blockade runner *Spreewald* south of Tahiti on 24 November to transfer the prisoners for passage to Europe, then sailed for Kobe in Japan, arriving there on 16 December.

23 Winter, op. cit., p.188.

24 ibid., p.175.

25 On 30 November, Gerhard Keller, who was Hrich's assistant, admitted to Farncomb that he had taken a film of the action. As for the fate of the film, Keller claimed he 'gave [it] to an officer for despatch to Germany'.

26 Summerrell, Richard, *The Sinking of HMAS Sydney*, A Guide to Commonwealth Government Records, National Archives, Canberra, 1997, p.87.

27 An exception was Lensch. Although in the *Trocas* group, Lensch appears to have been transferred to Harvey ahead of his group for admission to the camp hospital. He was interrogated at Harvey on 8 December.

28 Winter, op. cit., p.187.

29 National Archives (ACT), A9240, Set 2 Vol. 4.

30 National Archives (WA), K809/1.

The message quoted is that which was recorded by Geraldton. The message recorded in the SWACH logbook is as follows:

'Calling Darwin or technical telegraph operator from sea. Sydney calling send carrier men on board calling Frazer D/F Darwin cannot detect you Singapore call Darwin. This MSS Sydney calling message received frequency satisfactory will put through one more.'

31 National Archives (VIC), MP 1587/1, 164M.

32 National Archives (WA), K997/8, 1/15/2.

33 The attack on Pearl Harbor was launched on the morning of 7 December, but as the International Date Line lay between Australia and the Hawaiian Islands, it was 8 December when Australia learned of the attack.

34 National Archives (WA), K997/8, 1/15/2.

35 National Archives (VIC), MP 1049/5, 2026/19/6.

36 It is known that on his return to Melbourne, Dechaineux was given responsibility for following up the investigation into the reasons why *Aquitania* failed to report by W/T that it had picked up enemy survivors. Although Dechaineux completed his report on this matter on 9 December, he was still dealing with subsequent correspondence on 22 December.

37 National Archives (VIC), MP 1185/8, 2026/19/6. See also Summerrell, op.cit., p.26.

38 ADM 234/342 No.13, *Actions with Enemy Disguised Raiders 1940–1941*.

39 National Archives (ACT), A5954, 813/2.

40 National Archives (VIC), MP 1587/1, 164M.

 The cover note for the milk analysis report was prepared and signed by Rycroft and forwarded to Long's office in either January or February 1942. The annotation 'Resupply of Korman [*sic*] by Japanese Sub Date' appears to have been added by someone at a later date. This reference to a Japanese submarine, however, should be treated with caution. Staff at the National Archives believe that annotations on both reports are not part of the original documents. On 30 July 1993 a warning was issued, stating that 'the annotations are corruption's of the original, added to the documents by an unauthorized person'.

41 National Archives (VIC), MP 1587/1, 165K.

42 Miraculously, one of these souvenired milk bottles has survived and can be viewed in the Goldfield's War Museum in Boulder, Western Australia. Another *Kormoran* relic, a set of keys handed to a *Koolinda* crewmember by one of the survivors, is held by the Army Museum of Western Australia.

43 National Archives (VIC), MP 1587/1, 165P.

44 National Archives (VIC), B 1124 & B 1129, 2026/3/866.

45 National Archives (VIC), MP 1587/1, 165K.

46 Frame, op. cit., p.159.

47 National Archives (VIC), MP 1587/1, 165K.

48 National Archives (VIC), MP 1587/1, 165P.

Chapter 4 The tonnage war

1 Frame, T., 1993, op. cit., pp. 30–4.

2 Lenton, H.T., *British Cruisers*, Macdonald & Co. Ltd., London, 1973.

3 Churchill, Winston, *The Second World War*, Vol.1, Reprint Society Ltd., London, 1950, p. 320.

4 Roskill, S.W., *The War At Sea, 1939–45, Vol.1*, HMSO, London, 1954, p. 270.

5 Hardy, A.C., *Everyman's History of the Sea War*, Vol.1, Nicholson and Watson, London, 1948, p. 133.

6 Churchill, op. cit., p. 342.

7 Hardy, op. cit., p. 133

8 Churchill, Winston, *The Second World War*, Vol.2, Reprint Society Ltd., London, 1951, p. 445.

9 ibid., p. 564.

10 Winton, John, *Convoy*, Michael Joseph, London, 1983, p. 187.

11 Chalmers, W.S., *Max Horton and the Western Approaches*, Hodder and Stoughton, London, 1954, p. 276.

12 *The 1931 International Code of Signals, Volume 1*, HMSO, London, 1941 (reprint).

13 Campbell, Gordon, *My Mystery Ships*, Hodder and Stoughton, London, 1937 (reprint).

14 Naval Historical Society of Australia, *Naval Historical Review, Vol.20, No.2, 1999*, p.25.
15 Roskill, op. cit., p.549.
16 Brice, Martin, *Axis Blockade Runners of World War II*, Batsford Ltd., London, 1981, p. 96.
17 ibid., p. 67.
18 Brice, Martin, *Capture of Hannover, War Monthly*, Vol.10, No.1, War Monthly Publications, London, 1982, pp. 42–7.
19 Gill, G.H., *The Royal Australian Navy 1939–42*, AWM, Canberra, 1957, pp.118-24.
20 National Archives (VIC), MP 1714/1, Admiralty Fleet Order, Volume 1941, Part II— Confidential.
21 Muggenthaler, A.K., *German Raiders of World War Two*, Robert Hale, London, 1978.
22 Roskill, op. cit., p. 280.
23 Winter, op. cit., p. 40.
24 Poolman, Kenneth, *Armed Merchant Cruisers*, Leo Cooper, London, 1985, pp. 159–63.
25 Brennecke, J.H., *Ghost Cruiser H.K.33*, Futura Publications, London, 1974 (reprint).
26 The Weekly Intelligence Report was issued by the Naval Intelligence Division, Naval Staff, Admiralty. It was a secret publication distributed to British Officers and Officials. The report was to be destroyed upon receipt of the following issue though commanding officers of warships were permitted to retain copies for reference purposes. Cruisers such as *Sydney* were issued with three copies of each WIR.
27 Detmers was promoted to Fregattenkapitän on 1 April 1941.
28 Detmers, op. cit., p.13.
29 While an angle of 35° abaft the beam has been quoted, there is also evidence to suggest that the torpedo tubes were angled 135° from the bow, or 45° abaft the beam.
30 Many accounts state that *Kormoran*'s torpedo tubes were of 53-centimetre (21-inch) diameter, but there is evidence to suggest that this is incorrect. In his post-war account, Detmers indicated that *Kormoran*'s torpedo tubes had been 'taken from old torpedo boats which had seen action at the battle of Jutland'. Sources indicate that German First World War torpedo boats were equipped with 45-centimetre or 50-centimetre torpedo tubes.

    Further evidence that *Kormoran* was not fitted with 53-centimetre tubes can be found in *HMAS SYDNEY, Fact, Fantasy and Fraud*. Before sailing, *Kormoran* was supplied with twenty type G-7E and eight type G-7A 53-centimetre torpedoes for re-supplying Uboats in the Atlantic. Winter records on page 35 that Detmers wrote in the War Diary: '… I now have the submarine equipment on board as ballast for a long time, for the torpedoes and ammunition unfortunately do not fit my armament.'

    Information supplied to the author by Mr J. Greter, former Torpedo Officer of *Kormoran*, suggests that the torpedoes were of the type G-7 50-centimetre variant.

    The type G-7 50-centimetre torpedo was developed during the First World War. Between the wars the Germans developed a larger 53-centimetre model.
31 National Archives (VIC), MP 1587, 164N.
32 Brice, op. cit., p. 126.
33 National Archives (VIC), MP 1714/1.

34 Howe, Leslie, *The Merchant Service Today*, Oxford University Press, London, 1941, p. 146.

35 National Archives (VIC), MP 1582/7.

36 ADM 234/324, CB 3081(5), Battle Summary No.13, Actions with Enemy Disguised Raiders 1940–1941.

37 Payne, Alan, *HMAS Canberra*, The Naval Historical Society of Australia, Sydney, 1973, pp. 46–7.

38 Montgomery, op. cit., p. 96.

39 National Archives (VIC), MP 1714/1.

40 Poolman, op. cit., pp. 182–3.

41 These inconsistencies were noted in the action summary contained in Battle Summary No.13, Actions With Enemy Disguised Raiders 1940–1941.

    The German account of the action can be found in Brennecke, op. cit., p. 187.

42 Haines, Gregory, *Cruiser at War*, Ian Allan Ltd., London, 1978, pp. 56–7.

43 Winton, John, *Ultra at Sea*, Leo Cooper, London, 1988, pp. 22–4.

44 Gannon, Michael, *Operation Drumbeat*, Harper & Row, New York, 1990, p. 151.

45 At this time the Admiralty was still trying to identify each individual raider. As new raiders were identified they were listed in alphabetical order. Thus, the first raider identified was designated Raider 'A', the second, Raider 'B', and so on. The following are the correct names and designations of the seven raiders thus far mentioned.

    HSK 1 (*Orion*), or Ship No.36; designated Raider 'A' by the Admiralty.

    HSK 7 (*Komet*), or Ship No.45; designated Raider 'B' by the Admiralty.

    HSK 2 (*Atlantis*), or Ship No.16; designated Raider 'C' by the Admiralty.

    HSK 3 (*Widder*), or Ship No.21; designated Raider 'D' by the Admiralty.

    HSK 4 (*Thor*), or Ship No.10; designated Raider 'E' by the Admiralty.

    HSK 5 (*Pinguin*), or Ship No.33; designated Raider 'F' by the Admiralty.

    HSK 8 (*Kormoran*), or Ship No.41; designated Raider 'G' by the Admiralty.

    The letters HSK stood for *Handelsschutzkreuzer* (trade protection cruiser) or *Handelsstorkreuzer* (cruiser for harassing merchant ships).

46 National Archives (VIC), MP 1580, Weekly Intelligence Reports 1940–1945.

47 Winter, Barbara, *The Intrigue Master, Commander Long and Naval Intelligence in Australia, 1913–1945*, Boolarong Press, Brisbane, 1995.

48 National Archives (VIC), MP 1587/1, 775W/1.

49 WS 27 indicated that the reports of aircraft over Geraldton and Pearce had been investigated and it was considered extremely doubtful that the lights observed were from an aircraft.

50 National Archives (VIC), MP 1714/1, CAFO 1941.

    The instructions reproduced here formed Part A of CAFO 2302, and appear to be identical to those issued on 4 November; with the exception of the final sentence which had been amended.

    Part B of CAFO 2302 contained the procedure on boarding. It is understood that these instructions had been issued earlier in the year as CAFO 1069.

51 Beesly, Patrick, *Very Special Intelligence*, Sphere Books, London, 1978 (reprint), p.131.
52 Rogge, Bernhard, *Under Ten Flags*, Weidenfeld and Nicholson, London, 1957, p.183.
53 Western Australian Maritime Museum, MA 630/81/18.
54 National Archives (VIC), MP 1587/1/0, 1660.

Chapter 5   The interception

1   Gill, op. cit., p. 457.
2   Another prize officer, Diebisch, stated that his job was to transport wounded and to see that there was no panic.
3   As Bunjes was in the same lifeboat as von Gösseln, it is conceivable that he surrendered information supplied to him by the battle watch officer.
4   A similar 'after action report' was compiled by the senior surviving officer from *Perth*. On 1 October 1945, Lieutenant-Commander J.A. Harper, RN, following his release from a Japanese POW camp, submitted a detailed report on the loss of HMAS *Perth* to the ACNB. Harper finished his report in this way: 'The above report is compiled from a few brief notes made by me six months after the action and which I was able to retain throughout my imprisonment. Impressions of such an action are naturally very confused, and although I was able to discuss it with some officers and men during the ensuing five weeks, I was in no position then to commit any facts to paper. I was then separated from all but four other officers, and it was not until five months later that I was able to note down the few facts I could still remember'.
5   National Archives (VIC), MP 1587/1, 164N.
6   These ships, and the date of their sinking or capture, are as follows:

Antonis	sunk	6 January 1941
British Union	sunk	18 January 1941
Afric Star	sunk	29 January 1941
Eurylochus	sunk	29 January 1941
Agnita	sunk	22 March 1941
Canadolite	captured	25 March 1941
Craftsman	sunk	9 April 1941
Nicolaos D.L.	sunk	12 April 1941
Velebit	sunk	26 June 1941
Mareeba	sunk	26 June 1941
Stamatios G. Embiricos	sunk	24 September 1941

7   National Archives (VIC), MP 1587/1, 164M.
    To avoid excessive referencing, unless otherwise noted, all prisoners quotes or statements have been sourced from file 164M.
8   Montgomery was the first author to seriously pursue the Japanese submarine theory. Although his work *Who Sank the Sydney?* has proven popular, some of the evidence

used to support his argument could be regarded as suspect. For a critical analysis of Montgomery's claims of Japanese involvement, see Frame, pp. 158–77.

9   *Daily Telegraph*, 4 December 1941.

10 National Archives (VIC), MP 1587/1, 164N.

11 Some claim that Detmers and Ahlbach should have understood what 'NNJ' meant, and as a result, should have been able to remember the signal. Yet it is interesting that Kapitänleutnant Schneidewind, in command of the German minelayer *Doggerbank*, did not know how to reply to a 'NNJ' signal when challenged by HMS *Durban* on 11 March 1942.

12 On its previous escort mission to the Sunda Strait in early October, *Sydney* had returned to Fremantle at 17-18 knots. As there is no record of any signals ordering Burnett to return to Fremantle earlier than his amended ETA of 20 November, it is assumed that *Sydney* was making a similar speed on 19 November.

13 Detmers, op. cit., p. 180.

14 Von Gösseln, in his post-war account of the sinking of *Sydney* (*Readers Digest Illustrated History of World War II*. pp. 120–1), claimed they replied from Batavia to Lourenço Marques. Heinfried Ahl, *Kormoran*'s former flying officer (observer), however, stated that they signalled Fremantle to Batavia (*Australian Naval Historical Review*, December 1979).

15 Some have theorized that Detmers was in possession of *Straat Malakka*'s secret call sign. Such a claim is difficult to either prove or disprove, but the theory overlooks the fact that Detmers wanted to avoid combat. If Detmers had been in possession of the secret call sign, it is more likely that he would have used it to avoid being drawn into battle.

16 These theories range from Detmers signalling that he had a medical emergency, to the hoisting of a white flag.

17 Winter, 1991, op. cit., p. 61.

18 In order to be historically correct, all distances, measurements, tonnages and weapons calibres are given as recorded in the original documents. Wherever practicable, distances between *Sydney* and *Kormoran* will be standardized to metres, as this is the unit of measurement recorded in the interrogation statements.

19 Montgomery, op. cit., p. 112.

20 Detmers initially gave a battle position of 26° 32' South 111° East, but his post-war account gives a position of 26° 34' South 111° East.

21 Information supplied to the author by journalist David Kennedy.
See also, Joint Standing Committee on Foreign Affairs, Defence and Trade, *Submissions, Inquiry into the Circumstances of the Sinking of HMAS SYDNEY*, The Parliament of the Commonwealth of Australia, Canberra, 1998. Vol. 5, p. 961 and ibid, Vol. 18, p. 4322.

22 If Perth had received Detmers's Q signal, it would be logical to assume that a number of other stations, on land and at sea, would have heard the signal and either acknowledged or repeated it. Again, there is no evidence of this occurring.

23 Winter, Barbara. Paper presented at the HMAS *Sydney* Forum, Western Australian Maritime Museum, 21–23 November 1991.

24 There are a number of slightly different translations now available in archives. What appears to be the original translation, dated 15/7, is given here. It can be found in MP 1587/1, 165K.

A second decrypt and translation was apparently performed by Australian Military Intelligence in 1947, and forwarded to the DNI on 13 October 1947. A copy of this translation can be found in MP 1587/1, 164M.

In 1992, the Defence Signals Directorate prepared another decrypt and translation. This translation can be found in National Archives (VIC), Fleet Radio Unit, Melbourne (FRUMEL), B5823. Also contained in this file is what appears to be the cover page of the original decrypt and translation. This cover page is dated 20 July 1945.

25 The transcript prepared by the Defence Signals Directorate states, for example, that at 1715G *Sydney* 'cuts across starboard at range of 8 hm [800 metres]'. Another translation gives the distance as 9 hm (900 metres). This has led to the belief that the 90 hm (9,000 metres) figure is incorrect.

A range of 800 or 900 metres, however, is not consistent with the ranges given in Detmers's post-war account. In this, he indicates that *Sydney* was still beyond 3,000 metres before the request for the 'secret call', this being about 1725G (1825H).

Detmers also indicated in his post-war account that 3,000 metres was about the maximum effective range of his small calibre weapons, and that he wanted the cruiser to come as close as possible for these to be more effective.

Clearly, if the 800 or 900 metres figure is correct, Detmers would have opened fire at 1715G. As fire was opened at 1730G when the range was 1,300 metres (1,000 metres according to the post-war account), it would appear that the 8 hm and 9 hm figures are not correct. Therefore, *Sydney* must have been 9,000 metres (90 hm) away at 1715G.

26 It appears that Detmers did manage to get a copy of his report to Germany. In December 1943 the German Naval Command prepared an evaluation of the voyage of 'Ship 41'. The evaluation noted that the details of the raider's final operation had become available through the ship's doctor. Habben, it was noted, had recently returned home on a POW exchange and upon arrival in Germany had made a detailed report on the raider's loss.

The details of the report presented by Habben are almost identical to those found in Detmers's confiscated action report. It is not clear if Habben managed to smuggle out a copy of Detmers's report, or whether he had been forced to memorize it. Minor differences in detail suggest it may have been the latter.

27 Montgomery claimed that *Sydney* could not have closed from 9,000 metres to 1,300 metres in the specified time. This is incorrect. Given that *Kormoran*, steaming at 14 knots, would have travelled approximately 3.5 nautical miles between 1815 and 1830, *Sydney* only needed to cover an estimated 6.02 nautical miles in order to close *Kormoran*. The speed required to steam this distance in fifteen minutes equates to

24.08 knots. Given there was still a gap of some 1,300 yards between *Sydney* and *Kormoran* at 1830, *Sydney* could have covered the required distance at an average speed of less than 24.08 knots.

28 Detmers, op. cit., p.183.

29 Two books in common use at the time were Talbot-Booth's *What Ship is That?* and *Lloyd's Register*. While *What Ship is That?* provided basic information such as tonnage, dimensions and speed, it also gave each vessel's silhouette (where possible). *Lloyd's Register* did not give a silhouette, but gave more detailed information on each vessel.

30 It is known that *Sydney* carried sextant rangefinders, as a 1938 report on the ship's fighting efficiency noted that these instruments were supplied to each of the 6-inch turrets.

31 Western Australian Maritime Museum, MA 630.

32 Correspondence with Mr T. Fisher and Mr A. Templeton, both former *Sydney* crew members and both present at Divisions on 5 October. Although their recollections of what Burnett said differ, the statements of both men indicate that Burnett was aware of the possible presence of a raider in the area.

33 National Archives (VIC), MP 1049/5, 2021/5/596.

34 *Fleet Air Arm*, HMSO, London, 1943, p. 40.

35 ibid. p. 43.

36 *Australian Naval Historical Review*, December, 1979.

37 Poniewierski (Winter), Barbara. Letter to Western Australian Maritime Museum, dated 30 June 1997.

38 It was known that supply ships also acted as prison ships for seamen captured by the raiders. As the prisoners were normally accommodated in empty holds, if fire was to be directed at a suspected supply ship it was considered desirable to aim at the vessel's upper works in order to avoid casualties among the prisoners.

39 Although *Sydney* had emergency aerials, it is not known if these would have been rigged before the action. If not, there may have been a considerable delay before these could be rigged and an action report transmitted.

40 The Bass Strait field claimed *Cambridge* on 7 November and *City of Rayville* on 8 November, both vessels being sunk. On 5 December *Nimbin* was sunk off the New South Wales coast, while the fourth victim, *Hertford*, was severely damaged by a mine in the Spencer Gulf on 7 December 1940.

41 This scenario would appear to be supported by the statements made by one of the Chinese survivors, who claimed that *Sydney* elevated its guns during the exchange of signals.

Joint Standing Committee on Foreign Affairs, Defence and Trade, 1998, op. cit., Vol. 15, p. 3590.

42 National Archives (NSW), SP 551/1, Bundle 528.

The Royal Navy adopted a system whereby the whole, or only a portion, of the ship's armament was manned and ready for instant action. This system provided for four degrees of readiness. The First Degree of Readiness required all hands to close up at their action quarters. This was known as action stations. The Second Degree of Readiness was known as action stations relaxed. This required all hands to remain closed up at their action quarters but permitted a small proportion from each quarter to fall out for meals or relaxation. The Third Degree of Readiness was known as defence stations. This entailed one watch or a part of a watch remaining closed up at their action quarters. The proportion of the ship's armament actually manned would depend on the nature and the degree of threat. The Fourth Degree of Readiness was known as cruising stations. This entailed a part, or proportion, of a watch remaining closed up their action quarters. Normal duties would be carried out by the men not closed up.

43 Ross, W.H., *Stormy Petrel*, Pattersons Printing Press, Perth, 1943, p. 125.

44 Brooke, Geoffrey, *Alarm Starboard!*, Patrick Stephens, Cambridge, 1982, pp. 204–5.

45 1996 interview with Mr George Ramsay, who served as an Able Seaman in *Sydney*.

46 Ross, op. cit., p. 164.

47 Northcott, Maurice, HOOD, *Design and Construction*, Bivouac Books, London, 1975. Reports on the Boards of Inquiry into the loss of *Hood*.

48 Former *Kormoran* crew member Hermann Ortmann, when interviewed for the 1993 documentary *No Survivors* (Propero Productions and Storyteller Productions), said that one or two men could be seen wearing aprons; these he assumed were probably 'kitchen hands'.

49 A typical anti-scuttling party would have included specialists such as signalmen, W/T operators, engine room artificers, and stokers.

50 Captain Burnett took up the position of Assistant Chief of Naval Staff in 1939, permitting the previous appointee, Captain J.A. Collins, RAN, to assume command of *Sydney*. In May 1940 the title Assistant Chief of Naval Staff was changed to Deputy Chief of Naval Staff.

51 These warnings were in the form of Admiralty general messages, and were issued on the following dates: 16 December 1941, 14 March 1942, 11 June 1942 and 11 August 1942.

52 Public Record Office, London, ADM 1/12883.

Chapter 6   The action

1 National Archives (VIC), MP 1587/1, 164M.

Unless otherwise noted, all prisoners' statements and quotations are sourced from this file. All ranges will be given in metres as this was the unit of measurement most often used by the prisoners.

2 Support for such a hypothesis can be found in MP 1587/1, 164M. This file contains copies of the *Yandra* reports of 28 and 30 November 1941, as well as the notes of Bunjes's interrogation at Swanbourne on 1 December 1941. It also contains a report

titled 'SEA-BATTLE'. This is a four-page report of the action between *Kormoran* and *Sydney*, and although undated, bears Bunjes's name. This report is remarkably similar to Detmers's action report and contains information that was clearly not in Bunjes's possession before his interrogation on 1 December. The inclusion of details not given during his interrogation suggests that Bunjes was still gleaning information from other survivors (possibly Detmers himself), and modifying his view of the action, after 1 December.

3   British practice was to designate the turrets of a four turret warship 'A', 'B', 'X' and 'Y', but the German practice was to designate them 'A', 'B', 'C' and 'D'. The interrogation notes reveal that turrets were also identified by numerals.

4   National Archives (VIC), MP 1587/1, 165K.

5   National Archives (VIC), MP 1587/1, 165P.

6   The interrogation notes for von Gösseln indicate that *Sydney* was still firing at the end of the engagement. This is incorrect and would appear to be an error in translation.

7   Brinkman's statement implies that both torpedo tracks were visible to him. If they were, they were almost certainly also visible to *Sydney*.

8   This statement is a good example of how little most of *Kormoran*'s crew could see once they went to their battle stations. If the crew of the No.3 gun had been able to view *Sydney*'s approach, they would not have had their gun pointing in the wrong direction when the order came to decamouflage.

9   'Loaded below' probably referred to the fact that the 15-centimetre guns could be loaded while still camouflaged or that the ammunition came up from shell rooms below. Only the 2-centimetre guns were capable of being 'loaded below' before being raised hydraulically into the firing position.

10 National Archives (VIC), MP 1587/1, 164N.

11 According to Detmers (action report and post-war account), the 3-metre main rangefinder was withdrawn from view (for purposes of disguise) when the range decreased to 8,000 metres. Skeries was then forced to range *Sydney* with the auxiliary 1.35-metre rangefinders. Although very good instruments, these had to be supported manually by the user. As a result, Skeries may not have had complete confidence in the range figures produced.

12 Although Hildenbrand's claim that his gun was fired at a range of 1,100 metres does not fit in with this scenario, it is conceivable that 1,100 metres was the range employed by the No.5 gun in subsequent salvoes, remembering that he also claimed that they were instructed to aim for the waterline. If *Sydney* was approximately 1,200 metres away, shells fired at a range of 1,100 metres might have produced hits on the waterline, and shells fired at a range of 1,500 metres might have produced hits on the upper portion of the superstructure.

13 One of the more obvious errors in Detmers's post-war account was how he was able to recognize his opponent as a Perth class cruiser: 'It was one of the three Australian cruisers of the "Perth" class, the fellows I had seen in Sydney harbour when the cruiser *Koln* visited there in 1933.' Whether Detmers had confused the time and place

of his pre-war meeting with a Perth class cruiser is not clear, but it is certain that he did not see one in Sydney harbour in 1933. *Sydney* (ex-*Phaeton*) was not completed until September 1935. *Hobart* (ex-*Apollo*) followed in January 1936. *Perth* (ex-*Amphion*) was not completed until July 1936.

Another inconsistency in Detmers's post-war account, but one that is supported by his action report, is his claim that four seconds after the first shot was fired from the leading gun, the 'other three went into action'. The action report recorded: 'First salvo single shot short. Gun range 13. Second salvo. Third fourth fifth, up 400. About 4 seconds later scores hit on bridge and control position.'

One translation of the action report, prepared by Barbara Poniewierski in 1997, indicates that 'Third fourth fifth' represents Nos 3, 4 and 5 guns. In other words, the first salvo comprised a single gun (No.1 gun), and the second salvo the remaining three guns of the starboard battery (Nos 3, 4 and 5 guns). This interpretation finds support in the German Admiralty report prepared in December 1943, which states that the first salvo ('the first shot from the first gun') fell short, but 'the second, a salvo of three guns, hit the enemy's bridge and control tower'.

Clearly, Detmers believed only one gun fired in the first salvo, and the second salvo comprised three guns (Nos 3, 4 and 5). Whether Detmers was correct is open to debate. Skeries implied that two guns were used in the first salvo, and Kobelt said that the No.3 gun could not fire in the second salvo because it was facing the wrong way.

14 The 2-centimetre guns carried by *Kormoran* were of the Model c/30 variant. These guns were fed by twenty round magazines. The rate of fire was therefore dependent on how quickly the gun crew could change magazines. The nominal rate of fire for an average gun crew was 120 rounds per minute.

15 The 3.7-centimetre *Panzer Abwehr Kanone* (PAK) 36 was capable of penetrating 48 millimetres (just under 2 inches) of armour at 500 metres using standard high explosive shot. Penetration figures for ranges over 500 metres cannot be found, but performance over longer ranges is generally acknowledged as poor.

The lack of penetration was highlighted during the fighting around Arras in France in May1940 where many 3.7-centimetre PAK guns were abandoned by their disillusioned crews when they found their shells would not penetrate the armour of the British tanks. One disabled Matilda, stopped by mechanical failure, was found to have withstood 22 direct hits. Improvements in tank armour had, by 1940, made the 3.7-centimetre PAK obsolete. It is not surprising that Detmers had little trouble acquiring two guns for *Kormoran*.

16 Throughout its short career, *Kormoran* was noted as having a particularly heavy roll which, besides being unpleasant, was not conducive to good gunnery. On 16 December 1940, Detmers recorded in his log (*Kriegstagebuch*) that the ship 'rolls so heavily even in a slight sea that the use of the weaponry, especially the two guns in the hatches [Nos 3 & 4 guns], very quickly becomes impossible'. On the advice of his ex-merchant navy officers, Detmers decided to alter the trim of the ship by pumping

oil out of the double bottom and into the elevated storage tanks. On 22 December 1940, Detmers recorded that the change in trim had brought an improvement, and as more oil was used it was thought that the trim would become even more favourable. After *Kormoran* was re-supplied on 9 February 1941, Detmers recorded that '*Kormoran* fully loaded has again become the ROLLMORAN and thus with a heavy sea is not fully battle-worthy'.

On 16 October 1941, *Kormoran* rendezvoused with the supply ship *Kulmerland* and took on sufficient quantities of fuel-oil, ammunition, and foodstuffs to permit Detmers to record in the log that 'My sea endurance until 1 June 1942 seems to be ensured by this provisioning'.

Fully loaded again, it would seem certain that the trim of *Kormoran* would have been altered. As a result, the heavy roll would have returned. It would also be logical to assume that as an insufficient quantity of fuel would have been consumed before the raider's encounter with *Sydney*, there would have been little improvement in trim before Detmers was drawn into battle.

As Detmers had previously considered that his ship was not fully battle worthy in such a condition of trim, it would be logical to assume that the crews of No.3 and No.4 guns would have experienced considerable difficulty sighting and firing at *Sydney*.

17 Such a rate of fire appears acceptable when we compare it with an incident involving the raider *Thor*. On 10 April 1942, *Thor* intercepted and sank the British steamer *Kirkpool*. The raider fired fourteen salvoes in the space of five minutes.

18 Detmers also commented on this in his post-war account. He said that fire hoses had to be played onto the barrels of the over-heated guns to cool them down.

19 The only contemporary evidence of a torpedo having been launched before the first salvo was fired can be found in a poem written by prisoner Edmund Abel. It appears to have been written before the interrogations. Abel wrote:

> WE REPLY TO HIM IN HSK KORMORAN-LIKE MANNER.
> THE COVERS ARE OFF, THE GUNS ARE OUT READY FOR ACTION,
> ALREADY A TORPEDO IS SPLASHING THROUGH THE WATER,
> AND FROM THE GUNS THERE BREAKS THE MAD RHYTHM OF SALVOES.
> SHELL AFTER SHELL CRASHES, AND BRINGS MUCH DESTRUCTION.
>
> THE TORPEDO HAS FOUND ITS MARK.
> THE BOW LURCHES FORWARD.
> AND THEN THE SALVOES HIT THEIR MARK, SHOT AFTER SHOT.
> THE SYDNEY FIRES NO MORE. SHE HAS HAD ENOUGH OF THE FIGHT.

Some claim that Abel was describing the firing of an underwater torpedo before identity was declared, but it could also be argued that he was describing the firing of an above-water torpedo. The firing of the latter produced a large splash when the torpedo hit the water, whereas the firing of the former produced only bubbles.

Curiously, Edmund Abel was noted by the interrogating officers as being a 'torpedo mechanic'. If Abel served the below-water torpedo tubes, he would not have been in a position to witness the events he described. On the other hand, if he served the above-water torpedo tubes, given the angle of the below-water tubes, he would not have been in a position to witness a submerged firing.

20 Correspondence with former *Kormoran* Torpedo Officer Joachim Greter, March 1998.

21 The speed of 27 knots is based on the assumption that *Kormoran* was fitted with 50-centimetre torpedo-tubes; 27 knots was the maximum speed of the G-7 type 50-centimetre torpedo.

22 Gannon, Michael, *Operation Drumbeat*, Harper and Row, New York, 1990, p. 3.

23 ibid., p. 228.

24 Brennecke (1954), op. cit., p. 175.

25 *War Diary (KRIEGSTAGEBUCH) of the raider Kormoran-Schiff 41*. Translated by Barbara Winter. Copy held by the Western Australian Maritime Museum.

26 *Royal United Services Institute of Victoria News, Volume 2 Number 106*, article by Lieutenant A. Templeton, RANR (Retired).

27 It is possible that the turn to port was ordered without knowledge of 'A' and 'B' turrets having been knocked out. When *Sydney* went to action stations, the second in command (Commander E.W. Thruston, RN) should have gone to the lower steering position. This was done to avoid the possibility of the two senior officers becoming battle casualties at the same time, and was standard procedure.

   If command was passed to Thruston after *Sydney*'s bridge was destroyed, he may have ordered the turn to port not knowing the forward turrets had also been destroyed.

28 The sinking of *Afric Star* on 29 January 1941 revealed that *Kormoran*'s gunnery department was not as efficient as Detmers would have liked. *Kormoran* opened fire at a range of 8,700 metres, reducing to 7,200 metres. Of the sixty shells fired, only four hits were obtained. Detmers noted that the percentage of hits was below 7 per cent, and that in broad daylight was just not good enough.

   On 9 April 1941, *Craftsman* was attacked. Fire was opened at a range of 6,200 metres, reducing to 5,200 metres. Forty-five shells were fired, with an estimated twelve hitting the target.

29 National Archives (VIC), MP 1185/8, 2026/3/351.

30 AWM, PR 88/178, Papers of Capt. J.L. Hehir.

31 The fire on the poop deck apparently continued unchecked for the duration of the action. In describing the abandonment of the ship, Bretschneider claimed they had no worries about illumination as the poop deck and midships were in bright flames.

32 Some of the survivors claimed that *Sydney* fired 'dud' shells which did not explode. Clearly, several shells struck the raider and passed straight through without exploding. This, however, does not necessarily indicate that there was anything wrong with *Sydney*'s shells. Royal Navy practice was to employ armour-piercing (CPBC or SAP) shells when engaging enemy vessels, as it was considered that this type of shell would cause more serious damage by exploding deep inside the enemy ship.

CPBC and SAP shells were base-fuzed and were designed to explode inside a ship by means of a short time delay mechanism in the fuze. This mechanism was normally triggered by the shell penetrating a ship's side, but it was not uncommon for the shell to pass clean through without exploding, particularly when used against thinly plated vessels, the shell not encountering enough resistance to activate the fuze mechanism.

33 Skeries's claim that the 1-inch fire was mostly short indicates that he could either see the shots falling short, or some actually hit *Kormoran*. Because *Sydney*'s 0.5-inch machine guns fired standard (non-explosive) projectiles, it is doubtful that Skeries would have noticed them falling in the sea or bouncing off *Kormoran*'s plates. One in five bullets, however, contained a tracer element, which was designed to help the gunner spot his fall of shot. As these tracer bullets glowed red, they were also quite visible at the receiving end, and always looked larger than they actually were. It is therefore probable that the 1-inch fire Skeries witnessed was actually 0.5-inch tracer.

34 Detmers's action report records that after passing astern *Sydney*'s guns pointed to starboard, or towards *Kormoran*. This, however, would appear to be an error in this particular translation of Detmers's report. The long-hand translation contained in the Intelligence Memorandum No. 76 of July 1945 shows the entry as 'Enemy guns trained on port side', or away from *Kormoran*.
       National Archives (VIC), B5823.

35 When the aircraft carrier *Ark Royal* was torpedoed on 13 November 1941, the ship whipped so violently that five aircraft, which had just landed on and were waiting to be struck below, were thrown into the air three times.

36 Raven, A. & Roberts, J., *Town Class Cruisers*, Bivouac Books, London, 1975, p. 36.

Chapter 7 Possible & probable causes

1 Winter (1991), op. cit., p. 146.
2 Although this latter view cannot be discounted, the more reliable accounts of the action indicate that *Sydney* caught fire forward and amidships.
3 AWM, PR 88/178.
4 *Manual of Seamanship Vol. II BR 67*, HMSO, London, 1952, p. 496.
5 This low freeboard became apparent during trials of the lead ship, *Leander*. In May 1933 *Leander*, on passage to Devonport, had its boats damaged by waves. The freeboard of the ship could not be increased, so to give the boats more protection it was decided to raise the boats from upper deck height to forecastle deck height. As this proved effective, all ships of the class were subsequently modified.
6 Raven & Roberts (1980), op. cit., p. 9.
7 *Manual of Seamanship Vol. II BR 67*, op. cit., p. 504.
8 Manning, G.C. and Schumacher, T.L., *Principles of Warship Construction and Damage Control*, United States Naval Institute, Annapolis, Maryland, 1935 (4th edn), p. 243.

9   It is doubtful whether *Sydney* was equipped with these emergency lamps. When *Sydney*'s more modernized sister ship *Hobart* was torpedoed on 20 July 1943, the damage report noted that *Hobart* was not fitted with 'Automatic Emergency Lanterns'.

10 *Canberra*, completed in 1928, was not fitted with emergency generators. After suffering a complete loss of power as a result of damage received on the night of 8–9 August 1942, *Canberra*'s crew were reduced to fighting the numerous upper deck fires with buckets of sea water. Little could be done to fight the fires below deck because there was no steam available to operate the pumps.

11 HM Ships *Ajax* and *Achilles* were fortunate and emerged from the battle with light casualties and relatively minor damage.

12 Pope, D., *The Battle of the River Plate*, William Kimber, London, 1956.

13 Cunningham, A.B., *A Sailor's Odyssey*, Hutchinson, London, 1952 (reprint), p. 384.
    The same night (29–30 May) *Perth* was involved in another evacuation effort. Returning to Alexandria, the ship was attacked by German aircraft and struck by a single bomb. It glanced off the RDF gear on the foremast, then penetrated the upper deck before exploding in the forward boiler room. The explosion burst the main steam pipe, filling the room with scalding steam and forcing its evacuation. The main oil feed was also ruptured but fortunately the escaping steam extinguished the fire, preventing more serious damage.

14 Gordon E., *HMS Pepperpot*, Chivers Press, Bath, 1986 (reprint), pp. 125–35.

15 It is believed that Walton (sometimes named as Leading Seaman J. Walters) failed to recover from his ordeal and died a short time after his repatriation. If so, *Neptune* was, in effect, lost with all hands.

16 McKie, Ronald, *Proud Echo*, Angus and Robertson, Sydney, 1953, p. 130.
    Houston was sunk about twenty minutes after *Perth*. Of its complement of 1,020 officers and men, 652 were lost, the survivors becoming prisoners of war. Only 289 returned home to the United States at the end of the war.

17 TBS was Talk Between Ships, a short-range radio/telegraphy system used for passing voice messages between ships.

18 Harker, J., *Well Done Leander*, Collins, Auckland, 1971, pp. 298–309.

19 A board of inquiry into the 'circumstances attending the damage' to *Hobart* was conducted on board the ship on 22 July 1943.

20 Approximately 102 tons of oil-fuel was pumped from the port tanks to the starboard tanks. In addition, 20 tons of sea water was pumped from the firemain into an empty oil tank on the starboard side to more quickly correct the list. Even so, it was not until 2100 that the list was corrected.

21 National Archives (ACT), A 5954/1, 518/27.

22 The estimated loss of reserve of buoyancy is based on damage-control charts issued for *Sydney* in September 1940. These show that a torpedo hit on the bulkhead dividing the forward boiler and forward engine rooms would immediately flood both compartments. The effects were listed as an increase in draught of 5 feet at the

forepeak and 1 foot 4 inches at the after peak. This equated to a change in trim of 3 feet 8 inches by the bow. No list was anticipated, but the percentage of original reserve of buoyancy remaining was calculated as 77 per cent.

23 Although the Dido class cruisers were of a different design, they were similar in size, tonnage, and general layout to the Modified Leander class. The Dido class were anti-aircraft cruisers and were designed to mount three 5.25-inch turrets forward and two aft. The three forward turrets, when fitted, were designated 'A', 'B' and 'Q'.

24 Raven, A. & Lenton, H., *Ensign Z, DIDO Class Cruisers*, Bivouac Books, London, 1975.

25 That a large warship could be sunk by a single torpedo was shown by the loss of the 22,000 ton aircraft carrier HMS *Ark Royal* on 14 November 1941.

26 National Archives (ACT), MP 551/1, Bundle 177.

27 Information supplied to author by retired Senior Naval Architect R.H. Turner. See also, Joint Standing Committee on Foreign Affairs, Defence and Trade, 1998, op. cit., Vol.1, p. 101.

28 Northcott op. cit.

29 Alliston, John, *Destroyer Man*, Greenhouse Publications, Richmond, 1985, pp. 51–2.

30 Some former RAN personnel have expressed doubt that depth charges would detonate if struck by shrapnel or splinters. Support for this view can be found in an incident involving the destroyer HMS *Ledbury*.

On August 1942, *Ledbury*, while engaging enemy aircraft with its stern guns, suffered the misfortune of having a 4-inch shell fired by 'X' turret prematurely explode above 'Y' turret. The turret officer was killed and eight of the gun crew wounded, and the quarterdeck and the depth charges were riddled with shell splinters. None of the depth charges, which were primed, exploded.

On 24 October 1940, however, the destroyer HMS *Mendip* had its steering gear and part of the stern blown off when its depth charges exploded.

It would appear that the relatively stable bursting charge would not explode if struck by splinters, but if the sensitive primers are struck, the depth charges would explode.

31 Opinion is also divided over whether or not torpedo warheads (and depth charges) would explode in a fire. Many consider that the explosive filling would simply melt and burn. It is assumed, however, that if a torpedo warhead or a depth charge were subjected to sufficient heat, the sensitive pistol or primer would explode. This would then cause the warhead or depth charge to explode.

32 If *Sydney* sank as a result of a magazine explosion, the most likely cause would have been fire or heat reaching the 4-inch magazine. This magazine was protected by four oil-fuel tanks (A3, A4, A5 and A6) with a combined total capacity of 473 tons of oil.

33 *Janes Fighting Ships* (1943 ed.) credits the German 15-centimetre gun (Model 1909) as capable of defeating 5 inches of armour plate at 3,000 yards when firing base-fuze shell.

34 If *Sydney*'s forward boiler room did catch fire, there may have been another possible outcome that should not be overlooked. An oil fire in the boiler room would have

spread to the bilges and possibly the adjacent oil fuel tanks. If so, sufficient heat may have been generated to threaten the 4-inch magazine.

35 National Archives (VIC), MP 1587/1, 165P.

Chapter 8   With all hands

1 *Kormoran*'s complement on 19 November 1941 was 23 officers and 376 men (including the four Chinese). Two officers and 78 men were lost.

2 That approximately one third of *Sydney*'s crew may have been killed or wounded during the action is established by comparing the German hitting claims with the known number of men in certain locations. For example, 20 men were required to operate each of *Sydney*'s 6-inch turrets. As 'A' and 'B' turrets were claimed to have been destroyed, up to 40 men could have been killed of wounded in these two turrets alone. Similarly, upwards of 40 men would have been on *Sydney*'s upper and lower bridge, and inside the DCT and HACS. As this area was extensively damaged by shellfire, it is conceivable that many of these men became casualties. In addition, *Kormoran*'s 2-centimetre guns were directed against *Sydney*'s port torpedo tubes and 4-inch guns. Casualties in this area alone could account for another 20 to 30 men.

From the known casualties among the aircraft and catapult crew, the possible casualties in the forward boiler and engine rooms, and the probable casualties in the forward shell rooms and magazines (from the torpedo hit and associated flooding), it can be seen that well over 200 men could have been killed or wounded during the action.

3 AWM, PR 88/178.

4 Coppleson, V.M., *Shark Attack*, Angus and Robertson, Sydney, 1958, p. 195.

5 Photographs of HMA Ships *Australia*, *Shropshire* and *Hobart* taken later in the war reveal long cylindrical containers secured to the body of the float. These were salvaged American 5-inch cordite cases which were made of aluminium and had watertight caps. Two were supplied to each float or raft, one containing water and the other containing a small quantity of medical supplies, tins of milk, and a variety of survival items.

6 Walker, Allan S., *Medical Services of the RAN and RAAF*, Australian War Memorial, Canberra, 1961, p. 390.

7 Lech, Raymond B., *All the Drowned Sailors*, Severn House, London, 1984, p. 83.

8 It is possible that this time factor was taken into account when it was decided to conclude search operations on 29 November 1941, ten days after *Sydney* was presumed to have sunk.

9 National Archives (VIC), MP 1587/1, 164M.

Paul Schumann: 'Five days without water and bread in rough sea, and everywhere sharks in great numbers.'

Victor Schüttenberg: 'All around us were sharks and other animals, besides a raging sea.'

Walter Krahe: 'After 8 days of worry in a boat with 72 men and little food and water, and surrounded by sharks, whereby several of our comrades became delirious ...'

10 Busch, Harald, *U-Boats at War*, Putnam, London, 1955, pp. 127–31.

11 Public Record Office, ADM 1/12272, HMS DUNEDIN.

12 Gwinn had actually handed over control of the aircraft to his co-pilot so that he could repair a navigational antenna at the rear of the aircraft. It was while pondering how to repair the antenna that he happened to look directly down and saw the oil trail.

13 Lech, op. cit., pp. 157-8.

14 Simpson, Keith, *Forensic Medicine*, Edward Arnold, London, 1958, p. 14.

15 National Archives (VIC), MP 1587/1, 165P.

16 Personal communication with Mr John Dunn, August 1996.

17 A second lifebuoy marked 'HMAS SYDNEY' was found on a French beach (Saint Gilles-sur-Vie) in 1951. Given the location and year, it is extremely doubtful this lifebuoy came from the cruiser *Sydney*. A more likely source was the aircraft carrier *Sydney*. It had been constructed in Devonport and had done its trials and working up exercises in the waters around the United Kingdom early in 1949. The carrier then sailed for Australia through the Suez Canal, returning to Britain the following year for exercises with the Royal Navy. It is therefore much more likely that the lifebuoy found at Saint Gilles-sur-Vie came from the aircraft carrier *Sydney*.

18 Ashton, Challenor, and Courtney, *The Scientific Investigation of a Carley Float*, Australian War Memorial, Canberra, 1993.

19 The photograph in question shows *Queen Mary* and *Queen Elizabeth* astern of *Sydney*. It was taken on 4 September 1941.

20 Raven & Roberts (1980), op. cit., p. 9.

21 It is assumed that the letters OTRC stood for Olympic Tyre and Rubber Company and that the life-belt was manufactured in November 1939 (11/39).

22 National Archives (VIC), MP 1587/1, 165P.

23 Western Australian Maritime Museum, File MA 630/81/8.

24 In May 1949 the *West Australian* ran a story on the Chistmas Island corpse by the former Sergeant of the Christmas Island Platoon of the Singapore Volunteers, Mr J.W. Brown. In the article, the footwear was described as a pair of boots marked with a broad arrow and the letters 'Pty'.

25 Some have suggested that because the corpse was not wearing an identity disc the corpse was not that of a naval rating or officer, as regulations required all naval personnel to wear identity discs. The following Admiralty Fleet Order, issued on 25 December 1941, should therefore be noted: 'A recent report has shown that out of a number of casualties, some of them fatal, which occurred when one of HM Ships was damaged by enemy air attack, very few were wearing identity discs. Instructions concerning the wearing of identity discs were issued in AFO 2656/40 and the importance of complying with them is to be impressed on all concerned.'

26 Western Australian Maritime Museum, File MA 630/81/17.

27 Dr Frame's revised opinion on the origin of the Christmas Island float is apparently due to the work of Dr John A.T. Bye, of the Flinders University of South Australia. On 7 October 1994, 943 drift cards were released at position 27° 3' South, 111° 3' East. Of the nine cards subsequently recovered, one was found on the South Island of the Cocos-Keeling Islands, and the rest were found on the east coast of Africa. The results showed that the drift cards had initially been carried northwards in an anticyclonic drift pattern (towards the Cocos-Keeling Islands and Christmas Island), then westwards towards East Africa. This led Dr Bye to conclude: 'The results of the drift card experiment strongly support the possibility that a drifting object from the site of the sinking of HMAS *Sydney* could have arrived at Christmas Island.'

28 Marcus, Alex, '*DEMS¿ WHAT'S DEMS¿*', Boolarong, Brisbane, 1986.

29 Merchant navy rafts were constructed predominantly of timber and empty drums. Square or rectangular in shape, they could not be confused with oval-shaped Carley floats. The merchant navy type raft had a solid floor of planks, which helped prolong life by providing the occupants with a relatively dry and stable platform.

30 That non-specification materials were used in the construction of Australian manufactured Carley floats is evidenced by a float held by the Western Australian Maritime Museum.

Historic Boat exhibit No.26 is a Pattern No.20 Carley float. It is constructed of Australian made Lysaght 'QUEEN'S HEAD' brand galvanized iron. Its covering consists of canvas and Balsa wood.

31 Zincanneal appears to have come on the market in either 1937 or 1938. It is not mentioned in the 1934 edition of the Lysaght Referee, but it is described in the 1938 Lysaght Referee as the latest development in the treatment of steel.

32 The Christmas Island float was recovered but is understood to have been taken to the island rubbish tip and destroyed.

33 Dakin, William J., *Australian Seashores*, Angus and Robertson, Sydney, 1963, p. 206.

34 McKenzie-Smith, Graham, *Australia's Forgotten Army, Vol.1*, Grimwade, Canberra, 1994, p. 20.

35 Western Australian Maritime Museum, File MA 630/81/4.

36 McDonald's paper actually lists a water-damaged stick rocket type parachute flare that was recovered some time during the war. The report of the fired flare attached to a piece of packing case marked HMAS SYDNEY only became known to McDonald after the publication of her paper.

37 These descriptions and sizes were obtained from a wartime Walrus service and maintenance manual. Copy held by the Aviation Heritage Museum at Bullcreek, Western Australia.

Chapter 9 An honourable death

1   By definition, a W/T transmission such as the Q signal could have been regarded as a hostile act. On 8 June 1940, *Scharnhorst* and *Gneisenau* intercepted the tanker *Oil Pioneer*, the troopship *Orama*, the hospital ship *Atlantis* and the armed trawler *Juniper* off the coast of Norway. All except *Atlantis* were sunk. *Atlantis* was spared because it did not alter its non-belligerent status by transmitting a sighting report.

2   Detmers, op. cit., p. 144.

3   Although there is no documented proof to show that Detmers was aware of the British tactics, it is known that German radio intelligence had intercepted an Admiralty signal containing anti-scuttling instructions earlier in the war. Besides obtaining such knowledge from his own intelligence services, British newspapers freely reported the interception and capture of German blockade runners.

4   According to information contained in a diary kept by Oberleutnant Reinhold von Malapert (transcript contained in MP 1587/1, 165K) the sea on 20 November was 'quiet', and the wind was described as force 2-3 from the SSE. On 21 November he described the wind and sea as 'circa 3'. The following day the wind increased in strength and was estimated as '5 and 6 from SW', while the 'SSE and SSW sea was described as 'rough'. The sea on 23 November was still rough, with waves from the SW and a force '4/5/6' wind from the ESE. Conditions improved slightly on 24 November. The sea on this day was described as 'medium'. Von Malapert's boat, under sail for much of the time it was at sea, succeeded in making a landfall at Red Bluff on the morning of 25 November.

5   Shu Ah Fah did claim that he and his three companions refused to do the raider's laundry, but after 'being repeatedly locked up on biscuit and water rations, and being beaten and threatened with revolvers' they decided to agree to the German demands. It is doubtful that these claims were true but, if so, they indicate that the Chinese would not have been happy with their treatment. In which case they would have had little hesitation in telling the authorities of any wrongdoings on the part of Detmers and his men.

6   National Archives (VIC), MP 1587/1, 164M.

7   The only raider captain to be put on trial for war crimes was Fregattankapitän Hellmuth von Ruckteschell (Captain of *Widder* and *Michel*). He was charged with failing to secure the safety of the crews of *Anglo-Saxon* and *Beaulieu* and of continuing to fire on *Davisian* and *Empire Dawn* after they had signalled they were obeying instructions and abandoning ship. Von Ruckteschell was found guilty and sentenced to ten years' imprisonment.

8   National Archives (VIC), MP 1587/1, 165K.

9   As some of the photographs depicted *Kormoran* firing salvoes, they would undoubtedly have shown how the guns, and possibly the torpedo tubes, were concealed. Such information would have been of inestimable value to Naval Intelligence.

10 National Archives (VIC), MP 1587/1, 164M.

11 This story had a sequel. In 1995, Boyo and Johnny Mitchell, announced that they were going to search for Robotham's elusive chest. Their motive was the gold. When told that the gold, if it in fact existed, was still the property of the German government, their much publicized treasure hunt went quiet.

12 Memoirs of R.W. Mason 1941–1981, MS 7460, Mitchell Library, Canberra.

13 Winter (1995), op. cit., p.117.

14 Joint Standing Committee on Foreign Affairs, Defence and Trade, 1998, op. cit., Vol. 3, pp. 605–16 and Vol. 16, pp. 3925-31.

15 Joint Standing Committee on Foreign Affairs, Defence and Trade, 1998, Vol. 5, pp. 1123–4.

16 Joint Standing Committee on Foreign Affairs, Defence and Trade, 1998, Vol. 1, p. 133 and Vol. 9, p. 1977.

17 Joint Standing Committee on Foreign Affairs, Defence and Trade, 1998, Vol. 13, pp. 3143–4.

18 Joint Standing Committee on Foreign Affairs, Defence and Trade, *Report on the loss of HMAS Sydney*, The Parliament of the Commonwealth of Australia, 1999, p. 55.

19 During the parliamentary inquiry, it was suggested that Burnett did break W/T silence, but *Kormoran's* W/T operators 'jammed' his signal and prevented it from being heard. For this to occur the raider's transmission would have to have been powerful enough to drown out *Sydney's*. Such a transmission, usually in the form of a cancellation of a Q signal or a fake call to another vessel, should have been received at Geraldton, Perth, Coonawarra or *Harman*. Furthermore, because these types of transmission were often regarded as suspicious, D/F bearings were usually taken on them. These bearings, as well as the contents of the signal, would then be forwarded to the COIC for evaluation. To date, no record of such a signal has been found in the relevant RAN signal packs or the COIC or ASIS reports.

   It is acknowledged that *Kormoran's* Q signal could have been transmitted at the same time as a possible signal from *Sydney*, but the Q signal would not have been powerful enough to 'jam' *Sydney's* transmissions.

20 Gordon, op. cit.

21 Winton, John, *Carrier Glorious*, Leo Cooper, London, 1986, p. 206.

22 Muggenthaler, op. cit., p. 138.

23 Although Detmers initially claimed the action took place in position 26° 32' South 111° East (information given to Rycroft on 27 November 1941) his action report gives a sighting position of 26° 34' South 111° East. It should also be noted that although Detmers's action report gives a course of 25°, the navigation officer claimed the course was 24°.

24 Joint Standing Committee on Foreign Affairs, Defence and Trade, 1998, op. cit., Vol. 9, pp. 2035–42.

25 The naval vessels were *Tromp, Yandra, Olive Cam, Wyrallah, Heros* and *Gunbar*. The fifteen merchant vessels include those that were directed to pass through the search area as well as those whose courses took them through the search area.

26 Some sources indicate *Kormoran* had a gross registered tonnage of 9,400 tons.

27 If the 4-inch guns had been fitted with splinter shields, or if *Sydney* had been re-armed with twin 4-inch Mark XIX mountings (fitted with gun shields), it is conceivable that the gunners would have been given sufficient protection to enable them to bring their weapons into action. If this had occurred, the outcome of the battle might been vastly different.

28 Ross, op. cit., p. 125.

29 Much was learned about fire aboard ships following the Japanese attack on the US Pacific Fleet at Pearl Harbor. In 1942, as a result of American experience, *Hobart* had all interior bulkheads stripped of oil-based paint. The bulkheads were then painted with less flammable yellow chromate paint.

30 Despite the fact that Farquhar-Smith's signal was addressed to the ACNB, only one member of the board was directly responsible for *Sydney* when it was engaged in operations on the Australian Station. This was the First Naval Member (Chief of Naval Staff) Vice-Admiral Sir Guy Royle. Although Royle was Getting's immediate superior, he does not appear to have been informed of *Sydney*'s non-arrival until the morning of 24 November.

   The circumstances of Royle's briefing are unknown, but it is perhaps significant that Rear-Admiral Crace was not informed of *Sydney*'s disappearance until 24 November either. As RACAS, Crace was responsible for *Sydney*'s administration and operation, and should have been kept informed of any change in its disposition.

31 Acting Captain Heath was no stranger to naval disasters. From 1 December 1939 to May 1940 he held the position of Commander (Flying) aboard HMS *Glorious*. On 31 May Heath was relieved of his duties and transferred off the ship. Nine days later, *Glorious* was sunk off the coast of Norway. Only 39 men survived the sinking and the icy waters. A total of 1,207 officers and men were listed as killed or missing.

32 National Archives (VIC), MP 1185/8, 2026/3/452.

33 This assumption is based on the statements of former Pilot Officer R.M. Seymour RAAF, who was second pilot/navigator on Catalina A24-11. In 1995, in correspondence with the author, Mr Seymour stated that search planning had been based on visibility distance. On 27 November, when the search objective was to locate ships' boats or rafts, A24-11 was flown at a height of 'about 1000 feet'.

34 It is acknowledged that a search for *Sydney* may have been conducted on 23 November, but according to the claims made by former Group Captain Bourne, this search was to the south of Rottnest Island, well away from the area of the engagement.

35 Summerrell, op. cit., p. 113.

36 National Archives (ACT), A705/15, 163/113/137.

37 With 'A' and 'B' turrets knocked out and the port 4-inch guns and torpedo tubes untenable, *Sydney*'s offensive capability was reduced to 'X' and 'Y' turrets. Against *Sydney*'s broadside of four 6-inch guns and two quad 0.5-inch machine guns, Detmers

was able to use four 15-centimetre, one 3.7-centimetre and up to five 2-centimetre guns.

All of *Kormoran*'s guns were capable of rapid fire, and it was the volume of fire produced that gave Detmers fire superiority.

38 A seventh battle honour, 'Persian Gulf', was awarded to the guided missile frigate HMAS *Sydney* (*Sydney IV*) in 1990.

BIBLIOGRAPHY

PUBLISHED SOURCES

Alliston, John, *Destroyer Man*, Greenhouse Publications, Richmond, 1985.

Andrews, C. & Morgan, E., *Supermarine Aircraft since 1914*, Putnam, London, 1981.

Bancroft, A. & Roberts, R.G., *The Mikado's Guests*, Patersons Printing Press, Perth, 1945.

Bastock, John, *Australia's Ships of War*, Angus & Robertson, Sydney, 1975.

Beesly, Patrick, *Very Special Intelligence*, Sphere Books, London, 1978 (reprint).

Brennecke, J.H., *Ghost Cruiser H.K.33*, Futura Publications, London, 1974 (reprint).

Brice, Martin, *Axis Blockade Runners of World War II*, Batsford Ltd, London, 1981.

——, *Capture of Hannover, War Monthly, Vol. 10, No. 1*, War Monthly Publications, London, 1982.

Brooke, Geoffrey, *Alarm Starboard!*, Patrick Stephens, Cambridge, 1982.

Brown, David, *Warship Losses of World War Two*, Arms & Armour Press, London, 1995 (reprint).

Busch, Harald, *U-Boats at War*, Putnam, London, 1955.

Campbell, Gordon, *My Mystery Ships*, Hodder & Stoughton, London, 1937 (reprint).

Chalmers, W.S., *Max Horton and the Western Approaches*, Hodder & Stoughton, London, 1954.

Churchill, Winston, *The Second World War*, Vol. 1, Reprint Society Ltd, London, 1950.

Churchill, Winston, *The Second World War*, Vol. 2, Reprint Society Ltd, London, 1951.

Collins, J.A., *As Luck Would Have It*, Angus & Robertson, Sydney, 1965.

Coppleson, V.M., *Shark Attack*, Angus & Robertson, Sydney, 1958.

Cunningham, A.B., *A Sailor's Odyssey*, Hutchinson, London, 1952 (reprint).

Dakin, William J., *Australian Seashores*, Angus & Robertson, Sydney, 1963.

Davies, Jim, *The Lady Was Not a Spy*, Lamb Printers, Perth, 1992.

Detmers, T.A., *The Raider Kormoran*, Tandem Books, London, 1975 (reprint).

Dickens, Peter, *Narvik*, Ian Allan Ltd, London, 1974.

Durrant, Lawrence, *The Seawatchers*, Angus & Robertson, Sydney, 1986.

Fleet Air Arm, HMSO, London, 1943.

Frame, T., *HMAS Sydney*, Hodder & Stoughton, Sydney, 1993.

Gannon, Michael, *Operation Drumbeat*, Harper & Row, New York, 1990.

Gill, G.H., *The Royal Australian Navy 1939–42*, Vol. 1, Australia in the War of 1939–45, Australian War Memorial, Canberra, 1957.

Gordon, Ed., *HMS Pepperpot*, Chivers Press, Bath, 1986 (reprint).

Haines, Gregory, *Cruiser at War*, Ian Allan Ltd, London, 1978.

Handbook of Wireless Telegraphy, BR 230, Vol. 2, Wireless Telegraphy Theory, HMSO, London, 1940.

Hardy, A.C., *Everyman's History of the Sea War*, Vol. 1, Nicholson & Watson, London, 1948.

Harker, J., *Well Done Leander*, Collins, Auckland, 1971.

——, *HMNZS Achilles*, The Battery Press, Nashville, 1981.

Holmes, Richard, *Firing Line*, Penguin Books, Harmondsworth, 1987.

Hore, Peter, *HMAS Sydney II*, RAN Sea Power Centre, 2001

Howe, Leslie, *The Merchant Service Today*, Oxford University Press, London, 1941.

Hyslop, Robert, *Aye Aye, Minister*, AGPS, Canberra, 1990.

Janes Fighting Ships 1943–4, Sampson Low, Marston & Co. Ltd, London, 1944.

Jones, Geoffrey, *Under Three Flags*, Corgi Books, London, 1975 (reprint).

Jones, T.M. & Idriess, Ion L., *The Silent Service*, Angus & Robertson, Sydney, 1952 (reprint).

Keble-Chatterton, E., *Commerce Raiders*, Hurst & Blackett, London, 1943.

Landsborough, Gordon, *The Battle of the River Plate*, Panther Books, London, 1956.

Lech, Raymond B., *All the Drowned Sailors*, Severn House, London, 1984.

Lenton, H.T., *British Cruisers*, Macdonald, London, 1973.

Lloyd's Register of Shipping, Vol. 1, Lloyd's, London, 1940.

Lysaght's Referee, 17th Edition, John Lysaght Pty Ltd, Sydney, 1938.

Manning, G.C. & Schumacher, T.L., *Principles of Warship Construction and Damage Control*, United States Naval Institute, Annapolis, Maryland, 1935 (4th edn).

Manual of Seamanship Vol. I, *1937*, HMSO, London, 1939 (reprint).

Manual of Seamanship Vol. II, *1932*, HMSO, London, 1941 (reprint).

Manual of Seamanship Vol. II, BR 67, HMSO, London, 1952.

Marcus, Alex, 'DEMS? What's DEMS?', Boolarong Press, Brisbane, 1986.

McKenzie-Smith, Graham, *Australia's Forgotten Army, Vol. 1*, Grimwade, Canberra, 1994.

McKie, Ronald, *Proud Echo*, Angus & Robertson, Sydney, 1953.

Miller, Vicky, *No Survivors*, West Australian Newspapers, 1991.

Mohr, U., & Sellwood, A.V., *Atlantis*, Werner Laurie Ltd, London, 1955.

Montgomery, Michael, *Who Sank the Sydney?*, Cassell, Melbourne, 1981.

Muggenthaler, A.K., *German Raiders of World War Two*, Robert Hale, London, 1978.

Naval Electrical Pocket Book, BR 157, HMSO, London, 1953.

Naval Marine Engineering Practice, BR 2007, HMSO, London, 1955.

'Naval Staff History', BR 1736, *Mediterranean*, Vol. 1, September 1939 – October 1940, Historical Section Admiralty, London, 1952.

Newcomb, Richard, *Abandon Ship!*, Henry Holt & Co., New York, 1958.

Newton, R.N., *Practical Construction of Warships*, Longmans, London, 1941.

Northcott, Maurice, *HOOD, Design and Construction*, Bivouac Books, London, 1975.

Payne, Alan, *HMAS Canberra*, The Naval Historical Society of Australia, Sydney, 1973.

Poolman, Kenneth, *The Kelly*, William Kimber, London, 1954.

——, *Armed Merchant Cruisers*, Leo Cooper, London, 1985.

Pope, D., *The Battle of the River Plate*, William Kimber, London, 1956.

Raven, A. & Lenton, H., *Ensign 2, Dido Class Cruisers*, Bivouac Books, London, 1975.

Raven, A. & Roberts, J., *Ensign 5, Town Class Cruisers*, Bivouac Books, London, 1975.

——, *British Cruisers of World War Two*, Arms & Armour Press, London, 1980.

Readers Digest Illustrated History of World War II, London, 1989.

Rogge, Bernhard, *Under Ten Flags*, Weidenfeld & Nicolson, London, 1957.

Roskill, S.W., *The War at Sea, 1939–45*, Vol. 1, HMSO, London, 1954.

Ross, W.H., *Stormy Petrel*, Pattersons Printing Press, Perth, 1943.

——, *Lucky Ross*, Hesperian Press, Perth, 1994.

Scott, G., *HMAS Sydney*, Horwitz, Sydney, 1962.

Selwood, A.V., *HMS Electra*, Futura Publications, London, 1976 (reprint).

Showell, Jak P. Mallmann, *The German Navy in World War Two*, Arms & Armour Press, London, 1979.

Simpson, Keith, *Forensic Medicine*, Edward Arnold, London, 1958.

Summerrell, Richard, *The Sinking of HMAS Sydney, A Guide to Commonwealth Government Records*, Australian Archives, Canberra, 1997.

Talbot-Booth, E.C., *What Ship Is That?*, Sampson Low, Marston & Co Ltd, London, 2nd edn.

The 1931 International Code of Signals, Vol. 1, HMSO, London, 1941 (reprint).

The Navy List for November 1938, HMSO, London, 1938.

Walker, Allan S., *Medical Services of the RAN and RAAF*, Australian War Memorial, Canberra, 1961.

Winter, Barbara, *HMAS Sydney, Fact, Fantasy and Fraud*, Boolarong Press, Brisbane, 1991 (reprint).

——, *The Intrigue Master*, Boolarong Press, Brisbane, 1995.

Winton, John, *Convoy*, Michael Joseph, London, 1983.

——, *Carrier Glorious*, Leo Cooper, London, 1986.

——, *Ultra at Sea*, Leo Cooper, London, 1988.

Woodward, David, *The Secret Raiders*, Norton & Company, New York, 1955.

ARCHIVAL SOURCES

Australian War Memorial

AWM 54, 423/11/1. COIC Daily Summary of Operational Intelligence.

AWM 64, 0/2. RAAF Central War Room Operations Diary 6 November 1941 – 3 April 1942.

AWM 78, 329/1. Report of proceedings—*Sydney* (war diary) 1939–1941.

AWM 124, 4/224. Loss of HMAS *Sydney*.

AWM PR, 88/178. Papers of Captain J.L. Hehir.

National Library, Australian Capital Territory

MS 7460. Memoirs of R.W. Mason 1941–1981.

National Archives of Australia, Australian Capital Territory

1969/100/5, 105/30/AIR. HMAS *Sydney*—Search Operations.

A 5954/1, 518/27. HMAS *Hobart*—torpedoing of off Espiritu Santo July 1943.

A5954/1, 518/36. Advisory War Council Minute No. 842, 18 March 1942.

A705/15, 163/113/137. Air Board Minutes.

A9240, Set 2 Vol. 4. Background notes to War Cabinet Minute No. 1521.

MP 551/1, Bundle 171. HMAS *Sydney*, plans.

MP 551/1, Bundle 177. HMAS *Sydney*, plans.

National Archives of Australia, New South Wales

SP 551/1, Bundle 528. Log Books of HMAS *Sydney* 1940–1941.

National Archives of Australia, Victoria

B 1124 & B 1129. Subject Index, *Sydney*, 10/2/1942 & 17/2/1942.

B5823. Dietmar's Diary—Account of Action between *Kormoran* and *Sydney*. Decode and translations.

MP 138/1 603/263/538. HMAS *Sydney*, Alteration and Addition lists.

MP 138/1, 603/263/587. HMAS *Sydney*, Docking defect list.

MP 138/1, 603/263/602. HMAS *Sydney*, HA ammunition stowage.

MP 138/1, 603/263/624. HMAS *Sydney*, Alteration and Addition lists.

MP 981/1, 629/203/1274. *Canberra* and *Sydney* full calibre combined gunnery and torpedo firing, 3 August 1937.

MP 1049/5, 2021/5/596. Report on suspicious sighting by HMAS *Yandra*.

MP 1049/5, 2026/3/294. HMAS *Sydney* protection of fire control system and alternative controls.

MP 1049/5, 2026/3/429. *Sydney* protective shield for 4" Mk V gun.

MP 1049/5, 2026/3/441. *Sydney*—aircraft crane.

MP 1049/5, 2026/3/457. Search for HMAS *Sydney*.

MP 1049/5, 2026/3/511. Repairs to war damage of HMAS *Hobart*.

MP 1049/5, 2026/19/6. Interrogation of German survivors ex raider *Kormoran*.

MP 1074/4/0. Unclassified inward signals, 24 November 1941.

MP 1185/8, 2026/3/351. Report on *Bartolomeo Colleoni*.

MP 1185/8, 2026/3/452. HMAS *Sydney*—search area.

MP 1185/8, 2026/19/6. Loss of HMAS *Sydney*—report by Mr F.B. Eldridge on interrogation of survivors of *Kormoran*.

MP 1580/1. [Directorate of Naval Intelligence] Weekly Intelligence Reports 1940–1945.

MP 1582/7. Australia Station Intelligence Summaries 1939–1945.

MP 1587/1, 164L. *Kormoran*: (Raider No. 41) 'G'—German AMC.

MP 1587/1, 164M. *Kormoran*: (Raider No. 41) 'G'—German AMC Interrogation of survivors.

MP 1587, 164N. *Kormoran*: (Raider No. 41) 'G'—German AMC Translation of Log, Voyage.

MP 1587/1, 165K. *Kormoran*—Translation of diaries.

MP 1587/1, 165P. *Sydney – Kormoran* action signals etc.

MP 1587/1, 775W/1. Combined Operational Intelligence Centre—Weekly Summaries of Operational Intelligence, 1941.

MP 1587/1/0, 1660. *Ramses*—Blockade Runner, Destroyed.

MP 1714/1. Admiralty Fleet Orders, 1941, Part II—Confidential [CAFO].

National Archives of Australia, Western Australia

K 809/1. South Western Area Combined Headquarters logbook 2 July 1941 – 2 May 1942.

K997/8, 1/15/2. Admin—HMAS *Sydney/Kormoran* Action November 1941.

Royal Australian Navy, Naval Historical Section

ADM 234/342. Battle Summary No. 13, Actions with Enemy Disguised Raiders 1940–41.

B6259. Daily Movements, HMA Ships and Auxiliaries, Australia Station.

Western Australian Maritime Museum

HMAS *Sydney*, File MA 630/81.

War Diary (*Kriegstagebuch*) of the raider Kormoran-Schiff 41. Translated by Barbara Winter.

Public Record Office, London

ADM 1/12272. HMS *Dunedin*.

ADM 1/12883. Disguised Enemy Raiders and Blockade Runners; Conduct of HM Ships 1943–1944.

Reports, Newspapers and Periodicals

Ashton, J., Challenor, C., & Courtney, R., *The Scientific Investigation of a Carley Float*, Australian War Memorial, Canberra, 1993.

Bye, John A.T., *Results from Drift Card Releases at the Site of the Sinking of HMAS Sydney II*, Flinders University of South Australia, 1997.

Daily Telegraph.

HMAS *Sydney II: Proceedings of the Wreck Location Seminar, 26 November 2001*, RAN Sea Power Centre, 2002.

Joint Standing Committee on Foreign Affairs, Defence and Trade, *Submissions, Inquiry into the Circumstances of the Sinking of HMAS Sydney*, The Parliament of the Commonwealth of Australia, Canberra, 1998.

——, *Report on the loss of HMAS Sydney*, The Parliament of the Commonwealth of Australia, Canberra, 1999.

McDonald, Glenys, *Seeking the Sydney*, Western Australian Maritime Museum, 1993.

Naval Historical Society of Australia, *Naval Historical Review*, December 1979.

——, *Naval Historical Review*, Vol. 20, No. 2, 1999.

Olson, W.J., HMAS *Sydney: possible and probable causes of her loss*, Western Australian Maritime Museum, 1995.

——, *With All Hands*, Western Australian Maritime Museum, 1996.

Papers from the HMAS *Sydney* Forum, Fremantle, 21–23 November 1991, Western Australian Maritime Museum. Compiled by Kim Kirsner & Mike McCarthy.

Royal United Services Institute of Victoria News, Vol. 2, No. 106, 1995.

The Daily News.

The Sydney Morning Herald.

The West Australian.

INDEX